D0397918

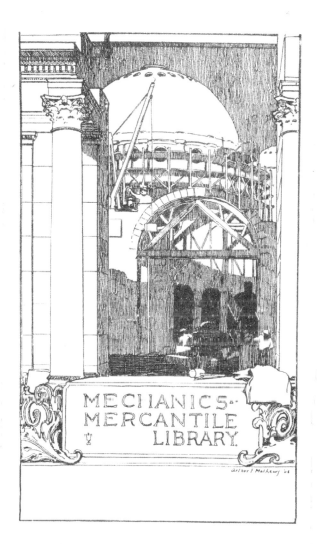

MECHANICS·
MERCANTILE
LIBRARY.

THE END OF CAPITALISM

THE END OF CAPITALISM

DESTRUCTIVE FORCES
OF AN ECONOMY OUT OF CONTROL

ROBERT H. PARKS, PhD

Prometheus Books
59 John Glenn Drive
Amherst, New York 14228-2119

Published 2011 by Prometheus Books

Inquiries should be addressed to
Prometheus Books
59 John Glenn Drive
Amherst, New York 14228–2119
VOICE: 716–691–0133
FAX: 716–691–0137
WWW.PROMETHEUSBOOKS.COM

15 14 13 12 11   5 4 3 2 1

Library of Congress Cataloging-in-Publication Data

Parks, Robert H.
    The end of capitalism : destructive forces of an economy out of control / by Robert H. Parks.
        p. cm.
    Includes bibliographical references and index.
    ISBN 978–1–59102–717–1 (cloth : alk. paper)
    1. Capitalism—United States. 2. United States—Economic conditions—2001–2009. 3. United States—Economic policy—2001–2010. I. Title.

HC106.83.p37 2011
330.12'20973—dc22

                                                    2011012102

Printed in the United States of America on acid-free paper

CONTENTS

APPENDIXES

DEDICATION AND ACKNOWLEDGMENTS

I dedicate this book to the many thousands of my former students at the Wharton School of the University of Pennsylvania, the Baruch Graduate Business School in New York, and Lehigh, Rutgers, and Pace universities. This dedication extends to the faculties of Swarthmore College and the Wharton School of the University of Pennsylvania. All taught me the indispensable and inextricable linkage of science to truth. Wharton Professor Charles R, Whittlesey and Nobel Laureate Simon Kuznets taught me to put science and ethics first. They insisted that good theory must be supported empirically.

I also dedicate this volume to my late wife, Inta, and our children, Karen, Robert, and Alison. Inta made many suggestions in this work for greater clarity and substance. Inta died from lung cancer on the day after Christmas 2007. Her death spurred me to write and complete this work as a very first priority. Life must go on despite inevitable grief. Duty to the living demands it.

I am also indebted to my mother, Amelia Parks, and my father, Charles Parks. They taught me a lot about charity, truth, and human compassion. I extend my grateful thanks to Steven L. Mitchell, Editor in Chief of Prometheus Books, for his help with this project.

Some readers may be displeased with a book that focuses on terrifying matters of life and death. But one cannot and should not try to please everyone. William Strunk and E. B. White make this clear in their *Elements of Style*:

> The whole duty of a writer is to please and satisfy himself, and the true writer always plays to an audience of one. Let him start sniffing the air, or glancing at the Trend Machine and he is as good as dead, though he may make a nice living.

Yes indeed.

RHP

7

Introduction

DESTRUCTIVE CONTRADICTIONS
OF CAPITALISM

Thus every part was full of vice. Yet the whole mass a paradise.
—Bernard de Mandeville, *The Fable of the Bees* (1705)

This book is about an economic forecast I made long ago in my 1998 work titled *Unlocking the Secrets of Wall Street*. In that volume I argued that US capitalism could not survive in what I called its present "ugly form." The ugly manifestations of capitalism hide behind many disguises, which will be unmasked as the present discussion unfolds introducing readers to the underlying causes of collapsing financial markets and the terrible aftereffects of major economic recessions. One of the more treacherous facets of capitalism looming in the background of every chapter is the ludicrous idea that free markets need little or no controls to bring about economic prosperity and to support social well-being. Economists dub this no-holds-barred approach an extreme *laissez faire* philosophy of markets. In other words, beyond bare security needs—safeguarding one's life and property from villains who would take either by force—government should have no role in the economic or social interactions of its citizens.

What markets? For the devotees of minimalist restrictions that serve as the hallmark of the laissez faire philosophy, a market could be any type of meaningful interaction between individuals, groups, or corporations. Those who advocate reducing or eliminating restrictions on such social and economic transactions fail to realize that it is the nature of such interactions to have embedded within them various core concepts—the rules

9

of the game, if you will—that guide basic interpersonal activity thereby demonstrating what each party can expect from the other in any specific transaction. If such implicit rules did not exist—beyond merely protecting life and property—who would feel safe engaging in trade, commerce, social relations, or any other type of human interaction? Clearly all markets within which we humans transact our social business require controls, not just the financial markets. Ultrafree markets—those that promote the no-holds-barred laissez faire approach and therefore possess few if any controls, or pitifully weak controls at best—do not protect the public from crippling injuries or death. Let's track the markets one by one to see just how an extreme laissez faire philosophy has pushed capitalism to the brink of destruction. We can easily count the varied ways in which capitalism is systematically destroying itself.

Countdown to the Last Days of Capitalism

Right-wing ideologists maintain that despite any faults of capitalism it is still the best economic system that exists. I beg to differ. Meaningful controls that protect all parties in social and economic transactions should and do count; and, due to their absence or their drastically weakened state in many cases, capitalism has already turned into a dangerous economic model that sets off self-destructive signals.[1] A society that cannot manage its own economic well-being, but instead permits wholesale disregard of the basic moral virtues, will not only reap a bitter harvest from its corrosive economic practices but will turn a blind eye to actions that unravel the very fabric of the community.

Our Out-of-Control Gun Violence and Death

In chapter 1 widespread gun violence and death are exposed. Here we meet the macho gun bullies who run gun-owner advocacy groups like the National Rifle Association (NRA). Sad to say, the NRA gets strong support from the federal, state, and local governments. Wrapping themselves in the flag, these gun advocates declare that they are the true patriots who are defending America. For the most part, they believe in very weak gun control laws despite an epidemic of gun violence across the country. Their plea for voluntary gun control is a sham.[2]

What does the plague of guns have to do with capitalism? Runaway capitalism, with its no-holds-barred approach to the creation of wealth and power, argues that the inherent collective self-interestedness (some would call it the selfishness) of individuals, and therefore of society at large, produces positive social change. Entrenched capitalists contend that placing restrictions on what they see as the inherent good judgment of individuals to make decisions that result in their personal and collective betterment only serves to undermine social progress. Strong gun controls would go beyond what capitalism views as government's legitimate role, i.e., maintaining very basic public safety and relying on its citizens to voluntarily control their own behavior, since it is in their own interest to do so.

This overly optimistic view of our core human nature, coupled with the prevalence of available guns in our society, has led to innumerable deaths. The NRA, the White House, as well as Democrats and Republicans in the Congress are responsible for this growing disaster. Since the United States has sought to ban or control the availability of many other types of dangerous weapons—explosives and bomb-making materials, surface-to-air missiles, and even dreaded nuclear weapons—why does it not ban guns? This mad culture of ours, one that cripples or kills through neglect or lack of concern for others, coexists hand-in-glove with the glorification of guns. And what happens when young people see guns being glorified? How do they react in such an environment during their formative years? By the time they reach the age of eighteen they may be just a step away from the macho war dogs, those who see the use of weapons as a way of achieving their objectives on the world stage. Maybe that's why so many of the war dogs are also ardent members of the NRA. Hurrah, they shout; keep controls away from our precious guns. We are the true patriots who defend America.

But the gun statistics tell quite another story—one of horror, tragedy, and death. For example, 34,000 people died from gun-related injuries in 2006. Firearm injuries were the eighth leading causes of death in the United States that year. Gun massacres occur far too often in our schools and our work places, on our streets, and in our homes. Media headlines tell the gruesome story. On Tuesday, April 17, 2007, Americans woke up to what was to be for its time the worst gun massacre on record. Headlines screamed that thirty-two people were shot dead at Virginia Tech. Despite such horror, not a single presidential candidate campaigning for the nomination of either major political party dared to mention the need for effective gun controls? Of course not; they had no desire to infuriate the gun lobby, whose votes and campaign contributions they coveted. The overwhelming silence of these politicians made clear the awesome power of the gun lobby in promoting its objectives instead of promoting the life, liberty, and happiness of citizens everywhere. Put another way, their claim to be super patriots is totally without merit.

New York City Mayor Michael Bloomberg would have no part of this gun lobby. On the contrary, he warned that the worst is yet to come regarding mass gun murder unless these firearms are banned from our streets and our schools. Mayor Bloomberg deserves high praise for speaking out. Why aren't more elected officials doing likewise? Given the number of political assassinations our nation has endured over the years, it should be clear to politicians and others in the public eye that the availability of large numbers of guns threatens their safety as much if not more than the population at large. Politicians in the public arena are huge targets for those who seek the spotlight by using a gun to gain a few minutes of notoriety in the media. My point is simply this: out-of-control gun violence, anemic gun laws, and a reluctance on the part of our leaders aggressively to enforce the laws we currently have combine to form just one of the many reasons why American capitalism, as a social policy, is in decline.

I also argue that the macho gun advocates think and act like the macho war dogs we meet in chapter 2. Their ties are strong. For example, both celebrate former President George W. Bush's brutal, illegal, and unjust military attack on Iraq. Still, gun violence can be stopped with meaningful gun controls that are actively and aggressively enforced, as I argue in depth in chapter 1.

The United States War Dogs

Chapter 2 tracks the war dogs, whose numbers include many members of the previous White House administration: the former president and vice president, the secretary of defense, the attorney general, the earlier hoodwinked secretary of state and his successor are all implicated. Hillary Clinton has replaced the former puppet spokeswomen for Bush as secretary of state. That certainly is great news. But the Bush crowd conspired in secret to attack Iraq on false grounds. When truly patriotic citizens contested their policies, these war dogs smeared, blamed, and shamed them. George W. Bush is now out of office and one hopes that his dangerous and failed policies in this troubled region have departed with him.

The war dogs threw innocent Americans and foreigners into secret prisons both here and abroad, tortured them in the name of intelligence gathering, deprived them of adequate food and medical care, detained them for months on end with no chance to see their relatives or a lawyer. Then for months or years the war dogs blocked these individuals from receiving a fair trial before a nonmilitary judge and jury.[3]

All this adds up to inhuman and cruel behavior for which leading members of the Bush administration should be brought to trial. To be sure, the former president still maintains that he is a compassionate man who also protected us from terrorists. But few Americans now believe anything Bush has to say about compassion, truth, justice, or democracy. He has self-destructed as a right-wing ideologue.

A Perilous Fallacy: The Global Nuclear Defense Argument

Chapter 2 also tracks the age-old "fallacy of composition," which contends that what seems true for one is true for all. Within the broader community of nations various individual countries insist that securing nuclear weapons and other weapons of mass destruction, presumably for defensive purposes, makes them more secure, so if more members of the world community possessed such weapons it would make the community as a whole safer. This defense pitch is both false and dangerous. As more nations seek nuclear capability and others increase the number of nuclear weapons they possess, the risks of a nuclear conflagration expand geometrically. Somehow, somewhere one of them will use this deadly deterrent through "accident, miscalculation, or design," as fourteen scholars we will meet would argue, including philosopher and mathematician Bertrand Russell.[4] I will always remember Russell for his astonishing prescience and courage. He was one of the first notables to fight against the proliferation of weapons of mass destruction.

The Religious Assault on Science

In chapter 3 we set our sights on head-in-the-clouds religious leaders as they contradict the views of leading experts who advocate for science and truth. These experts warn that religious superstition blocks out rational inquiry and the search for objective truth. Religion seeks to find out why the world is as it is and ponders what, if any, purpose we humans have as part of the natural order as it searches for meaning in sacred books and long-held myths. Science, on the other hand, uses rigorous investigative methods in its efforts to discover how the world works and to unlock nature's secrets so we may better understand the impact the natural world has on us and we on it. Through the centuries, religionists of various stripes have differed markedly—often to the point of fighting bloody wars—about the purpose of the world and humankind's place in it, and the god or gods that may or may not play a part in their respective explanations. Scientists share a collective desire to learn how the world works and its governing principles along with implementing a mutually accepted scientific method to reach empirically verifiable conclusions to support hypotheses offered to explain the world around us.

My fear is that extreme religious fanatics will someday get hold of nuclear arms and use them to wage their sectarian battles in the name of their respective views of some one-and-only God. For others this religious conflict could portend the arrival on Earth of the long-sought Armageddon that they believe signals the return of their savior, who will judge humanity. The *Economist* declared that such a risk exists between Islam and the Christian West.[5] It called this risk "the fundamental fear." I call it terrifying. In short, when religious superstition walks into the realm of empirical science and attempts to inject meaning and purpose where none can be sought, objective truth is crowded out. The more powerful religion becomes within the broader society the more willing people are to accept groundless myth and superstition over objective science and testable results. As capitalism continues to erode under the corrosive influence of an unchecked laissez faire mentality, fear and mass confusion provide religion with a fertile medium in which it can distort rational social objectives, convert advocates to its cause, and, in the end, the entire community is victimized.

Dishonest and Corrupt Business and Government Collusion

The systemic corruption by business and government is the focus of chapter 4. Conniving and cooperating scoundrels scam us on Wall Street, rig our public utilities in their own favor, and lie to us in the guise of using big government to legislate in the public interest. My most disturbing finding is the corrupt alliance between business, government, and the US Supreme Court. The Bush administration sought to add many ultraright-wing conservatives to the Court who would dilute and destroy many of our most precious rights. Such destructive and unjust alliances of business and the law weaken capitalism. A just capitalism without effective controls to eradicate corrupt internal processes and restrain those who engage in them cannot long endure. An extreme laissez faire philosophy with weak regulatory controls signals that capitalism is on its way out.

Vicious Industry Predators

In chapter 5 we track industry and the vicious predators who have been permitted to run amok within them. The abject failure of will on the part of government on all levels to shield adults and children of all ages from these predators is an outrage. My cast of predators includes **Fatmac** for Big Food; **Venom** for Big Tobacco; **Poison** for Big Pharmaceutical; **Distort** for Big Life Insurance; **Exploit** for Big Home Insurance; **Odious** for the Military, Industrial, and Big Oil Complex; and **Sick** for those who exploit uninsured Americans and immigrants.

To justify their greed, the predators who have infiltrated these industries constantly preach that the ultrafree market for the production and distribution of their respective goods and services knows best how to manage itself, and that government regulation and controls only make matters worse by restraining innovative ideas, lucrative avenues of wealth creation, and the inevitable progress that effective and efficient capitalism can bring to society. The sleaze and dishonesty that I document in this chapter are among the many ugly and destructive forces still at work to signal the death of capitalism.

Cultural, Racial, Sexual, and Economic Predators

Exposing the cultural, sexual, racial, and big economic predators in our midst is the overriding concern of chapter 6. These predators attack adults and children while at the same time suppressing and distorting the best of science. In addition, both age discrimination and sexual bias run wild and uncontrolled. Corporate-funded right-wing think tank venom masquerading as truth is passed off as sound political science. Macho misogynists (woman haters) show up as one of the most deadly of all predators. Most sickening are the predators who know they carry sexual diseases but who still deliberately infect prostitutes and others with the same diseases that cripple and kill. Can such barbaric abuse be stopped? Yes, but like battling alcoholism, the struggle will be long and hard, and perhaps never ending.

Chapter 6 also complements and updates the devastating culture of Wall Street and its scammers, its failed philosophy of success, the recent financial meltdown and the specter of deflation, depression, and the risk of devaluing the dollar. I have included in appendix C my full report of September 27, 2008, outlining the major components of a devastating decline in the US economy if the trends I was seeing then weren't confronted and corrected.[6] Here a few of the major questions I raise.

(1) Will the TARP (Troubled Asset Relief Program) ward off recession? No. As the lone approach it will not defrost frozen credit markets; stop the falling prices of properties; raise by much the crashed prices of bonds and mortgages now courting bankruptcy; end systemic foreclosures; or eliminate a frightening increase in lost jobs that leaves consumers without shelter, incomes, savings, or healthcare. The jobless rate has already shot up to twenty percent once part-time workers are included, as well as those who have given up looking for jobs that no longer exist, and those who work overtime for poverty wages and minimal or no benefits.

(2) Will the TARP bailout bring with it new criminal activity? Yes, because "that's where the money is," to quote the notorious bank robber Willy Sutton. This bailout will be managed by many of the same regulation-averse financial "experts" who got us into this terrible mess in the first place. Such attempts at economy stimulation, however well meaning they might be, will be manipulated by those who will find ways to profit from the misfortune of others. I forecast that the bailout could run far past its initial $700 billion into possibly many trillions.

(3) Could soaring unemployment degenerate into a deflationary depression in which consumers decide not to buy goods and services because they believe the prices will fall in the near future? Yes, especially when (a) major public works are slow to start, thereby reducing their intended stimulative effect and (b) an exit from the Iraq war has wasted trillions of dollars, leaving us with

a hollowed out economy that does not even replace or repair its roads, clinics, or other vital infrastructure components that have become obsolete.

(4) Will the right-wing block peace in Iraq and reject government-funded public works programs intended to spark domestic economic recovery? Yes. The ultraright is still locked into a trickle-down theory that believes giving economic incentives to those who are already better off will ultimately lead to the eventual trickling down of the benefits to those who are less well off. It wants nothing to do with a "bottoms-up stimulus" approach that would give people jobs through monetized or public subsidized works projects. Why? Because the extreme right hates famed economist John Maynard Keynes, the architect of America's successful recovery from the Great Depression. It despises big-government efforts to solve huge social and economic problems. It has little sympathy for the poor. It mocks and ridicules liberal economists and forecasters.[7]

(5) Could trickle-down theory, properly implemented, actually work for the general public welfare? It cannot. Trickle-down theory is inseparable from right-wing policies that are deliberately designed to benefit the wealthy through tax cuts, tax avoidance, and tax evasion.[8] The alternative to impotent trickle-down theory is trickle-up theory, which does work. Trickle-up theory, often called bottoms-up theory, argues that the way to ward off a major recession is to have the Treasury issue contracts for public works on a competitive bid basis to give people jobs and incomes.

(6) Will the Treasury and the Federal Reserve (or the Fed) avoid a major economic slump by implementing desperately needed public works much like what was put into place during the Depression? No. The ultralaissez-faire Republicans stridently oppose Keynesian economics to fight a downturn, even if it's close to being a depression. Economic naïveté is one reason. Also, the ultraright always blocks the efforts of big government to solve big problems. It hates anything liberal.

Hope with Obama

Has President Barack Obama moved in the right directions to ward off a major recession, or possibly another great depression? It's hard to say. He has continued the TARP money flowing to financial institutions and he and his advisors have worked to prevent the imminent collapse of financial institutions and major automobile manufacturers, and others. Efforts have been made to slow the rate of home foreclosures by refinancing at-risk mortgages. An $8,000 tax incentive for first-time homebuyers and the "Cash for Clunkers" program offered brief stimulation, but then they were gone. The tax incentive to homeowners was extended but then stopped. The congressional stimulus package was designed to put money into the economy and thereby create new jobs and stave off job losses, but the bureaucracy is churning so slowly that it prevents adequate amounts of money from reaching the very people the assistance was intended to help.

I hope that, first and foremost, President Obama does much more to tackle putting people back to work through immediate public works projects. Creating jobs and incomes brings with them spending power. With spending power in the hands of the middle class and the poor, we could see an upward swing in consumption and a rebound in related investment spending sparked by rising consumer spending. I also hope that Obama fires the supply-side right-wingers who got us into this financial maelstrom and who orchestrated the economic implosion we are now experiencing. But he must move fast.

The jobless rate has far exceeded the 8.5 percent that was thought to be the high point of job loss. The reported jobless rate has passed 10 percent but in fact it has already jumped to about 20 percent once we include among the unemployed all those who have stopped looking for jobs that have disappeared, those who work part-time but need full-time jobs, and those who work long hours at very low wages.

Environmental Degraders and Destroyers

In chapter 7 we meet the environmental killers. Many top scientists damn the selfish and ecologically defacing actions of countries like the United States, China, India, and others. These experts warn that our planet is fast heating up to perilous levels; humans are the villains, and, if our actions continue unabated, our present policies will destroy the planet. Meanwhile, government officials do little or next to nothing as we move ever closer to a global environmental catastrophe.

The Military, Industrial, and Big-Oil Complex

Continuing our countdown of the destructive components of ugly capitalism brings us logically to the intertwined and dangerous group I call "The Military, Industrial, and Big- Oil Complex." Chapter 8 discusses how this unholy coupling could bring on a global nuclear war all by itself. Corporations that manufacture weapons of war sell their wares to the Pentagon. Their profits depend on the government's desire for new, better, and more effective weapons systems. These corporations are the biggest supporters of war, though their words are couched in phrases designed to support what is euphemistically termed military preparedness.

Cartels revel in the loosely regulated manufacture of the instruments of war and the production and control of oil and gas prices. Sad to say, the United States also fails to curb the public's demand for oil by neglecting to employ innovative methods such as significantly raising the tax on (say) gasoline, forcing manufacturers to make cars that use far less gasoline per mile traveled, shifting production away from carbon-based fuels and toward hybrids and electric cars, aggressively seeking alternative sources of nonpolluting energy, and by prosecuting oil oligopolists and their cronies for their collusive acts. The coffers of global oligopolists overflow with many billions of dollars. As always, the poor consumers suffer most from soaring oil prices.

Self-Appointed Ascetics at War with Weapons of Mass Destruction

Chapter 9 features self-designated ascetics who are ready to wage war with whatever weapons of mass destruction (WMD) are at their disposal. In writing this chapter I am reminded of the Black Plague of the four-teenth century and how scrambling rats and fleas brought mass death throughout Europe. Compared to such a natural disaster, the threat posed by today's stockpiles of destructive weaponry is far greater. With so many areas of conflict in the world, countless self-styled ascetics, committed to one ideology or another, explode suicide bombs or engage in other forms of terrorism and in doing so they sacrifice their own lives *and ours* for their particular set of beliefs. If that weren't bad enough, just imagine the wholesale carnage they could bring about by engineering a global nuclear conflict. Key scientists warn that time is running out for the international community to avoid such cataclysmic consequences of radical beliefs running wild.

Can Science and New Leaders Save Capitalism?

Chapter 10 investigates the question of whether new leadership and new scientific advances, especially genetics and eugenics, can save or at least radically change capitalism to benefit all people. Put another way, are my dire forecasts for capitalism and humankind wrong? I still see solid evidence that humanity is oblivious to the horrifying risks of a global nuclear war. We can't even hear the repeated warnings of our very best and brightest minds.

The Evolution of Humankind in the Third Millennium

Early on I quoted J. C. Flugel's *Man, Morals, and Society.*[9] Flugel was adamant in attacking the idea, often voiced by conservative economists, that individual greed could have the cumulative effect of producing social harmony. He felt that quite the opposite is true. In all my earlier books and articles, and throughout this volume, I conclude that the sanctification of individual greed would bring with it a living hell for society. But can humankind succeed in casting aside its selfish and destructive ways in this new millennium?

That is the question I tackle in depth in chapters 11 and 12. I am especially interested to examine what roles science and new leaders might play in turning humanity from a violent and selfish species into truly benevolent creatures. How successful can science be in replacing hate and rage with love and compassion to usher in harmony and peace in the new century? Some readers may insist that I am naïve for even asking this question. Still, I am obliged to do so. At a minimum any helpful answers may serve as a counterweight to the dire forecasts I make in every chapter of this work.

Parallels of the United States Recession and the "Japanese Disease"

The recent dramatic US downturn has parallels with the collapse of Japan's megabubble stock market in 1990. In the wake of the market collapse, Japan's economic growth for the following ten years slowed to the point of what can only be described as a prolonged recession. I had earlier predicted (a) Japan's catastrophic stock market crash and (b) the economic collapse that then followed for many miserable years. I wrote that Japan faced by far the greatest economic collapse in its history.[10]

My current pessimism for the US stock market is deeply rooted in Bush's early refusal to use the full strength of the government to ward off a huge economic collapse with job-creating public works funded by the Fed. But wouldn't monetized deficit financing—the central bank creating money and credit on a substantial scale—be massively inflationary? Well, early on, severe oil and food inflation had already arrived even as housing prices continue to plunge. But if the current recession deepens much more it will quickly bring on a devastating deflation—falling prices coupled with reduced consumer demand as people with ever-dwindling resources wait on the sidelines to see if prices for the items they need will decline even more.

The Dollar and the President:
The Loss of Two Imperial Crowns

Over a longer time span, the lagging impact of government's overactive printing press will surely backfire. Raging inflation will then dominate the headlines. Sooner or later a rating agency or a senior government official will be pressured to cut the dollar's value among international currencies, a global valuation that has endured for many decades. To dethrone the dollar as a matter of policy would simultaneously undermine whatever administration happens to be in power at the time. The government's legacy would then be cemented for all time as one of the worst in America's history.

The Inextricable Bond Linking Science to Truth

A second constant theme that runs through each chapter is the indestructible bond linking science to truth. We all know that people bury truth under lies, superstition, myth, bad theory, and fake data.[11] Can we ever be *certain* that something is true? No. The philosopher Plato said long ago that happiness is the search for truth.[12] But you will never find *final truth for all time* in science. Why not? My short answer may help to guide readers through the chapters to follow:

1) Truth changes and evolves over the centuries with new research, new information, new experiments, new theory, and new data. "What is set forth as the unchanging gospel truth for all time cannot, therefore, be science."[13]

2) Truth must rest on the best theory and the best data. Either alone won't support it.

3) Truth must always walk hand-in-hand with honesty. Fake science in the service of extreme political, economic, or religious views can blot out truth for centuries.

4) Truth can never be locked up indefinitely. Sooner or later it will break out of any iron vault, secret meeting, or suppressed and doctored documents.

Truth and Consequences

I hope that my readers will judge this work to be a sincere search for truth and justice. But I am also convinced that it will infuriate many. They may simply hate to see the truth, especially when they are directly involved in the widespread abuses I document. I have already heard that I should not be partisan, that I should let the readers make their own judgments, that I should not be too opinionated, and that I should always present both sides of any issue.

I have no problems with such criticisms so long as I succeed in (a) identifying major problems, (b) offering solutions supported by good theory and good data, and (c) setting forth the truth forcefully to encourage others to help solve these problems. Most important, I will never accommodate the perpetrators of extreme abuse.

What a Good Preacher Does Best

The life's work of Reverend Martin Luther King Jr., was unfailingly to expose racism and ill treatment not only toward blacks but everyone. He always knew that any compromise with the harsh truth would be wrong and dishonest. In upholding the truth King was frequently ridiculed, hated, humiliated, often jailed, and finally murdered.

I believe one of King's primary goals was to hurl shame on evil people with the idea that some would listen and give up their evil ways. That's what a good preacher does best. My work also hurls shame on malicious people. My duty to justice and truth demands just that.

Chapter 1

THE PLAGUE OF GUN VIOLENCE ACROSS AMERICA

For everyone across America who's ever been counted out but refused to be knocked out, and for everyone who has stumbled but stood right back up, and for everyone who works hard but never gives up, this [message] is for you.
— Senator Hillary Clinton, on the campaign trail

Senator Clinton's words persuaded one reader to write, "That message resonates with voters who, when they are not bitterly clinging to their *guns* and *religion*, are having trouble . . . with their *mortgage payments.*[1] The wisdom of these comments as they pertain to guns, religion, and mortgage payments caught my attention.

This chapter deals with the plague of gun violence and the systemic nature of firearms deaths that continue to occur across America. Chapters 2 and 3 (the latter on the threat and reality of war) are logical extensions of a mentality that prompts political and religious leaders to ascend their proverbial soapboxes to persuade millions of people to fight and die as soldiers in often cruel and unjust wars. A mindset of cowboylike bravado concerning the use of guns feeds into a reckless and bellicose penchant to pick a fight. Uncontrolled gun slaughter and preemptive and illegal wars are just two of the deadly forces that can be found in an economy as it spirals out of control. And with the help of special interests that would benefit greatly from an influx of military spending, America's capitalist system took one more huge step toward a frightening financial meltdown and a major recession.

25

Today, many millions of desperate Americans have lost their homes, their savings, their jobs, and even their hopes for a brighter future.[2] The US economy is now hollowed out and seriously weakened by the Iraq and Afghanistan wars coupled with wasteful domestic spending on pork-barrel projects put in place not only by the administration of George W. Bush but by many previous administrations, as well as the earmarks of many a congressperson and senator. Huge opportunity costs show up in deteriorating bridges, potholed roads, shortages of good schools, a lack of modern hospitals, and less safe and efficient transit systems. The list of critical needs is endless and it will only grow so long as our resources are spent on wars that either should not have been started in the first place or appear to have no end in sight.

Deep Economic Slumps and High Suicide Rates

As confidence in the economy and hope for the future decline amid lost jobs, foreclosed homes, and failed businesses, the resulting atmosphere of despair give way to crime, family quarrels and shootings, mental depression, exhaustion, and a worrisome jump in murders and suicides as the unemployment rate continues to soar in a collapsing economy. The National Prevention Lifeline and other suicide-prevention groups have reported dramatically higher numbers of calls to their hotlines from anxious and desperate people who feel they have nowhere to turn. As I drive across the Tappan Zee Bridge in Westchester, New York, I see signs that say "Life Is Worth Living," yet people ignore these pleas and jump to their deaths into the Hudson River.

Multiple Self-Destructive Forces Imperil US Capitalism

Economic collapse, crime, murders, wars, and suicides are all linked. So are the forces of poverty, homelessness, acute inequalities of wealth, and the impact of an extreme laissez-faire doctrine. During the 2000 presidential election some right-wing Washington think tanks urged that the future administration of George W. Bush should emphasize loyalty to the commander and chief over experience when making key appointments. The predictable result was an abundance of unqualified hacks in office.

In the 1980s President Ronald Reagan declared, "Government is not the solution to our problem. Government is the problem." That kind of philosophy was directly germane to my forecast of the 1981-82 "maxirecession."[3] Runaway and extreme monetary and fiscal stimulus measures that featured major tax cuts led to a giant overinvestment boom that ultimately collapsed along with megabubble (speculative buying that drives up the price) stock gauges that crumbled. The resulting recession was easy to predict, at least for me. Deception and lying by federal officials contradicted their own beliefs. The same ludicrous right-wing and deceitful policies were carried out by George W. Bush. His bumbling ways made it easy for me to forecast the present financial meltdown and its economic implosion.[4] In sum, all of these closely interlinked forces now work to speed the downfall of US capitalism.

The Out-of-Control Gun Plague

Our discussion here of out-of-control gun violence in the United States is illustrative of an equally out-of-control economy, though it is not sufficient in and of itself to foretell total economic collapse. Many other destructive forces are at work simultaneously to destroy capitalism. They include selfishness, lying, arrogance, violence and murder, and a right-wing ideology that despises the idea that America needs a strong government to solve the many problems facing us.

I will try to document how an extreme conservative ideology feeds into gun horror, systemic shooting deaths, and injuries from gunshot wounds that maim or incapacitate innocent bystanders for the rest of their lives. Since the most seriously wounded often suffer constant pain, their exit strategy is sometimes suicide. Even the killers often choose suicide after they have murdered their wife, husband, and/or children; their schoolmates; or their own parent(s).

Shooters often kill dozens of people in what are officially called gun massacres, and then shoot themselves as their final gruesome act. The many millions of easily available and loosely controlled guns for sale in this country make this litany of horror all so easy. Needless and terrible carnage brought on by out-of-control gun availability grows worse by the day.

The National Rifle Association (NRA): Propaganda versus Truth[5]

Let's look first to the National Rifle Association (NRA) as one source of this plague of gun deaths. The NRA sees itself as a powerful and benevolent force. Yes, it is powerful but it can hardly be viewed as benevolent, and in my opinion it is seldom truthful. For example, the NRA insists that it promotes public safety through programs geared toward personal protection and gun safety for all who wish to participate. It glowingly describes itself in countless pamphlets and press releases as a nonprofit organization dedicated to the protection of the Second Amendment of our Constitution's Bill of Rights, which it believes safeguards an individual's right to own guns.

The NRA defends the right to own firearms and is an unceasing advocate for marksmanship, firearms safety, and the protection of hunting, as well as the right to individual self-defense with the use of a gun. That being said, the group's strong objections to effective and meaningful gun control and the use of its considerable resources through lobbying efforts to defeat any legislation that would enact such controls is couched in words that describe such laws as daggers aimed at the heart of the Second Amendment. However, it is precisely the proliferation of guns, the pitifully weak controls over these weapons, and the absurd pro-gun propaganda of the NRA and other gun-advocacy groups that helps to explain the growing number of horrible incidents that take place at the hands of gun-wielding individuals who seek their fifteen minutes of fame (notoriety) or who desire to settle some imagined score against those they believe have harmed them, or just against society at large by endangering whoever happens to be in their path at the time. Headline news reports every week tell us of the many injuries, deaths, and massacres that occur as a result of our gun culture.

The NRA is recognized as one of the most powerful political lobbies in the country. No doubt that's true but surely it is unfortunate for most Americans. Its lobbying is always at the expense of effective controls to stop gun violence. Gun ownership, it declares, is a civil liberty protected by the Second Amendment. That's debatable, but in any case the NRA does nothing to curb the plague of gun deaths across America. Its own website glorifies the assertion that its membership is over four million strong. Again, in my opinion, this is a fact that is extremely unfortunate for all those each day who are killed, whether intentionally or unintentionally, by someone brandishing a firearm.

Many Americans would be alive and well today if they had not been the victims of accidents or violence in which guns played a major role. It is my personal view—and I hope I am not alone in this—that the people of the United States would be far safer if the NRA and similar likeminded organizations were to become extinct. Oftentimes one sees flyers, bumper stickers, or ads that claim: "Guns Don't Kill People, People Kill People." This preposterous slogan is at once false and dangerous.

The Unholy Alliance

The truth, of course, is that guns *plus* people kill people. We often hear ourselves saying that "It takes two to tango." Well, it is also true that easily available guns end up in the hands of violent people, and all too often they are in the possession of criminals. Wide-ranging gun ownership rights coupled with few meaningful controls, or little or no enforcement of the gun controls that do exist, is a perfect recipe for widespread injury and death. Thanks to gun advocacy groups and their supporters in the Congress who defeat meaningful regulations, the executive branch in many administrations who have been reluctant to confront powerful lobbies, as well as many state and local governments, even criminals find it possible to carry concealed guns outside their homes, and they use these weapons to rob and kill with little fear.

But criminals are not the only ones running wild with guns. We have a pervasive gun culture in this nation, populated with cowboy-style advocates of individual freedom and self-defense who consider restrictions on gun ownership, the elimination or restricting of various types of guns, and other related regulations as gross violations of basic rights granted to us by our Constitution. Gun massacres in our schools and on our streets are now headline grabbers in the news each day. In this chapter I will show how out-of-control gun violence is closely linked to an economy on the edge of collapse. My emphasis will be both on the NRA's twisted and fallacious logic but also the terrifying data on how gun violence generates widespread injuries and deaths that cultivate a crippling attitude of fear in America.

Dissenting Comments of the AMA and the Brady Center

I am hardly alone in my caustic criticisms of the NRA. I believe its pitch is nothing more than self-glorification with no evidence to support its claims for superpatriot status. As Detective Joe Friday would say on the once popular television show *Dragnet*, "Please give me the facts, Sir." Yes, that's my task in this chapter.

But first let's hear briefly from the Brady Center to Prevent Gun Violence and from the American Medical Association.[6] They are my allies against gun terror. These two organizations accept none of the NRA's half-truths and absurd slogans that I document. Nor should they.

The Brady Center

The Brady Center to Prevent Gun Violence has long tracked gun-related violence and deaths. It also takes legal action in our courts to protect Americans from gun-toting killers. Here are just three recent instances it cites in its effort to ward off gun violence. First, it documents that law enforcement agencies and communities in general are less safe since the September 2004 expiration of the ban on oversized and extremely lethal rifles, often known as assault weapons, that are frequently used in shootouts with police. It says that the availability of assault weapons has changed the balance of power between law enforcement and criminals. At least fifteen police officers have been killed and twenty-three wounded since the gun ban expired. [7]

In a second case, the Brady Center hails a court ruling blocking domestic abusers from obtaining guns.[8] Such abusers anywhere throughout the country are prevented from buying guns because they would have to go through a mandatory background check, which would flag their convictions for abuse. A variety of persons are excluded from buying guns in the seven-day waiting period for background checks. But many still find guns illegally and there are few if any restrictions on buying guns by mail, on the Internet, or at the many gun shows that take place throughout the country.

In a third case the center brought a successful lawsuit against a gun dealer for supplying a rifle to a criminal who then used it to commit a murder. The family of the victim sued the gun dealer because the killer, a fugitive from justice and a methamphetamine user, was prohibited from buying or possessing guns. Yet he was able to purchase a rifle without the mandatory background check. Two days later he used the same gun to kill his victim. The Brady Center lawsuit contended that the gun dealer was liable for the victim's death because the dealer negligently and illegally provided the gun to the shooter. There are many gun deaths and crippling gun injuries such as this that I address in this chapter.[9]

The American Medical Association (AMA)

In 1997 the AMA concluded that gunshots caused almost 32,000 thousand fatal injuries and 100,000 nonfatal injuries in the United States. In addition to the enormous human toll from gun violence, the AMA calculated the average cost from gunshot injuries that included acute care and follow-up treatment costs. It estimated the average medical cost per injury at roughly $17,000. Its lengthy and complex mathematical set of confidence levels suggested, however, that the $17,000 estimate might be far too low.[10]

School-Related Shooting Deaths[11]

The term "school-related shootings" refers to gun violence in educational institutions, including any mass murder or spree killing that involves any educational institution. These shootings are perpetrated by any number of persons: those who are mentally unbalanced, those with a known mental disorder, expelled students, alumni, faculty members, outsiders, and even regular students who never seem to pose a problem to their classmates or to their teachers. Such shootings frequently involve numerous victims, some of whom may have been targeted, but often the actual victims are random individuals who are just in the shooter's path. Many of the killers commit suicide after their rampages.

The most frequently mentioned school killing is that which took place at Columbine High School, in Columbine, Colorado, on Tuesday, April 20, 1999, involving the murderous acts of students Eric Harris and Dylan Klebold. But the most deadly shooting, labeled a massacre, took place on the campus of the Virginia Polytechnic Institute and State University (Virginia Tech) in Blacksburg, Virginia, on April 16, 2007. The shooting spree consisted of two separate attacks occurring two hours apart. The perpetrator, Seung-Hui Cho, killed thirty-two people and wounded many others. The massacre stands as the deadliest shooting incident by a single gunman in US history, on or off a school campus.

The Disguised Santa Claus Shooter

It seems that even a disguised Santa Claus can unleash a bloodbath with guns. In news reports around the globe, a Santa Claus killing spree got under way about 11:30 P.M. on Christmas Eve 2008 in Covina California.[12]

When an eight-year-old girl attending a Christmas Eve party answered a knock at her door, she admitted a man dressed as Santa who was carrying what was thought to be a present but turned out to be a handgun instead. He shot the little girl in the face, and then began shooting indiscriminately as partygoers tried to flee. Police said the shooter was Bruce Pardo who had just reached a settlement with his ex-wife. Pardo's ex-wife and her parents were listed among those killed. The gift-wrapped box Pardo carried was a pressurized container he used to set fire to the house. The body of the ninth victim was found the next morning. Pardo committed suicide with a bullet to his head, which is typical of mad or deranged killers who have easy and cheap access to guns.

Worldwide Gun Horror: April 1981 to October 2008

I was sickened to discover the breadth and magnitude of school-related gunshot injuries and deaths worldwide. Since I am mainly interested in the gun horror experienced in the United States, I spent several days isolating the gun incidents in America from the international listing of all gun incidents. A brief scan of these terrible acts makes clear the stark horror of gun availability that has long been permitted to remain unchecked.[13] Each incident (attack) includes the date, the location, the attackers, and the number of injuries and deaths. Sources such as Wikipedia and others estimate that a complete worldwide list of nonmilitary gunshot incidents for the last one hundred years would total at least 500 million. I purposely use the term "incidents" because these cases could easily have multiple deaths and/or injuries making the number of persons involved potentially dramatically higher.[14]

Recent Gun Horror in the United States 2006 to 2008

Let's focus on the most recent US data for the years 2006, 2007, and 2008, applicable solely to school-related attacks in elementary and secondary schools as well as universities and colleges. Each incident includes the date, the location, the attackers, the number of injuries and deaths, and brief published details on the alleged cause of the attacks. The list covers primary and secondary schools first, then colleges and universities. The sequence is in ascending chronological order and intended to show the enormity of the social challenge we face as a nation.

Primary and Secondary Schools[15]

January 13, 2006; Longwood, Florida; Charles Penley (age fifteen); 1 dead. Penley held his class hostage with a handgun before being fatally shot by police.

August 30, 2006; Hillsborough, North Carolina; Alvaro Castillo (age nineteen); 1 dead, 2injured. Castillo fired a rifle and shotgun eight times to wound two students at Orange High School. Castillo killed his father with a firearm before driving to the school.

September 27, 2006; Bailey, Colorado; Duane Morrison (age fifty-three); 2 dead, 5 injured. Morrison took six female hostages at Platte Canyon High School. He sexually assaulted them. When sixteen-year-old Emily Keyes tried to run away, he shot and killed her before killing himself.

September 29, 2006; Cazenovia, Wisconsin; Erich Hainstock (age fifteen); 1 dead. Hainstock brought a shotgun and handgun to Weston High and killed the principal.

October 2, 2006; Lancaster County, Pennsylvania; Charles Carl Roberts (age thirty-two); 6 dead, 5 injured. Roberts entered an Amish school, killed five young girls and injured five other students before killing himself.

October 9, 2006; Joplin, Missouri; Thomas White (age thirteen); no injuries; White fired an assault rifle inside his school. After firing one shot the gun jammed.

January 3, 2007; Tacoma, Washington; Douglas Chanthabouly (age eighteen); 1 dead. After a dispute, Douglas shot and killed Samnang Kok in one of the schools hallways.

January 19, 2007; Sudbury, Massachusetts; John Ogdren (age sixteen); 1 dead. Ogdren stabbed a fellow student to death. No guns were used.

February 8, 2007; Prineville, Oregon; Marc Hollingsworth (age eighteen); 1 dead. Hollingsworth committed suicide with a gunshot wound to the head in the high school's parking lot.

March 7, 2007; Midland, Michigan; David Turner (age seventeen); 1 dead, 1 injured. Turner shot seventeen-year-old Jessica Forsyth four times, critically wounding her before turning the gun on himself.

March 7, 2007; Greenville, Texas; Joey Horn (age sixteen); 1 dead. Horn shot himself.

April 10, 2007; Gresham, Oregon; Chad Escobedo (age fifteen); 10 injured. Escobedo shot windows out of classrooms, injuring ten students. He missed the instructor who was his intended target.

April 18, 2007; Huntersville, North Carolina; Josh Emerson Cook (age sixteen); 1 dead. Cook threatened two students with a gun in the high school parking lot and then died of a self-inflicted gunshot wound.

May 4, 2007; El Maton, Texas; Alison Camacho (age fifteen); 1 dead. Camacho fatally shot herself in a restroom of her high school.

September 28, 2007; Oroville, California; Greg Wright (age seventeen); no injuries. Wright held a group of students and a teacher hostage in the band room at Las Plumas High School, firing at the ceilings until police arrived.

October 7, 2007; Crandon, Wisconsin; Tyler Peterson (age twenty); 7 dead, 1 injured. Peterson, a part-time police officer, murdered three current and three former students of Crandon High School who were attending a party at a private home. He then reportedly committed suicide.

October 10, 2007; Cleveland, Ohio; Asa H. Coon (age fourteen); 1 dead, 5 injured. Coon went on a shooting spree in Success Tech Academy and later committed suicide after a police chase.

February 7, 2008; Portsmouth, Ohio; William Michael Layne (age fifty-six); 1 dead, 1 injured. Layne walked into his wife's fifth-grade class and wounded her and was later killed by police.

College and University School Attacks[16]

September 3, 2006; Shepherdstown, West Virginia; Douglas W. Pennington (age forty-nine); 3 dead. Pennington killed his two sons while visiting them at the university they attended, then fatally shot himself.

September 17, 2006; Pittsburgh, Pennsylvania; 5 injured. Gunshots are fired outside Duquesne University after a dance party, injuring five members of the basketball team.

April 2, 2007; Seattle, Washington; Jonathan Rowan (age forty-one); 2 dead. Rowan fatally shot his girlfriend, Rebecca Griego, and then committed suicide on the University of Washington campus.

April 16, 2007; Blacksburg, Virginia; Cho Seung-Hui (age twenty-three); 33 dead, 25 injured. This attack soon became known as the Virginia Tech massacre. It took place at the Virginia Polytechnic Institute and State University. Cho Seung-Hui also took his own life after his shooting rampage.

August 4, 2007; Newark, New Jersey; Jose Carranza and three Delaware State University Students; 3 dead, 1 injured. The attackers forced three university students to kneel against an elementary school wall. Then they shot them, execution-style.

September 21, 2007; Dover, Delaware; Loyer D. Braden (age eighteen); 2 injured. Braden, a student at Delaware State University, fired four to six rounds hitting two seventeen-year-old students.

September 30, 2007; Memphis, Tennessee; DeeShawn Tate (age twenty-one), Victor Trezvant (age twenty-one) and Courtney Washington (age twenty-two); 1 dead. These three men were arrested for the fatal shooting of University of Memphis football player Taylor Bradford in what was believed to be a targeted attack.

February 8, 2008; Baton Rouge, Louisiana; Latina Williams (age twenty-three); 3 dead. Williams opened fire in a classroom at Louisiana Technical College killing two before committing suicide.

February 14, 2008; DeKalb, Illinois; Steven Kazmierczak (age twenty-seven); 6 dead, 16 injured. Kazmierczak opened fire with a shotgun and three handguns at Cole Hall on the campus of Northern Illinois University, killing 5 and wounding 16, then he committed suicide.

The easy availability of guns, absent a society dedicated to enforcing strong controls that monitor who can obtain these weapons and under what circumstances, serves to place the entire social structure at risk. Increasing numbers of lethal weapons on the market coupled with a high demand for them among people who fear for their own safety and who wish to protect their property in an unstable economic climate in which moral commitment is weak, all serve to make conditions ripe for a lethal perfect storm of instability that threatens to shred the social fabric. These frequent rips and tears become commonplace, often serving as convenient excuses for justifying self-aggrandizing behavior, whether personal, economic, or political, that promises short-term gain but risks damaging the nation's social structure in the long term.

Murder and Gun Madness in New York City

Before investigating the many reasons why people kill people with easily available guns, I thought I would check the city's newspapers on a daily basis for gunshot injuries and deaths. In the New York City area alone I counted fifteen people who were shot dead in just twenty-two days.[17] Please check my count and pay special attention to the many reasons given to explain the bloodshed:

1) A shooting tied to a divorce leaves 2 dead
2) Ex-trooper fatally shot his wife, her lawyer, and himself
3) A 14-year-old boy shot a 15-year-old dead
4) A businessman shot and killed Mr. Wang
5) (Mr. Chase) was killed by a drive-by shooting
6) (Mr.) Casanova and [Mr.] Watkins were shot dead
7) Gunshots into a passing car lead to bystander's death
8) In three separate outdoor parties gunmen opened fire leaving two people dead and injuring three, one critically
9) An armed man and his (young) daughter, whom he (used) as a shield, died in a shootout with the police.

Hail to God; the NRA; and the Red, White, and Blue

I continue to follow the news reports on gun deaths and injuries every week. The dark string of firearms-related deaths for men, women, and children is a forewarning of even greater and more needless carnage yet to come. I can only conclude that the number of gunfire incidents is probably understated, often deliberately. Internet sources, the Brady Center, and the AMA, among other groups, share my outrage. They repeatedly warn, for example, that their own tallies of gunshot deaths are probably far too low.

In any case, the American public, the Congress, and most certainly the NRA are oblivious, or pretend to be oblivious, to the ghastly magnitude of gun horror. Still, before we can fully appreciate the enormity of this gun quandary, we must first analyze the many reasons that account for the deaths and injuries stemming from out-of-control firearms.

To use an analogous situation, most American families and many municipalities try to gain the upper hand on out-of-control fireworks when celebrating the Fourth of July and other holidays. We seem concerned enough about personal and public safety to mandate regulations restricting the sale of these explosives even though the number of deaths and injuries from fireworks are miniscule compared to the escalating number of gun injuries and fatalities. Why is this? For an answer let's look at the reasons that underlie the carnage from firearms.

Evidence of NRA Deception and Fake Slogans

One reason rests with the patently false assurances the NRA and others offer about gun safety. While the NRA's favorite gun slogan makes no sense, it is still taken as the gospel truth by both the membership and millions of Americans. Their slogan is worth repeating. It reads:

**The NRA Protects America. Guns don't kill people.
People kill people.**

You may have seen this on bumper stickers, lamp posts, or even some buildings. Once several rough and tough NRA superpatriots tried to convince me of the truth of their slogan. I responded by offering my counter-slogan in an attempt to demonstrate their logical error. Instead, they swore at me with profanity best described as unprintable.[18] My slogan reads:

Atomic bombs don't kill people. People kill people.

Still, the NRA members had enough sense to understand that if my parallel but ludicrous slogan made no sense, as I intended, then their slogan must also be dismissed as illogical.[19]

The Multiple Reasons behind the Gunshot Crimes

We must examine closely the many reasons for the violent storm of gun deaths across America. One reason is that many people are consumed by hate and rage or are afflicted with a serious mental disorder. What were the causes of the shooting massacre at Columbine High School in 1999 that left fifteen people dead?[20] What were the causes of the Virginia Tech Massacre on April 16, 2007, that killed thirty-two people? Who knows for sure?

Yet there was little argument over another shooting that made headline news: "Mentally Disturbed Killer Shoots 8 to Death in a Postal Rampage."[21] Just add up the fifteen dead at Columbine High School, thirty-two dead in the Virginia Tech massacre, and eight dead in the post office attack. That's a total of fifty-five people shot dead in just three attacks out of the hundreds already tracked. My key point is that criminals, mentally sick people, and many others get their hands on guns that are easily available because ours is a morally sick culture with pitifully weak gun controls.

Consider this Halloween incident: "[A] 16-year old knocked on a door as a prank. [The] homeowner mistook him for a burglar and shot him dead."[22] Some may claim that the boy caused his own death because he tried to trick or scare the homeowners. The property owner might have genuinely believed that his life and the lives of his family members were at risk. At least that's what the NRA would have us believe. A better logic is the need for strict gun controls to reduce the numbers of illegally owned firearms augmented by gun safety programs (possibly like those the NRA offers) for those who can obtain such weapons legitimately, both of which would help to prevent these regrettable accidents from happening.

Another report on careless hunters was featured in the *Wall Street Journal*.[23] Many readers may be unaware that the journal is happy with weak and voluntary gun controls. One need only peruse the journal's editorial pages to appreciate my point. The paper ranks hunter fun first and safety for all others dead last. Still, the journal listed four safety rules for hunting quail: (1) As the quails take flight, shoot at an "upward angle." But the shooter shot "low." (2) "Make sure you know where all the [hunters] are." But the shooter did not. (3) "Be certain of what is in front of or behind the target." The shooter was not certain. (4) Drink "no alcohol." The shooter drank alcohol shortly before the shooting.

The careless shooter in question also opposes safe gun controls. I believe you have heard of him. It was none other than Dick Cheney, then vice president of the United States and a long-time avid supporter of the NRA.[24] He wounded a fellow hunter and covered it up for days. So, what was the cause? The incident was caused by a deadly mix of careless hunters, alcohol, weak controls, and poor law enforcement. It's that simple.

One alert gun analyst concluded, "In [one year] seventy-nine people died hunting, but only eight college and high school players died from football injuries,"[25] a sport that is known for injuries and the occasional accidental death. Query: Is hunting a deadly sport (for those other than the designated prey)? Yes. Without strong controls hunting has always been a deadly sport. Many hunters die. Yet NRA counterfeit patriots pretend to be blind to these gun tragedies.

Relevant here are Brady Center advertisements containing a picture of a gun and a warning: "Thinking about a Florida vacation? Make sure your family is safe." That warning makes sense in view of the concealed pistols people carry in their jackets in Florida. The NRA acts very much like the old-time rough and ready cowboys who consistently shot first and then celebrated with whiskey later. A cowboy gun mentality still shames America.

The Second Amendment Fight

The NRA is an avid defender of the Second Amendment, which reads:

> A well regulated militia, being necessary to the security of a free state, the right of the people to keep and bear arms shall not be infringed.

For many decades the courts ruled that a *well-regulated militia* meant the police and the military, not *private individuals*. The language is a bit muddy and therefore has remained a topic of debate for decades. What is clear is the curse of death brought on by the prevalence of guns, whether they be legally or illegally obtained, and the feeble gun controls coupled with equally feeble enforcement of the laws we do have on the statute books. To aggravate matters further, the District of Columbia Court ruled on March 7, 2007, that individuals could keep their guns and carry them in public. I can reach only one grim conclusion from the court's opinion: that "life, liberty, and the pursuit of happiness" are now empty words for those who have been fatally shot or risk being victims.[26]

One thing for sure is that the NRA will always block strong gun controls. One city mayor said, "The NRA is…out to stop anything that would get guns off the streets of this city. There's going to come one [more] massacre when the public says, 'We're not going to have it anymore.'"[27] The mayor is right. The NRA's efforts to stifle gun control must be stopped.

The Deadly Celebration of Ultrafree Gun Rights

In extreme laissez faire style the NRA and its millions of supporters demand that guns be free of regulation and controls. In that sense the gun lovers are linked to the right-wing ideologues who brought us the ongoing financial meltdown and economic implosion. The gun advocates are also tied closely to those who glorify war on false grounds. They think alike and act alike to spark powerful forces that destroy an economy already on the brink. In short, they are also helping to destroy capitalism.

Is there a way out of the ongoing culture of guns and death? Yes. Strong gun controls must replace weak ones and we must enforce the laws we have to their full effect. Otherwise, those who possess the guns will continue to increase the death toll across America and a dark future looks very likely. Presently, America has a cruel cowboy culture of out-of-control gun possession. This culture of death and war in the guise of personal freedom and public safety shows up everywhere. It has invaded popular culture in books, films, and in the lyrics to popular songs.

We know that hunters with guns all too often kill innocent bystanders. How about hunters with guns plus alcohol? Together they kill thousands of people every year across America. The gun plague is here and now. Consider the evidence:

✓ In 2006 there were over 34,000 gun deaths in the United States [close to 37,000 in 2007]. Suicides accounted for 54 percent, homicide 41 percent, and accidental deaths 3 percent. Firearm injuries are the eighth leading cause of death in the United States. For every fatal shooting there are roughly three nonfatal ones.[28]

✓ In 1998 handguns murdered 373 people in Germany, 151 people in Canada, 57 people in Australia, 19 people in Japan, 54 people in England and Wales, and 11,769 people in the United States (excluding suicides).[29]

✓ Among twenty-six industrialized nations, 86 percent of gun deaths among children under age fifteen occurred in the United States.[30]

✓ Every two years more Americans die from firearm injuries than the total number of American soldiers killed during the eight-year Vietnam War.[31]

✓ States with the greatest number of guns in private homes also have the highest rates of homicide. In the 25 percent of US states with the highest level of gun ownership, the overall homicide rate was 60 percent higher than in those states with the lowest 25 percent of gun-owning households. The rate of homicides involving guns was more than twice as high in the former group than in the latter.[32]

Gun Possession and Carry Laws[33]

Guns are everywhere. It's no wonder, then, that gun carnage abounds. Several studies tell us that some 40 percent of American households own one firearm or more. Many are legally owned. The owners say they are used for sport shooting, hunting, or protection from intruders in their homes. An estimated 75 percent of gun owners insist that the main reason is for personal and family protection or to protect their property or business. Americans now hold 192 million firearms, including 65 million handguns. Almost 40,000 firearms are sold every day in the United States, including about 18,000 handguns.[34]

Just who are the gun owners? In a recent year about 25 percent of the guns were obtained through robbery or burglaries. In other words, criminals break into homes and business and steal the guns they find on the premises. Many young people possess guns. One in seven juveniles was reported to be carrying a gun outside the home. In our central cities gun ownership is far higher. One study of 800 inner-city high school students reported that roughly one-fifth of them carried pistols or small handguns. Upwards of 88 percent of juvenile offenders reported carrying firearms.[35]

In 1994 the Bureau of Alcohol, Tobacco, and Firearms responded to almost 90,000 requests by police departments to track the sources of guns involved in criminal activity. Among juvenile drug dealers, over 40 percent were reported to have used a gun to commit a criminal offense. Many were gang members.[36]

The Many Reasons People with Guns Kill People

Let's expand further on this plague of guns and death in America. Have you ever thought about what may happen when a little child pulls the trigger on a gun he or she has found in a desk drawer, in a closet, or under the parents' bed? The child mistakenly thinks the gun is unloaded. Bang, bang. The trigger is pulled and a best friend lies dead. How about the hunter who aims at a deer and the bullet whizzes by to kill a little girl or a fellow hunter?[37]

Suppose a man and his wife get into a violent argument: will one of them resort to shooting the other? It happens every day. The gun in the drawer makes killing easy. If you drink too much alcohol and become angry in public, would you ever shoot someone? It happens every day. A gun under your jacket makes that possibility all too easy.[38]

Hunters who do not kill for survival but for sport shoot birds, deer, bears, tigers, jaguars, elephants, and other animals for the thrill of it. Their macho pride, one of the seven deadly sins, is at work. They glorify killing for the fun—the challenge—of it. Their egos demand the biggest trophy antlers for their walls. They make false pitches for weak gun controls even as many thousands of Americans are either killed or suffer crippling wounds for life. Hunters seeking full gun rights but pathetically weak gun controls disgrace America even as they parade proudly but falsely as great patriots.

Guns and Gangs in Major Cities[39]

It is estimated that in 1996 some 31,000 gangs with 846,000 members, were shooting and killing people in almost 5,000 cities and towns in the United States. The risk of gang members being shot dead is 60 percent higher than for the overall population. Gang members also get involved in drug use, drug sales, and the inevitable gun violence that occurs with such illegal activity. In some cities, for example, Los Angeles, Chicago, and St. Louis, gun deaths and injuries are far higher. St. Louis has a gang homicide rate one thousand times higher than the overall homicide rate for the entire country. Young gangs have invaded the schools in cities, towns, and rural areas across the country.

Innocent Bystanders in the Line of Fire

In researching why and where these gangs sprout up, it should come as no surprise that they flourish in areas of extreme poverty. Garfield Park, for example, is one of Chicago's most violent neighborhoods and it is steeped in poverty. With the easy availability of guns, gangs go to war. Bystanders, including little children, are also shot dead in the mayhem. Gangs at war retaliate for losing one of their own who may have been shot during turf wars with other gangs. The retaliation leads to many more deaths of opposing gang members as well as innocent residents who happen to be unfortunate enough to find themselves in the line of fire.

Weak Gun Controls Foreshadow Record Gun Massacres

To be sure, the theoretical and empirical evidence point to an epidemic of gun violence. Weak local, state, and federal gun controls offer little protection. Voluntary gun controls by private groups are a cruel joke since they are imposed on those who are least likely to violate them. In the absence of major new substantive gun controls to keep weapons out of the hands of those who cannot use them responsibly, we should look for more gun massacres in our schools, on our streets, in our parks, and elsewhere.

Despite alarming headlines, the pro-gun lobby still has strong support from the White House and the Congress, Republicans and Democrats in general, the NRA, and even the Supreme Court. The Court recently declared that the Second Amendment does not block individuals from owning or carrying guns in public. That's an avalanche of very bad news. Contrary to NRA falsehoods and Supreme Court decisions, the best of science warns that gun carry laws end more lives than they save. Concealed or not, those with guns kill people. The evidence shows up in fourteen recent mass shootings in Western democracies. Seven of these killings took place here in the United States.

America bans its citizens from owning or making bombs, and the sale many explosive materials are carefully monitored, and these procedures work. We know that guns cause needless deaths for adults and children every day. Thus, one solution is in plain sight: ban private guns everywhere. Is there any politician who will demand strong gun controls?

Mayor Bloomberg of New York City does, and he deserves high praise for his courageous stand.

Sinful Silence: Political Candidates Keep Quiet on Gun Controls

Sad to say, most political candidates avoid the gun issue. They rail against violence and promote stiff penalties for violating the current laws but they offer few, if any, critical comments about the NRA, and for one major reason: They want the votes and the campaign support the NRA and other gun advocates control. Is not their silence itself a sin that puts many Americans, including politicians, at risk of being shot dead? Well, this short list of assassinations and attempts leads me to answer the question with a resounding yes.[40]

> Lincoln, dead (1865); Garfield, dead (1881); McKinley, dead (1901), Theodore Roosevelt, bullet deflected (1912); Franklin D. Roosevelt, bullet missed (1933); John F. Kennedy, dead (1963); Senator Robert Kennedy, dead (1968); Martin Luther King, dead (1968); George C. Wallace, paralyzed (1972); Gerald R. Ford, unharmed (1975); Ronald Reagan, wounded (1981).

Who is next? Well, this frightening history and the current lack of resolve to ban guns signals to me that the present horror will get worse, a lot worse. Good theory and good data make clear that the United States fails to shield its own leaders from the threat of being killed by firearms. Still, out-of-control gun violence is but one reason I look for an end to capitalism in the United States. Another is the terror of guns in the hands of the war dogs among us.

Close Links between Gunslingers and War Dogs Threaten US Capitalism

So just how does this widespread plague of gun violence relate to my ominous forecast for US capitalism? The answer is simply that uncontrolled killers running wild, wherever they may be, are a menace to capitalism. Even now guns (and bombs) kill millions of people in India, Russia, Africa, and elsewhere across the globe. Will the United States do nothing to stop our own *home grown horror* from getting far worse?

I try to answer that question in chapter 2, where I assess the strong and growing links between the gun-happy US cowboy culture and our bellicose war dogs. But a short answer should be obvious. The gunslingers and the war dogs are one and the same. They think alike, act alike, and together pose a terrifying threat to any future for US capitalism.

Chapter 2

THE MACHO WAR DOGS

My purpose here is to point out the close linkage between the gun bullies we discussed in chapter 1 and what I call the macho war dogs, who are eager to use the flimsiest of excuses to justify their desire for battle. You'll recall the deceptive and illogical slogan touted by the macho gun bullies: "Guns don't kill people. People kill people." It's easy to show such a slogan to be false by making up a similar but fatally flawed counterexample. I created the slogan "Atomic bombs don't kill people. People kill people." Any fool can see instantly that both slogans are false. It is people *with guns* who kill people *and* people at war *using bombs* who kill.

It is the height of absurdity to separate guns or bombs from the people who use them to kill others. It takes people using either form of weaponry to destroy their fellow human beings. So, the next time you see or hear a slogan you believe to be highly questionable, try (a) identifying the slogan or other statement you think is false, (b) making up a similar slogan that is also patently false, and (c) supporting your view with sound theory and first-class data.[1] One should reason like a scientist, always demanding solid theory and empirical support. There is no other way to arrive at the truth.

Sound Reasoning: We Must Have Theoretical and Empirical Support

Suppose that a big, strong school-yard bully throws a smaller and weaker schoolboy to the ground just for the fun of it. Assume further that the small boy (a) had no warning of the attack and (b) was at no time a threat to the bully. In such a case many would have to conclude that the macho bully committed an evil first strike attack without provocation. (A macho is anyone who mistakenly thinks he or she is superior to most people. A macho may also be selfish and cruel.)

History has certainly taught us that nations, like individuals, can also attack another nation without warning and on false grounds. That's an evil first-strike military attack. The surprise Japanese attack on Pearl Harbor is one well-known example. The US first-strike attack on Iraq that started the second Iraq war is another. Both lacked legitimacy.

The Common Denominator of Evil

In chapter 1 we discussed gun advocates, and in this chapter we are concerned with war dogs (warmongers) or international bullies. Both possess the power to do great harm.[2] We'll listen in on the plans of the war dogs for a secret first-strike military attack. But first let's rank them by the degree of power each one has. The ranking helps us to appraise who is responsible for the policy failures that brought great damage to America and the world.

The Ranking of Power and Blame for Failed Policies

1) Former US President George W. Bush was the most powerful of the war dogs. He had a reckless propensity to rush into war for false reasons. He claimed that God made him president. Really? As it turns out, Bush showed himself to be an egotistical bungler, a hypercritical compassionate conservative, a deceiver, and a bellicose warmonger. His credibility at home and abroad dropped so low that, toward the end of his second term, few had confidence in anything he had to say.

2) Former Vice President Dick Cheney was also a first-strike war dog who allegedly was willing to break domestic and international law to get his way. He supported the gun bullies we met earlier. They love him. He loves them. They all love the NRA. Cheney also provided indirect support to the military, industrial, and big-oil complex (see chapter 8).

3) Former Secretary of Defense Donald Rumsfeld liked to charge headlong into a full military attack. He constantly invented reasons for his first-strike assault on Iraq even as his "shock and awe" military attacks backfired. Criticized severely and repeatedly for his poor military judgment, Rumsfeld finally resigned. Bush then appointed another defense secretary who continued to parrot whatever his commander-in-chief demanded.

4) Former Attorney General Roberto Gonzales was fond of jailing the guilty and the innocent alike. He was responsible in part for the cruel imprisonment and torture of alleged terrorist detainees. Like the president, the attorney general operated under the barbaric rule that a detainee was guilty until proven guilty, and should have no access to legal representation or a nonmilitary judge and jury. Gonzales eventually resigned because many on Capitol Hill viewed him as cruel, dishonest, and inept. Like many others, I was utterly dismayed by his arguments justifying the alleged torture of those detained from Iraq, Afghanistan, and elsewhere. As President Barak Obama has made clear recently, torture can never be justified!

5) Former Secretary of State Colin Powell, during his short term in office, reminded me of a caring and concerned man who had been tricked by his political superiors into supporting an immoral and illegal preemptive war. Eventually, when Powell disagreed with Bush's actions and his less-than-adequate justifications, he was fired by the president and replaced by Bush's security adviser, Condoleezza Rice. She struck me as a loyal and obedient robot. She, too, seemed unable to see, hear, and speak ill of an evil president, or was she just afraid or confused? It is up to the public to decide.

Sneer, Smear, Blame, and Shame

We all know people we would classify as aggressive war dogs. Their more public counterparts hit the news headlines daily. Whatever their actual names, their actions and motivations fall into four major categories, which I have named Smear, Sneer, Blame, and Shame.

Smear says bad things about you if you disagree with the president about almost anything. Sneer watches you with sharp eyes and a twisted and wicked smile. Blame accuses you of bad things that you never actually did. Shame reminds you constantly of those same bad things you never did. All four work together as a cruel team. They justify their behavior as good American patriots fighting terror. But honest American patriots they are not. Until these four character assassins are stopped they will continue to destroy liberty and free speech.

Evil Plans for a Preemptive War

It's not hard to imagine finding plans that Bush and Cheney drew up for their first-strike attack on Iraq. Here is my "transcript" of how the imaginary planning session would proceed:

Bush: I am the commander-in-chief. Either you are for me or against me. Secretary Powell, you said some things that disturb me about your loyalty.

Powell: Sir, you are planning a first-strike attack on Iraq. But we have little evidence that Saddam Hussein plans to attack us or that he has any weapons of mass destruction (WMD).

Bush: Cut it. Iraq is a major threat to democracy and freedom. It has WMD andwill use them. Did you forget that the 9/11 terrorist sympathizers are still our enemies?

Powell: Sir, we must have stronger evidence on Iraq's plans and. . . .

Cheney: And nothing! We must bomb their military leaders. Our quick victory will shock and overpower their army.

Rumsfeld: The Iraqi army and citizens will welcome us with love and flowers.

Powell: The photos you have on WMD are fuzzy. They may be OK but. . . .

Cheney: No buts. Look, the 9/11 terrorists destroyed our World Trade Center.

Powell: Sir, could a first-strike attack that bypasses United Nations support backfire and. . . .

Bush: General Powell, are you with me or against me? This meeting is over!

Torture Defined

Among his other nefarious policies, Bush appeared to be a stronger believer in torture, as I stressed in the introduction. But before we proceed further, we need an accurate definition of torture, not the broad and sweeping terms Bush and his cronies have used to describe it. *Webster's New Universal Unabridged Dictionary* defines torture with startling precision:

Torture (1) is the act of inflicting excruciating pain as punishment or revenge, as a means of getting a confession or information, or for sheer cruelty and (2) a method of inflicting pain and the extreme anguish [and] agony of body and mind [that] causes extreme pain.

As I'll shortly document, this definition fits perfectly the horrors of torture we have learned about from the media. Surely everyone in power in the present Obama administration should memorize every word.

Torture as Defined by the United States Army Basic Field Manual

However, former President Bush was unlikely to read, much less memorize, the real meaning of torture. Indeed, he was upset with its description in the *United States Army Basic Field Manual*. He argued that the army rules were too constrictive.[3] Well, the manual requires the Central Intelligence Agency and other government agencies "to abide by the restrictions on holding and interrogating prisoners." The manual contains a blanket prohibition of torture when interrogating prisoners. It also identifies the specific examples of torture that are strictly prohibited:

1) Forcing a prisoner to be naked, perform sexual acts, or pose in a sexual manner.

2) Placing hoods or sacks over the head of a prisoner and using duct tape over the eyes. Applying beatings, electric shocks, burns, or other forms of physical pain.

3) Waterboarding (forced dunking into water to create the fear of drowning).

4) Using military working dogs to terrify prisoners.

5) Inducing hypothermia or heat injury.

6) Conducting mock executions that may frighten a person to death.

7) Depriving a prisoner of necessary food, water, or medical care.

8) Jailing a prisoner and subjecting him to freezing temperatures and loud and blaring music so that he can't sleep or rest and may therefore risk death.

Bush and Cheney needed to specify the acts of "interrogation" that they would condone within the guidelines of the army field manual.

The US Torture of Detainees at Guantanamo Bay

On Tuesday May 20, 2008, a former US imprisoned detainee, Murat Kurnaz, testified before the US Congress that he had suffered extreme torture that included but was not limited to "electric shock, simulated drowning, and days spent chained by his arms to a ceiling."[4] The lawmakers were enraged, since the Pentagon had repeatedly denied any use of torture.

To make matters worse, Kurnaz was held for four years *after* US intelligence agencies had already concluded that he had "no known links to terrorism." Of course, the Pentagon and the White House were not likely to tell us how many other detainees suffered unjust imprisonment and torture. But the whole story of US torture and false imprisonment would some day burst into the open. Truth cannot be locked up indefinitely. In fact, President Obama's recent disclosure of CIA memos outlining such alleged torture techniques and their use on detainees has brought a firestorm of criticism against the Bush administration and those who offered a legal justification for their use.[5]

Recently declassified reports showed that both US and German intelligence agencies knew as early as 2002 that Mr. Kurnaz had no links whatsoever to terrorism. Despite this knowledge, he was still held for four more years in Guantanamo.[6] His testimony to Congress and a report of the FBI made it clear that harsh and inhuman torture by the United States at the Guantanamo Bay detention center was pretty much the rule, verifying what many worldwide perceived as America's brutality in its conduct of an illegal war on Iraq. The reaction of the Congress was explosive. Both Republicans and Democrats, who had earlier believed the denials of torture by the Pentagon, reacted with outrage and regret at Kurnaz's statements. For years former President Bush, his submissive Republicans, and nervous Democrats denied legal safeguards for the detainees. They were labeled as "unlawful enemy combatants." That action placed these persons in a legal, political, and military limbo, which, in itself, took away any pretense of justice and human decency for the prisoners.

Habeas Corpus Denied

The suffering of the detainees did not end with these public disclosures. How would any of us feel if we were falsely charged and then had no way to contest our confinement or the extreme torture we suffered? That's the way Bush and his high-level advisers wanted it. Had any American citizen been subjected to such treatment a howl of injustice would have been heard from every corner of our nation. The legal right of habeas corpus is guaranteed to all in our Constitution. It means that anyone so confined has the right to be confronted with the accusations or charges against him and to challenge both their veracity and his manner of confinement before a nonmilitary court, judge, and jury. Relevant here is a recent ray of legal hope, for after many years of lawbreaking and hideous treatment of detainees by our federal government, the US Supreme Court finally awakened. It ruled that detainees also have that prized legal right to challenge the government and to get their chance for freedom.[7]

After all, Bush often tried to deny habeas corpus. He saw to it that prisoners seized in Afghanistan and elsewhere were piled into the Guantanamo facility. He claimed that since Guantanamo detention center is in a foreign country the detainees could not then challenge their status in a United States court. To be sure, the Supreme Court handed the Bush administration a major defeat. It concluded that the Military Commission Act violates the Constitution.[8]

Readers will note that I have used Bush's name rather than one of his senior officials. These abuses of basic human rights represent a moral outrage; and while anyone who may have been complicit in authorizing them should share legal responsibility as well, the commander-in-chief as chief executive for the nation must be held ultimately responsible. I sincerely hope someday that Bush will be forced to testify under oath for his wanton destruction of liberty, free speech, and democracy.

"Dying in Detention"[9]

It's the responsibility of the United States to provide medical care and good food to those individuals it jails. That's rule number one for humane treatment under any international convention one might want to reference, whether those detained are enemy combatants or hardworking immigrants. But in fact the *Washington Post*, the *New York Times*, and CBS News have reported quite the opposite. They found alarming evidence of "shoddy care, poor staffing, lax standards, secrecy, and ineptitude in the United States immigration detention system."[10] Maybe that's why detained immigrant Boubacar Bah of Guinea died after fracturing his skull. His injuries remained untreated for some fourteen hours. Maybe that's why Francisco Castañeda died of cancer. Both his diagnosis and treatment were tragically delayed. These are just two of the many immigrants who have been tortured, hurt, or killed by our immigration system. Representative Zoe Lofgren, a Democrat from California and the House Immigration Subcommittee chairwoman, put the vile treatment best: "Whether immigrants are legal or illegal has nothing to do with their right to human care. You are not supposed to kill people in custody.[11] Representative Lofgren and Senator Robert Menendez, a Democrat from New Jersey, have jointly sponsored the Detainee Basic Medical Care Act that would provide the protection that so many thousands of immigrants never received under the Bush administration. On the other side of this issue, New York Congressman Peter King, the ranking Republican on the subcommittee asked, "Why should the American People be responsible for paying for Rolls Royce medical care for illegal aliens?"

You, the reader, have a choice. Senator Menandez and Representative Lofgren insist that all immigrants and detainees be treated with basic human decency. Republican Peter King offers the opposite view, one laced with selfishness and rage against immigrants. Here you have two widely divergent approaches: one emphasizing kindness and love and the other selfishness and rage. Which would you choose? These competing and deeply entrenched forces, kindness and justice versus selfishness and rage, will show up in every chapter as we work through the corrosive undercurrents of contemporary capitalism. These starkly conflicting views reinforce the reason I wanted to write this book from the very first day I began studying economics and finance. Capitalism needs to have a moral focus and a compassionate heart. Ugly capitalism has neither and is rotting from the inside out.

The Inextricable Links of Sound Disciplines to Science

As a young doctoral student in economics and finance at the Wharton School of Business at the University of Pennsylvania, I was required to study Raymond T. Bye's *Applied Economics,* a bestselling textbook then used in many colleges and universities across the country.[12] But there was a huge problem with the work, at least for me. Bye's constant message was that the economist's job was to explain how any policy could work to match the end result with the identified initial policy goal. Stick to economics, Bye argued. Leave politics, philosophy, and ethics out of your work. Don't get sidetracked, he would insist, time and time again.

Well, I could not accept Bye's counsel. After all, most of the great classical economists called themselves political economists, which demonstrated their concern that a linkage exists between ethics, society, politics, and economics. Further, to leave ethics and politics out of science is to ignore completely monumentally important actions such as the US atomic bombing of Hiroshima and Nagasaki in 1945. The moment that America dropped those nuclear bombs no one could ever again pretend to divorce ethics, politics, mathematics, philosophy, logic, or any other discipline from science. I have tried to abide by my own counsel of integration in every chapter of this work.

The Null Theory on Law and Justice

Relevant to the injustice we have reviewed above, it is helpful to think of the null theory as applied to law and justice. This is also what is often called the presumption of innocence, a cornerstone of British common law and one that remains firmly planted in our legal system. The null theory means that anyone charged with a crime is presumed in a free society to be innocent until proven guilty beyond a reasonable doubt. Put another way, a person is presumed not to have committed a crime until the state proves beyond a shadow of a doubt that the person did the deed. Thus, given the Court's recent decision, a detainee is presumed to be innocent until the war dogs can prove him guilty *before a nonmilitary court and jury*. At least that's the law in a democratic America.[13]

The problem is that the war dogs tend to break American laws they don't like. They also break international laws. They ignored the United Nations and waged war that they justified on bogus grounds. Bush declared that Iraq was an imminent threat with its alleged WMD. He lied. What about Cheney and others in the White House? Well, they all planned in secret to embark on a first-strike unilateral attack. They all lied to the American people.[14] Bush not only broke international law but also failed to find any weapons of mass destruction in Iraq. Meanwhile, Bush sought to create new weapons that could be used from space. That surely is a first step that could lead to war in space as well as pollute the sky and the earth beyond repair.

Remembering Black Saturday

It has been nearly half a century, but for those who lived through it Black Saturday was one of the darkest days of the cold war between the United States and the former Soviet Union. On that day, October 25, 1962, American, Soviet, and Cuban militaries faced a nuclear confrontation. Ten days earlier an American U-2 spy plane provided photographic evidence that the Soviets were sneaking nuclear missiles into Cuba. Writer

Michael Dobbs reported what happened in his work *One Minute to Midnight: Kennedy, Khrushchev, and Castro on the Brink of Nuclear War.*[15] On that day a Soviet missile team in Cuba shot down an American U-2 plane. The pilot was killed. The United States Joint Chiefs of Staff decided to embark on an immediate military retaliation. Castro wired Khrushchev that Cuba faced an immediate invasion by the United States. Then Khrushchev dispatched a tough and angry letter to President John F. Kennedy. Richard Holbrook, in his review of *One Minute to Midnight*, writes:

> That night men in Washington went to sleep not knowing if they would awake in the morning. Their wives debated whether they should stay in Washington with their husbands or go to safer rural hideaways. (Almost all stayed, including Jackie Kennedy.)[16]

You know what happened. Fortunately, cooler heads prevailed. Both Kennedy and Khrushchev knew that a nuclear war would only end in horror and death. They knew that many millions of people would die or be horribly burned or crippled. So Kennedy and Khrushchev blocked their military forces—each at the ready for all-out war—from launching their respective missiles. In truth, Lady Luck was on both sides despite widespread confusion, time pressure, and military demands for a quick nuclear strike, poor communication, and jumbled messages.

Lady Luck is not likely to make an appearance for the next potential nuclear confrontation. Now some ten nations own nuclear bombs or other weapons of mass destruction. In 1962 only two nations had such destructive capacity. What does proliferation mean for the risk of nuclear war?

Countdown to a Nuclear War

It seems that little has changed since World War II. After all, the United States was the first to drop a nuclear bomb on another nation. Many thousands of innocent civilians died immediately on impact or were sickened and died in the days, weeks, and months that followed. People debate whether the bombings were necessary. What's not debatable is the terrible precedent their use set for future nuclear proliferation.

Long ago Bertrand Russell, a philosopher and mathematician, warned against nuclear bombs. He argued that the greater the number of nuclear bombs owned worldwide (arithmetically), the greater would be the risk (probability) that they would be used. In plain language, the risk of nuclear war would soar. But why would nuclear bombs be used? Russell's short answer was simple: these weapons would be employed as a result of "accident, miscalculation, or design."[17] Nation after nation would rush to obtain nuclear bombs for their own defense and to join the atomic league of powerful nations to be dealt with when issues of importance are discussed. Just note the recent disclosure by North Korea that it exploded a new nuclear weapon and has tested long-range missiles that could carry such weapons hundreds of miles away.

But the defense argument can easily backfire to produce a global nuclear war. At least nine nations now have countless nuclear warheads.[18] They are the United States, 10,350; Russia, 7,200; China, 400; France, 350; Britain, 200; Israel, up to 200; Pakistan, possibly 60; and India, 50. The total of nuclear warheads is 18,810, and still counting. North Korea now has a nuclear capacity and others also may rush to get warheads for "defense."

Is there any real defense possible with the widespread ownership of nuclear bombs? No. Just one nuclear bomb could destroy any major city in the world. The total number of nuclear warheads in the world is more than enough to destroy all life on the planet.

Another Deadly Fallacy: The Fallacy of Composition

There's another huge problem in addition to the ownership (proliferation) of nuclear bombs worldwide. The age-old "fallacy of composition" dictates that what may be true for one nation can backfire as false for all nations. If one nation attacks another with WMD, then the attacked nation would surely retaliate. Both could be blown away. Any nation attacked would likely strike back (if it were able to do so). If one nation bombs another, the crippled nation will seek to bomb the aggressor.

If one nation has a missile shield for "defense," others may try to obtain a similar or better shield for their defense. Even now both China and Russia are upset over America's plan to build a missile shield in Europe. Missile shields, they declare, "do not support strategic stability and they harm international efforts to control arms and the proliferation process."[19] In plain English, the huge problem is widespread ownership of nuclear weapons and the risks that they will be used in war, just as Bertrand Russell warned.

A Deadly Mix

President Dmitri Medvedev of Russia and President Hu Jintao of China met recently. They condemned American proposals for a missile shield in Europe and called the plan a setback to international trust that would upset the balance of power. Their criticisms were not about the cold war but the newer tensions over an array of military and economic issues, including rivalry over oil in central China. They are annoyed by US naval ships in their waters, angered by American plans to place missile shields in the Czech Republic and Poland, and insistent that America stop meddling in how they address human rights within their respective nations.

They declare that every state has the right to encourage and promote human rights based on its own special features and circumstances. Both China and Russia lectured former President Bush on his repeated failures regarding the faltering US economy and our own human rights foibles. However one interprets their statements, it is clear that the United States has lost credibility and power among the community of nations. Given its own stance on torture, trumped up military attacks, and international law-breaking, the United States now has little ability to lecture other nations on matters of ethics and decency. During his administration George W.

Bush had largely destroyed respect for the United States and our capitalist system both at home and abroad.

Religions at War with Nuclear Bombs

The refusal by the United States to work in meaningful ways with other nations to block the proliferation of nuclear warheads is yet another potentially earth-shattering problem. Will rogue nations, political splinter groups, or religious suicide bombers some day acquire nuclear bombs, laser death rays, or other WMD we have not yet seen? Who could doubt that they would try. We need only link (a) the deadly fallacy of composition to (b) the proliferation of WMD and the Strategic Defense Initiative (SDI) missile shields to (c) the refusal of nations to destroy all such weapons to envisage the likely result. This scenario could only lead to a collapse in the defense argument with all nations at risk of embarking on nuclear war for their own peculiar ends.

Indeed, my biggest fear is that competing religions rather than nation states will someday manage to get hold of such weapons for their own defense (see chapter 3). But the fallacy of composition tells us there is no defense against proliferation. Call it what you will, to me the defense argument is a mad delusion of totally unenlightened minds. There is no escape for anyone anywhere in a global war using nuclear or the vastly more powerful hydrogen bombs. Everybody dies.

Benjamin Franklin versus George W. Bush

One of the notorious seven deadly sins is extreme pride (meaning self-importance), which is often accompanied by other unsavory qualities such as vanity, conceit, and arrogance. All of these devil-like words could describe George W. Bush's morality (his "moral" character). Maybe I am too harsh. So, let's review the seven virtues (outstanding moral traits) found in the *Autobiography of Benjamin Franklin*.[20] How would you grade Bush's morality against this seven-point checklist of Franklin's virtues?

1) **Temperance**: "Eat not to dullness; drink not to elevation." Bush drank a lot in college but declared he was born again, and stopped drinking. With a fresh passion for truth and justice, he said God put him on Earth to be our compassionate leader.

2) **Resolution**: "Resolve to perform [and] perform without fail what you resolve." Bush rushed into a preemptive and illegal war. He promised peace and democracy but his mad bombing destroyed much of Iraq's industry, housing, agriculture, electrical systems, and its food and water supply. As of November 2006 some 3500 American soldiers have been killed. (It's above 5000 now.) Further, over "600,000 civilians died in violence across Iraq since the 2003 American invasion and occupation.[21] Bush's "Stay the Course" slogan now looks like the road to hell. Worst of all, his preemptive attack on false grounds made other countries feel less safe and helped exacerbate a dangerous global race to own WMD in the name of defense.[22]

3) **Frugality**: "Make no expense but to do good to others and yourself; waste nothing." The promises to rebuild Iraq (and New Orleans after hurricane Katrina) or to provide US soldiers the best of armor and medical care were in ashes. Bush also threatened to veto a bill that would provide free college education to anyone who has served in the military three years since the 9/11 attack. He said he needed soldiers to fight, not go to college. He also believed that if the bill were passed, many more soldiers would leave the army. The real solution, of course, is to get Americans out of Iraq, but this option was hardly on the mind of bellicose Bush.

Headlines in 2009 screamed about the violent behavior of returning American soldiers from Iraq and Afghanistan.[23] For several years, the Fort Carson Army base in the Rocky Mountains has become, "a way station for American soldiers cycling in and out or

Iraq." Nine soldiers have been charged with killing someone after returning from Iraq. Many more returning soldiers have been charged with domestic violence, rape, and sexual assault. Some of the badly wounded soldiers have tried to commit suicide. The problem, of course, is post-traumatic stress disorder (PTSD), a matter the *New York Times* reported on at length in January 2009.

Then the *Times* counted at least 121 cases in which combat trauma and the stress of redeployment to Iraq "set the stage for these crimes, and suicides." Yet military commanders still ask, "Where is this aggression coming from and how do we explain such violent behavior?" The military questions strike me as a cover-up to suppress the truth, which is embedded in the horrors of protracted combat in illegal wars—it teaches humans to kill, kill, and kill again. The truth is PTSD.

Beyond the military, New Orleans is still in deep trouble and Walter Reed Hospital remains mired in deep scandal.[24] Thus waste crowds out frugality; dishonesty destroys truth; and wars without end kill the prospects for peace.

4) **Sincerity**: "Use no harmful deceit; think innocently and justly." Bush's slogan of "compassionate conservatism" has been a cruel joke on the poor, the sick, the jobless, the uninsured, and on immigrants. His tax cuts were for the rich at the expense of the poor and middle class. His borrow-and-spend antics for pork-barrel earmarks and continuing the Iraq war produced record budget and trade deficits.[25] Bush's war has been like that of a giant economic grinder. Labor, materials, and capital enter and come out as bullets, tanks, and death. A fraction of US war costs could finance universal healthcare for every man, woman, and child in America, including immigrants.

5) **Justice**: "Wrong none by doing injuries." As already documented, Bush justified torture. He ran secret prisons. The organization Human Rights Watch has charged Bush with failure to acknowledge how and why innocent detainees disappeared. Bush arrested innocent foreign citizens and sent them to countries where they

were tortured. This "extraordinary rendition" is hideous, but he seemed untroubled. Despite such widespread cruelty the Bush administration still classified (censored) its own records. Bush's excuse for secrecy and censorship was always that it was necessary if he was to fight terror effectively. Fanning fears of terror, he kept war spending out of the formal budget and shifted moneys spent on war to additional secret accounts.[26] His most dangerous attack on justice was the 2006 banning of *habeas corpus* for "detainees" and "enemy combatants." Even the innocent would then have no right to challenge their incarceration before an impartial judge and jury. The facts demand that this commander-in-chief be labeled "Bush the Unjust."

6) **Moderation**: "Avoid extremes." To kill justice is brutally extreme.

7) **Humility**: "Imitate Jesus and Socrates." Bush the religious shouted praise for his God but his actions bore the mark of his personal devil. Bush the insecure crucified reason and science, did not admit his worst blunders, and became visibly angry when criticized. Bush the irrational said God made him commander-in-chief. Bush the lawbreaker insisted on passage of a bill in 2004 to enhance his administration's intelligence-gathering capability despite the Justice Department's conclusion that it was illegal. He backed down only when his attorney general at the time and many other top Justice Department aides threatened to resign.[27] Bush the infallible lived in a dream world of grandeur, personal omnipotence, and certainty of final truths for all time. It comes as no surprise that a former US attorney general[28] demanded that Bush be impeached for his illegal war, secret prisons, false arrests, and torture.[29]

So, does Bush get a failing grade on Franklin's virtues? You decide. Where does America go from here? Well, as I write we are in a recession that gets worse and worse with each passing week and month. I think back to my April 25, 2008 *Money and Capital Markets Monitor* titled: "Triple Nightmare: The Risk of Depression, Deflation, and Dollar Downgrade" (available on request). Yes, the economy was falling apart. It now faces the high risk of an outright depression, support for which I provide in chapter 12.

As a lame duck president, Bush's ability to push legislation through the Congress was traditionally weak. Americans no longer trusted their president, those around him, or those in his party. Foreigners viewed Bush as a pathetic loser. What about the Iraq War? For many it was an immoral and lost war with no end in sight. Violence, war, and economic misery still dominate the news headlines every day. US marines, including officers, have been charged with the *murder* of unarmed civilian men, women, and children.[30] New data and a long list of problems signal that the United States faces the immediate future with a 75 percent chance of falling into a full-blown depression. America's refusal to sign a treaty banning weapons of mass destruction continues to generate fears of a nuclear clash of nations in our future.

Iraqi Maelstrom: Guns, Bomblets, and Bombs

Bush and his obedient senior officers declared over and over again that the "surge" of troops sent to Iraq was a success. By success they meant that the surge brought greater stability, safety, and security to the Iraqi people and its government. None of this is true. Gun fights and exploding suicide bombs continued everywhere. Consider the June 23, 2008 report compiled by reporter Richard A. Oppel Jr.[31] Below is my outline of the horrors Oppel recorded from Iraq.

1) The latest in a wave of suicide bombers killed 15 people and wounded more than 40 others in a heavily fortified courthouse and government outpost in central Baquba. The bombing followed four attacks by guerillas in Diyala Province that killed 25 people and wounded almost 60 others. These attacks have prompted concerns about the endurance of any security gains and why guerillas can still operate freely.

2) Hours after the explosion in Baquba, a mortar volley struck north of Khalis in the western end of Diyala, killing 7 people and wounding 12. The bomber who struck in Baquba wore a vest padded with powerful explosives and laced with small projectiles like iron ball bearings. The magnitude of the huge explosion left three police officers torn to pieces, which raises more questions on the greater sophistication of the bomb makers. Does this mayhem remind you of the "cluster bombs" used by the US military?

3) The bomber struck inside a cordon or barrier of the government center designed to admit only government and police vehicles. The explosion blew shrapnel across a wide radius and into a crowded area that people believed had been made safe by the barrier. But it failed to keep out a female suicide fanatic with bombs hidden under her cloak.

4) Fifteen other women carried out suicide bomb attacks in Diyala Province. Strict Islamic rules prevent all men, including security officers, from conducting searches or even touching women. If they can't touch and they can't search, they can't stop suicide bombings by women. One senior military officer said, "Most of the women wear black cloaks that can hide anything, and we can't prevent that."

5) Compounding the predicament is a scarcity of female Iraq police officers and soldiers who could search female suspects. If the female officers don't exist, they obviously can't search and can't stop suicide bombings. Do you know of any tangled web of war, religion, politics, lies, and death worse than the one in Iraq? If not, see chapter 3 on the "US Religious Assault on Science."

Chapter 3

RELIGIOUS ASSAULTS ON SCIENCE

We may be witnessing the end of capitalism as we know it.
—Tom Wolfe, quoted in *New York Times*, June 24, 2008

In a *New York Times* article by Andrew Ross Sorkin, he tells us of the time that noted *Bonfire of the Vanties* author Tom Wolfe, dressed in his trademark white suit, was on the floor of the New York Stock Exchange. His tour of the exchange took place in June of 2007. The real excitement then, traders whispered, was that Wolfe was there to celebrate the Blackstone Group going public with the largest initial public offering in the United States since 2002. At that time the Dow Jones Industrial Average (DJIA) stood at 13,337, considerably above what it was at the end of 2009, and well above what it is now.

My point is that happy deals were zipping across the ticker in this mania-driven stock market boom. Blackstone's stock also crashed along with most other stocks. Wall Street later sent out pink slips to several hundred thousand employees worldwide in the face of a brutal financial meltdown and a major recession. Sorkin tells us that a CNBC reporter pulled Mr. Wolfe aside to ask him what he thought the hubbub was all about. Mr. Wolfe, with a wry smile, delivered his prophetic declaration. Wolfe said: "We may be witnessing the end of capitalism."[1]

Economist Joseph A. Schumpeter on "Evaporated Property"

It looks like I am hardly alone in my unqualified forecasts of the demise of capitalism. The epilogue of my *Unlocking the Secrets of Wall Street* is in a sense a preface to the present work. Published in 1998, the content of virtually all of the headlines one has been reading today on Wall Street for many months about deception and systemic theft was spelled out chapter by chapter.[2] Thus I am far from alone in my dire forecasts. The many experts we will meet in this chapter made similar dire warnings like that of Wolfe.

Economist Joseph Schumpeter (1883–1950) coined the term "evaporated property." He, like John Maynard Keynes (1883–1946), has always been one of my favorite economists. How prescient Schumpeter looks today. Once we understand the vanishing value of subprime debt, the near bankrupt state of bond and mortgage insurers, plunging stock prices, massive layoffs, falling profits, a muddled Federal Reserve, a confused US Treasury, and the pitifully poor regulation of US financial markets, then we should have no problem understanding Tom Wolfe, Andrew Ross Sorkin, and Joseph H. Schumpeter on evaporated property. Here are Schumpeter's words in plain English.

> Stocks and bonds are evaporated property. People completely lose touch of the underlying assets. It's all paper, these esoteric devices. It has become evaporated property cubed [a number raised to the third power].[3]

The Missing Ethic: Freedom from Religion

This chapter takes us now from Wall Street's assault on science and truth to the religious assault on science and truth. In chapters 4 and 5 full attention will be paid to Wall Street's economic, moral, and social indiscretions. Yes, business deceit, religious superstition, and bellicose war dogs all work together to undermine capitalism's survival. One might think that the deceit and corruption found in government and the business arenas would surely not be found in religion. Do not religious leaders teach us honesty, kindness, and compassion? Yes, but the major religions also lie, deceive, torture, and wage holy and murderous wars among themselves and against many other groups and nations. I shall document all this, but surely any understanding of the religious crusades and their bloodletting and torture should put us on our guard. Fanatics at war with massively destructive weapons should not be lightly brushed aside.

To be sure, capitalism and religion together made great strides over many centuries. In the Great Depression Franklin Delano Roosevelt ushered in freedom from want by giving people food stamps, jobs, incomes, free medical care, and shelter. Much earlier our War of Independence from Great Britain gave the American colonies not only democracy but freedom of religion. Each of us can choose any religion we like, then and now, an unheard-of option for many other nations. But even today a key freedom gets no respect from any religion. What's missing now is freedom *from* religion.

Freedom from Religion: A Vital Freedom Still Missing

Tom Wolfe often stressed in his novels and lectures the importance of freedom from religion. Many top scientists and experts make the same point. My own conviction is that freedom from religion is absolutely required to produce an educated, enlightened, honest, and productive working force. Unfortunately, I don't see that taking place, which is just one of many reasons capitalism, in my view, is fading fast.

Research on genetics, stem cells, technology, health, industrial production, farming, medicines and medical techniques, engineering, space science, robotic mechanical tools, and just about everything else of value is at risk when religion crowds out science. That means new sciences, new inventions, and new discoveries that hold the promise of dramatically increasing productivity and wealth are at risk. The experts I track in this chapter have reached the same dire conclusions. Consider now their comments as a preface to the detailed theoretical and empirical evidence I include in this volume.

Fourteen Famous Experts Fault Religion

✓ **Tom Wolfe (1931–), novelist**: I listened in awe to Wolf on CNN television May 30, 2008, at which time he explained at length a missing freedom, the freedom *from* religion.

✓ **Nicolaus Copernicus (1473–1543), astronomer**: His revolutionary science contradicted church myths. He was so afraid of the church that he hid his research from public view for years.

✓ **Galileo Galilei (1564–1642), astronomer and physicist**: His support of Copernicus's work on the stars and planets enraged the church. Religious leaders demanded that he be silent or risk prison or death.

✓ **Bertrand Russell (1872–1970), mathematician and philosopher**: He said that fear begets religious superstition of heaven and hell.

✓ **Richard Dawkins (1941–),[4] ethologist, evolutionary biologist**: He says belief in God is a pernicious and deadly delusion.

✓ **James Joyce (1882–1941), writer**: He condemned all of the religious concepts of heaven and hell.

✓ **Francis Crick (1916–2004), biologist, physicist, neuroscientist, and Nobel laureate**: He faulted religion as an attack on science and truth even as he unraveled DNA and the blueprints of life.

✓ **Stephen Hawking (1942–), theoretical physicist**: He warns that global nuclear war can end all life on Earth. He views science as a philosophy of discovery and religion a philosophy of ignorance.

✓ **Martin Rees (1942–),**[5] **cosmologist and astrophysicist**: He says humans face a high risk of extinction in this century. Like Stephen Hawking and other scientists, he fears the specter of global nuclear war.

✓ **Carl Sagan (1934–1996),**[6] **astronomer, astrochemist:** He slayed religious demons and myths with science and truth.

✓ **Carolyn Porco (1953–), planetary scientist**: She says the glory and wonder of the universe beats holy myths.

✓ **Charles Darwin (1809–1882), naturalist; Albert Einstein (1879–1955), physicist; and Karl Marx (1818–1883), political philosopher**: Each attacked religious fallacy and superstition.

Religious Leaders Who Fault the Experts

Here are just a few of the many religious leaders who assault those who hold to a scientific view of the world (the papal dates refer to their reigns as pontiff):

✓ Pope Clement VI (1342–1352): He claimed that God brought on the plague (or the Black Death) in 1348.

✓ Pope Clement VII (1523–1534): He threatened Galileo with imprisonment and death.

✓ Pope Urban VIII (1623–1644): He subjected Nicolaus Copernicus to a callous grilling.

✓ Pope Benedict XVI (2005–), the present pope: He asks why God allowed Auschwitz. Recently, many publications have alleged that the pope protected, or failed to take action against, pedophile priests.

✓ Several evangelical preachers attribute devastating floods, famines, tornadoes, earthquakes, and war to divine intervention. Other strident preachers say these same calamities were God's punishments for our (or specific groups') various sins.

The Fire-Breathing Dragon
and the Meaning of Proof

Religious myth and superstition still run wild across the globe. Far too few young people and as well as grown adults have ever heard of, much less read about, many of the great scientists. A tragic fact is that there remain in our midst people who are actually not sure whether the Sun revolves around the Earth or the Earth around the Sun. They have never heard of evolution or Darwin or Copernicus. They know little about critical thinking and the need for empirical evidence. Unenlightened, these people often struggle desperately to survive in a harsh world.

The illiterate, the uneducated, and the unenlightened accept without understanding all kinds of nonsense. So, what better way to explain science than to start with a great twentieth-century example like the late astrophysicist Carl Sagan and his fascinating tale about a fire breathing dragon. Here is Sagan's story of how to spot truth from falsehood. Notice that I also put you in his story.

Sagan: A fire-breathing dragon lives in my garage.

You: Show me. (Sagan leads you to his garage. You look inside and see a ladder, empty paint cans, an old tricycle, but no dragon).

You: Where's the dragon?

Sagan: Oh, she's right here. [But] she's an invisible dragon.

You: Let's spread flour on the floor to capture the dragon's footprints.

Sagan: Good idea, but this dragon floats on air.

You: Let's use an infrared sensor to detect [the heat of] the invisible fire.

Sagan: Good idea, but the invisible fire is also heatless.

You: Then let's spray paint the dragon and make it visible.

Sagan: Good idea, but it's incorporeal (spiritual). Paint won't stick.

Sagan then asks, "What's the difference between an invisible, incorporeal, floating dragon that spits heatless fire and no dragon at all?" He answers, "If there is no way to disprove my contention, no experiment that [counters] it, what does it mean to say that my dragon exists? Your inability to invalidate my hypothesis is not the same as proving it true. Claims that cannot be tested and assertions immune to disproof are worthless."[7]

Mystics, Fortune Tellers, Witch Doctors, and Faith Healers

Scientists dismiss fortune-tellers,[8] mystics, witch doctors, and religious faith healers. Sagan reminds us that religion has little ability to forecast since it has no scientifically credible evidence upon which to base its claims, prophecies, or folktales. He says there isn't a religion on this planet that doesn't long for the scientists' skills to forecast. He is right, for nobody can match the accuracy of scientific prediction based on strongly supported theoretical and empirical evidence.

Often Confused Religious Jargon

Let's turn now to religious terms that are common but often confused. First, what is the difference between "theism" and "deism"? A quick but incomplete answer is that both believe in a god. But there are important differences. Theism is the belief in a god as the creator and ruler of the universe. Many theists also believe this god reveals himself to all his creatures, whether humans or cats. Theists call this "revelation."

On the other hand, deists do not accept supernatural revelation. Also, deists believe the existence of a god must be found in the evidence of reason and nature alone.[9] Deists believe that we come to understand the creative capacity of a god by using the methods of science and critical reason to learn more about the world we live in. Put another way, deists put much more faith in good science than theists do.

The Close Brotherhood of Atheists and Scientists

How about the atheist? For some atheism is an absence of belief in any god or gods, while for others it is the flat denial of the existence of any deity whatsoever. The thinkers I have listed are in the latter mold. Indeed, most true scientists are atheists, but not all would wish to admit it. Historically, scientists feared unenlightened and cruel discrimination, and in some countries they risked execution if their views became public knowledge. In our enlightened and techno-savvy world it is hard to believe that just a few decades ago German Nazis included atheists among the many millions they executed and starved to death in concentration camps.

Like the scientist-atheist, many theists also reject such religious concepts as heaven and hell, the virgin birth of Jesus, eternal life, and ghost-like contacts with a god, among others. They believe strongly, though, in church teachings that oppose killing and promote honesty, charity, and compassion.

Religious Dictators:
Their Cruel Actions and Threats

Pope Urban VIII and Nicolaus Copernicus

Let's turn the calendar back now to the sixteenth century. I'll review first how Nicolaus Copernicus managed to survive the wrath of Catholic Pope Urban VIII. What follows is my rendition of the arrogant cross-examination by the pope of Copernicus and his views of astronomy. Admittedly it is simplified and shortened, but nevertheless fundamentally true.

Copernicus: I worked the past four years tracking the planets, the moon, and . . .

Pope Urban VIII: Quiet. That's enough. I read your manuscript, but have questions. You say Earth is not the center of the universe. You believe that?

Copernicus: Earth is the center of the moon's orbit. But the Sun is the center of our universe, not Earth. Earth moves every day around its own axis. It moves every year around our Sun. Stars are the suns in the distant universes.

Pope: But don't your views contradict Ptolemy, Aristotle, and other great scientists? Also, many of my papal predecessors have taught for centuries that Earth is central to man and all creation. You don't fault the Church. Correct?

Copernicus: Correct. My work tracks the planets as they revolve around our Sun. In fact, I intend to call my book "On the Revolutions of the Celestial Spheres."

Pope: Your work does not deny God's word. Is that right? Your work does not mock the Bible and its teaching of Earth's creation. Correct? You surely don't mean to rank science ahead of God and the Church. Correct?

Copernicus: Correct.

Pope: Good. I'll permit you to publish your book.[10]

Pope Clement VII Threatens Galileo with Prison and Death

In the seventeenth century Galileo made his own telescope, with which he tracked how the planets revolve around the Sun and confirmed the findings of Copernicus. Pope Clement VII was perturbed with Galileo's support of Copernicus, and he quickly became enraged.

> **Pope Clement VII**: Galileo, the Church is terribly upset with you. So am I. We find you guilty of having held and taught the Copernicus doctrine. We order you to recant (take back) your views. Your *Dialogue Concerning the Two Chief World Systems* mocks the Church. You must confess that your writing is full of errors. You must state that you published under false pretenses. We must prosecute. You are therefore ordered to stand trial for heretical dissent (making claims contrary to Church teachings). Your trial will take place in Rome this February 1633.

> **Galileo**: I understand. I'll admit my errors and lack of clarity.

> **Pope**: Still, I must dictate your conclusions.

> **Galileo**: Holy One, I'll abide by your orders and correct my mistakes.

Later: Pope Clement VII charges Galileo with heresy

> **Pope**: I have had enough of you. Your work is still heretical. Let me tell you that God can bring about effects that man can only imagine. But you don't bend to God's omnipotence (all powerful nature), to God's omnipresence (His existence everywhere and at all times) and to God's omniscience (His ability to know and see all). Given our power and responsibility to God, we now must sentence you to be imprisoned for heresy. Still, you confessed your errors and said you would rectify them. Thus I agreed to change your imprisonment to house arrest and seclusion. But you still must confess here and now.

Galileo: Yes, I confess. (Galileo thinks silently: "It vexes me when they constrain science by the scriptures [but these scriptures] are not bound by reason and experiment."[11] These church officials have their heads in the clouds. They have neither the will nor the vision to see truth and science on earth.)

Galileo's confession of having sinned was forced upon him to save his life.[12] Still, his house arrest lasted eight years. In January 1642 a fever killed him. I wonder whether the pope ever had Galileo tortured. Well, torture takes many forms. For one thing, just imagine how Galileo must have felt to see his revolutionary findings blocked. Just imagine how he felt to see the Church's power and its superstitious creeds dominate science.

Just imagine that you have finally unraveled, after many decades of work, a major myth of the universe. Imagine that you are mocked, ridiculed, tried for heresy, and sentenced to house arrest and seclusion for your revolutionary gift to science. Imagine religious authorities trying to smother your best work. Imagine how you're forced into seclusion away from those who could console you. Imagine your terror that the Church could always change your sentence to death. The Church stomped as a huge and enraged bull on Galileo, science, and truth. That's torture.

The Monster Sin of Torture[13]

The Pew Research Center for the People and the Press recently made a survey in 2007 asking Americans if torturing suspects to get important information was ever justified. Ask yourself what you think of the survey. Here are the groups and their percentages saying that torture is never justified:

> Total Population: . . . . 27 percent
> White Evangelical: . . . . 28 percent
> White Mainline Protestant: . . . . . 31 percent
> Roman Catholic: . . . . 26 percent
> Secular: . . . . 25 percent

What's your judgment? I was saddened to see how low the percentages were across the board. I had no idea how motivated US citizens are to inflict extreme pain and suffering on their fellow human beings. I believe torture should be abolished without exception. I agree with those who say torture should be banned just as we ban slavery, genocide, and rape.

Nor am I convinced that torture can produce honest and reliable information. On the contrary, the tortured will lie when subjected to extreme pain and suffering, or even commit suicide. Torture is often a death warrant for the victim. Torture disgraces and marks its perpetrators as ugly and depraved in the eyes of the world. It's a monstrous sin against humanity and contrary to any notion of decency and justice.

Discourse with Enlightened Scholars (Continued)

In the following exchange I joined in my imagination with many famed scholars, some long deceased, who provided me with support for my own research and convictions.

RH: It's an old story. When superstition and anger sneak in, science is crowded out.

Dawkins: But science eventually slays myths. That's what it does best.

RH: Yes, it does. Science tells us of the discord and danger that show up in competing religions. For example, Christianity is the religion with the largest number of believers. Christians say that Jesus is the son of the only true God. The road to salvation is only through Christ.[14] No others need apply to heaven. Their holy book is the Bible, the only true word of their one true God. So the Christians claim.

The second most populous religion (numbering 1.3 billion adherents) is Islam. It's prophet is Mohammed (570–632 CE) and its one and only God is Allah. A ticket to heaven comes only through Allah.[15] Mohammed, though illiterate, often spoke to his followers. They compiled in the Koran the teachings of Allah that were claimed to be divinely revealed to Mohammed. The Koran is viewed as the only true word of Islam's one true God. So the Muslims claim.

Religion versus Science on Life and Death and Heaven and Hell

It is clear that conflicting religious dogmas can cause a lot of trouble, even lead to war. It is relevant here to ask ourselves if we can think of any truth that is final and absolute for all time? I asked my son (who happens to be a surgeon) that question. He answered without hesitation: "Everybody dies."

Maybe he was also thinking of Charles Darwin who said evolution (biological adaptation to environmental conditions over long time spans) is the only final truth. The dilemma, however, is that many people still believe in life after death. They surely are entitled to their belief, especially if such thinking helps them to face death. But the fact remains that nobody anywhere has ever come back to life after being buried or cremated. Neither theoretical nor empirical evidence supports the claim of life after death. I often try to explain this fundamental principle of science to my students with a simple syllogism.

Query: What's wrong with this argument?

> Major Premise: . . . . .If all men are immortal,
> Minor Premise: . . . . .and Aristotle is a man,
> Conclusion: . . . . .then Aristotle is immortal.

Again, the scientist knows instantly that the conclusion is false. He knows that nobody is immortal (the major premise is false). He knows that everybody dies and that the dead don't come back to life. The advocates of immortality have taken the structure of a valid logical argument, namely:

Major Premise:	. . . .	.If all A is B,
Minor Premise:	. . . .	.and X is an instance of A
Conclusion:	. . . .	.then X is an instance of B

and inserted an untrue major premise. To be sure, the conclusion of the original argument would be flawless provided that the major premise had been true. But the major premise is false. No empirical evidence exists that Jesus, Allah, or any other religious leader, or anyone else ever returned to life after having died.[16]

Most Americans ignore the requirement of science to support with evidence their deeply felt convictions on religious matters. In matters religious they don't seem to care about science and truth. Instead, they are content to reach important conclusions about life and death in a fairy tale land of superstition.

What do they really believe? Well, a current groundbreaking study of a representative group of some thirty-five thousand adults found that seven out of ten Americans with a religious affiliation believed in salvation and eternal life. Seven out of ten! The Pew Forum on Religious and Public Life released the study.[17] Here are its findings broken down for eleven religions. The first number is the percent representing those who believe that many religions can lead to eternal life, whatever the specific religious affiliation. The second number reflects those who believe that only their specific religious affiliation can provide salvation and eternal life. Here are the data.

Total:	. . . .	.70 percent, 24 percent
Hindu:	. . . .	.89 percent, 5 percent.
Buddhist:	. . . .	.86 percent, 5 percent.
Mainline Churches:	. . . .	.83 percent, 12 percent.
Jewish	. . . .	.82 percent, 5 percent.
Roman Catholic:	. . . .	.79 percent, 16 percent.
Orthodox:	. . . .	.72 percent, 20 percent.
Black Churches	. . . .	.59 percent, 34 percent.
Evangelical:	. . . .	.57 percent, 36 percent.
Muslim:	. . . .	.56 percent, 33 percent.
Mormon:	. . . .	.39 percent, 57 percent.
Jehovah's Witnesses	. . . .	.16 percent, 80 percent.

We can see from the first set of figures on the left that a large majority rejects religious "exclusivity" (i.e., that only a specific religion guarantees eternal life). Put another way, the majority preferred "pluralism" (many religions guarantee eternal life). Of course, these numbers overstate to some degree the hegemony of myth over science. Why? Well, American agnostics and atheists, who are among our leading scientists, were not included in the study.

Nor does the data touch at all on how the Bush administration attacked and vilified science for eight long years (see chapter 4). I was dismayed and saddened to read the extent to which myth overtook reason and science. Let me sum up: I believe good theory *and* good data, the hallmarks of science, are required for truth. Religious dogma that rests on metaphysical theory without empirical support cannot approach the status of truth. Religious dogma not supported empirically must be classified as superstitious nonsense.

Finally, I will be forever grateful to the Pew Research Center and other media for their findings on the plague of religious myth racing across America.

Back to the Wisdom of Top Scholars

Please join me once again in my imagined conversation with some of the best scholars in the world, whether living or dead. My latest exchange relates to the concept of absolute authority. For example, the pope says God gave him absolute authority as head of the Catholic Church as the direct religious descendant of the Apostle Peter, who is believed to have founded the Church. I always ask my students what they think about such claims to possess absolute authority. Some respond that if it is in the Bible it must be true. Many think these claims are nonsense.

The next time you hear such claims ask the self-styled absolute authority how such a view can be defended. Some will simply declare that it's true because they say it's true. Such circular reasoning is illogical and unconvincing. The same claimant to absolute authority may offer up a divine book, such as the Bible, as further proof. To do so contradicts the claim of absolute authority. If the person making the claim has the alleged authority then it can't have been obtained from a book of scripture for then the holy book would be the absolute authority and not the claimant. It should be obvious that absolute authority instantly begets contradictions. The immediate victims are those who are taken in by such broad and baseless assertions, but, in the end, the search for truth is the real victim.

Dawkins: You speak of religious claims of absolute authority. Indeed, religious claims about the divine origin of certain books, the virgin birth of certain people, and survival after death all purport to be about reality. But religion, especially intelligent design, is a philosophy of ignorance. Anything scientists can do to weaken the hold of religion may be our greatest contribution to civilization. Science is a philosophy of discovery. God is a pernicious delusion.

Crick: You know and I know that there are no absolute and eternal truths. One thing I do believe in fiercely, however, is that life spans could soar as we learn more about DNA and life's blueprints. Science has the power beyond any religion to help humankind.

Darwin: Yes, the mystery of the beginning is insoluble. I am an agnostic. That means any ultimate reality, like God, is unknown and probably unknowable.

RH: An atheist flatly denies the existence of a God since believers have not provided compelling empirical evidence to support their claim. Who most effectively debunks religious superstition? That would be scientists who insist that the scientific method and empirical evidence be offered for any claim of existence. And these scientists are often agnostics or atheists.

Einstein: Religion must give up the source of fear, hope, and vast power in the hands of priests. A foolish faith in authority is the first enemy of truth.[18]

Marx: Religion is the sigh of the oppressed. . . . It is the opiate of the people. . . . The first requisite for the happiness of the people is the abolition of religion.

RH: What's intelligent design? Is that also a religious view? I'll answer my own question. Intelligent design is extreme religious superstition regarding the evolution of humankind.[19]

Porco: I am a research scientist at the Space Science Institute. Science offers a far better alternative to religious myths. Let's teach our children at a very young age the true story of the universe with all its incredible richness and beauty. It is already so much more glorious and awesome and comforting than any scripture or God concept.[20]

Russell. Most of the greatest evils of man on man [are] feeling certain about something that is false. Religion should only be taught to consenting adults.[21]

Crick: Biological science now offers great promise. We might some day banish the demons of religious superstition as scientists learn more about the genetic code.

RH: But many of the church's views on heaven and hell are still false to this day. The church promises eternal reward in heaven if we are good. It threatens eternal damnation in hell if we are bad. Is not this tradeoff of reward and risk immoral? Don't heaven and hell appeal to our most selfish side?

Should not people do good deeds independently of any reward they are promised on earth or in an imaginary heaven? Should not people cease from doing harmful acts simply because those acts are wrong and not to avoid the imagined horrors of hell? We must fight religious threats based on superstition and cruelty.

James Joyce: Maybe. Consider the church-contrived fears in the preacher I invented.[22]

> The preacher began to speak in a quiet and friendly tone. . . . This evening we shall consider for a few moments the nature of the spiritual torments of hell. [The first] and by far the greatest is the pain of loss. . . . The second pain which will afflict the souls of the damned in hell is the pain of conscience . . . the third the pain of extension and the fourth the pain of intensity. . . . [The] last and crowning torture of that awful place is the eternity of hell. . . . To bear even the sting of an insect for all eternity would be a dreadful torment.

> What must it be, then, to bear the manifold tortures of hell forever? . . . Try to image the awful meaning of this. You have often seen the sand on the seashore. How fine are its tiny grains! And how many of those tiny little grains go to make up the small handful a child grasps in its play?

> Now imagine a mountain of that sand, a million miles high, reaching from the earth to the farthest heavens, and a million miles broad, extending to the remotest space, and a million miles in thickness. . . . [Imagine that] a little bird came to that mountain and carried away in its beak a tiny grain. . . . How many millions of millions of centuries would pass before that bird had carried away even a square foot of that mountain? . . . Yet at the end of that immense stretch of time not even one instant of eternity could be said to have ended.

RH: Joyce's sermon is a beautifully crafted satire on hell. He knows that religious concepts of heaven get no support from science. He knows that if there is such a thing/place, heaven is found in the good deeds of good people on earth, and hell in the cruel deeds of brutal people.

Pope Benedict XVI: His Outrageous Question on Auschwitz

RH: Pope Benedict XVI asked why God could permit the Holocaust to take place. But why blame a mythical entity? The Nazi leadership killed six million Jews and an equal number of minority groups while many people (some place the Catholic clergy among them) stood by mostly in silence. Man did the killing, not God. Nor should we blame some mythical devil when things go wrong. We should blame ourselves. We need to keep God and the devil out of matters of right and wrong, good and bad.

In September of 1348 Pope Clement VI spoke of the "pestilence [Black Death]." He blamed "God for afflicting [the Black Death] on the Christian people."[23] That is pure superstition. It's much better to have faith in love. With that thought in mind, here is one of my favorite poems of love, compassion, and charity by a deeply religious woman.[24]

At my back door the other eve, a youth was standing, hat in hand.

It didn't take long for me to see the makeshift patch that hid his knees.

His grimy shirt and worn-out shoes. His downcast look of "What's the use?"

He forced a smile as I heard him repeat, "Ma'am could you spare a bite to eat?"

As I hastened his food to prepare, I thought "A mother's son is standing there."

So, somehow, I just cannot deny some bread to the stranger passing by—

> So, I break a piece and let him share. I just can't say, "I have
> naught to spare."

And we all know that some superstitions can help make people happy. I
was once asked, "Is Santa Clause a fake?" Is Santa also a lie, a deception?
Well, most people would say that Santa is a white lie. Once I asked my
little grandson, Jason, what his best Christmas present was. He said, "My
I-pod." "Who gave it to you?" I asked. "Santa," he answered. "Did your
father or mother help?" I asked. "No, I got it from Santa," he said. What
could I say to him? I smiled and said, "Merry Christmas."

RH: Words like "love," "generosity," "devotion," "beauty," and "joy" are
all part of human kindness, the bright side of ourselves that we show at
special times when we give of ourselves to others. But millions of children are still left far behind. Their parents can't afford to buy them nutri-
tious food or medical and dental care. They are months late in paying the
rent. They have no money left to buy presents for the special times in
their children's lives.

The dark side of society exists side by side with the spending of the
rich for mansions, yachts, cars, and personal services. Economist
Thorstein Veblen called this "conspicuous consumption" in his work
titled *Theory of the Leisure Class*. Perhaps one of the seven deadly sins,
obscene gluttony, is a better way to depict this dark side. There are other
far more deadly sides to religion. We know religious groups wage wars
with other religious groups. Suppose warring religions get hold of WMD.
What then?

Rees: Let me answer. Scientists have reset the Doomsday Clock close to
midnight. There is a fifty percent chance that a global conflict could
destroy civilization by 2100.

Hawking: Life on Earth is at the ever-increasing risk of being wiped out
by global nuclear war, a genetically created virus, or dangers we have not
yet thought of.[25]

RH: Will scientists or politicians some day find ways to abolish our destructive weapons and with them war itself? It's true that both say they want to do good deeds. They also decry killing, but it goes on and on around the globe. Some religions continue to revel in their holy wars.

The Cruel and Inhuman Treatment of Agnostics, Atheists, and Others

Remember that Jesus supposedly said (Luke 6:23): "Blessed are you when men hate you, exclude you, and reject you as evil." Do you know any people who are hated, excluded, and rejected? I do. They show up in huge numbers in chapter 5 on industry-by-industry predators and chapter 6 on cultural, racial, and sexual predators. But what about religious predators, the subject of this chapter? Who are the religious predators?

RH: The facts are that many scientists and others who employ the scientific method are also atheists or agnostics. They have challenged church teachings for centuries and have suffered persecution and death. I searched the Internet and found this statement of belief in the *American Atheist*.

> The atheist strives for involvement in life, not escape into death. He seeks to know himself and his fellow man, builds a hospital instead of a church, does [good] deeds on Earth rather than prays to a god, and strives to end disease, poverty, and war. The atheist believes in love for his fellow man, not in an afterlife existence.[26]

These carefully crafted words of love and compassion for humankind contradict the ugly but mistaken notion many people have of atheists. To me the atheist creed solidifies the importance of the missing freedom, the freedom *from* religion. If there is a merciful god anywhere, I feel sure he must have created the atheist in his own image.

Religious Discrimination against Women

Discrimination takes many forms. Consider several vile examples as applied to women.[27]

✓ In an interview for Vatican Radio, Monsignor Amato reiterated that the church did not feel authorized to change the will of its founder, Jesus Christ, in barring women as priests and demanding that those who act as priests be excommunicated. The Vatican, he added, felt in good company because the Orthodox and ancient Eastern churches have also preserved what he said was a two-thousand-year-old tradition.

✓ In March of 2008, the archbishop of St. Louis, Raymond L. Burke, excommunicated two women in his diocese and another living in Germany after they were ordained as priests by the Roman Catholic Women Priests organization. In the past six years, the organization says it has ordained more than fifty women and some men as priests and deacons in North America and Europe. But in 2002, the Vatican again excommunicated the first seven women shortly after the organization had designated them as priests.

✓ The Vatican repeats again and again that excommunicated Catholics cannot participate in the sacraments or public ceremonies or hold ecclesiastical jobs.

Christian and Muslim Discrimination and Violence[28]

Fueling all discussions of violence is the unavoidable fact that in an age of instant communication, offenses against Muslim sensitivity, such as the cartoons of the Prophet Mohammed published in a Danish newspaper, can easily trigger a global chain reaction and cause everything from murderous riots in Pakistan to a collapse of European exports to Muslim countries. Many demand censorship as the solution. But that's no answer.

Prince Turki Al-Faisal, a senior Saudi official, said, "I can never accept that freedom of speech is morally right when it offends my faith."

But the prince ignores another question: How can freedom of speech ever be reconciled with the Muslim or any other religious demand for a ban on public statements or even cultural products such as art that offends sensibilities? My conviction is that truth and science should never be locked up by twisted politicians, governments, religious doctrine, or anybody who declares that his particular religion has been maligned. To censor the truth is evil despite the fact that truth eventually flees its shackles. It's evil because cruel behavior can easily get out of control while truth is smothered for a day, a year, or, in the case of religion, for centuries.

The Age–Old Questions

Heaven and hell do exist here and now on Earth. Your choice to be good or bad is here and now, not in some imaginary hereafter. Still, countless millions of atheists worldwide are "closet" atheists. They fear to declare the truth about themselves. They fear being "hated, excluded, or rejected as evil," or in some countries executed. We know that many religious people demean and hate atheists. But is not hate an unspeakable sin?[29] Yes, hate is a destroyer of truth and happiness everywhere.

Better News but Not Good News on the New Evangelicals[30]

Years ago members of the extreme religious right evangelicals were riding high. They were just about the only white evangelicals in the news. Their policy agenda included an abolition of the capital gains tax, a war on Islam, an attack on what they called a myth of any desired separation of church and state, and criticisms of gay rights and abortion. The Republican Party welcomed them as members. Together the extreme evangelicals and the Republicans tried to break the constitutional barriers that keep religion out of government and the rule of law. While they championed freedom of religion, they never believed in freedom *from* religion.

Today new evangelicals are on the scene. Many have chosen to vote for Democrats. They were favorably impressed with Barack Obama and his plans for health care and his moral opposition to the Iraq war. They also lobbied Congress to join the fight against global warming, and denounced the virulent and anti-immigrant talk of Republicans in the 2008 primaries. What a breath of fresh air. Still, the new evangelicals are hardly ready to embrace science, scrap myth, and accept freedom from religion. My conviction is that they still possess considerable power to do great harm to America.

A Question of Certainty

It is worth repeating that most of the advocates of science I listed are atheists or agnostics. I was asked how I can be certain of that. My response is always the same, namely, that evolution and change are the closest things I know of to certainty. We can thank Darwin and other scientists for that simple truth. I christened them and the other experts I cite as "The Apostles of Science and Truth." Listen to them, not to the old or the new evangelicals. Evangelicals cannot and will not guide us to the high road of science and truth.

Chapter 4

BUSINESS AND GOVERNMENT COLLUSION

It is not the role of the Supreme Court to pronounce the Second Amendment extinct.

—Antonin Scalia, Supreme Court Justice
Majority opinion, *District of Columbia v. Heller* (2008)

Supreme Court Justice Antonin Scalia has no use for liberals. His extremely conservative court decisions make this clear. In the case of *District of Columbia v. Heller* (2008) his majority decision gave the National Rifle Association reason to celebrate. To me this foreshadows even greater horror from the proliferation of guns. In any case, assaults take place in all walks of life. On that consistent theme, I shift now from the religious assaults on science in chapter 3 to the lawbreaking assaults of business and government in this chapter. Government and private business conspire to break laws and in so doing sicken, injure, and often kill people. Like the Roman Empire, capitalism has within itself the seeds of is own destruction.

Ugly US capitalism now heads for its downfall. Sick examples abound of dishonest companies out of control. One example is General Electric. Having worked as a senior economist at GE, I witnessed firsthand the company's right-wing ideology, professing free and open international competition even while it demanded that its employees not purchase foreign-made automobiles, televisions, and the like. During my tenure with the company, GE management also broke the antitrust laws involving the manufacture of light bulbs and steam turbines. Some individuals were convicted and sent to jail. Further, GE sent letters to its employees, myself included, urging that any documents we might have on antitrust matters be destroyed. I had no such documents, but still I expressed my annoyance to management for its hypocritical and unlawful acts.[1]

Even as GE deceived its employees, the authorities, and the public, it was dumping poisonous waste into the Hudson River. That was many years ago, but as I write this I see that the company is again in the headlines. Columnist Floyd Norris of the *New York Times* writes, "This week General Electric agreed to pay $50 million to settle a suit filed by the SEC [Securities and Exchange Commission] that it fiddled with its books [to hype earnings] early in this decade."[2] I also document in this chapter dishonest acts of the federal government and those on Wall Street who repeatedly practiced to deceive. Having worked as chief economist for several Wall Street companies, I found among my various employers the same dishonest policies. What does this mean for capitalism? Dishonest business and government may well self-destruct together.

Later in this chapter, I will also track the evils of what economists call "monopolistic competition." Be aware that corporations never use the word monopolistic to describe their own policies and actions. Rather, they regularly pride themselves on their competitive practices that help keep prices down. But they leave out their anticompetitive practices that push prices of products and services higher than those of their competitors and far higher than the prices of "generic" goods and services. In a nutshell, monopolistic competitors charge higher prices for a wide array of goods and services that you can actually buy at much lower prices. They get away with this by claiming that their products are superior to all others. They are not. I will offer details later in the chapter.

Let's turn now to lawbreaking by business and governments. Of special interest is how major industries break laws in concert with a conspiring federal government. I will focus here mainly on several villains, including **Scam** for Wall Street, **Rig** for the electrical industry, **Lie** for the federal government, and **Strip** for the corrupt alliance of government and the Supreme Court. By stuffing the Court with right-wing advocates, recent administrations have diluted the inalienable rights of the people.

The US Supreme Court's Twisted Ideology

I am deeply saddened by the Court's decisions on gun control. In effect it has placed ideology far above any priority of law, justice, mercy, or the protection of life itself. In the five-to-four majority decision mentioned above, the justices ruled that the nation's most effective gun control ordinance, one passed by the crime-ridden District of Columbia, was unconstitutional. Among other measures, the ordinance had banned handguns and required rifles in the home to have trigger locks to make them inoperative until they were unlocked for use.

Since 1976 the ordinance had been the law in the district, but not now. The Court's June 2008 narrow majority ruling goes a long way toward destroying effective gun controls designed to keep many people from killing and injuring others. In chapter 1, we learned that over thirty thousand people are killed or murdered and hundreds of thousands injured by firearms every year. The Supreme Court's decision signaled yet more carnage could be on the way—forty thousand dead?…fifty thousand?

What so dismays me is the specious rationale of the majority opinion written by Justice Antonin Scalia. He declares that it is not the role of the Supreme Court to pronounce the Second Amendment extinct. What? No doubt it would take a new amendment to the Constitution to repeal the Second Amendment, but Scalia's opinion in this important case in fact proves to be a dreadful blow to effective gun control designed to protect human life. Justices Anthony M. Kennedy, Clarence Thomas, Samuel A. Alito Jr., and the Chief Justice John G. Roberts Jr., also joined the majority. Each member of this majority is tainted with a far right ideology that helps to explain former President George W. Bush's own strong support for pitifully weak gun controls.

What is most tragic and ironic is that Justice Scalia's opinion came on the heels of his dissent (also in June of 2008) in the habeas corpus case that gave detainees at Guantanamo Bay the legal right to be heard in court. He was annoyed. He fumed that the right of habeas corpus would mean that information about the trials would be made public and would incite the anger of radical Iraqi extremists, which he believed could mean that many more American soldiers would be killed in Iraq. Really? One astute editorial writer declared: "[Scalia's] words apply with far more force to [his] decision in the District of Columbia case."[3] Yes, it does indeed.

The world is likely to view this Supreme Court decision as one that protects sloppy and ineffective gun rights first and human life dead last. The most recent estimates are that as many as 250 million guns are now in the hands of Americans. Guns are easily available. Thus it comes as no surprise that many people with guns kill many other people. Some people with guns also kill themselves by accident, as a result of acute depression, or intentional suicide.[4] The usual view is that newly appointed Justice Sonia Sotomayor will be much like Justice David Souter, the man she replaced on the Court. Many Court watchers think that the liberal-conservative mix on the Court will not change much. But I expect that, over time, Justice Sotomayor will shake up and defuse the right-wing ideologs on the Court and that its extreme right will be weakened. Now there is even more to speculate about since Elena Kagan's confirmation as associate justice to replace Justice John Paul Stevens on the Court as it convened for its a latest session in October 2010.

Relevant to this plague of gun death, I noted in chapter 1 the thirty-three people shot dead in the 2007 Virginia Tech massacre. Six more were killed by firearms in 2008 at Northern Illinois University. On the very day before the Court handed down its decision, a worker in a Kentucky plastics plant "shot his supervisor, four co-workers, and himself to death."[5] Does America put any value on human life ahead of its out-of-control gun plague? Apparently not, for ours is still macho cowboy country.

In the introduction I noted briefly that ours is an extreme laissez faire government. *Webster's Dictionary* defines laissez faire as a "system of government that upholds the autonomous [self-directed] character of the economic order and the belief that government should intervene as little as possible in the direction of economic affairs."[6] Does that not sound wonderful for anyone in love with freedom and progress? Well, as a veteran economist I have a far better definition integrated with good theory, hard facts, and ethics. I would define extreme laissez faire as a system of government out of order, out of control, and the single most corrupting force in US capitalism.

Political Hiring and Discrimination in the "Department of Injustice"

With its recent embrace of the Second Amendment, I am compelled now to classify the Supreme Court as just another extreme right-wing ideological body. It relegates reason, justice, and law to the back seat and sits with its brother, limited government, in the front seat. The two act together to strip away American justice, honest democracy, and truth. Since truth sooner or later breaks under the weight of its own suppression, we know now that the Justice Department under former President George W. Bush became politicized. It devolved into a "Department of Injustice."

Headlines in the press cited political and extreme ideological factors in recruiting candidates for career positions. The reports cited were prepared jointly by the Office of the Inspector General and the Office of Professional Responsibility, both of which found that the government would quickly hire law school graduates who were members of the conservative Federalist Society or who attended conservative schools. They weeded out the candidates who demonstrated any trace of being liberal or left leaning. The federal government often relied on Internet searches for evidence that job seekers for civil service were ideologically acceptable. Candidates were summarily disqualified if they showed any signs of political sin. What might that be? Showing any signs of being liberal? Consider now just a few examples of government-sponsored illegal discrimination.[7]

- ✓ One rejected candidate from Harvard Law worked for "Planned Parenthood."

- ✓ A second wrote articles critical of the US Patriot Act and the nomination of Samuel A. Alito Jr., to the Supreme Court.

✓ A third applicant worked for Senator Hillary Rodham Clinton and posted an unflattering cartoon of President George W. Bush on his My Space page.

✓ A fourth applicant, a student at the top of his class at Harvard who was fluent in Arabic, was relegated to the "questionable" pile because he was a member of the Council of American-Islamic Relations, a group that advocates civil liberties.

✓ A fifth was rejected because he was "personally conflicted' about the National Security Agency's program of wiretapping without warrants.

How to Get a Job in George Bush's Federal Government: Be a Hack Conservative

Bush's Justice Department hired law school graduates with conservative credentials at a much higher rate of pay than those with resumes that appeared more liberal. Here are the data on this huge ideological gap, a clear case of vicious and illegal discrimination. The numbers represent the percentages of conservatives versus liberals as defined by the Justice Department and cited frequently in the press. For 2002 the Justice Department accepted 91 percent of those who appeared to be conservative versus only 20 percent who looked or acted in some way liberal. In 2006, the acceptance rate was 82 percent for conservatives versus 45 percent for liberals. Now we can understand better why many government officials under Bush's rule were best classified as incompetent right-wing conservative hacks who attack science and truth. But things can backfire. Any strong alliance with the former Bush administration, in some people's eyes, may well taint an individual as dishonest and incompetent.

US Capitalism's Ardor for Weak Controls and Lawbreaking Regulators

Capitalism's present philosophy of pitifully weak regulation and lack of controls on industry fosters systemic fraud and lawbreaking that makes headline news every day. Many industry senior executives put maximum short-term profits above everything else. That's why they (1) support weak government controls that won't limit industry sleaze and law-breaking, (2) preach that the free market private sector always knows best for the people, and (3) declare that strong government limits on industry's actions cripples corporate America's ability to provide good jobs and innovation to benefit consumers and workers. All three reasons are spurious. Yes, unfettered laissez faire in ugly US capitalism allows criminals to run free to fleece the people.

Villains Out of Control

This chapter highlights the acts of three big marauding villains. The first I have named **Scam** for the countless ways Wall Street manages to get our money and lose it for us, often illegally. I saw dishonesty first hand as chief economist for three major Wall Street firms. I dub the second villain **Rig** for the electrical industry and its violation of antitrust laws. I came to know Rig well when employed by the General Electric Company as a senior economist in its economic forecasting division. The third and most destructive villain is the federal government. I will focus on government first.

For more than a quarter century I hosted joint conferences attended by (a) my invited clients, all senior investment executives, and (b) senior government officials whom I also invited to make short presentations. The subject was always the same, namely, the outlook for the economy, the financial markets, and the prospects for the dollar against key foreign currencies. As host, I always stressed the value of spirited interchange and argument.

In these conferences I also stressed that any valid conclusion must always have theoretical and empirical support. One alone won't do. You may wonder what I thought of the short lectures given by the invited government officials. Their lectures were sometimes useful, but in many cases they were best viewed as right-wing ideology having nothing to do with economic science. It was after the formal conference that I learned what my government guests really thought. Truth then crowded out falsehoods, usually at a nearby bar in Washington, DC. I'll return to this point with the details, but first let me try to explain why I believe otherwise honest people can turn abruptly into criminals.

Devil Pressure, Demon Insecurity, and Satan Selfishness

The quick answer is that otherwise honest people may suffer simultaneous attacks of pressure, insecurity, and selfishness. Take, for example, the nervous would-be whistle-blower, one who would like to speak out about his dishonest employer, but he remains quiet. He may fear being fired, so he rationalizes that his first priority is to his job and family. Immediately, Demon Insecurity and Devil Pressure steal his integrity while Satan Selfishness infects him with greed. The good man is abruptly caught off guard because these three underworld fiends work quickly and efficiently as a team.

The Unholy Trinity on Earth

Remember the scholars in chapter 3 who put their trust in scientific reasoning? They all declared that heaven shows up in the good deeds of good people on Earth, and hell in the bad deeds of bad people. They also warned that pressure, insecurity, and selfishness can tempt otherwise honest people to do some very bad things. Shakespeare made the same warnings in his classic *Macbeth*. The three witches he casts in Act I, Scene I ask, "When shall we three meet again, in thunder, lightning, or in rain?" I borrowed from these three demons of pressure, insecurity, and selfishness and dubbed them the Unholy Trinity. They can be seen running wild across all the chapters of this work as we watch them bring on thunder, lightening, rain, and unremitting misery.

Scam and Corruption on Wall Street

These three demons are alive and well and at work on Wall Street. Just imagine these netherworld fiends around a fiery cauldron at Wall and Broadway, a few steps from Trinity Church. Listen to their shrieking and incantations:

> Boil and Bake too much confidence. Stir in too little knowledge. Throw in craw of hog diseased from selfishness, heart of dove ruptured from pressure, and bowel of chicken shriveled from insecurity. Sprinkle lightly a shredded rabbit of regulation. Chant and Howl glory be we worship thee: Selfishness, Pressure, Insecurity. In the caldron we see the fall of triple, triple, troubled Wall.[8]

Let's be specific: many ugly capitalists head up corrupt companies. Examples include Arthur Anderson, Pete Marwick, Citigroup, Enron, Global Crossing, Health South, Imclone Systems, Merrill Lynch, Bear Sterns, and a wide array of hedge fund managers and investment "experts" who make huckster pitches on TV and radio.[9]

Lawbreakers are widespread (systemic) across the financial world. They include corporate board chairpersons, CEOs (chief executive officers), CFOs (chief financial officers), CIOs (chief investment officers), investment brokers, analysts, insurance executives, mutual fund managers, mortgage executives, and economists. They dishonestly hype (overstate) projected investor earnings. Meanwhile, retained earnings (i.e., profits not paid out but held for future needs) between 1997 and 2002 somehow vanished. Why? Earnings were frittered away in leveraged buyouts of other corporations that went bankrupt. Firms went on a borrowing binge to buy back their own stock at highly inflated prices, which then plunged. Top executives lied and deceived to fill their pockets with stock options, huge salaries, and bonuses, while racking up large nonrepayable loans. Shareholders lost their investments and their pensions, and workers lost their savings and jobs.

Wall Street's mantra of *always* investing for the long run (or even the short run) was false. Still, the street kept prodding investors to buy stock just before they crashed in 2002. In the mega-bubble stock and property market of 1997 to 2002, major US stock gauges soared and predictably burst. Some firms, like Fidelity, had full-page advertisements touting why stocks were a bargain just before the bubble burst. Companies urged their clients to engage in *momentum investing*. Follow the market up, up, up to get rich, they said. Such corrupt advice, which was widespread, cost investors dearly. Many investors lost everything when the bubble burst with full force.[10]

The NASDAQ Composite gauge (high-risk financial stocks that mania-driven buyers pushed to extremely high prices that predictably crashed, and the closest stock index to the mania-driven Japanese stock market) gets top honors for dishonest earnings projections. Its analysts forecast that "operating earnings" (which can mask a company's fixed costs) would continue to soar higher and higher in 2000, 2001, and 2002 even as "trailing earnings" (defined as revenues minus all legitimate costs) collapsed. It should be stressed that operating earnings are calculated *before* any deduction of interest, taxes, depreciation, amortization, and often marketing costs (often called ebitdam). Marketing costs alone often exceeded total revenues. Projected operating earnings (hyped up profit forecasts) were the common way to lie. The higher the profit forecasts, the more investors wanted in on the action.

The buying mania lifted the NASDAQ Composite price-to-earnings (P/E) ratio to 289 on March 3, 2001. In other words, the price of stocks was 289 times the actual earnings! By the summer of 2001 the NASDAQ Composite had an infinite P/E. Infinite? Yes, the losses for all the companies in the NASDAQ index exceeded the total earnings of other companies in the same index.[11] Think of it: this major indexed stock gauge had zero net earnings. So, what do you get when you divide a positive price by zero? You get a price-to-earnings ratio of infinity. Simple P/E ratios made clear the evidence of a mania-driven megabubble stock market.

Worse, "trailing earnings," (previous actual earnings as opposed to prospective future ones) were much lower than projected "operating earnings." Most NASDAQ companies had no profits. Still, they dreamed that profits in general would rise and give them a dominant market share. Like many dreams, they tripped over the oldest of fallacies, the fallacy of composition (what's true for one is true for the group). The overinvestment boom produced excess capacity (more production capability than needed) followed by plunging profits and stock prices. The NASDAQ stock gauge burst (along with the other major stock gauges). Pipe dreams vanished. Then Federal Reserve Chairman Alan Greenspan's "new-era-wealth-effect" nonsense was blown away by crowd mania. He dreamed and forecast a new and wonderful economic world. But his excessively easy and sustained monetary expansion (i.e., expanded money supply) was the principal force that created mania-driven property and stock market inflation that was fated to burst and bring down with it a terrible financial meltdown and recession. Greenspan never could make good forecasts. His mumbo-jumbo finally caught up with him to his dishonor.

A Litany of Failure: Chief Investment Officers and Chief Financial Officers

Chief investment officers (CIOs) and chief financial officers (CFOs) stayed in stocks with inflated prices far too long. They and their shareholders lost heavily when stock prices fell. CFOs were chiefly responsible for buying back their own stock at these dangerously inflated prices. They were blind or pretended to be blind to the practice of treating stock options provided to corporate executives as a cost to the company. They raided (stole from) their own pension funds and declared the money as income just so they could report higher profits to their shareholders. They failed to raise a dime of net new equity capital from 1997 to 2002 despite the ultralow cost of equity financing.

Ultralow cost of equity? Just turn the price to earnings (P/E) ratio upside down. The result is an earnings/price ratio. For example, if the price of a stock is $1000 per share and the earnings are $10, the P/E ratio is established by dividing 1000 by 10, or 100. Now divide the $10 by 1000 to calculate an ultracheap cost of equity financing of one percent. In summary, "extraordinary popular delusions and the madness of crowds"[12] held dominion over common sense once again. Individual and institutional investors kept buying stocks at inflated prices, making the prices go even higher and their projected earnings appear even more impressive. It looked like the party would never end.

Megabubble stock prices were even more extreme in Japan just before the collapse of its stock exchange, known as the Nikkei 225, in 1990. I then counseled two major Japanese firms to sell their stocks, immediately convert the yen to dollars, then raise new equity money in yen at an ultralow cost of equity capital, and again convert all the yen to dollars. They did not take my advice. Like many Americans they were caught up in a runaway mania. The Japanese missed a golden opportunity to buy up the world with equity money raised at an ultracheap cost of equity capital.[13]

Were Wall Street analysts and economists sound asleep or were they, like many others, sucked into a runaway mania mode? Well, there were far more serious problems than sleeping.[14] First, senior executives and analysts were looking at the wrong data. They focused on the "coincident data," namely, income, production, employment, sales, and gross domestic product. But these rearview indicators cannot tell us where the economy or the stock market is headed. Second, they failed to track all the "forward" or "leading" indicators (i.e., orders, contracts, housing starts, construction permits, private placements, etc.). Third, and most important, they failed even to understand the initial and lagging effects of fiscal and central banking policies. They were blind during the period 1997 to 2002 to how extremely easy fiscal and monetary policies fueled the overinvestment boom that collapsed. They never once identified inflated stock prices that were destined to crash. The crowd mania for higher and higher stock profits displaced good judgment and any science of investing and forecasting.

Let's continue being specific: federal and state governments were on a runaway spending and borrowing spree. Federal Reserve monetary policy was sustained and inordinately easy. Broad money (M2) growth ran ahead of the Federal Reserve's own targets. Money (M2) velocity soared. M2, broadly, is the money in circulation that includes demand deposits and short-term savings deposits. Velocity is the speed of turnover of money being spent. A high velocity signals that buyers of stocks and property are taking risks to spend in order to make big profits. Both excessive money growth and higher money velocity defined the runaway mania that signaled to me a major bursting of the economy and a severe recession ahead.[15] Fast money growth multiplied by soaring money velocity fueled a dangerous "asset inflation" in stocks and real estate. The Fed was the principal villain.[16]

Consumer price inflation, though, remained fairly stable because record imports of high-quality goods at low prices kept the Consumer Price Index (CPI) from soaring. Still, never once did the Federal Reserve chairman acknowledge record imports as a powerful counterinflationary ally. Worse, he said it was no business of the Fed to tame inflating stock prices. With such policy blindness firmly in place, stocks predictably climbed to "megabubble" heights.

My overall grade for fiscal and monetary policy from 1997 to 2002 shows both with failing marks. As of 2008, exploding trade and budget deficits and our high levels of borrowing to finance our wars in Iraq and Afghanistan still marked fiscal failure. Borrowing heavily to finance military spending is the very worst way to manage a major war that appears to have no end in sight.

Micro and Macro Economic Blunders

For those readers who remember the ship the Titanic, you'll recall that the experts said the ship was unsinkable. But this British luxury liner did sink to the bottom of the North Atlantic on April 14-15, 1912. It ran at excessive speed into a huge iceberg. The analogy of the Titanic tragedy with bungling investment managers makes good sense. During the period from 1997 to 2002 both fiscal and monetary policies backfired from a huge effort on the part of the Federal Reserve to maintain excessively easy credit for an inordinately long period of time.

Consensus Economists and Biased Forecasts

How can one possibly explain why just about everything goes wrong on Wall Street? Is it possible that Wall Street is poorly trained, or dishonest, or both? To be sure, many Wall Street executives have their impressive MBAs from noted business schools, but they apparently didn't learn very much. Economists with their PhDs must have been asleep, too. Actually, the problem with economists is far worse. To see why first read this portion of a letter to me dated January 1989:

> Forecast accuracy guaranteed or your money back. Take a subscription for the Blue Chip Economic Indicators at absolutely no risk. If you're dissatisfied with the quality of forecasts…we will refund [your money].

Blue Chip economists make up a supposedly elite group of economists who are regularly cited in the press, but their forecasting record is terrible. Nobody can really guarantee the accuracy of forecasts. Nobody knows for certain what the future holds. Moreover, you probably know by now that most Wall Street economists, including the Blue Chip ones, are reluctant to walk out on a pessimistic limb and predict anything all on their own. So the broad consensus among economists is all too often skewed to the bright side no matter how bleak the outlook. Listen to the plight of Wall Street senior economists as the Unholy Trinity on earth whispers into their ears:

> Look, shade to the bright side. If the entire pack of economists is optimistic, don't walk way out on a limb as a pessimist. If you're wrong, that could cost you your reputation, even your job. But if you're in the pack, you'll still be in good company, respected. Who could fault you? Play it safe. You're only human. [17]

It seems that little has changed to bring much confidence in the Blue Chip consensus forecasts. Here is what *New York Times* reporter Louis Uchitelle had to say about them:

Economics as the Dismal Science? Not in some quarters. In the midst of the deepest recession in the experience of most Americans, many professional forecasters are optimistically saying the worst may soon be over. If the dominoes fall the right way, the economy should bottom out and start growing again in small steps by July [2009] according to the December [2007] survey of 50 professional [Blue Chip] forecasters.[18]

I compliment Mr. Uchitelle. He had the wisdom and, I suspect, the doubts over the Blue Chip forecasts to include other forecasters who project no recovery in sight. He knows that the Blue Chips missed completely both the financial meltdown and the grave recession now changing from bad to worse every day. The Blue Chip performance was no better, for they missed earlier cyclical downturns completely. In *Unlocking* I write that shading to the bright side is always a problem when the Blue Chip forecasts seem constantly biased to the upside. But I also argue that poor theory, the mother of all bad policy and poor projections, is far more important.[19]

The "Quants" and Their Broken Mathematical Models

One of the most devastating forces that led to the present financial meltdown and recession was the inane work of financial "quants," the quantitative mathematical economists. The quants substituted mathematics and patterns of past data in place of sound economics. But their models suffered major flaws. One key missing ingredient was their total inability to identify in advance the initial and often the lagging destructive impact of bumbling monetary, fiscal, and international financial policies. I have already reviewed that utter breakdown in depth. Today nobody would pay a nickel to rely on econometrics, including the once prized work of Wharton econometrics.

Another broken-down mathematical model goes by the name VaR, meaning "value at risk." Grounded on centuries-old statistical and probability theories, the VaR came into being in the early 1990s according to

Joe Nocera, a business columnist for the *New York Times* and a staff writer for the *New York Times Magazine*.[20] Well, I was around in the early 1990s as a harsh critic of these brand new and highly egotistical "quants."

One of the most appealing enchantments of VaR was that it was supposed to measure both the amount of risk in a single stock trader's portfolio and the broader risk posed to the stock brokerage firm as a whole, all in one single number. For example, VaR would compel traders to assign risk to individual stocks and then calculate an *average* expected risk for all the stocks in their portfolio. These were useless averages that had no support from economic science. What rot! Still, the Securities and Exchange Commission, tasked with regulating the activity of stock and bond traders, and the Basel Committee (an international counseling group on stocks and bonds) both validated VaR. Incredible but true, both regulators said that firms could rely on their own internal VaR calculations to set their capital reserves, the amount of money they needed to have on hand to cover unexpected and major costs or a fall in revenues and any expected demand by investors to redeem their stock for cash.

But Mr. Nocera wisely concluded, "The widespread institutional reliance on VaR was a terrible mistake." Indeed, VaR and related quant nonsense was all part and parcel of the attempt by financial economists to carve out a separate and higher-valued niche for themselves that would find investors paying ever higher prices for stocks and bonds with brokerage commissions increasing proportionally. But all of this was done in a manner that was viewed as separate and superior to sound economics. That attempt failed miserably and predictably. As was pointed out earlier, a major flaw is the failure to track the initial and lagging effects of monetary, fiscal, and international financial policies that often bring about huge cyclical swings in the economy. In other words, very few economists are trained, experienced, or capable macroeconomic forecasters. That's why they fail to forecast bubbles or recessions until after they occur. This fact has ruined the reputation and value of financial quants and has cost millions of investors their jobs, their incomes, their homes, and in many cases their life savings.

The Victims of Recession:
Frantic Consumers with No Money

Consumers are now stricken with falling house prices and loss of their jobs and incomes. They borrow on their 401(k)s. They sell or borrow against their life insurance policies for immediate cash. They may even sell their houses to raise desperately needed cash with the understanding that the buyer shares as much as 50 percent of any future gain in price.

Perhaps most humiliating is not to have any money to pay hospital bills. The hospitals are also operating on very tight budgets. So if American citizens and immigrants do succeed in getting hospital treatment, the hospitals will often auction their unpaid bills to collection services. Imagine the agony of being pounded day after day by collection agencies you never heard of after having lost your house, your job, your income, your health insurance, and whatever meager cash savings you might have had. This is the extreme agony and the economic torture many people are experiencing throughout America today.

Others are resorting to expensive and risky options to get ready cash. Whether through overextending their credit card debt or pawning valued possessions, they take what few dollars they can get. But these people also give up precious liquidity (their access to ready cash) for a rainy day and finally lose their power to borrow at all. Meanwhile, those heavily in debt may be besieged by scam artists on Wall Street and elsewhere. These scammers pop up everywhere in times of recession and despair. Those who have lost the most are at greatest risk. Their desperation makes them easy targets for con artists.

Bungling and Fumbling Government Policies

In contrast to the misery and woe I have spelled out for consumers, my fellow economic forecasters repeatedly and mistakenly paint rosy scenarios despite the hard evidence of troubles ahead. Even worse, bungling and fumbling fiscal, monetary, and international financial policies put investors, consumers, and businesses in trouble. Check out the havoc wreaked by poor theory and government incompetence on most of us.[21] The Fed normally constricts (i.e., raises) interest rates (thereby reducing the amount of available money in the economy) to ease inflationary pressures, or it eases these same rates and increases the money supply to fuel economic expansion by making credit more affordable and easier to obtain.

	Federal Reserve Policy		What Followed?
1)	1948	Fed Policy Constriction	Recession
2)	1953	Fed Policy Constriction	Recession
3)	1957	Fed Policy Constriction	Recession
4)	1960	Fed Policy Constriction	Recession
5)	1969	Fed Policy Constriction	Recession
6)	1973-74	Fed Policy Constriction	Recession
7)	1980	Fed Policy Constriction	Recession
8)	1981-82	Fed Policy Constriction	Recession
9)	1990	Fed Policy Constriction	Recession
10)	1997-02	Fed Sustained Ultra Ease	Boom-to-Bust Collapse
11)	2008	Fed and Fiscal Ultra Ease	Financial meltdown and recession

The tenth and eleventh cases were completely different.[22] The Federal Reserve's excessive easing of the money supply and interest rates between 1997 and 2002 ignited the overinvestment boom that predictably collapsed causing overpriced stocks to plunge in value. Did the Fed question the wisdom of targeting interest rates? No. Were its fiscal and monetary "experts," those at the Treasury, or even those in the private sector (1) blind, (2) confused, and (3) themselves trapped by the same "extraordinary popular delusions and the madness of crowds" that favored continued unrealistic expansion of the economy and higher stock prices? Yes. You should check all three.[23]

Eleven strikes and you're out. In nine consecutive instances, excessive Federal Reserve constriction of the money supply and interest rates preceded recession. Each time the Fed governors had pursued an excessively easy monetary policy that sent the economy booming, which eventually led to concerns about potential inflation. These concerns brought on an abrupt constriction of that same money supply (intended to prevent inflation), which in turn precipitated a recession. The Fed also embarked upon a concurrent policy of "targeted" interest rates, a policy that predictably backfired every time.[24]

Targeting Interest Rates: A Failed Policy Every Time[25]

To understand how and why the Federal Reserve can strike out eleven times in a row we need first to understand what targeting rates means. Briefly, targeting interest rates in the late 1970s meant that the Fed provided the additional bank reserves to permit lenders to expand credit and money at a fast pace In an attempt to keep Interest rates down. Since interest rates are a barometer of the ease with which credit can be obtained, the lower the interest rate the easier one can secure a loan and the greater the likelihood that the economy will expand as more people seek loans for personal and business uses. But the attempt backfired because excessively fast money and credit growth produced boom and inflation, which triggered higher interest rates. The Fed's failed policy of boom and bust induced me to forecast "a post-election blow off in rates" as the Fed was then forced to restrict credit and money, which in turn brought on the extreme recession of 1981-1982. Let's explain step-by-step the Fed's monetary idiocy:

(1) + MONEY SUPPLY: It tries to keep interest rates from rising too much because it is concerned that its policy will choke off economic expansion. So it shoves additional bank reserves into the banking system and speeds the growth of credit and money with the aim of keeping interest rates from rising above its expressed target.

(2) – INTEREST RATES: Interest rates decline temporarily in response to the huge influx of money and credit that the Fed has engineered. Monetary economists call this the "liquidity effect."

(3) + INFLATION: With a short lag, inflation speeds up in response to the liquidity infusion brought about by the rapid and excessive expansion of money and credit. The total effective demand for goods and services speeds ahead at a faster pace than the economy can effectively supply them, thereby fueling greater demand, which hikes prices up and fuels inflation. Economists call this lagging or deferred impact of rapid money growth on inflation the "Fisher Effect," after famed economist Irving Fisher, who first took note of it.

(4) + INTEREST RATES: With a short lag, interest rates rise in response to sizzling economic activity, rising loan demands, and the accelerating inflation set into motion by the Fed itself. Inflation and the expectations of higher inflation induce lenders to protect themselves by raising interest rates, by demanding that an "inflationary premium" be tacked onto interest rates. The lagging rise of interest rates is also part of the Fisher Effect.

(5) + MONEY SUPPLY: The Fed then tries to keep interest rates from rising too much. It is concerned that policy should not choke off economic expansion. It therefore shoves reserves into the banking system and speeds….

Wait a minute! We are back to (1) where we started. By pouring reserves and money into the economy in the futile attempt to keep interest rates down, or within acceptable limits, the actual outcome is to produce yet another roaring economy that will eventually push interest rates higher. That makes a bad situation worse, and an inflationary situation even more inflationary. The word to describe this policy is *procyclical*, an antonym for *countercyclical*.

Instead of stabilizing economic activity, which is supposed to be the number-one function of a nation's central bank, the Federal Reserve has done just the opposite. It destabilizes, but it will never tell you that. The

Fed also targeted interest rates from 1997 to the present. Targeting backfired yet again. Query: How did the central bank try to keep interest rates
from falling too much? Just reverse every step I have set forth in the Fed's
attempt to keep rates from rising too much. If you succeed then you can
easily see why I called its actions "idiocy circles." If you have trouble, I
refer you to pages 91 and 92 of my *Unlocking the Secrets of Wall Street*
for a step-by-step explanation of a backfiring central bank.

Mephistopheles on Wall Street

I decided that Faust's devilish Mephistopheles must be ruling our Federal
Reserve, the Department of the Treasury, and Wall Street. To make my
point consider another real-life example in March 1974 of how a top Wall
Street executive who headed up retail sales at a major brokerage house
tried to force his chief economist (yours truly) to lie.[26] I'll call him Twist
in this actual exchange:

> **Twist**: Let me get to the real reason I wanted to talk with you.
> What's this I hear about a "maxirecession"? Look at these lousy
> headlines. You are quoted all over the press saying we're going to
> be hit with a big recession. What the hell is that? You've got
> every branch manager calling me. How did the press get this?

> **RH**: The press called me. They always do. You know that. Also,
> editorial mails all my reports to the press.

> **Twist**: Yeah, but whoever heard of a maxirecession? Look, you
> are our biggest prospecting tool for the RRs [stock brokers]. They
> use your reports. But you are now frightening them out of their
> minds. Why this maxirecession scare?

> **RH**: Oil prices have shot up. This cuts buying power. Worse, it
> looks now as though central banks around the world are preparing
> to strip away money growth and raise interest rates to fight infla-
> tion. This will cripple buying power and spending power. The for-

ward indicators are crashing. I called our institutional clients and warned them of that. They have to be alerted to the . . .

Twist: Stop! I don't want an economic lecture. You are killing retail business.

RH: I didn't know I had that much power.

Twist: Don't get smart. We made you first vice president and chief economist. You're supposed to be a partner with us in this firm.

RH: I'm doing my best. What do you want? If you don't agree with my forecast, then tell me why. I'm willing to listen. Nobody has prescience.

Twist: Press what? I've had enough of this. Kill that maxi stuff.

RH: But that would be shading.

Twist: What?

RH: Shading. You know, slanting or twisting the truth. That would be dishonest.

Twist: Don't you understand? I don't care whether you are right or wrong. I don't want to hear of a maxirecession again. Get out of my office. Get out!

I understood all too well. Twist wanted me to paint my reports always to the bright side no matter how bleak the outlook. Instead, I changed my forecast from a maxirecession to a minidepression and called the press to report just that. What happened? The 1973-74 recession lasted sixteen months. At the time, it was the worst recession since the Great Depression.

One might ask: Where were the financial regulators and the rating agencies whose actions are supposed to reduce the likelihood of wild swings in the economy? Had they been asleep all this time? My conviction is that they were either asleep or dishonest. Indeed, pitifully poor federal and state regulations always pose a big risk of needless economic damage.

Poor regulation and enforcement of laws was even more of a problem under George W. Bush. He declared, "We must get government off the backs of the people." He succeeded. Government inaction let the robber barons run free to lie, steal, and deceive. A few corporate executives were jailed, but most got away scot-free because the White House refused to bring their supporting business cronies to trial. Corruption ran amok.

Lawbreaking "Rig" in the Big Electric Industry

General Electric preached free trade publicly in the daylight. In the dark it practiced protectionism. As mentioned at the beginning of this chapter, GE sent a memo to its employees, including me, in which it asked that we not buy foreign cars, appliances, and TV sets. I was the only one who complained about the letter to the executive office in Manhattan.[27] I began by quoting the famed economist Frederic Bastiat (1801-1850) from his classic work *Economic Sophisms*.

> We are subjected to the intolerable competition of a foreign rival, who enjoys such superior facilities for the production of light [at a price so low] that French industry is reduced to a state of complete stagnation. . . . The rival [is] none other than the sun. We must block out [the light of the sun].[28]

That's not all. GE also practiced protectionism at home. When it was not dumping waste poison into the Hudson River it secretly conspired to restrain trade and block competition for light bulbs and steam turbines. Some GE officers ended up in prison.[29] Consider this exchange I had with the manager (TC) of GE's industrial and economic forecasting division in Schenectady, New York, where I worked as a senior economist:

RH: I can't believe you asked me to destroy records on light bulbs or turbines. I have none. Anyway, it would have been unethical and illegal for me to do so.

TC: I did not ask anybody to break the law. Nobody else complained about my request. What's your problem? I made myself clear that the executive office wanted those records destroyed. Also, the memo you sent to [New York] on Bastiat was out of order. General Electric is not a university. Be careful.

RH: The other senior economists have been here forever. They won't speak up. They don't want to jeopardize their promotions and their jobs. But you put them in a terrible bind, to put loyalty over everything else. What did they do?

TC: That's not your business. You're all wet. I have a meeting to attend.

"Lie" for the Federal Government

It's worth repeating how economics professors graded the views of then President-Elect George W. Bush.[30] Over a quarter of the professors responding to a poll by the *Economist* "reckoned the [future] President's plans merited a grade of D or F." The academics were referees of the *American Economic Review*, an extremely prestigious economics journal. I then graded Bush with an F-. In reviewing his eight years in office, there is every reason now to keep the failing grade.

Still, Bush was not the first to bungle and fumble with damaging policies. In 1981 President Ronald Reagan and his supply-side ideologists went on a wild borrowing-and-spending spree. A terrible financial meltdown followed, and the 1981-82 recession was the unfortunate result. It was, predictably, one of the nation's worst recessions.[31] Sad to say, the extreme right-wing supply-side ideologists returned with a vengeance when George W. Bush entered the Oval Office. None deserves to be called a professional economist. They gave Bush the same bad counsel provided to Reagan nearly twenty years earlier.

Bush's soaring budget and trade deficits in 2008 looked eerily similar to those that preceded the 1981-82 collapse. The dishonest conservative pitch to downsize big government shows up in fact as a huge expansion of government pork barrel spending, spying on American citizens, jailing people unjustly, waging war on false grounds, and condoning torture. These actions only serve to destroy the moral and economic foundation of capitalism.

Suppression of Science: We All Lose

It gets worse daily. Testifying under oath, former Surgeon General Richard H. Carmona said he was muzzled by the Bush administration.[32] He testified that he was forbidden to speak or issue warning reports on emergency contraception, AIDS, sex education, global warming, cigarettes, and prison abuse, as well as mental and global health issues.[33] He says the White House delayed for years a study on why even brief exposure to cigarette smoke can cause immediate harm. Are there two morals here? Yes. First, everyone loses when such disclosures are not made in the public interest. Second, never trust a declared ultraconservative president who regularly breaks laws but who also claims to be compassionate and kind.

This chapter would not be complete without stressing the diluted role of science in America. I have already written of how the previous administration under Bush elected to put its ideological officers far above their level of expertise. The repeated Bush mantra was to deny that global warming posed a danger, that the ultrafree market without controls is a problem, and even that millions of Americans are short of food, healthcare, and a roof over their head.

The truth is that many Americans also remain ignorant of the most elementary dictates of science and the importance of theoretical and empirical support for any scientific conclusions. The National Science Board points out that many Americans can't tell whether Earth moves around the Sun, or the Sun moves around Earth. They are decidedly more ignorant than people in other developed countries of the cosmological Big Bang view of our universe, of Charles Darwin and the meaning of evolution, or the basic rules of mathematics, biology, and physics.

What bothers me most is that many Americans who are in the dark don't understand or accept the simple fundamentals of science, critical reason, and searching for the truth. The National Science Board asks whether the decline in science and reason also feeds into extreme religious views that have neither theoretical nor empirical validity. Creationism is one example. The simplistic idea that Earth was created just a few millennia ago is another. The extreme religious view that rejects medical care in favor of divine intervention is yet another. Add to this list the growing belief in ghosts, flying saucers, witches, fortune-tellers, fakes, and charlatans and we discover that popular acceptance of science evaporates as each new groundless belief gains acceptance and thrives. The list of unscientific nonsense is endless. But what is lasting is the absence of scientific training for millions of Americans. Its absence represents an expanding roadblock to learning, invention, discovery, and a renewed surge in productivity, progress, and national wealth. Surely the former Bush administration's devaluation of science has been a huge force in destroying capitalism.

The Macho Cultural, Sexual, and Racial Predators

Children of all ages are the losers to Scam on Wall Street, Rig in Big Electric, and Lie in big government. We next meet in chapter 5 a wide range of corrupt predators in the food, tobacco, pharmaceutical, and insurance industries, among others. Their prey includes both adults and children of all ages. I'll document the terrible harm and even the deaths these corrupt and selfish predators inflict directly or indirectly on all Americans and their role in the demise of capitalism.

Chapter 5

INDUSTRIAL CORPORATE PREDATORS

The rich and the fortunate do well to keep silent, for no one cares who and what they are. But those in need must reveal themselves.
— Rainer Maria Rilke, *Selected Poems* (1990)

Rilke and Martin Luther King: Famed Fighters for People Most in Need

I quote the acclaimed poet Rilke because he cared dearly about those people most in need. So did Dr. Martin Luther King Jr., a truly compassionate man who fought for truth and justice. King relentlessly exposed abuse and racial discrimination. He identified and shamed lawbreakers, killers, and cruel racists.

The bitter truth is that far too many Americans offer neither charity nor compassion for their fellow human beings who are most in need. My goal here is to identify abuses that rampage across America. To have any success in solving social problems we must first spot their causes using the best theory and data. Without further ado, let's meet the enemies of good health and happiness.

Cast of Evil Predators

The roster of bad industry predators includes **Fatmac** for big food; **Venom** for big tobacco; **Poison** for big pharmaceutical; **Deny** for big health insurance; **Distort** for big life insurance; **Exploit** for big home insurance; **Odious** for the military, industrial, and big-oil complex; and **Sick** for those who exploit uninsured Americans and immigrants.

Public enemy number one also shows up again in this chapter as an enemy of life, liberty, and happiness. Here, again, I mean the despicable philosophy of extreme laissez faire. It worships ultrafree markets and pathetically weak government controls. Its policies block effective regulation to prevent suffering and death in every one of the industries on the list above, a list of the damned and the lost. Government's hands-off policy regarding regulation and controls permits industries to fill their pockets with huge profits at the expense of fraud and deceit inflicted on all of us.

To justify their greed these industries constantly preach that the free market knows best and that government controls only make matters worse. The sleaze and dishonesty I document is just one of the forces that foreshadow an end to ugly capitalism. I'll start with the misery and death that the food industry inflicts on millions of consumers both young and old.

The Horrors of Fatmac

Children face many dangers. Librarian and author Chris Roberts offers this parody of the well-known Mother Goose rhyme "Georgy Porgy":

> Rowley Poley, pudding and pie,
> Kissed the girls and made them cry.
> When the girls began to cry,
> Rowley Poley runs away.[1]

Rowley Poly (aka Roley Poley) is a fat child who eats too much. Does he remind you of two of the seven deadly sins that Pope Gregory I listed: sloth (inactivity) and gluttony (excessive eating)? Both sloth and gluttony can sicken and kill people.

For years I rode the subways and trains to my office in downtown New York City. During these commutes, I was amazed at the many obese men, women, and children I would see almost every day. I wondered if they knew of the dangers obesity brings with it: heart, liver, kidney, and other organ diseases; terrible pain and discomfort; sometimes the amputation of a limb due to the complications of diabetes; and, all too often, premature death. I talked with many of these fellow commuters. They thanked me sincerely for my warnings, but I was saddened to hear that few had ever been alerted to these dangers, either from their friends or their parents, let alone their physicians.

No matter what their age, people who are more than a little overweight or those who are morbidly obese (extremely fat) are at high risk for contracting disease and succumbing to an early death. Obese children who fail to exercise regularly face a whirlwind of suffering. Many don't even realize their dreadful fate until it's too late. And the federal government doesn't help much either. Yes, it warns us about smoking, drug abuse, and food that could sicken or kill people. But to please these killer industries it does very little to control or prohibit dangerous products. I must stress at the outset that overeating coupled with inactivity can bring on pain, diabetes, heart disease, muscle damage, loss of limbs and blindness due to poor circulation and complications of diabetes, and even death. That's why scientists list obesity as an epidemic.

In the face of the scourge of obesity, the food industry, with few exceptions, continues to spend enormous sums to market a wide range of drinks, candies, and fast foods the consumption of which can, in excessive quantity, bring on the massive weight gain that cuts life prematurely short for millions of Americans. Very young children often suffer the most with type-2 diabetes, heart failure, and muscle deterioration.

John Kenneth Galbraith:
Millions of Americans Eat Themselves to Death

Starvation surely can kill but so can gluttony and sloth. Economist Thomas Malthus (1776–1834) made dire forecasts that population growth would put pressure on the food supply, which would not be able to grow fast enough to feed all of the people. He said it would lead to sickness, misery, and widespread death. Another economist and noted scholar, John Kenneth Galbraith (1908-2006), quipped that the food supply now presses against the population. True, too many people starve in the United States. "Thirty-five million families, one-third [of whom are] children, don't get enough food."[2] But millions of Americans also eat themselves to death! The two demons of sloth and gluttony often lead to premature death, while the food industry mainly stands by and does nothing to monitor or prohibit sales campaigns that encourage people to eat themselves to death.

Pope Gregory I didn't have the science and facts we have today. Even so, he was far ahead of his time. There's a moral here. What do you say if your friends want you to join them every day for sweet colas, candy, cake, French fries, and giant hamburgers? I will put myself (RH) in this exchange I have often had with children of all ages.

RH: What do you say to your friends?

All: NO, NO, NO. Overweight people get diabetes and die young.

RH: The real demon is the choice to eat far too much each day. Eating less high fat food, then, is no answer if you are still gorging yourself.[3] So, how do we encourage children to cut back on foods that are bad for them? As a start, parents should not let children make the choices of what they eat. The parent should do that. Second, it's not a good idea to single out a child as overweight and in need of a special diet. Instead, have everyone eat the right foods as a family. Third, make sure that your children exercise on a regular basis, which probably means cutting down their television time. Fourth, take your children to a good doctor if you suspect they are overweight. Ask the doctor to calculate their "body-mass index." Fifth, and most important, don't procrastinate. These simple rules can ward off needless horror.

Caution: Don't Confuse Simple with Absolute Rules

I have often stressed that simple rules may not always apply to all people. For example, some overweight people seemed to be happy and healthy. Of course, "some" does not mean "all." A recent medical study found that one-half of overweight adults and one-third of obese adults are "metabolically healthy."[4] Despite their excess pounds, these overweight and obese adults have healthy levels of "good" cholesterol, blood pressure, and blood glucose. But about 25 percent of supposedly healthy, thin people have at least two cardiovascular risk factors linked to obesity.

Part of the confusion may be related to what it means to be overweight. As I noted, one is often judged to be of normal weight based on the body-mass index (BMI). It measures weight relative to height. A normal BMI ranges from 18.5 to 25. At 25 one is considered overweight, and at 30 or higher, obese. One other factor is always relevant: just about every medical report I read insists that those who are overweight should exercise regularly to strengthen their muscles, bones, and hearts. So use those exercise machines or a bike, or walk daily for forty minutes. Walk for health and happiness.

Try to get your weight down before you start any fast walking or running. Don't end up in later years with knee injuries or arthritis in your ankles and toes. Elephants have four strong and thick legs to stand on and run. Darwin tells us that our two legs are weak relative to the weight of our body. That's why hockey, basketball, and football players; ballet dancers; and ice skaters often end up crippled and in pain. If your key goal is to make podiatrists happy and rich, then run, run, run as long and as fast as you can.[5] Wherever you run, I forecast you will sooner or later end up in a podiatrist's office.

Venom for Tobacco and Poison for Drugs

RH: Other killers also stalk children in the name of free enterprise and with few if any controls to stop them. Those who reject the concept of controls seem far more comfortable with the old adage "Let the buyer beware," but this approach has its own problems. For example, many young adults simply don't understand the dangers of addiction, or they believe that they will never fall victim to it. Another huge problem is that neither private industry nor governments (local, state, or federal) have a strong control program to prohibit these products from being sold in the first place. Also, keep in mind that these government entities make money off of the sale of tobacco and alcohol through the sales taxes that are placed on them.

Some of the other killer substances include drugs such as cocaine, ecstasy, heroin, and methamphetamine (called "meth" by addicts and drug dealers).[6] What do you say to these murderers? Let me hear you loud and clear.

All: NO, NO, NO. All are killers. We can get sick and die young.

RH: Yes, you don't want to become an addict. What about beer, whiskey, and cigarettes? One way to fight tobacco addiction (getting hooked) is to get 100 percent of the nicotine out of cigarettes.[7] A better way is not to smoke at all. Also, beware of second-hand smoke, which is defined as the smoke you inhale from smokers around you. Avoid it whenever possible. In recent years, many municipalities across the country have legislated smoking bans in public places to curtail secondhand smoke. New scientific research makes clear that secondhand smoke can turn children into tobacco addicts quickly, sometimes in a matter of days.

All: Does that mean "light" cigarettes offer little protection against disease?

RH: That's exactly correct. The tobacco companies have begun creating feminized versions of their macho male-oriented brands. Many women may fall for the phony advertising. Menthol flavored cigarettes are also heavily marketed to minority populations. Smoking is still the leading cause of lung cancer in women, not to mention emphysema and heart attacks. What do you say, children, when someone tempts you with whiskey, beer, or cigarettes?

All: NO, NO, NO. They are all drugs. We can get very sick. But what's an addict?

RH: An addict is someone hooked on a drug, whether it be alcohol, nicotine, or crack cocaine. He can't stop without terrible pain. True, it takes a bit longer to become addicted to alcohol and cigarettes than to the hard drugs. Many doctors say a little alcohol actually improves health for some adults. Moderate consumption of red wine, they now say, can add years to the human life span unless other diseases or self-destructive behavior is involved. But many people cannot drink in moderation. They risk drinking too much, too often, and then turning into alcoholics.

On a personal note on poisonous tobacco, let me tell you what I ask my graduate students in the very first class meeting. I ask them to raise their hands if they smoke cigarettes. Invariably two or three hands shoot up. Then I describe what head and neck surgeons often do. Since smoking causes cancer, the surgeon may cut away part of the smoker's lips, cheeks, nose, or even their voice boxes. The goal is to keep any cancer from spreading (in the surgeon's jargon, to metastasize) to other body organs.

The instant I mention the voice box, the same three students shout they will stop. Good, I respond, even as I wonder in silence if they really can stop. Addiction is hard and extremely painful to break. That's why tobacco companies spend millions of dollars to get people hooked, including many teenagers. The bank robber Willie Sutton was asked why he robbed banks. He said, "That's where the money is." Why do tobacco companies strive to get people addicted to tobacco? That's where they make the most money.

Alcohol is as deadly as tobacco. Many adults can't stop with one alcoholic drink. That's one reason why alcohol-related traffic deaths stood at almost 17,000 in 2004, or 39 percent of total traffic fatalities.[8]

The death rate is higher now, close to 40,000. Put another way, an adult or a child dies every thirty-one minutes from accidents caused by drunk drivers. That's why parents must warn their children again and again of the danger of drugs.

One deadly drug is caffeinated alcoholic energy drinks. A major distributor, Anheuser-Busch, allegedly failed "to adequately disclose the negative health effects of its Tilt and Bud Extra drinks. It also made false claims on how to stay up late for partying, and illegally targeted minors with its advertising."[9] Even some cough suppressant drugs and sleeping pills can be deadly. The Center for Disease Control reported that in 2004-2005 over-the-counter cough suppressants made 1519 children sick. Three died.[10]

Stronger Warnings Demanded for Byetta®[11]

I have already noted the terrible dangers of diabetes. The drug Byetta is widely used to fight diabetes. Marketed by Amylin Pharmaceuticals and Eli Lilly and Company, the drug has run into a problem. Apparently two patients died and thirty others were made terribly ill by Byetta, according to the Food and Drug Administration (FDA).

One dangerous side effect of the drug is pancreatitis. The regulators said that patients should stop taking Byetta immediately if they develop signs of acute pancreatitis. The disease causes nausea, abdominal pain, and potentially dangerous complications. Marketed for patients with type-2 diabetes, more than 700,000 patients have used the drug since it was introduced in June 2005.

Another related problem exists that put the Consumer Product Safety Commission (CPSC) in the headlines. It is tasked with ensuring that roughly fifteen thousand products in the US marketplace are safe to use. Apart from its acute shortage of funds and employees, a constant problem in recent administrations has been that when a product is cited as a hazard, little is done to alert the consumer. Often more than two-thirds of recalled products "go unaccounted for and leave children and adults vulnerable to injuries."[12] Does that include disease and death from drugs? Yes it does, including the much-reviled Vioxx.

Merck Charged Again with Bogus Vioxx® Claims[13]

It seems that Merck is again in the headlines. Merck and Co. said that a 1999 clinical study was done to test the side effects of the painkiller Vioxx. In fact, the "study" was conducted primarily to support a *marketing* campaign *before* the drug's launching" (emphasis added). Researchers said their findings, based on internal Merck records disclosed during litigation, are among the first to document what many scientists had already suspected. It was common practice in the drug industry to conduct so-called clinical studies "masquerading" as clinical science to bolster marketing plans.

Fake studies raise questions about whether participants were "unknowingly and needlessly put in harm's way." Dr. Kevin Hill, a psychiatrist at McLean Hospital in Belmont, Massachusetts, was the lead author of the study. He said, "Patients and physicians were not told of the marketing objectives of the study." He added, "Participants in the studies expose themselves to a drug's potentially dangerous side effects, and they need to know what they're risking their health for." Another critic of the Merck studies was Edward Scolnick, Merck's head of research at the time. He called the study "intellectually redundant and extremely dangerous because it could yield data that might compromise more meaningful clinical trials."[14]

Youth Access to Drugs Increases

According to the National Center on Addiction and Substance Abuse (CASA), 23 percent of twelve- to seventeen-year-old youths said they could buy marijuana in an hour or less. CASA Chairman Joseph Califano Jr. says, "A substantial number of American parents have become passive pushers. A few decades ago, parents used to have a lock on the liquor cabinet. Maybe there should also be a lock on the medicine cabinet." The Partnership for a Drug-Free America lists the drugs teens prefer, with marijuana at the top of the list.[15]

Let's look at the data on the percentage of teenagers who have abused drugs at least once, according to the Partnership for a Drug-Free America. It reports that roughly one-third of the teenagers surveyed abused marijuana at least once. The lowest level of abuse was for (11) GHB (gamma–Hydroxybutyric acid).

(1) MARIJUANA, (2) INHALANTS, (3) PRESCRIPTION DRUGS, (4) COUGH MEDICINE, (5) COCAINE/CRACK, (6) ECSTASY, (7) METH, (8) LSD, (9) KETAMINE, (10) HEROIN, (11) GHB.

Deny for Big Health Insurance Companies

RH: Please answer five questions: (1) Do you make enough money to pay for housing, food, and medicine? (2) Do you earn a lot more than the hourly minimum wage of $7.25? (3) Do you get regular medical and dental checkups? (4) Are you now in poor health? (5) Do you have a history of serious medical problems? Did you answer (1) through (3) with no, and (4) and (5) with yes? Then you stand little chance of buying good health insurance. The private insurance companies won't sell you insurance coverage, or if they do it is at a very high price that few can afford. They are, in effect, denying you health protection. Private insurers pick and choose (cherry pick) among the likely consumers in an effort to cover only the healthy and those who can afford the monthly health insurance premium. This selective practice allows the insurers to enjoy low costs and big profits while their executives draw huge salaries and bonuses.

Those individuals who are healthy are less likely to get sick, which cuts the number of insurance claims and saves the insurance companies money. The wealthy will also pay insurance premiums on time. Private health insurers can then spend heavily on attractive marketing campaigns to bring in more healthy clients, further boosting profits. Private health insurance is a cruel joke. Listen to noted economist Paul Krugman:

> The best way for an insurer to avoid paying medical bills is to avoid selling insurance to people who really need it. An insurance company can accomplish this in two ways, through marketing only to the healthy and by denying coverage to the sick, or charging the sick very high premiums.[16]

The Major Value of Mandatory Health Insurance

Is there any sound solution? Yes. The federal government should provide mandatory (required) health and dental insurance for every man, woman, and child in the United States. A universal federal program can operate cheaply and efficiently. There need be no bloated marketing costs or huge salaries and bonuses. Since the government would run the program, there are no competitors and thus no one to require splashy ads to attract new clients to this or that insurer. A federal program could operate like Medicare, Social Security, and veterans care. It could operate fairly and cheaper for everybody.[17] People in poverty should not be charged a nickel for preventive checkups, needed medicines and surgery, and short- or long-term hospital and clinical care. I hope that the Federal Healthcare Reform Bill that has recently been signed into law by President Obama will in fact address these concerns. We shall have to wait and see as provisions of the legislation go into effect over time.

Many states now try to provide health coverage, a role the federal government had largely abandoned. But when a severe recession hits, like the one we are currently experiencing, the funding for many state programs dries up because their much smaller budgets can't accommodate the costs. The states run out of money as jobs and tax revenues evaporate. Unlike the combined efforts of the federal government and the Federal Reserve, states and cities have insufficient power to create money, thus they lack the very ability they need in a recession to provide healthcare at the very time when it is most needed.

Policy Madness and Perverted Capitalism

Neither private charity nor state health programs can assure they will be there when the populations they serve are most in need of them. Federally mandated and funded preventive care alone would take the huge burden off private and teaching hospitals. Now many private hospitals and clinics face bankruptcy as federal and private funds are cut back sharply. Many were forced under the Bush administration to close their doors to the poor. Only a sick and perverted capitalism would permit such outrages.

Distort for Big Life Insurance

We recorded how both General Electric and Blyth Eastman Dillon, a Wall Street investment firm, practiced to deceive. The same holds for the life insurance industry. I worked for all three industries. In the 1960s I was hired as the research director for the Life Insurance Association of America (LIAA).[18] In the exchange to follow I had to conclude that Mephistopheles must run the life insurance business.

Let me explain. I had many duties. One was to keep track of research the LIAA funded. For example, the board of directors had already decided to spend $300,000 for a study on taxes. It wanted to prove that income tax rates destroyed incentives to work, save, and invest. It also wanted to prove that high corporate tax rates cut into corporate profits and cripple investment spending and economic growth. Economist and emeritus professor Daniel Holland of MIT agreed to head up the research overseen by the National Bureau of Economic Research (NBER). Holland's job would be to interview business executives to see how they might react to higher tax rates.

I objected and will explain why shortly. But first let me cite for perspective how this all got started. At the outset I tried to persuade the LIAA board that few people would take the study seriously. I reminded them that Dr. Holland was an economist, not a psychologist trained in human motivation. I argued that the interviews could not support the "proof" that income taxes destroyed incentives. I warned the LIAA that it was about to throw $300,000 down the drain. I lost the argument and the board approved the study.

Shortly thereafter I was offered a job as chief economist for DuPont Glore Forgan, then the second largest Wall Street firm behind Merrill Lynch. But I wondered what had happened to the study. To find out I telephoned Dr. Holland. The following is a short transcript of our talk.

RH: What happened to your study? I can't find it. I want to include your research findings in a book I'm writing.[19]

Dr. Holland: I believe you can find some of the research in the *1969 Proceedings of The National Tax Association*.[20] Let me remind you that what I published in the proceedings was not cleared by the National Bureau of Economic Research or the LIAA. The study was scrapped because they were furious with the findings.

RH: I am not surprised. Most of the LIAA presidents never heard of the concepts "tax incidence" and "tax impact" and how both are crucial in understanding taxes. Simply put, the impact of the tax is its initial resting place, that is, on the corporation. But the incidence of the tax, in other words, who actually pays it, is on the consumer. The corporation shifts the tax onto the prices of the goods it produces and sells with no reduction of net profits. This truth is seldom understood.[21]

There is a major exception, however, to the shifting theory. In a recession corporations have trouble shifting both costs and taxes into higher prices. In that case profits and jobs are hit hard. In severe slumps costs and taxes may in fact be shifted backward, not forward. Profits suffer. Jobs are lost. This is the exception to the rule. The general rule, supported theoretically and empirically, is that corporate taxes are shifted forward into higher prices, other things being equal. When such a shift of costs to the consumer is not possible (as in a deep recession), corporate productivity gains may keep total costs and prices down to offset a rise in corporate tax rates.

Right-Wing Supply-Side Nonsense on High Taxes

Let's now meet Dr. Martin Feldstein. He is a Harvard professor of economics and former chairman of the Council of Economic Advisers under President Reagan. He (MF) was my guest for two conferences I hosted for him and my institutional investor clients. One was held in New York City on April 28, 1977. Here is our brief exchange on corporate taxes.

RH: Dr. Feldstein, we are all delighted that you could join us.

MF: Thanks. Let me first summarize my main conclusions. The corporate tax absorbs cash flow that otherwise would be available to finance capital formation in machinery, plant and equipment, new technology, and research and development. By absorbing cash flow, the corporate tax cripples the rise in productivity and slows growth in real output. Corporate shareholders pay a double tax, first on corporate income and second on corporate dividends.

RH: I have one question. You set forth the "absorption" theory. It argues that taxes soak up profits. But you contend in your books and articles that the corporate tax is shifted forward into higher prices. Thus consumers pay the tax. True, the initial "impact" of the tax is on the corporation. But the "incidence" of the tax, the real burden, is quickly shifted forward into higher prices. Economists call that the "shifting" theory. So how can there be a double tax if, as you say, the corporate tax is shifted forward?

MF: Taxes impair incentives no matter who pays them. You see that?

RH: No, I do not. You did not answer my question.

Dancing Around the Question

It looks like Dr. Feldstein danced around the question. That's what people do, whatever their education or training, when they become enmeshed in contradictions of their own making. They do an ideological dance. But science has no interest in ideology. It is concerned with the truth. I have often met many people who have become trapped by their own contradictions. Sad to say, extreme ideology perverts economic science and it in turn perverts US capitalism. But here is a positive note about people who don't fall into ideological traps. Listen in on an exchange I had with a senior officer of the US Chamber of Commerce in Washington, DC. I'll call him **AP** for his anonymous protection.

> **RH**: The chamber argues in this week's *Economic Intelligence* that the corporate income tax sops up corporate cash flow. Yet, just last month you wrote that consumers pay the tax. I saw your full-page advertisements arguing that the consumer pays the tax through the nose in higher inflation. How can you reach opposite conclusions every other week?

> **AP:** Robert, I was just hired for this job. I had nothing to do with that double-talk baloney on taxes.

Industry-by-Industry Corporate Cheating on Taxes

There are other ways corporations fail to pay taxes. I'll just note two here. First, they avoid paying taxes with offshore tax havens. Many of these schemes are legal, but unethical. Second, they illegally evade taxes. Avoidance and evasion cost the US Treasury many billions of dollars each year. *Effective* tax rates on US corporations are not high. Indeed, they are far lower than any US president or corporation talks about. They have no interest in talking about *effective* tax rates. The truth tells us that US adjusted corporate tax rates are lower than those of foreign corporate competitors. But the former Bush administration still published phony research denying the truth, often written by their right-wing extreme laissez faire think-tank cronies in Washington, DC.[22]

In short, the evidence is clear that corporate America is not bleeding to death from killer taxes. On the contrary, many US presidents and their officers have worked in lock step with executives from many industries to support low taxes for business and the wealthy. So, just whose wallet is bleeding red ink? First, as already documented, the loss of tax revenues from the wealthy cuts into the funds that could alternatively be directed to help the poor and the middle class. That's intentionally extreme right-wing ideology at work to cripple America. Second, tax evasion and avoidance cuts into the funds necessary to repair and rebuild what I have repeatedly labeled as a hollowed out US economy, one weakened by the huge opportunity costs of misguided wars and pork barrel spending.

So the trains crash, the cranes fall, the bridges and roads crumble and tumble, and the health clinics, hospitals, and modern schools disappear. Already half dead as of January 2009, ugly US capitalism could well vanish in just a few years.

The Sick: The Exploitation of Uninsured Americans

Dr. David Ludwig of Children's Hospital warns of dangerous bacteria that still infest the meat-packing and produce industries.[23] Food experts repeatedly decry the dangers of poor regulation.[24] Bias is also rampant in trade association research.[25] Other studies slam drug companies for hosting expensive dinners for doctors. Worse, some companies pay money kickbacks to doctors who prescribe anti-anemia and other questionable drugs.

I learned a lot listening to medical doctors about the poor and lower middle class. Say that you have no insurance and your children become seriously ill. So, you walk into a free emergency clinic and wait and wait and wait. Maybe it's already too late to ward off a killing disease. If you have any income at all, the hospital will bill you. Your bill will probably exceed that of the healthy and the wealthy. They are already fully covered by private insurance. Worse, as already noted, private hospitals may be forced to close their emergency doors to the poor. Our "compassionate" conservatives also seek to cut benefits for Social Security, Medicare, and Medicaid.

It gets worse month by month. How do the poor, uninsured, and desperate immigrants get medical care? Many don't. Others try to borrow. They use credit cards to pay for unexpected sickness and surgery. One study says that 30 percent of poor families are loaded up with debt. Another study reports that, "the average American's consumer debt has doubled since 1994 and now tops 130 percent of his or her income."[26]

Even worse, a study put out by the Labor Department documents that the unemployment rate is far worse than reported. Using an alternative measure of the jobless rate, it estimates that as of April 2008 the unemployment rate hit almost ten percent or roughly double the 5 to 5.5 percent the Bush administration had publicized. The higher rate includes (a) discouraged workers who can't find a full-time good job and (b) desperate workers who agree to work part time for wages below the poverty line and with no health insurance or other benefits.[27] It's worth repeating the words of columnist Bob Herbert. He is always a valued source on the frightening debt burden on the backs of millions of poor Americans and immigrants. Herbert writes:

> A society is seriously out of whack when loan sharks close in on those who are broke and desperately ill. Even then they [the borrowers] don't know whether or not they are buying fake drugs or possibly drugs spiked with poison.[28]

Tangled Web: Drug Companies, Secret Compensation, and Consulting Scientists

One nauseating practice of doctors involves being paid millions of dollars by drug companies as secret consultants.[29] Several Harvard University professors are in that category. Drug companies pay these huge amounts in violation of federal law and Harvard University's own ban on secret consultation. To make matters worse, the Harvard professors failed to include consulting incomes on their tax returns.

One Harvard professor, recognized as a renowned child psychiatrist, touted the value of antipsychotic drugs. Therein lies another problem, for doctors were well aware for many years that these drugs can have damaging side effects on children such as excessive weight gain and other metabolic changes by which protoplasm (the living matter of all tissues and cells) is produced, maintained, or destroyed. In plain English, science still does not know whether or not these medications can improve or worsen the lives of children over time.

What incenses me most are four matters: First, why did not the university monitor and enforce its ban against secret compensation? Second, why did not Harvard remind its employees that such compensation is illegal under federal law? Third, why is the Food and Drug Administration so lax in enforcing federal laws? Fourth, how many other professors in academia have accepted secret and illegal consultation fees?

Laissez Faire Destructive Philosophy: Find No Evil

We already know the answer to my third question. For one thing, the administration is understaffed. The huge opportunity costs of the Iraq war and now the economic bailout, the stimulus package, and the huge deficits we are incurring explain understaffing throughout federal agencies that are supposed to protect Americans. Far more important, however, has been the right-wing philosophy of the former Bush administration that abhorred big government efforts to solve all manner of big social problems. The destructive philosophy shows up in every chapter of this work. Indeed, it seems that federal inspectors are taught to see no evil, speak no evil, and most assuredly find no evil. The three evils fairly well sum up the essence of extreme laissez faire self-destruction under US capitalism.

Odious Oil Oligopolists

Many schemers work to support Big Oil. Corporate oil senior officers lie. Trick oil writes warped research for slick oil. The US federal slush fund employs sleaze and secrecy to shower money on Big Oil. It's no wonder that the Organization of Petroleum Exporting Companies (OPEC) and US officials are ever so friendly and cooperative in making huge amounts of money for themselves. Together they generate (a) obscene profits, salaries, and bonuses for oil industry executives and (b) noxious gases such as carbon dioxide, methane, and sulfur dioxide that kill people. Scientists have warned repeatedly how these gases can cause global warming with catastrophic effects.

I will document in detail in chapter 7 the multiple dangers of global warming. What we already know about are the obscene efforts of the oil industry and the US government to *amplify* our dependence on oil. A huge red flag of danger smeared with black oil tells us we are running out of time. Consumers and workers, wherever they live, are now the victims of the noxious oil industry. They all pay inflated prices for oil to heat their homes; gasoline to drive their cars and trucks; electricity to turn on their lights and to power their TV sets, microwaves, toasters, washing machines, and air conditioning units. Meanwhile, the coffers of the Big Oil producers overflow. The billions of dollars OPEC earns come on the backs of consumers here in the United States and everywhere.

What precisely are some of the other effects of wildly fluctuating oil prices, with crude oil futures reaching highs of $142 a barrel on July 10, 2008? One direct effect is inflation. It cuts deeply into the sales revenues and profits of the airlines, trucking, and car manufacturing industries. They try to offset huge losses in many cases by cutting services, charging new fees, and raising prices. Even so, twenty-four airlines were forced into bankruptcy in the first six months of 2008.[30]

Bubbles in Oil and Commodities Burst

Truckers now park or try to sell their rigs. They simply cannot make any money when diesel fuel reaches $4.50 a gallon, up from $2.50 the year ago. Further, a whole range of industries including plastic, rubber, toys, clothes, and many others depend on oil for the products they make. Their prices are up, too.

Indeed, prices explode as speculators and mania-driven investors pour their money into oil. But the huge bubble in oil and key commodities will go the way of all bubbles. They will burst and usher in a rash of new hedge fund bankruptcies.[31]

As always, the poor are the ones who suffer the most as oil prices deplete buying power. Often the poor live in rural areas with no public transportation available to them. Every dollar they pay for $4.00 a gallon gasoline means they must cut back *somehow* what they spend on food, housing, medical and dental care, and many other necessities of life. I put the word "somehow" in italics to signal that many fail to cope. Many go hungry and fall into despair. Some commit suicide.

But does not higher wage income help them? No, quite the reverse. The inflation we experience with high commodity process is not a wage and price spiral of the kind we witnessed in the 1970s. On the contrary, real wages adjusted for higher inflation have moved way down. As the present recession worsens, as I expect, wages will collapse far more even as the jobless rate soars. The double blow will devastate the poor and the sick. With this preface of woe let me now summarize the seven sins of the oil industry and the US government. (I'll return to this subject in chapter 8 on "The Military, Industrial, and Big-Oil Complex.")

Can you spot any collusion of government with executives of the Big Oil industry who become richer and richer? Well, consider this list of multiple failures:

- ✓ The failure year-after-year to fight the dire effects of global warming.

- ✓ The failure to eliminate or at least reduce the number of coal-fired furnaces, and to modify drastically the jet planes that spew deadly fumes into the atmosphere.

✓ The failure to force auto makers to cut production of gas guzzling vehicles.[32]

✓ The failure to develop new sources of energy to end US dependence on oil.

✓ The failure to prosecute oil companies for systemic cheating, lying, fraud, and recently (May 2010) catastrophic oil spills that have wrecked the infrastructure and the precious land and clean water of the Gulf of Mexico and New Orleans, as well as destroying property, jobs, and lives.[33]

✓ The failure to block oil cartels that restrain trade and break antitrust laws.

✓ The failure to crack down on the multibillion dollar tax breaks and government subsidies showered on oil executives here and abroad.[34]

Unfinished Business

I will try in chapters 9 and 10 to find good data and good reasons to counter the widespread convictions that the Earth will catch fire or that humankind faces extinction. I hope I succeed but I just don't know. In any case, don't classify me as another crazed and loud fanatic walking the streets and forecasting doom. Such criticism no longer makes much sense in a world filled with nuclear weapons and occupied by political and religious fanatics.

Chapter 6

RACIAL, SEXUAL, AND ECONOMIC PREDATORS

[This] brings us to the main problem: credibility. Wall Street and our senior regulators seem to be running out of that precious commodity almost as quickly as cash.
— Gretchen Morgenson, *New York Times*, July 13, 2008

The Cultural Climate in America: Sick and Inflamed

In this chapter I focus on cultural, sexual, and racial predators. By culture I mean "the sum total of the ways of living built up by a group of humans and transmitted by one generation to another.[1] Some aspects of American culture are cruel and discriminatory. I also analyze the cruel and deadly social and racial policies of American society, among other conniving and dangerous policies. Since rage, hate, and violence are widespread, it should come as no surprise that inflamed arguments and anger now sweep across the United States.

I must confess that the intense rage that now erupts on the economic and financial fronts caught me by surprise. The wild and raucous arguments between liberals and conservatives are, in my view, loaded with faulty logic, fake data, and ugly slogans bathed in hate and rage. At the other extreme many pundits and several of my fellow economists declare without evidence that the worst recession since the Great Depression is over. They bellow that a satisfactory economic recovery lies straight ahead. *New York Times* columnist Paul Krugman writes how, "big government saved us from depression."[2]

Saved from depression? Hardly. Where is there a powerful program to give the unemployed jobs and incomes? I answered that question in the "Ten Forecasting Sins of Capitalism" and listed the "missing policy stimulus that now foreshadows the high risk of a major economic collapse."[3] I warned that the present jobs program is "peanuts."

> President Obama provided funds to the states for the repair and rebuilding of America. But its size is peanuts in relation to what is needed. Have we already run out of time? Well, no satisfactory and sustained recovery is possible without a swift program to put people to work that matches or *exceeds* the massive federal jobs stimulus of the Great Depression. Deflation has sunk its teeth into the economy and fosters expectations of continuing price declines and huge job losses. A full-blown jobs program is critically needed here and now.[4]

The Fed apparently agrees with Krugman and other optimistic economists who see blue economic skies ahead. Reporter Edmund Andrews of the *New York Times* writes, "The Federal Reserve said . . . that the recession is ending."[5] Is the recession truly ending? No. Keep in mind that this is the same Fed that was in denial two years ago that any financial meltdown and recession would take place. This is the same Fed, under Alan Greenspan and then Ben Bernanke, whose members failed to forecast the financial meltdown and the recession that followed.

I had earlier sent to Bernanke, then editor of the *Journal of Finance*, my article titled "Ex Ante Recognition of Bubble Stock Gauges and Forecasts of Their Bursting in the United States and Japan."[6] He told me that his referees said the article was too long. So Bernanke rejected it. I sent my rejected article to another refereed journal that quickly published it and for which I garnered a best author award. I often pondered why Bernanke rejected the article, for I had previously published in Bernanke's extremely prestigious refereed journal. The second paragraph of my abstract to the article may provide a clue:

Excessively expansionist monetary policies, including Federal Reserve ultra-easy policy 1997-2002, were paramount in fueling overinvestment booms that predictably collapsed and flyaway bubble stock gauges that predictably crashed. Failure of the regulatory authorities and central banks [including the Federal Reserve] to suppress crowd mania and systemic fraud was also a deadly mix, a strong forward indicator of the destructive legacy of bursting bubbles.[7]

I sensed that if the *Journal of Finance* had published my article, both Greenspan and Bernanke would have been instantly blamed for creating the huge financial meltdown and major recession that now bedevils America. Consistent with my view that the truth cannot be locked up, the two Fed chairmen are already being judged as incompetent.

I have never paid much attention to what the Treasury, the Fed, or any given White House administration says it does or what it forecasts. But I always paid full attention to what the Fed actually does, focusing on its initial actions and my own forecasts of the lagged effects of Fed actions that often prove extremely damaging. With that rule, I managed to forecast every recession since 1969–1970 to 2009.[8] As of the end of the fourth quarter of 2010, *we still don't have a massive jobs program by the Fed and the Treasury to ward off a looming depression!*

Profits and Toxic Financial Instruments

Where are the profits of corporate America? Yes, profits and the stock market have shot up recently. But left out of most news reports are two worrisome facts. First, revenues, profits, and market prices are still far below earlier peaks and still far below the prices investors paid for financial instruments. Many of these financial instruments held by banks and Wall Street, among other holders, are called "toxic" instruments.

"Toxic" means that major holders are not eager to sell at big losses that show up on their accounts. They are afraid that sales of toxic bonds, stocks, or mortgages would show up as a fall in profits and thereby induce stock and bond rating agencies to cut sharply the estimated value of these securities. A major rating downgrade could then spark bankruptcy. Current prices of individual houses, apartments, and business properties are in the same toxic shape. The recent rally is, in my mind, a false dawn. Market prices of toxic securities could easily plunge back to their earlier lowest prices.

Why would toxic securities fall again a lot more? One reason is that consumer buying and investment spending continue down, down, down. Retail and wholesale sales still fall. Investment spending still declines. Worst of all, where is the audacity and insistence of the Treasury and the Fed to provide jobs programs for the millions of unemployed and desperate workers? Where is the needed "Bottom-Up" jobs stimulus?

To repeat, I firmly believe that President Obama's biggest mistake was his lack of audacity (a) to speed a huge jobs program and (b) to fire all of the right-wing and enraged Republicans who helped get us into this mess in the first place. With no jobs program and no audacity, I have raised my forecast in the epilogue from a 60 percent probability to a 75 percent probability of a renewed and major collapse in consumer and investment spending that could easily bring on a second great global depression lasting years.

But what about Wall Street firms and the many banks, mortgage companies, and others who are now loaded with cash they received from the Treasury bailouts? Is that not a signal of good times ahead? No. Major financial firms seem most interested in giving their senior officers huge bonuses and guaranteed high salaries while simultaneously investing in some extremely risky investments. Is that why they worry over inadequate capital? Is that why bank loans are mostly frozen? Are we headed now for another financial bubble that will most assuredly collapse in the midst of a growing economy? It looks that way to me. Lots of cash cannot propel this economy forward unless it is spent. Put another way, the velocity of money must rise, and sharply. Also, a surge in cash holdings by banks and other financial institutions reminds me of the failed Republican "trickle down" theory. It won't work to spark recovery. The only macro stimulus force that could work is a massive jobs program to put spending power into the hands of millions of unemployed and desperate workers. In the absence of a huge "bottoms-up stimulus" to spark growth, financial and other companies will be unable to survive, much less recover. Instead, they will fall together from the horrors of depression and deflation. Sad to say, a weak jobs program foreshadows a needless economic catastrophe straight ahead.

I draw readers to the quote from Ms. Morgenson that began this chapter. She has long been one of my favorite news reporters in exposing deception, lying, and fraud in the financial markets.[9] She was repelled by the repeated but false assurances made by the government, the Federal Reserve, and private investment executives. Together they declared confidently that the problems in the mortgage market were confined to sub-prime loans. Both Fed Chairman Benjamin Bernanke and former Treasury Secretary Henry Paulson sang that same mistaken tune starting in early 2007. Christopher Cox, chairman of the Securities and Exchange Commission, insisted in March of 2008 that the investment firm of Bear Stearns was doing well. All were in denial—a strong signal that the economy was in trouble.

So, Bernanke, Cox, and Paulson were all wrong in 2007. But they still painted a bright economic picture for much of 2008 despite the dark, if not bleak, outlook. Morgenson was right in 2007. I believe she remains correct in saying that the worst is yet to come.

Cultural, Sexual, and Racial Predators

On that somber note, I'll turn to an equally dismal and worrisome concern: six vicious predators. While there are many predators preying on consumers, I am focusing on those I believe to be among the most brutal and dangerous. They include (1) racial prejudice, (2) age discrimination, (3) employment preferential treatment, (4) sexual harassment, and (5) disability injustice in conflict with simple compassion and the law. These five predators are in turn linked closely to (6) government itself as a predator. In its federal, state, and local forms government is among the very worst of predators.

To be sure, I document that government predators operate on a variety of levels, but my main focus in this chapter is on the biggest government predator of all, namely, the federal government under former president George W. Bush. The Bush administration simply failed to enforce existing laws designed to protect consumers from great harm. It operated under an extreme laissez faire and warped philosophy that a free and unbridled market can do no harm. That hands-off philosophy is, in my view, dead wrong. Minimal or in some cases zero controls fostered great injury, injustice, and needless deaths for millions of Americans.

Update on the Severe Financial and Economic Meltdown

I'll begin with the role of government as a major contributor to the financial and economic shock waves that now appear to exceed the worst of the 1981-82 major recession. I had then dubbed the downturn a "minidepression" that just barely avoided tumbling into a deflationary depression. Currently, the bungling and fumbling US government is in a cyclical crisis. The Fed and the Treasury had argued endlessly over whether the key risk was recession or inflation. The hard evidence I cited in chapter 5 pointed unambiguously to deflation and major recession as the primary risks we face.

Indeed, it would be foolish now to rule out the risk of a deflationary depression with dreadful long-term consequences. In that scenario, the current bubbles in oil, gold, and grains would all burst. This is exactly the huge risk we face despite the recent uptick in the economy that still fails to stop foreclosures and falling prices of homes, as well as unemployment that plagues millions of people. As deflation then sweeps from coast to coast, a gush of bankruptcies follows as surely as night follows day.

Deflation's falling prices severely undermines revenues, profits, and stock and property values thereby ushering in serious recession or worse. Spending on both the consumer and the investor level fall precipitously.

Economic Recovery and the Risk of Severe Deflation

Confidence in the Federal Reserve, the Department of the Treasury, the Congress, and the president has already evaporated. Deflation and slump are the critical problems today, ones the Fed and the Treasury belatedly but finally recognized. Good, they have shifted again their position to better mesh with bottoms-up stimulus measures, including President Obama's "vast" government contracts for public works to create jobs. (But these programs are not "vast." Weak is a better description at this point.) If these job-creation programs do in fact lift the economy out of its slump into a recovery mode in, say, two or three years, we can bet that inflation fears will quickly return unless all government spending programs are effectively monitored for waste and fraud. That is Obama's challenge, which in effect requires blocking any right-wing and extreme Republican opposition to effective regulation. Obama has placed people like Lawrence Summers and Austan Goolsbee as his economic advisors to help him accomplish this but it has proven to be a very difficult task given the current Congress. The president's 2011 State of the Union Address is good news. It is evidence that Obama will, as he has warned, act to veto any bill emerging from Congress that would dilute or eliminate his proposals to pursue new actions to create jobs and avoid a depression even greater and longer than the last. His recent White House speeches warning that he would veto Republican efforts to cut Medicare or Medicaid, his newly enacted healthcare program, or any other liberal programs to help American workers acquire good jobs should be supported.

Forecast: Right-Wing Hate and Rage to Block President Obama

Perhaps President Obama's use of the inspector general's office to investigate misuse of TARP and other bailout finds will start the process of effectively restoring sensible controls and trust once again in a US government that has failed so miserably for the past eight years. I hope Obama succeeds, but I expect to see a fury of opposition from the ultraconservative Republicans who will fight hard to destroy the liberal programs Obama introduces. The ultraright is extremely angry for having lost power and influence in he 2008 elections. Consumed with hate and rage, it will fight Obama's liberal programs with false propaganda and lawbreaking the very way the now disgraced Bush did in all his years in office. Of all the forecasts I have made in this work, I feel most certain about this one. I see no apology coming from the extreme right. Their all-consuming goal now is to undermine the liberal Obama policies.

Many government and central bank executives are still tainted with an ultralaissez-faire philosophy. Each rejects using big government in time to ward off big dangers facing the economy. Even now, they try to block bottoms-up stimulus for public works to ward off deflation and an even more brutal recession. The same extremists still fight the need for strong regulation and control over markets. In short, the sick philosophy of "hands-off" government is still very much alive, signaling more destruction and despair if their views prevail.

Angry America in Turmoil

Angry words now exchanged by the Democratic liberal left and the extreme right-wing Republicans are making headline news. Republicans appear to be the most enraged and inflamed as they scream at just about everybody. Reporter Kelefa Sanneh of the *New Yorker*[10] cites many instances of poisonous exchanges loaded with hate. Others have made the same point. Consider these examples:

- Newt Gingrich used Twitter to call Obama's Supreme Court nominee, Sonia Sotomayer–and her "wise Latina" remark—"racist."

- Sergeant James Crowley of the Cambridge Police Department on July 16 responded to a 911 caller who said two men were trying to get into a house. After a dispute, the officer arrested Henry Louis Gates, a Harvard professor who lived there. President Obama, when asked about the incident, said racial profiling was a nationwide problem, and the police "acted stupidly."

- Thomas McCotter, a Michigan Republican, demanded that Obama apologize.

- The *National Review* online accused Obama of "racial self-aggrandizement."

- The radio and TV host Glenn Beck said that the president revealed his "deep seated hatred for white people," and that "this guy [Obama] is a racist."

- Republican critics of the president said that, "Obama's healthcare proposals would create government sponsored 'death panels' to decide which patients live or die."[11] This is the most revolting and totally false Republican charge to date.

- Reporters Jim Rutenberg and Jackie Calmes of the *New York Times* cite many other Republicans who make these horrible charges. They listed the former Republican vice presidential candidate Sarah Palin, Iowa Senator Charles Grassley, and the *Washington Times*, among other news pundits, who defeated President Clinton's healthcare program with bogus charges ten years ago.

The wrangling is likely to get even more intense over the huge salaries and bonuses paid to executives of Wall Street firms and banks bailed out with government money. Reporter Eric Dash of the *New York Times* writes that a guaranteed bonus seems like a contradiction in terms. But Wall Street investment companies and banks are so eager to hire top traders that they are offering multimillion-dollar payouts, guaranteed no matter how an employee [or the firm?] performs. The guaranteed bonus is surely likely to become "a hot button issue for the Obama administration's pay czar, Kenneth Feinberg." It raises questions in my mind of whether Obama can be and will be audacious enough to rein in obscene money payments to bankers as the rest of the working class moves deeper into debt and jobless poverty.

Government Predators

For some reason, which is foreign to me, social scientists seldom list the US government as a vicious predator. Yet the plain facts scream out government plunder, mismanagement, collapsing financial markets, and an economy moving down, down, and down. The economy and the financial markets are plunging as the vice of a major recession grips investors and freezes new private lending. The government steps in to provide cash to commercial banks, investment banks, and the giant mortgage firms Fannie Mae and Freddie Mac. These developments alone are hard evidence that an unbridled US capitalism is already half dead. The bad economic and financial news is everywhere.

Self-Generating Downhill Economic Spirals

As of July 18, 2008, share prices for the federal mortgage lending institutions known as Fannie Mae and Freddie Mac were down 80 percent. The two had recovered a bit as of August 2009 but they were still priced far below their initial purchase prices. Put another way, they still remain as "toxic bonds." The weak efforts of the government have failed to restore confidence. A self-generating and perilous downhill spiral is now well underway. As housing collapses, the economy grows weaker and weaker, which further magnifies the collapse in housing, which further depresses consumer and investment spending, and the overall economy. This economic maelstrom will get worse month by month as job losses continue to mount.

Businesses are desperate to secure capital before the rating agencies classify their bad debts as junk. Lending to the private sector is frozen or very sluggish at best. Home prices continue to fall. Foreclosures rise sharply as consumers can no longer afford to pay higher monthly payments resulting from hikes in adjustable-rate mortgages as well as the loss of their jobs and health insurance. Meanwhile, government spokespersons issue unending statements of progress: productivity levels are touted as strong and the mantra is offered that the US economy will recover as it always has in the past.

The Myth of Automatic Economic Recoveries

There is no classical economic theory of automatic recovery that would bring strong growth in 2010 or even 2011. Keynes made that clear long ago in his 1936 work titled *The General Theory of Employment, Interest, and Money*.[12] Pleasant and optimistic talk will not work this time. What is needed is major central bank funding of public works to produce jobs, spending power, and economic recovery. President Obama has signed a stimulus package of hundreds of billions of dollars for just such spending, but will the financial stimulus be injected into the system quickly enough to bring about the needed recovery? In my opinion, the answer must be a resounding no unless the president acts quickly to expand major new jobs programs to emulate the brave steps taken by President Franklin D. Roosevelt in the 1930s to create new jobs and incomes and thereby end the huge depression that swept the nation.

History as a Guide to the Future

In thinking about how we come to find ourselves in these economic disasters from time to time, it may be useful to scan our early history as a nation. As the list below shows, great progress was made during America's early years. But things have changed. Contrast these earlier gains with the current assaults on freedom, liberty, and civil rights. In studying each entry always ask yourself if the laws to protect freedom, liberty, and justice were in fact enforced.

1776: The Declaration of Independence declares all men to be created equal.

1865: The Thirteenth Amendment abolishes slavery but does not give blacks equality.

1866: The Civil Rights Act gives all persons the same rights to make and enforce contracts, to be parties to legal suits, to give evidence, and to receive full and equal benefits.

1868: The Fourteenth Amendment states that all persons born or naturalized in the United States are citizens and that no state can deprive any person of life, liberty, or property without due process of law or deny any person the equal protection of the law.

1920: The Twentieth Amendment provides that the right of citizens to vote shall not be denied or abridged on account of sex.

1963: The Equal Pay Act prohibits sex-based pay differentials on jobs.

1964: The Civil Rights Act prohibits employment discrimination based on race, sex, national origin, or religion. Title VI of the act prohibits public school discrimination. Title VIII is the original "Federal Fair Housing Law," later amended in 1988.

Defining Opinions in a Right-Wing Government and Supreme Court

Here are three "Defining Opinions" by the US Supreme Court.[13] Note the strong right-wing bias, the poor writing, and the absurd reasons that underlie these opinions.

1992: *Planned Parenthood v. Casey*: In this case, the US Supreme Court upheld the right of the State of Pennsylvania to place certain restrictions on the right to obtain an abortion. The Court reaffirmed the constitutional right to abortion by a vote of 5 to 4. Three Republican-appointed justices were in the majority. Sandra Day O'Connor, Anthony M. Kennedy, and David Souter said that while they would not necessarily have voted with the

Roe v. Wade majority eighteen years earlier, they believed it would damage the Court to repudiate that precedent under political pressure. "The promise of constancy, once given, binds its maker," they said. Constancy? What does this word mean for truth, justice, and women's rights?

2000: *Bush v. Gore*: This case ended the Florida recount and effectively declared George W. Bush the president-elect. In deciding the case in Bush's favor the Court stated the following in its unsigned opinion: "We are presented with a situation where a state court with the power to assure uniformity has ordered a statewide recount with minimal procedural safeguards." A debate continues to this day over whether the five justices in the majority were motivated by policies or by the neutral principles invoked. Neutral opinions now determine the fate of the land. What does that mean? Will Democrats ever get around to demanding court hearings with testimony by Bush and Cheney and others under oath on what many see as Bush's rigged election?

2008: *District of Columbia v. Heller*: In this case the Court held that the Second Amendment protects the right of individuals to keep a loaded gun at home for self-defense. Justice Antonin Scalia wrote for the 5-to-4 majority, and Justice John Paul Stevens for the dissent. Each dissected the history of the Second Amendment. They came to opposite conclusions but based their opinions on the premise that the original understanding of the amendment's framers was the proper basis for the decision.

Constancy with previous judicial decisions, neutrality of their opinions, and returning to idiosyncratic interpretations of the original framers' intensions for clarification—where is the logic here? What the United States needs is a chicken in every pot, not a loaded gun in every home. I set forth in chapter 2 strong reasons for banning all handguns to ward off gun massacres of men, women, and children. The courts seem interested only in protecting gunslingers.

A Politicized Supreme Court of Right-Wing Ideologues

The Bush administration sought to confirm justices whose views mesh nicely with the laissez faire right-wing ideologues in the Federal Reserve, the White House, the Department of the Treasury, and the Congress. Meanwhile, since the 2008 elections the Democrats still waffle as they constantly fail to develop a powerful and credible position that effectively counters what is now a Republican minority in Congress. As a liberal and registered Democrat I am distressed with my own political party. But let's turn now to the six predators I identified as being among the most brutal and dangerous.

Government Discrimination

Discrimination is everywhere in the United States. Why? Well, I have left out of my remarks so far the huge influence of Nobel Prize winning economist Milton Friedman. I knew the man well. Friedman debated Dr. Pierre Rinfret in New York at the Plaza Hotel on May 23, 1972, for which I served as moderator. Friedman lost.

Friedman's overriding idea was simply that prosperity required government to keep its bungling hands off private markets. In other words, Friedman was an ultra-extreme *laissez faire apostle* of the economy. His archenemy was John Maynard Keynes, as I noted earlier. I can only repeat my long-held view that pitiful controls have now placed the US economy out of control and falling fast into a dreadful slump.

Looking Back to Document the Present Turmoil

Sometimes it is useful to look back at earlier forecasts and see how they have worked out. We already know that the federal government, the Federal Reserve, and the wide range of financial institutions were in denial. They seemed to keep asking "Bubble, bubble, what bubble?" They were wrong, as usual. Maybe these excerpts from my August 11, 2005 *Money and Capital Markets Monitor* can help to explain why so many were in such denial.

The Money and Capital Markets Monitor:
Robert H. Parks & Associates, Inc.

THE PREDICTED BURSTING OF THE HOUSING MARKET

Reporter Jay Loomis stated my warnings on housing in the
Journal News, June 6, 2005:

"Robert H. Parks, a finance professor at Pace University, estimated that 70 percent of housing markets nationally are showing bubble characteristics. A downturn in real estate markets, he said, could spill over to the economy, leading to a recession, drops in consumer spending, stagnant real estate prices, and overextended property buyers struggling to cover their loans. 'All bubbles burst, but nobody can say when,' Parks said. 'Only unenlightened gamblers would be making major bets on real estate now.'"

Here are several questions and my answers on the huge housing bubble.

1) Is there a giant housing bubble? Yes indeed. The theoretical and empirical evidence spell a giant housing bubble. Housing is not unlike stocks. The fundamental value of each is simply the discounted value of net future income. But the net rental income after all costs is flat-to-falling. Moreover, the climb in the risk of holding bubble real estate is pushing that discount rate higher. Higher risk and higher discount rates are already translating into lower present values, lower fundamental values of houses. The data bear that out. Fundamental values based on discounted net rental streams now run 25% to 75% below market prices. House prices have soared. In the last four years house prices for the United States raced ahead some 50% in contrast with the BLS [Bureau of Labor Statistics] estimate for average rentals at roughly 27% over roughly the same time span. In some places rentals are flat to down.

2) Why don't [Federal Reserve Chairman Alan] Greenspan and Bush warn of a bursting housing bubble? To do so they would have to admit complicity in manufacturing dangerous bubbles. Consider

Greenspan first. He provided the ultra-easy monetary fuel to fire the giant overinvestment boom and flyaway bubble stock gauges [from] 1997 [to] 2009. Both the overinvestment boom and bubble stock gauges collapsed (Exhibit 1).

3) Does it make any sense to analyze monetary policy or fiscal policy separately? Never. Consider George W. Bush's madness to spend wildly for pork and for war even as he argued for more tax cuts. The result is trillion-dollar budget deficits with no end in sight. What's frightening is that the huge spending for war is now being largely monetized (funded via the money printing press), the worst way to finance a war. Query: Have you heard even once any concern by [former Fed chairman] Greenspan over war finance? Of course not. Both George W. and his sycophant Greenspan are in the same pea pod, prisoners of each other in the very worst of fiscal and monetary policies. [(The new Federal Reserve Chairman Benjamin) Bernanke seems more puzzled than ever.]

4) Could the housing bubble deflate slowly? Possibly. The "hissing sound" economist Paul Krugman notes may have already started (the *New York Times*, August 8, 2005). Other headlines now report that rents are falling absolutely in many areas. As compared with bubble-inflated housing prices, it is now much less costly to rent than to buy. The gap grows as vacancy rates for rental homes continue to rise. Still, I expect to see a big bang bursting bubble for housing. Why? Well, this is the biggest property bubble in US history. According to the *Economist* (June 18. 2005), the "global housing boom is the biggest financial bubble in history." Pay attention to the *Economist* this time around.

5) Has speculative mania taken over in the rush to buy houses? Yes, no-money down loans, interest-only loans, low-interest loans, and adjustable-rate loans now leave borrowers in a precarious state should interest rates suddenly jump higher across the entire yield curve. Over one-half of all consumer debt and over one-quarter of all mortgage debt is now adjustable. Much of the mania buying is for purely speculative purposes. You buy, and hopefully sell 20 percent higher to another fool. That's the way with crowd mania.

6) What can you do to protect yourself? Assume you already own, that you paid $300,000 for your apartment, that you can now sell it for $500,000, that you just had a baby, and you want a place with three bedrooms. If you sell now you will be dismayed to discover that mania buying has pushed out of your reach the larger house with that extra room you need so desperately. You suddenly realize that you are partly locked into this bubble.

Perils of Being Locked in a Bubble

Your best course is (a) to look for a rental that meets your needs, (b) to sell and lock in your paper gains before they evaporate in a bursting bubble, (c) to put your sales proceeds at least temporarily in high-grade money market funds, and (d) to relax without worry over bursting bubbles. When this major house bubble bursts, as it will, a financial meltdown will accompany it. The stock market (still at bubble prices), the auto market, the airlines, and the bond and mortgage markets including Fannie Mae and Freddie Mac will all be at risk of collapse. After the predicted bust, you will be better able to buy at lower prices the dream home you wanted.

Conclusions

1) The housing bubble, like the stock market bubble [of] 1997-2006, is mainly a product of sustained and excessively easy monetary *and* fiscal policies [undertaken during the period] 1997-2006.

2) The "new-era-wealth-effect" passion [of] 1997-2000 was blown away with the wind of crowd mania. But crowd mania still exercises absolute dominion over housing.

3) Federal Reserve policy restraint via its tiny boosts in the funds [interest] rate [in an attempt to curb inflation] comes too little and too late to mop up *massive* excess liquidity sloshing through markets.

4) All big bubbles burst; housing is a huge and dangerous bubble. RH

Exhibit 1

**Press Documentation for the Crash of the S&P 500
and NASDAQ Composite**

- B*arron's*, November 29, 1999, article by Alan Abelson, "The Grand Illusion." [Abelsom states,] "That's what...Parks calls the popular conception that Fed policy has been restrained. In fact, Fed policy, he insists, has been wildly expansionary."

- The *Christian Science Monitor*, January 3, 2000, article by David Francis, "[Parks] is betting the NASDAQ bubble will burst in the next few months."

- The *Journal News* (Westchester, New York), July 1, 2000, article by Phil Reisman, "Parks said [that] excessive Federal Reserve stimulation [created] a runaway boom, runaway stock market bubble, runaway real estate prices, and a mountain of debt."

- The *New York Times*, December 31, 2000, article by Alex Berenson, on the "over investment boom": "[Parks] said 'all of a sudden you wake up with overcapacity.'"

- *Associated Press*, January 18, 2001, article by Dunstan Prial, "[Parks says that] speculation within the technology sector represents 'the biggest stock market bubble in US history. . . . Perform or die mania turned investment managers into gamblers.'"

- The *Christian Science Monitor*, January 25, 2001, article by David Francis, "[Parks] said companies bought back their own stock at bubble prices."

- The ·[*Baltimore*] *Sun*, September 29, 2002, page 1 (Business). "On January 3, 2000, in the *Christian Science Monitor*, Parks described the boom in technology stocks as 'the biggest bubble in US history' and said the NASDAQ would deflate within months. In August last year [2001] after the NASDAQ had fallen to the then-unthinkable floor of 2000, Parks wrote that 'the bursting equity bubble has not run its course, especially NASDAQ stocks. He was right."

Note: Forecasters get zero credibility unless their predictions are (1) documented by the press and (2) reviewed by their peers in the refereed journals of finance and investment. You may be interested in two of my refereed articles accepted for publication. They expand in great detail on the theory and the empirical evidence inadequately noted in this monitor. They also make explicit the parallels in property and stock markets. If interested, please let me know and I'll make sure you get copies. The two articles are:

1) "U.S. Monetary Policy, Bubble Stock Gauges, and the Over-Investment Boom-to-Bust Cycle 1997-2002," *International Journal of Business Disciplines*, October 2005.

2) "*Ex Ante* Recognition of Bubble Stock Gauges and Forecasts of Their Bursting in the United States and Japan," the *Journal of the American Academy of Business,* Cambridge, Best Author Award, Vol. 8, Number 1, March 2006 (see appendix C).

Other Government Abusive and Cruel Policies

In chapter 2 in which we discussed the war dogs, I documented in detail how the former Bush administration tortured detainees in the name of the president's "war of choice" on Iraq in violation of the US Constitution and international law. In making further inquiries, I read extensively the many reports via the Internet of confirmed torture practices. What I found was consistently hard evidence of a depraved Bush administration. What particularly disgusted to me was the evidence provided by a US government lawyer before a panel of the US Court of Appeals for the Seventh Circuit on government-released torture memos obtained using the Freedom of Information Act. Here is just one of many that brought tears to my eyes despite the extremely mangled English.

The draft report (submitted to CNN) made the near-ridiculous suggestion that if the purpose of torture was to extract information, not to cause pain, it wasn't really torture. "Even if the defendant [a US government agent] knows that severe pain will result from his actions [and] if causing harm is not his objective, he lacks the requisite intent even though the defendant did not act in good faith.

Let me put into simple English this badly written statement: If someone tortures you to inflict unbearable pain, that person cannot be accused of torture even if he knows that you will suffer severe pain but no harm. How in the world can you suffer severe pain without harm? Does not severe or unbearable pain cause harm, sometimes death?

I found many other instances of torture. One had to do with an Iranian, Amhad Batebi.[14]

Nine years ago, Ahmad Batebi appeared on the cover of the *Economist*. He was one of thousands who protested against Iran's government that summer. He was photographed holding aloft a T-shirt bespattered with the blood of a fellow protestor. Soon afterwards he was arrested. During his interrogation he was blindfolded and beaten with cables until he passed out. His captors rubbed salt into his wounds to wake him up so they could torture him some more. They held his head in a drain full of sewage until he inhaled it. . . . He suffered a partial stroke from the beating and solitary confinement for years in a small cell that was little more than a toilet hole with a wooden board on top. . . . Later Amhed escaped to the U.S.

Doesn't this inhuman torture remind you of the torture inflicted on Guantanamo detainees by the US Army, documented in chapter 2? Any torture shames those who perpetrate it, and the nation they represent.

Race and Religious Predators

Racism takes many forms. It includes but is surely not limited to the following: fear and hatred of foreigners (xenophobia), interracial mixing, ethnic nationalism, social discrimination, racial segregation, violence, pogroms, massacres, ethnic cleansing, religious and political persecution, and genocide. Again, while this list is illustrative it is far from complete.[15] Here are random news quotes on racial discrimination, hate, and fighting among opposing religions.

1) "President Mahmoud Ahmadinejad claims [the Holocaust] is a myth created to justify the creation of the state of Israel."[16]

2) "These are the children of the Lebensborn...bred to be the next generation of the Nazi elite. Children were kidnapped as infants from their families. To be accepted into the Lebensborn, pregnant women must have the racial traits of blond hair and blue eyes."[17]

3) "The genocide in Darfur is getting worse. Innocent men, women, and children continue to be maimed and killed in a conflict that's spreading beyond the borders of Sudan."[18]

4) "The National Association of Evangelicals rebuffed leaders of the Christian right who call for action to fight global warming. The Family Research Council says 'the global warming controversy shifts away from abortion, homosexuality, and sexual abstinence.'"[19]

5) "One American citizen among many others have fumed, 'If you [an immigrant] are here illegally, you are breaking the law–like the guy who robs the liquor store or the guy who waits to case your house and rob you. You are a criminal.'"[20]

6) "More than one of every hundred Americans is in prison. The incarceration rate is skewed by race. One in nine black men and one in 36 adult Hispanic men aged 24 to 34 are behind bars."[21] "Black men are nearly twelve times as likely to be imprisoned for

drug arrests as adult white men, according to the Human Rights Watch."[22]

7) "Racial discord also follows the presidential candidates. More than 80% of black voters had a favorable opinion of Barack Obama versus only 30% of white voters."[23]

The Deadly Racial Tragedy in South Africa: Genocide

I cited Gretchen Morgenson of the *New York Times* for her extraordinary work as a reporter in spotting fraud and dishonesty in finance and government. Kudos also go to Nicholas D. Kristof for his relentless reporting of racial abuse. Consider these excerpts from his article on "Prosecuting Genocide."[24]

> Many aid workers and diplomats suffered a panic attack when the chief prosecutor of The international Criminal Court sought an arrest warrant this week [in July 2008] for the President of Sudan, Omar Hassan al-Bashir, for committing genocide. They feared that Mr. Bashir would retaliate by attacking peacekeepers and humanitarian workers.
>
> But instead of wringing our hands, we should be applauding. The prosecution for genocide is a historic step that also creates an opportunity in Sudan, particularly if China can now be induced to and shamed into suspending the transfer of weapons used to slaughter civilians in Darfur.
>
> If China continues—it is the main supplier of arms used in the genocide—then it may well be in violation of the 1948 Genocide Convention. . . . According to United Nations data, 88 percent of Sudan's small arms come from China. . . .
>
> Throughout most of history, genocide was simply what happened to losers in a conflict. . . .
>
> Now the prosecutor's pursuit of a head of state suggests that *human standards truly are changing*–and that is a prerequisite for ending genocide itself. (Italics added)

I surely hope that "human standards are truly changing." But this troubled world is fast running out of time to change human behavior, as I argued in chapters 2 and 3.

Hate, Benevolence, and Racism

Here is what British philosopher David Hume (1711–1776) said about hate versus benevolence:

> [The] vulgar dispute concerning the degree of benevolence or self-love [is] never likely to [be resolved]. There is some benevolence [in] our bosom, some spark of friendship for humankind, some particle of the dove kneaded into our frame, along with the elements of the wolf and the serpent.[25]

Hume has long been one of my favorite economists in promoting truth, honesty, and justice. Yet he wrote this racist piece in his *Race and Racism* that saddened me.

> I am apt to suspect the Negroes to be naturally inferior to the Whites. There scarcely ever was a civilized nation of that complexion, nor even any individual, eminent either in action or in speculation. No ingenious manufacture, no arts, no sciences. [26]

Did Hume, a great economist, have elements of the serpent in him? It looks that way.

Age and Employment Discrimination

Discrimination based on age typically takes three forms. One is discrimination against youth (sometimes called adultism), discrimination against those forty years or older, and discrimination against elderly people. The Age Discrimination in Employment Act (1967) prohibits discrimination nationwide for people forty years old or older. The act also addresses the difficulty older people face in obtaining new employment after having lost a job. Some people believe that teenagers and young people between fifteen and twenty-five years of age suffer discrimination. Employers may stereotype them as adolescents, immature, violent, rebellious, and hung up on rock music and drugs.

Well, some do fit that negative characterization. But many millions of other youths do not. My point here is that discrimination based on age or perceived inability to perform specific tasks may be prohibited by law, but the law is often not enforced by regulatory authorities.

I have witnessed firsthand racial and sexual discrimination as a veteran economist on Wall Street. Age and sex discrimination always start at the hiring stage. That was true for each of the three firms I worked for as their chief economist. When I would ask, "How many women did you interview for chief economist?" all would reply, "None." On one occasion a prospective employer laughed about women even as he offered me the job. The interviewer considered any woman to be unfit for the top job of chief economist. A case of misogyny if ever I saw one![27] I refused the position. My experience was hardly isolated. Consider these headlines on discrimination against women both here and abroad:

- Wall Street Will Settle Sex Bias Suit Against Women[28]
- Japan Accused of Role in World War II Sex Slavery[29]
- Indian Women Seek Protection Against Violence[30]
- World Health Finds Women at Home Suffer Great Violence[31]
- Sexual Parity Ranks Sweden 1, US 22 where 1= Equality[32]
- Bride Burning, Honor Killings, Sex Abuse, and Rape Run Wild[33]
- Polygamy for Immigrants Makes Slaves of Women[34]

Who Are the Hominids?

Did you ever hear of the super family that scientists call the *Hominidae*? No? Well, scientists say the *Hominidae* consist of (1) gorillas, (2) chimpanzees, (3) orangutans, and (4) humans. The four are known collectively as the great apes. Why do I bring this subject up now in a discussion of cultural, sexual, and racial predators?

Well, one reason has to do with the chimp's DNA. It is 95 percent to 98.7 percent the same as that of humans, depending on how DNA is measured. So, the chimp can feel fear and happiness, create tools, use language, remember the past, plan the future and show compassion, just as humans do. Yet humans torture and kill chimps in the name of medical research. Humans threaten the existence not only of our closest living relative, the chimpanzee, but also tigers, elephants, jaguars, and many other animals.[35] If human cruelty and slaughter of our closest living evolutionary relatives can go on in the name of financial benefit or sick self-interest, and we can extend this repulsive view to other animal species, then these actions demean the principles of capitalism as cruel, uncaring, and unjust. That's one reason the Spanish Parliament seems determined to grant limited rights to our closest nonhuman relatives, all four of the great apes.[36] I hope Spain succeeds. Maybe its quest is to start ending human attacks on the great apes as well as vicious human attacks on other species and on other humans. Would that not be a grand and glorious change in the character of the human being? Yes, but it is not likely.

The Monster: "I Am Malicious Because I Am Miserable."

Eighteenth century human rights advocate and social philosopher Mary Wollstonecraft, who wrote the influential books *Vindication of the Rights of Men* (1790) and *Vindication of the Rights of Women* (1792), had a daughter, whom she also named Mary.[37] Later her daughter married the poet Percy Bysshe Shelly. She then became known as Mary Shelly.

Do you recognize her? Mary Shelly is the author of *Frankenstein*. The most startling thing I recall about her classic novel is an exchange between the monster and Frankenstein. The monster asks, "Create a female for me?" Frankenstein replies, "Create another like you, whose wickedness might desolate the world. [No!]" The monster, still pleading for a female mate, says, "I am malicious because I am miserable…. Am I not hated by all mankind? Yet you, my creator, would [destroy] me. [But] if any being felt emotions of benevolence towards me, I would return them a hundred and a hundred fold."[38]

I read Shelly's classic over and over again. Her first truth is that misery (e.g., poverty, hunger, sickness, prejudice, joblessness, and war) is one of the major causes of bad behavior. The second is that society must fight with compassion and love to reduce bad behavior. The third is that society does not fight hard enough, or in even the right way. Shelly dramatized these three vital truths in *Frankenstein*. I have tried hard to make Shelly's truths one of the guiding principles in the present work.

Religious and Political Drivel versus Truth

Chapter 2 on the war dogs and chapter 3 on the assault by religion on science document a long history of religious and political discrimination, and war. Still, internecine fighting continues. Current news reports in papers and magazines all across America make crystal clear widespread discrimination on many counts:

- The president (George W. Bush) expressed a strong vote of confidence in Attorney General Gonzales despite charges that his dismissal of US attorneys was illegal.

- Episcopalians argue heatedly with Anglicans over homosexuality and abortion.

- Pope Benedict XVI supports the Church's opposition to abortion, euthanasia, and gay marriage despite the strong views of "Right to Choose" women. The pope remains ambivalent toward pedophile priests whose actions undermine the priesthood and the expressed values of the Church.

- Ideas collide on condom bans versus abstinence as a solution to the AIDS crisis.

- The US government is accused of undermining the separation of church and state. Faith-based initiatives, for one example, favor religious applicants in violation of the First Amendment that prohibits government establishment of religion.

This list makes abundantly clear the wide abuse that involves wrong-doing and fighting among humans.

Distortion of Economic Science

Could dishonest political and religious forces destroy America? Yes. It could happen here. Indeed, destruction is well underway. We have put together many instances of how fake economists on the far right distort economic science. The supply-side, right-wing ideologists are in this group. A crass example here is the ridicule that supply-side ideologists heap on John Maynard Keynes, one of the most brilliant economists who ever lived, though many supply-siders have never even read his major works.

Here are excerpts from a foreword I wrote on the works of Keynes. It includes my criticism of supply-side deliberate distortions of Keynes's key books and articles (see appendix A for the text of the entire foreword).[39]

Keynes's most influential works included *The General Theory of Employment, Interest, and Money* (1936) and *How to Pay for the War* (1940). In the *General Theory* Keynes renounced the classical doctrine of automatic recoveries from economic slumps as fatally flawed. Government intervention must replace laissez faire to ward off a deepening depression, he said.

To spur sustained economic recovery, Keynes counseled, the government should monetize (create brand new money and credit) to finance budget deficits for tax cuts and spending for public works. He was right. In 1940 Keynes declared that the best way to finance a huge war and avoid inflation was to tax as much as possible, to save as much as possible, and to restrict borrowing mainly to nonmonetized (little money creation) sales of treasury obligations to the public. He was right again. Keynes would irrigate to fight drought and drain to fight floods.

Supply-Side Fake Economic Science

We are all indebted to Keynes's genius, not just economists. Still, the detractors of Keynes stereotype him as a wild deficit spender for all times. The right-wing, supply-side ideologists who counseled Bush are in a real sense the new "popularizers" and "vulgarizers." These were Keynes's earlier words for fake economists. Others as well continue to swap warped ideology for economic science. The dangers of confusing one for the other are greatly understated. Keynes so warned in his revolutionary contributions to economic science and their just-in-time applications to the major geopolitical problems of his era.

Extreme Right-Wing, Think-Tank Nonsense

Extreme right-wing twisted ideology has a long history. It has its roots in the works of Ludwig Von Mises (1899-1973), Friedrich A. Hayek (1899-1992), and Bernard de Mandeville (1670-1733). They argued that only the power of competitive demand and supply forces could operate efficiently. The very early "vulgarizers," as Keynes dubbed them, included de Mandeville. He was a physician and word master, not an economist. He twisted individual selfishness (a vice) into a virtue with this couplet in *Fable of the Bees* (1714):

> Thus Every Part was full of vice.
> Yet the whole mass a paradise.

Keynes identified Adam Smith (1723-1790), John Stuart Mill (1806-1873), David Ricardo (1772-1823), and many other classical economists who richly deserved to be called professional economists.[40] He noted that the best of them extolled competition, *but competition with limits*. Mill once said that your freedom ends where my nose begins. Keynes made clear that a key role of government is that of regulation and control. His aim was to make sure robber barons didn't run free under full-blown laissez faire policy.

Is there a parallel today with the supply-side goal "to get government off the backs of the people"? Yes, corporate deception, accounting trickery, looting, and systemic fraud blossomed in the mania-driven, boom-to-bust cycle from 1995 to 2002, even as government restraint was irresponsibly weak.[41] Lack of regulation and control is now killing America in 2011. The absence of effective regulation and controls and strong programs to provide good jobs to millions of unemployed Americans signals another major downturn that could easily degenerate into a depression worse than that of the Great Depression.

But is the new "Libertarianism" just another name for the discredited and extreme laissez faire? Have not both failed? Libertarianism is, to my mind, right-wing nonsense passed off spuriously as genuine liberal policies to help the unfortunate poor and sick. During his administration Bush seemed to give up trying to privatize Social Security. He left office with his attack on Iraq in shambles. "Libertarians at the Cato Institute make no headway now in convincing people that global warming—the archetypal free market failure—is a hoax."[42] My conclusion: supply-side, right-wing theory is fast fading away. That's good news but hardly enough to save capitalism from its ultimate demise.

Extreme Right-Wing, Think-Tank Toxin

Author Sally Covington warns that the Cato Institute, the Heritage Foundation, and other research groups pass off right-wing half-truths as economic science. Her listing of ultraright-wing groups also includes wealthy patrons, corporations, think tanks, and associations with All-American but deliberately misleading patriotic titles.[43]

Look at the evidence: Covington identifies twelve conservative foundations that support pitifully unregulated markets, privatization of government services, deregulation of industry, tax cuts for the wealthy, and major cuts in antipoverty programs. The private institutions include the National Bureau of Economic Research (NBER),[44] the Hoover Institution, Brookings Institute, the American Enterprise Institute, the Manhattan Institute, the Club for Growth,[45] and the Center for the Study of American Business. They all love trickle-down tax cuts for the very rich. Supply-side, right-wing ideologists are the darlings of major think tanks.[46] Equally important, conservative in-house journals often bear names that resemble objective journals. What a hoax. They spew out counterfeit economic science.

The American Civil Liberties Union versus George W. Bush

The American Civil Liberties Union (ACLU), which conservatives loathe, publishes its "ACLU Congressional Scoreboard." For example, on September 28, 2006, it supported the right of detainees to seek court hearings on wrongful detentions, actual innocence, abuse, or torture. On September 14, 2005, it supported a federal criminal acts statute to include violent acts directed against a person's sexual orientation or gender identity.

Fair: The Question of Accuracy and Fairness in the News

Complementing the work of the ACLU is Fairness and Accuracy in Reporting (FAIR). In its March 11, 2007 article titled "What's in a Label?" FAIR denounces what it calls "Missing Labels." Its point is that right-wing, think-tank articles are often quoted but the reader is unaware of the source. To see how top think tanks are identified in the media, they found that many were not identified at all, or labeled improperly.

The FAIR list included the Brookings Institution, the Heritage Foundation, the American Enterprise Institute, and the Cato Institute. The

Brooking Institution, for example, "was given no identification in 78 percent of the 228 [media] citations." In another it was identified only as being in Washington, DC. Twice it was referred to as "liberal," twice as "nonpartisan," and once as "centrist." These specific labels are simply inaccurate. They fail to identify the extreme right orientation at work.

Most of the think tanks listed here are indeed ultraright wing, which comes as no surprise to me, yet they are often quoted by the best newspapers across the country. The studies are largely financed by major corporations, always with a message to sell some corporate goal or product regardless of the truth. Objective and honest scientists are not to be found in these Washington-based think tanks that constantly pander and distort.[47]

Some Slithering Reptiles and the Damage They Can Cause

The following names may remind you of truly lethal snakes. Good, for that is my intention. Indeed, ultracruel humans are analogous to dangerous snakes. Maybe this short primer will help us to recognize the brutality of the six human predators we tracked. In any case, I tried to limit my list to some of the very worst human predators. I could not track all of them but did succeed, I think, in documenting some of the worst.

1) **Coil** revels in vicious age and sexual discrimination here and abroad.

2) **Pierce** is a pure racist bully that enslaves and often kills his fellow humans.

3) **Strike** spits and ejects religious myths and superstition in conflict with science.

4) **Bite** invents false legal arguments to support hideous torture and first-strike wars.

5) **Venom** produces distorted research that makes a mockery of economic science.

6) **Rattle** makes up political gibberish that has no bearing on political science.[48]

7) **Slither** passes off Washington think-tank toxins to support selfish industry goals.

8) **Intap** is the human counterpart of the "Inland Taipan," the most dangerous snake in the world. Intap reminds me of inhuman xenophobia (hatred of foreigners).

This list of deadly snakes, both imagined and real, and their parallels to human killers is far from fictional. On the contrary, the day after I had prepared this killer list, radio, television, and first page press headlines of January 1, 2009, featured terrible racist killings.[49] The *New York Times*, for example, wrote that a group of young Staten Island men gathered on November 4, 2008, to watch election returns. Then they took to the streets when it became clear that the country had elected its first black president. But they were not out to celebrate. Armed with a police-style baton and a metal pipe, they attacked a black teenager, pushed another black man, harassed a Hispanic man, and ran over a white man they mistakenly thought was black. A federal indictment charged three men with conspiracy to interfere with voting rights. If convicted each of the men faced a maximum of ten years in prison. According to prosecutors, they and a fourth man decided to find blacks and assault them in retaliation for an African-American becoming president. Cruelty and exploitation of blacks seems never to end in capitalistic America.

Latinos Testify to Constant Racist Attacks

Racist beatings of blacks sparked wide press coverage in Westchester County, New York. But blacks are hardly the only minority group spit upon, assaulted physically, and all too often murdered. One must include other minority groups in this oppressed group, including immigrants and Latinos.[50] Consider here the fate of Latino Carlos Orellana in Pathogue, New York. On walking home from his job as a construction worker in this small Long Island town, about a dozen teenage boys on bicycles knocked him to the ground and kicked and beat him. They shouted together, "Go back to Mexico." Mr. Orellana, thirty-nine, said he lost consciousness. When he came to, his shoes and twenty dollars were missing.

Attacks like those on Mr. Orellana have soared. Eleven Latinos told the *New York Times* of thirteen hate attacks over the last two years. I'll cite just three of them.[50]

1) On November 8, 2008, seven boys of age sixteen or seventeen attacked and stabbed to death an Ecuadorian immigrant. The youths had a casual and derogatory word, "beaner bopping," for their hate crimes. One youth told the authorities, "I don't go out doing this very often, maybe once a week."

2) On September 22, 2007, a thirty-eight-year-old Hispanic male was sitting on his porch with friends. Sixteen to twenty youths, thirteen to eighteen years old, threw rocks, sticks, and logs of firewood at them, cursing these "Spanish people." The youths fled in their car before police arrived. The victim went to a hospital for eight stitches.

3) On July 11, 2008, six boys surrounded a forty-five-year old Hispanic male on a dark Patchogue street. They sprayed liquid into his eyes, kicked him, and beat him with baseball bats. They stole his three hundred dollars, his wallet, his clothes, and his shoes. Five months later, the victim said he had headaches, blurred vision, and was no longer able to work.

The Question of Safety for Barack Obama

This and other criminal attacks bring up again the question of safety for Barack Obama.

I have long felt that widespread racial hate and xenophobic rage puts Obama in danger of assassination. That's why I earlier included a list of the many presidents and other officials who fanatics have wounded or killed with firearms. Fanatics include many groups other than those espousing racial and xenophobic hate and rage. It seems to me that the ultralaissez-faire, right-wing conservatives have also emerged as a real threat to Obama.

They are sizzling mad for having lost their jobs and their power in Obama's great election victory. Perhaps they will now admit to their ghastly role in creating the financial meltdown and economic implosion now slamming America, but I doubt it. That's why I would not allow a fanatic of any stripe to get within gunshot range of President Obama, his wife, and children. All Americans must now make sure that nobody shoots and kills our president.

A Short Primer on Real and Dangerous Snakes

Here is a short primer on real snakes and how to avoid them. As we proceed, ask yourself if real snakes have any parallels with vicious human predators. I'll start with rattlesnakes. You know that most snakes are poisonous. But are they as deadly as the Tiger Snake, the Inland Taipan, and the Red Bellied Black Snake, all in Australia? Not often realized, the Mojave rattlesnake is the most venomous snake in North America.[51]

I often visit my daughter and grandchildren in Laguna Niguel, California. In the park playground, the warning signs read, "Leave the rattlesnakes alone and they won't bother you." The sign is only partly true. Unless a rattlesnake is threatened it will slide away, but not always. Instead, they may strike instantly, much like a human predator. Indeed, the Mojave Rattler[52] is more deadly than the Indian Cobra.

Bush's military attack on Iraq on false grounds is a perfect parallel to the no-warning preemptive strike of the Mojave rattler. Even a baby Mojave rattler has enough venom to kill a person. I take that as yet another parallel to the juvenile Bush who never grew up to act like an intelligent and compassionate adult. Coiled into an S shape, a rattler can jump forward over two thirds of its body length. It strikes with lightening speed, just as Bush did in his illegal but lightening attack and terribly botched occupation of Iraq.

My list of poisonous snakes is scary. Are humans really like rattlesnakes? Not exactly, humans are by far the most dangerous animals on Earth.

Commander in Chief Bush: Parallel with Humpty Dumpty

I have repeatedly argued that the US federal government is the most dangerous of the vicious predators. This takes me to Humpty Dumpty—not the character in the children's nursery rhyme, but what some historians say was a massive cannon. It was supposedly mounted on top of the Wall of St. Mary's Church in Colchester, England, in the English Civil War (1642-49). The king's men held onto the city for eleven weeks. But they lacked the skill to fire Humpty Dumpty. Instead, they managed to blow it to pieces.[53] Like Humpty Dumpty, I doubt that former President George W. Bush can ever be put back together again. Humpty Dumpty and Bush are now past tense.

What relevance do cruel US predators have for the future of capitalism? The poisonous predators in this chapter are just a few examples of the destructive forces of an economy out of control. Together the manifold destructive forces tracked chapter-by-chapter make up the essence of the evil within contemporary capitalism, now headed for oblivion.

Chapter 7

ENVIRONMENTAL DEGRADERS AND DESTROYERS

Our dangerous overreliance on carbon-based fuels is at the core of three challenges—the economic, environmental, and natural security crises.

We're borrowing money from China to buy oil from the Persian Gulf to burn in ways that destroy the planet. Every bit of that has to change.

—Former Vice President Al Gore
New York Times (July 18, 2008)

The Environmental Alliance of Malevolence

The United States is the world's biggest and most dangerous polluter as we spew millions of tons of poisonous gas into the atmosphere. China is second and India third. This alliance of malevolence blocks efforts to combat global warming even as the earth heats up. As our former leader, George W. Bush, heaped shame on America in the eyes of the world as a global polluter and arsonist whose policies degraded and destroyed the environment.

Arsonist? How so? Webster's dictionary defines arson as the malicious burning of another's house or property or, in some state statues, the burning of one's own property.[1] Given this definition, one that would allow for the destruction of public and private property as a result of fires brought on by drought and failure to attend to the needs of the nation and the global environment, one must conclude that the United States is a

177

global polluter and arsonist, along with China and India. Of the big three polluters America is the worst. Regardless of whether anyone is intentionally evil, one must always judge a nation by its acts, not its words. On that count Bush offered nothing but counterfeit compassion. His policies degraded and destroyed the environment and aided in inflicting suffering and death on Earth's inhabitants.

To be sure, the frequent firestorms in California and across much of the country have many origins. But scientists tell us that man-made global warming is at the top of the list of causes. Al Gore's classic film, *An Inconvenient Truth*, made the case clear and strong that global warming was largely man made, and must be stopped.[2]

The Denials of Global Warming

I write this at a scary time for our planet and its people. Wars, revolutions, and other forms of unrest keep global tension high even as nation after nation pollutes and heats up the atmosphere. Global warming by itself brings with it forest fires, hurricanes, floods, tornadoes, drought, poverty, sickness, disease, death, and population displacement. I have already tracked the perils of wars with WMD.[3] We'll turn now to the many bogus denials of global warming.

Government Alteration, Distortion, and Lying on Global Warming[4]

1) Former President Bush delayed, altered, and minimized findings of government scientists on global warming. Some scientists assert that the White House pressed them to alter or distort research. They repeatedly noted that good climate-related science and key data inexplicably disappeared from their work desks and their web sites.

2) The Fish and Wildlife Service forbade government biologists to discuss "climate change, polar bears, or sea ice." Former Department of the Interior official Deborah Williams said, "This sure sounds like a Soviet style directive to me."

3) J. Steven Griles, the former second in command on global warming at the Department of the Interior, now an oil and gas lobbyist, pleaded guilty in federal court to obstruction of justice and lying.

4) Philip Cooney, chief of the White House Council on the Environment, resigned after allegations that he deleted, altered, and distorted scientific work on global pollution.

5) Economist Stern, formerly of the World Bank, warned constantly of toxic emissions and that the costs to slash emissions would be in the "hundreds of billions of dollars."

6) The Department of the Interior's inspector general reported that a senior political appointee without training in the natural sciences rewrote the conclusions of the Fish and Wildlife Service to downgrade the threats of global warming. Policy trumps science on many occasions, said one interior lawyer in his statement to the inspector general.

7) Stripped down to its essentials, the Bush administration's position was that global warming was a problem that would either solve itself or it wouldn't. The White House consistently opposed taxes or regulations or mandatory caps to reduce, or even just stabilize, greenhouse gas emissions.

US Censorship on the Dangers of Global Warming

A July 2008 congressional investigation on global warming cited how the Bush administration lied and suppressed the truth. The administration had earlier agreed that greenhouse gases "could endanger the public and should be regulated under the clean air laws." Indeed, the report by the US House Select Committee on Energy Independence and Global Warming confirmed that the Bush administration had earlier supported policies to combat global warming.

Then these policies were abruptly reversed by then former Vice President Dick Cheney's office. Big oil corporations celebrated. His reversal of plans to fight global warming was coupled with suppression and censorship of opposing views. Truth was the victim once again in the White House.

The House committee report leans hard on the testimony of a former official of the Environmental Protection Agency (EPA). It is also based on official and confidential interviews with EPA staff and documents subpoenaed from the agency. Committee Chairman Ed Markey lashed out at the administration with this simple truth: "The dysfunctions and motivations of the Bush administration [are] laid bare." Of course, the White House rejected the committee's findings. A government spokesman said, "Chairman Ed Markey's report is inaccurate to the point of [being] laughable." Really? Who could believe any spokesman for the Bush White House? Answer: Extreme right-wing ideologues.

That's not all. For months, Congress focused on a series of decisions by EPA administrator Stephen Johnson. One of his decisions was to stop the State of California from regulating motor vehicle greenhouse gas omissions. This seemed odd because earlier Mr. Johnson had sided at least in part with the EPA staff on several matters, including the fear that greenhouse gas emissions pose a danger to the public and should be regulated.

That was then, but not after Cheney reversed the policy.[5] Jason Burnett, a former EPA administrator, told the House committee that people in Mr. Cheney's office and the White House felt that global warming controls would hurt Bush's legacy. It's doubtful that they would have hurt his legacy since it was already half dead. The reversal of policy seems to have included just about every loyal Bush supporter who did whatever the boss demanded regardless of the significant risks to personal integrity and public safety. These loyal supporters seemed to have collectively memorized a single line to be repeated over and over again: "The Clean Air Act is not the appropriate way to regulate carbon emissions."

Bush's Team Players Who Practice to Deceive

The report of the House Select Committee on Energy Independence and Global Warming identified government officials and oil industry executives who exerted great pressure in their attempt to destroy controls on greenhouse emissions. They include:

> F. Chase Hutto III, Mr. Cheney's energy adviser; individuals within the Exxon Mobil Corporation and the American Petroleum Institute; Bush's deputy chief of staff, Joel Kaplan; Secretary of Energy Samuel Bowdman; Secretary of Transportation Mary Peters; and Secretary of Commerce Carlos Gutierrez.[6]

Of course former President Bush was the first one to deny illegal or incompetent actions or policies. Consistent with his disgust with the *New York Times*, he consistently faulted the liberal press. Yet he declared that he did not read newspapers but received his news directly from the White House staff. "I don't read biased reports," the president declared. I suppose that means Bush never bothered to read the rebuke the Supreme Court made of the EPA.

The Rebuke of the Bush Administration

The Supreme Court reprimanded the EPA for its "arbitrary, capricious, and unlawful conduct." Their words leave no room for doubt. Here's a sample of the front-page news quotes that followed the Court's ruling.[7]

1) *Business Week*: "The Court's case is a rebuke to the US administration."

2) *Washington Post*: "The ruling could also lend authority to the states to force the federal government to reduce greenhouse gas emissions, or to do it themselves."

3) **Reuters**: "This is a stinging defeat for the US administration."

4) *Scientific American*: "The Court [said] that the EPA injured cities and states."

5) *New York Times*: "[The decision] is a victory for a world increasingly threatened by climate change. It could [now] impose mandatory limits on carbon emissions."

6) *Christian Science Monitor*: "The US illegally suppressed the views of dissenting scientists when it eased logging restrictions in the Pacific Northwest."

7) **The Gallup Poll** reported an overwhelming majority of Americans support (a) government restrictions on greenhouse gas emissions and (b) more taxpayer money to be spent on developing alternative sources of fuel and energy.

Bush's Spurious Riposte

Bush's rejoinder was predictable. He countered that these reports were off base. He added that he had taken measures to fight global warming, and they were sufficient. Bush constantly pointed out: "The real problem lies with China, not me. China will produce greenhouse gases that will offset anything we can do. I have no need for the [EPA] to regulate emissions of gases."[8] Again Bush assured those concerned that "What we do is quite sufficient."

Bush's Specious Criticisms of China

To those who insisted that a clear policy to fight global warming was needed Bush's rejoinder made little sense. With only five percent of the world's total population the United States produces one-quarter of the world's deadly emissions.[9] Relatively speaking, Bush's criticisms of China were misplaced. Our pollution problems are internally manufactured and yet Bush continued to blame China in part for the poor air quality that we had failed to clean up in our own back yard and for a huge trade and budget imbalance that we brought upon ourselves. The truth is that America's budget and trade deficits are mainly homegrown. America spends billions of dollars to wage an illegal war and to purchase foreign oil even as it tries to block imports from China of relatively high-quality, low-priced manufactured goods. If these claims sound familiar, readers may well recall that not all that many years ago the United States was insisting that our economic rival, Japan, was the culprit behind our fiscal woes.

The Great Global Warming Swindle[10]

Not everyone agrees that global warming is a major problem. There are always exceptions to any rule. Former President Bush was just that, an exception to the rule. As absurd as Bush's actions were, a British documentary titled *The Great Global Warming Swindle* was equally absurd. Reporter Andrew Revkin wrote that Britain's watchdog agency, the Office of Communication, rebuked Britain's television Channel 4 for its broadcast of the film. The agency said the film unfairly portrays several scientists and the Intergovernmental Panel on Climate Change. The watchdog agency also concluded that the film focuses on a small group of scientists who reject the idea that global warming poses big dangers. Since its release the film has been widely circulated by opponents of restrictions on greenhouse gases. Criticism has been especially sharp regarding the film's assertion that depiction of human-caused global warming is a willful deception. In one particularly jarring line, the narrator says: "Everywhere you are told that man-made climate change is proved beyond doubt. But you are being told lies."

What? Good scientists, as I have often stressed, never pretend to find truths valid for all time. The various scholars I have mentioned throughout this book don't even feel comfortable using the word "proof." All of their conclusions are tentative since they are hypotheses that, if confirmed, remain so until subsequent evidence is found that potentially demonstrates otherwise. They know that better theory, better data, and new discoveries lie ahead. Relevant here, the film's conclusions were also criticized by several top scientists, including Dr. Carl Wunsch, an ocean and climate expert at the prestigious Massachusetts Institute of Technology. He said that his comments on the film were taken out of context and made him appear, inaccurately, to question the seriousness of human-driven warming. The report upheld his complaint, but it did not go far enough for Dr. Wunsch. In his view, the film clearly misled the public in harmful ways. He said that the film claimed to be a science documentary. He added that it politicized an extremely complicated science problem without enlightening anyone. A film that claims to be a scientific documentary but is really a nonscientific political tract can be quite poisonous to the public perception of an issue as important as global warming.

Nonscientific Political Tracts

Is it any wonder that I emphasize the need to include science when addressing socioeconomic matters of considerable social importance? The rules of science, especially good theoretical and empirical support, can always help us to spot dishonesty. If the science-based criticisms of *The Great Global Warming Swindle* are accurate then the film itself is a mockery of science and truth.

One reason I include a critique of this film here in a work on the demise of capitalism is to make clear the close parallel of points the film made to the actions of the former Bush administration. Bush and his cronies constantly attacked science in an effort to support their own extreme ideology but it has failed to help America. The destructive acts of Bush and his advocates served only to undermine the nation. These acts include calls to reduce foreign imports, decrease the number of immigrants seeking only to work, and falsely charging non-Americans with being possible terrorists.

Backfiring Trade Policies

If the United States were to succeed in blocking imports from China, such actions would surely backfire, thus harming not only China and other nations but itself as well. When we start blocking imports, other nations will retaliate by doing the same. Clearly we are back to that old logical fallacy of composition that we saw injecting confusion into the nuclear arms debate. It also applies to economic trade wars as well.[11] If only one nation were to erect barriers for imports, the global impact may not be all that significant, but when other nations retaliate by creating their own trade barriers, the international economic impact is considerable. Such tariffs threaten a total world trade collapse, as happened during the Great Depression, in which case everyone loses. To be sure, some trade barriers to imports are desirable, as in the case of imported counterfeit products or poisonous drugs, knock-off products that damage the domestic manufacturers, and similar items. But the general rule is that trade wars quickly boomerang globally not only to kill trade but also to bring on a global economic slump.

If only the Bush administration had brushed up on the benefits that the concept of "comparative advantage" for world trade offers the international community. When a country demonstrates lower costs and higher quality of particular goods and/or services, then that nation has a comparative advantage for these products and services until another nation achieves a better economy of scale and thereby attracts more of the market. Had they paid attention to this concept—an internationally recognized one—then Bush and his spokespeople might have understood the nonsense they were spewing forth. Bush and his policies could have also benefited from an understanding the views of classical economist David Ricardo, who first explained fully the comparative advantage concept.[12] But he most likely never did. Clearly Bush's extreme conservative philosophy forever blocked his road to straight thinking and sound economic science.

A Lost Art for America: Setting a Good Example

During the latter part of his second term, former President Bush simply lost the confidence of foreign countries and his own people, including many who voted for him. While in a state of deep denial about the environmental challenges facing the world and its various ecosystems, he opposed strong policies to curb global warming. The governments of China and India, with their growing economies, are in the same denial camp. How can America ever expect the rapidly developing nations of Asia, let alone smaller and poorer countries, to cut their respective carbon emissions if larger and more affluent national economies fail to do so? The richer, more developed nations must lead by example. To this day, the wealthier economies, including America, are not part of the solution to global warming. Instead, they are often the biggest part of the problem.

The Destructive Forces of Global Warming

Al Gore, former vice president in the Clinton administration, has proved himself to be a fierce fighter against global warming. We already know that many people in the world's largest economies now suffer from shockingly high rates of obesity and the deadly health conditions that result from it. Many of these same advanced societies have substantial military forces that risk being drawn into international conflicts on less than compelling grounds.[13] Will unchecked global warming precipitate an ecological disaster that could conceivably threaten all life on Earth? The damage is well under way. Perhaps this lethal list can help clarify the specter of global environmental risk:[14]

1) Glaciers, from the South American Andes to the European Alps, are shrinking at an accelerating pace. Countries are already haggling over water rights. From 400 million to as many as 3.2 billion people face serious water shortages over the next twenty to fifty years.

2) A visiting scientist at the Potsdam Institute for Climate Research and an author of a report by the Intergovernmental Panel on Climate Change said, "There is going to be massive species extinction unless [warming] is limited."

Humans: The Major Cause of Global Heating

3) Global warming is "unequivocal, and humans [are] the main driver[s]."

4) Since every extra increment of carbon dioxide leads to extra warming, addressing the effects of climate change without dealing with the root cause is like treating diabetes with doughnuts.

5) Dumping sewage, plastic, garbage, and drugs into the oceans strangles, suffocates, and kills fish and birds worldwide. This leaves behind dead zones, toxic zones, and further increases the temperature of the oceans. Primordial algae and toxins take over, and a kind of reverse evolution transforms the oceans to a state of dense microbial growth they haven't experienced in many millions of years.[15]

Floods and Loss of Species Habitats and Homes

6) The Alps are the warmest they have been in 1,250 years. An increase of just a few more degrees would [wipe out] most ski resorts.

7) The sudden disappearance of islands is a symptom of an ice sheet [melting]. Greenland has 630,000 cubic miles of ice, enough to raise sea levels twenty-three feet.

8) The panel[16] concludes that global warming signals loss of species' habitats, increased acidity of our oceans, loss of wetlands, and the bleaching of coral reefs. Hundreds of millions of Africans and tens of millions of Latin Americans will be short of drinking water in twenty years. By 2050 more than a billion Asians will face water shortages.

Disease, Military Conflict, Uninhabitable Cities, and Death

9) The Military Advisory Board concludes, "Global warming could lead to large scale migrations, increased border tensions, the spread of disease, and conflicts over food and water. All could lead to direct involvement by the United States military." Other studies show that drought, disease, and scarce water already fuel conflict in Afghanistan, Nepal, Sudan, elsewhere.

10) A hurricane storm surge in New York City would disable power lines, flood the subways, choke basements, breed mold, and make buildings uninhabitable. Flying debris from buildings will crash through windows and create interior suction to cause windows and walls to blow out. How could New York City survive if we lose one airport, if 20 percent of the city it is flooded, if nothing works, if waste-water systems are destroyed, and waves flood the Roosevelt Tunnel?

11) "Call for Change Ignored." The levees along the Mississippi River show a patchwork of damaged banks. Some are tall and earthen, while others are aging and sandy.[17] Hurricane Katrina has also weakened and destroyed the levees in New Orleans.

12) "Congress Wary of Oil Speculation." As energy prices soar, Congress is under the gun to find a way out for American consumers—or, failing that, someone to blame: big oil, commodity speculators bidding up the price, or the opposing political party.

13) "Losing the North Pole." Unusually warm weather has accelerated the melting of Arctic ice, so much so that by the year 2030 the Arctic Ocean may be ice-free each summer.[18]

14) "Energy Watchdog Warns of Oil Production Crunch." The International Energy Agency fears that oil-producing regions can't meet future needs.[19]

15) "With Oil's Rise, Floridians Shift on Oil Drilling." Consumer anger over high gasoline prices is driving a reconsideration of the

US ban on coastal drilling for oil and natural gas even in Florida, where conservation and tourism concerns have long bolstered a bipartisan consensus against offshore production.[20] This desire to drill had diminished somewhat with lower oil prices, but the British Petroleum Gulf of Mexico platform disaster and the resulting spill has dampened the popular urge to increase drilling offshore.

16) "Two Decisions Shut Door on Bush Clean-Air Steps." Taken together the [decisions] make it clear that any significant new effort to fight air pollution will fall to the next president.[21]

17) "India's Growth Outstrips Crops to Produce Food Crisis." Forty years ago the Green Revolution drove hunger from an India synonymous with famine and want. Now, after a decade of neglect, India is growing faster than its ability to produce rice and wheat.[22] The specter of famine once again haunts India, and other nations.

18) "Air Travel and Carbon on Increase in Europe." Airlines are already the fastest growing source of climate-warming carbon dioxide emissions.[23]

New York City Unprotected in the Next Major Hurricane?

Under the previous Bush administration New York City would not been likely to survive a major hurricane like that of Katrina in 2006. In that case federal apathy, arrogance, and incompetence were evident, with deadly results. After such a fiasco, how could anyone expect then Commander-in-Chief George W. Bush to protect New York City from a similar ferocious hurricane? Here is my reaction to the disaster, which appeared in a Pace University student newspaper interview I gave on the power of the Katrina storm that devastated New Orleans.[24]

> . . . a Pace University finance professor who was born in New Orleans . . . said that the President should be held criminally negligent in his failure to respond promptly to the catastrophe that hit

New Orleans and the lower delta Mississippi region. Many of its victims suffered and died because of the abysmal mismanagement and incredible delays in getting food, water, and medical aid.

The very poor and the blacks and other minority groups suffered the most. They lacked the money, the transport, and government help to flee a stricken New Orleans. The federal failures in New Orleans came on top of the Bush administration's preemptive first strike military attack on Iraq on false grounds. The president has shamed the United States at home and abroad.

Dr. Parks added that the present administration has done little to deal with the oil and petrol crisis. Its failure to push for energy conservation or fight global warming puts no limits on gas guzzlers. He forecast that huge budget and trade deficits will devastate financial markets and the economy.

How indeed could New York City survive a hurricane the size of Katrina? One part of the solution is to reduce the risk of global warming and the potential increase in violent weather patterns that may result by reducing emissions of carbon, whether from buildings, factories, autos, airplanes, or ocean liners. Part of the solution to a problem like global warming is to realize that our actions contribute to environmental degradation and that we need to do our part to reduce our negative impact.

Looking Ahead by Looking Back

I often look back to disasters of the past and wonder if they will be repeated. I have in mind the terrible mistakes made that resulted in the release of large amounts of toxic gas in Bhopal, India, killing many thousands of people, and the risks currently of massive pollution of the world's giant oceans. On December 3, 1984, something terrible happened in Bhopal.

A tank inside a Union Carbide factory released forty tons of methyl isocyanine gas killing thousands who inhaled it while they slept. At the time it was called the world's worst industrial accident. At least three thousand people were killed immediately. Thousands more died in the aftermath. More than 500,000 people suffered health problems. The toxic remains have yet to be carried away. They have seeped into the soil and water and left pesticide residuals in the neighborhood wells far exceeding permissible levels.

Nobody has bothered to address the concerns of those who have drunk that water and tended kitchen gardens on the soil. But now present ailments loom for children who have been born with everything from mental retardation to clef palates, among other sicknesses. Why it has taken so long to deal with the disaster is an epic tale of the ineffectiveness and seeming apathy of India's government and its failure to make the factory owners do anything about the mess they left.

Bhopal becomes the tragedy that India forgot. Those who try to help the sick and injured claim that the Dow Chemical Company, which bought Union Carbide in 2001 also bought its liabilities and should pay for the cleanup. Dow, based in Michigan, insists it bears no responsibility to clean up a mess it did not make. Scot Wheeler, a Dow spokesman said, "As there was never any ownership there is no responsibility and no liability—for the Bhopal tragedy or its aftermath." Mira Shiva, a doctor who heads up the Voluntary Health Association countered, "Had the toxic waste been cleaned up, the contaminated ground water would not have happened. Dow was the first crime. The second crime was government negligence." Mira Shiva and others have long pressed Dow to take responsibility for the cleanup, apparently without success.[25]

The Bhopal disaster in the 1980s, the earlier US toxic waste site controversy in Love Canal area of Niagara Falls, New York, in the 1970s, and the aftermath of Katrina are just a very few reminders of the many disasters that cause untold misery yet are often met with anemic and late-arriving government action. Then, of course, there are the lesser disasters: droughts, wildfires, floods, crushing poverty, lost homes, lack of health insurance, rapidly increasing unemployment, and the destruction and degradation of the environment. The need to address these tragic situations with care, compassion, and desperately needed aid is vital if any society is to survive.

The biggest disaster at present is the failure of the US government to implement wide-ranging programs to solve major social problems. The administration and the Federal Reserve risk failure here and now if they do not ward off the current well-entrenched recession, one that could easily push us into depression if immediate action isn't taken, by having the nation's central bank fund public works to provide jobs for millions of Americans. We need to do more than commit dollars to the problem. We need to make sure that the funding enters the economy quickly, that public works projects are started, and that real jobs are created. Only in that way will confidence be restored and the economy finally begin to regain strength. The potential for massive economic disaster in the form of a deflationary depression remains high if living-wage jobs aren't created that will begin to reverse the existing intense recession.

Human Apathy and the Plight of the World's Oceans

We need far more than hope. This takes me now to a discussion of "Planet Ocean." The Nature Conservancy wrote, "Admittedly the name 'Planet Ocean' doesn't have a ring to it. But after a bit of thought, you might agree that it makes sense." Here are the reasons the Nature Conservancy sets forth:[26]

> After all, oceans cover over seventy percent of planet Earth's surface. Those vast reaches of water—be they rolling waves or frozen ice flows—conceal an outstanding diversity of life: An estimated 100 million creatures (an almost incomprehensible number) from blue whales to the tiniest plankton.
>
> The wealth of our oceans can be measured economically. The value of goods and services derived from the world's oceans totals a mind-boggling $21 trillion. Each year on average the oceans yield 85 million metric tons of fish and other raw materials that accounts for 16 percent of all animal protein consumed by people worldwide.

It's so distressing that the oceans' trove of riches is threatened today as never before from destructive fishing practices, land-based sources of pollution, poorly planned coastal development, and the wide-ranging impacts of climate change. The Coral Triangle, regarded by scientists as the epicenter of our planet's marine diversity, stretches across the seas of six countries: Indonesia, the Philippines, Malaysia, East Timor, Papua New Guinea, and the Solomon Islands. The Triangle provides feeding and breeding grounds for whales, dolphins, sea turtles, sharks, and mantra rays.

But like so many places around the world, the seas of the Coral Triangle are increasingly at risk. Destructive fishing practices and pollution are weakening the regions' reef habitats and depleting its fish stocks. Warming waters brought on by global climate change are leading to mass coral bleaching and the devastating loss of live coral. . . . While New Yorkers do not directly depend on coral reefs for their food and livelihood, they are directly dependent on the natural world, including the shellfish industry of Long Island to the forests of Tug Hill, the shores of the Finger Lakes to the waters of the Catskills. . . .

The Urgency of Action to Cut Greenhouse Emissions

However, these natural systems—and the lives they support—are now threatened by climate change. Higher temperatures, rising seas, stronger storms, increased droughts, shifting landscapes the list goes on and on.

Even if all the world's carbon sources were turned off like faucets—right this second—we would still face up to a century of temperature increases and related changes. Just as an egg will continue frying in a skillet after the burner is turned off, the Earth's atmosphere will continue to warm even as greenhouse gas emissions diminish. (Emphasis added.)

Folly and Farce of Voluntary Controls on Greenhouse Emissions

An important if not indispensable step to curb greenhouse gases would be to tax fuel and gasoline consumption heavily. Voluntary reductions of pollutants with carbon emissions credits bought and sold in the market place won't solve the problem. Instead, absolute limits on pollution emissions should be mandated by law. Most important, government and industry must work with the scientific community to find alternative fuels to replace coal, oil, and gasoline. The solutions require that everybody must fight global warming. One critical need is to fight cartel price fixing and lawbreaking. Such action will help to curb the likelihood of an economic depression, but in the long run it should spur us to develop competing energy sources that will not leave a "carbon footprint." We will review that shortly. For a start, however, here's a partial list that also includes what many Americans can do.[27]

The Many Solutions to Global Warming

1) Increase the fuel economy of two billion cars from 30 to 60 miles per gallon.

2) Replace the 1,400 large coal-fired electricity plants with gas-fired plants.

3) Add twice today's nuclear output to displace coal.

4) Increase solar power 700-fold to displace coal.

5) Cut electricity use in homes, offices, and stores by 25 percent.

6) Install carbon capture and sequestration capacity at 800 large coal-fired plants.

7) Halt cutting and burning of forests that cause 20 percent of the world's carbon emissions.

8) Replace incandescent bulbs with low-cost-longer-lasting fluorescent bulbs.

9) Reduce the speed limits nationally to no more than fifty-five miles per hour.

Most of these suggestions are obvious but all too often ignored.

The Fate of High-Tech Trash[28]

One huge problem facing environmental experts (and all of us) is what to do with the mountains of trash we produce. Take high-tech electronics as just one example. A growing percentage of the hardware components do get recycled but most still wind up in landfills. That's where the troubles begin. The elements and compounds in electronic waste (e-waste) can leach into the soil and water and scatter into the air. The health risks of e-waste are many and dangerous.

1) Lead used in creating computer boards is a neurotoxin that can harm the kidneys and the human reproductive system. As we have learned with lead-based paints, even low-level lead exposure can impair a child's mental development.

2) PVC, a versatile plastic, can produce highly toxic dioxins.

3) Brominated flame retardants may cause thyroid troubles and harm fetal development.

4) An elevated exposure to barium can cause gastrointestinal disturbance, muscle weakness, breathing difficulty, and a rise or fall in blood pressure.

5) If inhaled, chromium can damage liver and kidneys, increase the risk of lung cancer, and cause asthmatic bronchitis.

6) Mercury, linked to brain and kidney damage, is harmful to a developing fetus and can be passed through breast milk.

7) Beryllium is a carcinogen, and beryllium dust can cause lung cancer.

8) Long-term exposure to cadmium damages kidneys and bones.

Many of our high-tech computers, TVs, cell phones, and other devices contain these poisonous substances. Given these serious risks, science and technology must find less dangerous ways to manufacture these devices that we depend upon so much.

Outsourcing Disease and Death

All toxins can damage and kill. To be sure, the 1989 Basel Convention, a 170-nation accord, requires that the developed (or richer) nations notify developing nations (most of which are struggling economically) of incoming hazardous waste shipments. The European Union (EU) also requires manufacturers to shoulder the burden of safe disposal of their e-waste. In spite of these safeguards, untold tons of e-waste still slip out of European ports on their way to the developing world. Here are a few telling examples of what happens to e-waste as told by Chris Carroll in the *National Geographic*.[29]

> June is the wet season in Ghana but here in the capital, Accra, the morning rain has ceased. . . . As the sun heats, in the humid air pillars of black smoke begin to rise above the vast market.... I follow one plume to its source, past stalls of used tires and through a clanging scrap market where hunched men bash on old alternators and engine blocks. Soon the muddy track is flanked by piles of old TVs, gutted computer cases, and smashed monitors heaped in a pile.

This sad saga continues to describe desperate men, women, and children working to earn a few pennies salvaging e-waste. What they don't know is that the e-trash they handle daily contains the many deadly toxins outlined above that may sicken or kill them. Now you know why I labeled this section "Outsourcing Disease and Death." Rich nations create e-trash and then look for a place to dump it, creating disease and death in developing countries. That's yet another social sin we must add to the growing list of economic and environmental insults for which America must eventually answer.

Racing to Hug Those Trees[30]

Just recently my daughter Karen was nearly brought to tears when several of her Laguna Niguel, California, neighbors demanded that she cut down her beautiful palm trees in the back yard. The neighbors insisted that Karen's trees blocked their view of the ocean. Karen eventually won the day and her trees still stand as beautiful as ever. Shortly thereafter, I came across a magnificent piece in the *Economist* titled "Racing to Hug Those Trees." Since the writers don't sign their articles, I couldn't send the author a well-deserved word of praise. Here are a few excerpts from the article.

> Next week [early April 2008] the United Nations will convene yet another meeting to debate a successor to the Kyoto protocol, its treaty on climate change. As usual there will be long discussions on how to preserve forests, since deforestation accounts for about one-fifth of all greenhouse gas emissions. The new treaty, which is due to come into force in 2012, is supposed to include incentives for reducing emissions from deforestation and degradation (REDD in the jargon).
>
> But many conservationists and financiers won't wait: they are devising tree-saving ideas on their own. . . . One solution is to ignore the UN altogether. A scheme called Plan Vito, for example, would channel money to villagers in Mexico, Mozambique, and Uganda who pledge to protect nearby forests or plant trees. Others hope that such voluntary credits might eventually gain UN approval. Merrill Lynch, an investment bank, recently announced a plan to preserve a huge swath of forest in the Indonesian province of Aceh.

Talk Is Cheap and the Hour Is Late

Will any of these programs, in addition to private funding, cool down a burning world? Not likely. The private sector cannot fight alone and expect to succeed. Moreover, many national governments are still ideologically blind to their great power to solve huge problems. Those governments that believe it is the responsibility of the unregulated private sector to deal with pollution emissions will continue to wait only to see global warming speed ahead at an accelerating rate until they recognize that this is a social threat to human well-being that must be engaged and overcome at the highest political levels. We are wasting valuable time.

Cartels and "The Military, Industrial, and Big-Oil Complex"

Many other problems remain. In chapter 8 we will encounter global cartels, including the Organization for the Petroleum Exporting Countries (OPEC), Russia, major oil producers, and big importers and refiners of petroleum. Together they make up a global price-fixing cartel. All are loosely linked to what I have dubbed "The Military, Industrial, and Big-Oil Complex." They seek to get very rich very fast, and they have succeeded.

Consumers worldwide suffer cartel dominance when oil and gas prices reach record high levels. A large part of these soaring prices lies in the rapid growth and the energy demands of China and India as well as systemic price speculation on the world oil market. Our discussion will focus on the damage that has been done and on how to bring lawbreaking cartels under control.

Bellicose Macho Man: A Short Life Span for This Single Species?

Will modern humans survive much longer? Maybe not. Unlike the many species of ants, termites, and others that have been on the planet for millennia, *homo sapiens* constitute a single species and scientists tell us that a single species either evolves or risks extinction. For thousands of years we humans have struggled to survive and adapt to our world only to begin fighting one another in more recent centuries. We humans not only attack each other but the very planet we call home. It comes as no surprise that some scientists now predict that humankind will disappear in the present century.[31] Obviously, we must appraise these fears in our relatively new age of proliferating weapons of mass destruction. We humans have a lot to learn about staying alive and getting along with one another.

Chapter 8

THE PERILS OF THE MILITARY, INDUSTRIAL, AND BIG-OIL COMPLEX

Exxon-Mobil, Total, and British Petroleum--original partners in the Iraq Petroleum Company—are in the final stages of discussions that will let them formally re-enter Iraq's oil market, which expelled them 36 years ago. The contracts also include Chevron.

—Andrew Kramer, *New York Times*, June 30, 2008

US Key Officials Posing as Advisers to Iraq?

Mr. Kramer tells us that the disclosure of these contracts, "coming on the eve of the contracts' announcement, is the first confirmation of direct involvement by the Bush administration in deals to open Iraq's oil to commercial development." Kramer adds that US involvement was "likely to stoke criticism," which may be the understatement of the year.[1] Indeed, disclosure of the secret US plans brought scathing criticism of the Bush team in a *Times* editorial.[2] The editorial merits wide coverage.

Kramer's report makes clear that long before the United States attacked Iraq, Bush and Cheney had their eyes on Iraq's oil. They secretly planned to take over "the world's largest untapped oil fields and its potential for vast profits." Kramer's article and the earlier *Times* editorial were devastating:

1) These "deals" could provide additional support for the view held by many of the world's Arabs "about oil being America's real reason for invading Iraq."[3] The deals will once again ignite American anger over the real reasons for the US war of choice in Iraq.

2) Apparently, "American advisers led by a small State Department team played an integral part in drawing up these contracts between the Iraq government and five major Western oil companies to develop some of the largest oil fields in Iraq."[4] Indeed, this does look like a great "Iraq Oil Rush," the title of the *New York Times* editorial.

3) Query: Were senior US officials posing as advisers? Is it not more likely that the US goal was to lock up quickly and secretly profitable contracts for Iraq oil? Should not the Senate and House subpoena Bush, Cheney, and other US officials to testify under oath about these lush oil contracts?

4) The contracts were made without competitive bidding, and only to companies that advised Iraq's oil ministry on how to increase production.[5] Other oil companies were not a party to these contracts. The editorial states, "Given that corruption is an acknowledged problem in Iraq's government, the contracts would have more legitimacy if the bidding were open to all…."[6] Of course, but systemic and constant corruption in the US government is never acknowledged by the White House. America's dishonesty and greed has long included getting hold of Iraq's oil wealth. Fair dealing in oil was hardly possible as long as the Bush administration remained in office.

5) Add to this the fact that these negotiations were conducted "even though Iraq's parliament has failed to adopt oil and revenue sharing laws—critical political benchmarks earlier set by the Bush administration. That is evidence of continued deep divisions in Iraq over whether oil should be controlled by central or regional governments, *whether international oil companies should be involved in how profits should be distributed.*"[7]

Marauding Oil Oligopolists

Let's turn now to an expanded cast of bad characters beyond those Kramer cites. I mean those who helped to push oil and gas prices to record high levels.[8] To be sure, the fast pace of economic growth in China and India has contributed to soaring oil and gas prices, and higher general inflation. But oil oligopolists also played a big part by fixing the price of oil at record levels. Just what are oligopolists? Can they in fact determine prices in order to get ultrarich?

The answer is yes. If any given industry is dominated by four or five of its biggest producers then an oligopoly has been born. These entities grow obnoxiously rich and happy through "tacit collusion." Simply put, cooperating oligopolists informally agree among themselves to raise oil prices and then maintain their efforts to keep these inflated prices at record levels. The firms agree with each other to maintain this secret pricing strategy. This is also known as "price leadership."

Tacit Collusion by Oil Oligopolists with Oil Middlemen

Firms stay within the law but still tacitly collude by checking each other's prices to make sure no one member is shaving prices to boost its own sales. If the profits of collusion are greater than the payoffs for anyone who cheats, then the firms will happily agree to collude. The result is predictable: Money and huge profits overflow the coffers of oligopolistic oil exporters such as members of the Organization of Petroleum Exporting Countries (OPEC). OPEC also sets up shady and favorable deals with cooperating and silent partners. They include salespeople, oil traders, oil brokers, refineries, and some major oil importers. Oil exporters and even some importers and others get richer and richer.

The Growing Economic Maelstrom for Consumers

Meanwhile, consumers grow poorer and poorer as electricity firms, delivery service, taxicab, and other companies add on special fuel surcharges in an attempt to recover some of their costs of doing business.[9] Consumers, already hit by high oil and gas prices, now suffer other losses of spending power. Many have lost their jobs, their incomes, their health insurance, their homes and cars, and even their hopes and expectations for a better life anytime soon. A major financial meltdown and recession gains accelerating force even as the Federal Reserve and the Treasury issue their usual optimistic reports.

The Sorry State of American Capitalism

I am hardly alone in my bleak forecasts. The *Economist* in a lead article in July of 2008 offered an extremely pessimistic outlook on the economy and the war titled "Unhappy America."[10]

> If America can learn from its problems, instead of blaming others, it will come back stronger. The United States, normally the world's most self-confident place, is glum. Eight out of ten Americans think their country is heading in the wrong direction. The hapless George Bush is partly to blame for this: his approval ratings are now sub-Nixonian.
>
> One source of angst is the sorry state of American capitalism. The "Washington consensus" told the world that open markets and deregulation would solve its problems. Yet American house prices are falling faster than during the Depression, petrol is more expensive than in the 1970s, banks are collapsing, the Euro is kicking sand in the dollar's face, credit is scarce, recession and inflation both threaten the economy, consumer confidence is an oxymoron, and Belgians have bought Budweiser, "America's beer."
>
> Abroad, America has spent vast amounts of blood and treasure to little purpose. In Iraq, finding an acceptable exit will look like success; Afghanistan is slipping; America's claim to be a beacon of freedom in a dark world has been dimmed by Guantanamo [and] Abu Gharib. Most revolting is the US flouting of the Geneva Convention.

The *Economist* is mostly right. Even the 9-11 terrorist attack on the World Trade Center is no excuse for torture of "enemy combatants and other detainees." Torture can never be justified! Still, one subject the *Economist* leaves out of its fine report is that all big bubbles collapse, including oil and a wide range of other commodities.

The Second Great Depression?

As of January 9, 2009, worldwide major recession slammed oil prices down from a bubble peak of $145 a barrel to $50 and lower. Dreadful deflation crushed commodity prices and consumer and investment demand, and it signaled far more property foreclosures, bankruptcies, and job losses. Worse, once deflation sinks its teeth into the economy it becomes extremely difficult (a) to exit from the current financial meltdown, (b) to spark any satisfactory economic recovery, or (c) to head off a major economic implosion that could easily degenerate into a second great depression. Oil prices have recovered somewhat from their lows—they now stand about $85 per barrel as of fall 2011—but deflation remains a serious risk.

Runaway Deflation and Apathetic Policymakers

As prices tumble, expectations grow that they will continue to tumble. Such expectations, as Keynes wisely warned, lead consumers to postpone spending in the hope of even lower prices later. Lowered demand and reduced spending sends prices still lower to attract willing spenders, which in turn further weakens consumer and investor spending as they wait for prices to decline even more, which in turn weakens prices even more, and the spiral continues. The downhill and self-reinforcing deflationary cycle grows even worse if attempts at government bottoms-up stimulus come too late. Sharp bickering now over vast public works projects proposed by Obama suggests we may have already run out of time. The ultraright wing seems oblivious to the quagmire of a runaway cycle of deflation. Supply-side ideologues refuse to learn anything from history or from Keynes.

Multiple Federal and Central Bank Economic Blunders

The *Economist* then discussed briefly a wide range of problems I have reviewed in detail in this work. Its reports point out that by employing ultra-easy and sustained monetary and fiscal policies both the Treasury and the Federal Reserve fueled (a) the overinvestment boom that predictably collapsed, (b) flyaway megabubble stock gauges that predictably burst, (c) the economic slumps that followed and are now deepening, and (d) the mortgage and housing boom that collapsed on a hollowed out US economy strangled by wars and mountains of corporate and consumer debt.

The federal government had to step in to rescue Fannie Mae and Freddy Mac, which either own or guarantee fifty percent of all outstanding home mortgages, all at market prices far below the cost of acquisition. We ended up with a mountain of direct Treasury debt and supposedly *de facto* federal guaranteed mortgage debt. The huge debt load will adversely constrict federal efforts to fund critically needed spending to create jobs and repair a severely damaged economy. Thus, when Barack Obama entered the Oval Office, he inherited a whirlwind of problems left unsolved by the corrupt and amateurish actions of his predecessor.

A Cast of Bad Characters

I turn now to the core of this chapter on government and the big-oil industry. Who are the worst of the bad characters in big oil? Check this listing:

- ✓ The petroleum cartel (OPEC) fixes oil prices ultrahigh to make obscene profits.

- ✓ Oligopolistic exporters and US oil companies are ever so friendly with OPEC price gouging policies. Their common objective is to get very rich very fast.

- ✓ Oil and gas brokers become wealthy from skyrocketing oil prices.

- ✓ US federal officials secretly support the huge profits of the big oil companies.[11]

Like Pulitzer Prize winning *New York Times* reporter Gretchen Morgenson, I do believe Andrew Kramer also deserves high praise for uncovering duplicity and deceit in the Bush administration. Most important, he helped to confirm long-held suspicions of a key but hidden motive of the Bush White House in its preemptive attack on Iraq. It was oil all along.

Science and the Free Press: Two Powerful Forces for Truth

Thus truth has finally burst its shackles many years after the Iraq occupation, thanks to the dogged and tireless work of great news investigators. I have said repeatedly that the one great success of the free press is to liberate truth and expose selfish right-wing ideology that constantly masquerades as truth.

Bush never realized the awesome power of a free press in catapulting political thugs out of office. He never understood just how low he and his cronies in deception had sunk because of their spurious attacks on science. Yet the two most powerful forces for truth and justice in America are science and a free press. Did Bush ever know this? Did the Bush-loyal Republican Party know it? Judging by their failed policies and questionable tactics, I must conclude that they have learned very little about the meaning of a free and honest America. Their destructive acts foreshadow the end of capitalism.

The 1973-1974 "Minidepression" and Dreadful "Stagflation"

This takes me now to the oil oligopolies and the ties they have to the US government. I will first turn my attention to the major oil crisis of 1973 and 1974. One aim is to point up the parallels between that economic downturn and the financial meltdown and exploding energy prices we faced in 2008 and that continue to threaten us today.

Consumers were tapped out, so to speak, by high oil prices in 1973 and 1974. Real inflation-adjusted oil prices[12] jumped from $8.00 to

$27.00 per barrel on top of a higher overall level of consumer prices. People worried about the damaging effects of "stagflation" (extremely weak economic growth coupled with extremely high inflation). Economists have long argued that accelerating inflation could not exist in a major and prolonged recession. But the consensus of economists was wrong once again. Inflation in fact accelerated even as the economy fell into a major recession. Early on I had forecasted a "maxirecession" that would be classed as the worst in post-World War II history. That's what we got, a 1973-1974 deep slump that lasted sixteen dreadful months. It almost degenerated into an outright depression because of prolonged and excessively tight central bank monetary policy.[13]

US Policy to Fight Stagflation Backfires

Let's track step-by-step the repeated blunders of policy in 1973 and 1974. Then we will be in a better position to identify any parallels between that period and the turmoil in oil and gas markets and government policy missteps in 2008. In this first case, OPEC cut oil output, which reduced the supply and raised the price of oil and gasoline. Then price inflation accelerated to strip away real buying power. Higher prices at the pump and elsewhere forced consumers to cut back their spending on all but essential items. Next, policymakers, fearing the onslaught of inflation, tightened money and credit growth to raise interest rates to fight the inflation. But their excessively constrictive policies backfired: they made interest rates so high and credit so hard to get that they produced a major recession. The US tight money policy became a big part of the oil problem. Bungling policymakers made matters worse.

It must be stressed that the 2008 and the current storm clouds for the economy are not at all like those preceding the 1973-74 maxirecession. In 2008 the problem was the lagging impact of sustained and excessively easy monetary and fiscal stimulus. Fast money and credit growth plus an exploding federal budget and foreign trade deficits were a perfect mix for economic collapse.[14] With that said, lets turn now to the inept policy makers in 1973-74.

The Happy-to-Cooperate Oil Oligopolists

The cooperative oil oligopolists were a big part of the problem. Many define oligopoly as "a market of few producers who affect but don't control markets." This definition does not make sense today in understanding the oil oligopolists. I never thought that it made much sense, because the big oil oligopolies do in fact exercise enormous control over oil prices. Nor does the standard definition apply well to the 2008 financial meltdown, recession, and soaring oil prices. We will take note of the parallels in a moment, but first let's count the reasons for turmoil in the oil markets and the world economy in 2008:

1) OPEC, Russia, and US big oil companies conspire secretly to cut the oil supply.

2) Oil is already in very short supply even as oil demand soars in India and China.

3) Conflicts of one sort or another throughout the globe beget huge oil demands from militaries and governments. In addition to our own military campaigns in Iraq and Afghanistan, there were other conflicts in Asia, Africa, and elsewhere. All of these require the buildup of oil, armor, and personnel.

4) OPEC and other oil oligopolists contrive secretly to push oil prices yet higher.

5) High oil prices flood the Military, Industrial, and Big-Oil Complex with profits.

6) Exporting oil oligopolists and others still seek to get very rich very fast.

7) The Bush administration's links with big oil in effect permit the oil and gas industry to do pretty much what it pleases. Weak government controls let them run wild.

The 1973-1974 Oil Embargo and the Great Minidepression

Consider now the incredible blunders of monetary policy and skyrocketing oil prices in 1973 and 1974. All hell broke loose in response to the Arab oil embargo. The runaway panic led me to forecast a major recession, which I dubbed a "minidepression." That's what occurred—a recession of sixteen dreadful months that barely avoided outright depression. As noted above, the massive slump was brought on by extreme monetary and fiscal constriction to fight inflation. We got the minidepression, as predicted, but lost the war on fighting inflation.

Consumer price inflation jumped higher and higher even as recession struck with its full fury. Indeed, the consumer price index was higher at the end of this sixteen-month slump than at its beginning. The Federal Reserve was a huge part of the problem as it attempted to confront a terrible economic slump made far worse by stagflation.

Wage Demands and the Self-Generating Cycle of Stagflation

Stagflation is a word combining major economic stagnation and high inflation. But how in the world can the two go together? Shouldn't a major recession kill inflation by depressing prices since recession causes demand for goods and services to drop? This was not the case in 1973-1974. For one thing, as prices ratcheted up and up, huge wage demands from workers seeking to maintain their relative standard of living contributed to a self-reinforcing inflationary spiral. Higher and higher wage costs quickly fed higher and higher wholesale and retail prices. Then inflationary expectations and powerful unions kicked in. Both consumers and business began to spend early in the hope of avoiding higher prices later, or they bought as speculators to make big profits later because they expected prices to rise even more. These actions—both sensible in their own way—caused demand for goods to rise and the prices right along with it. Production had to increase to restock the goods purchased. This gave power to the unions, which at the time had the power to demand higher wages or make good on their threats to strike. These forces led me to write a short piece titled "Dialogue of the Insane."

Dialogue of the Insane

Central bankers speak in an obscure and suffocating jargon. Even so, that does not subtract from their insane arguments once we convert their jargon into plain language. I took the time to translate their suffocating speech into understandable English.[15] I focus hard on monetary and fiscal theory and practice in my research and teaching. As a Wall Street economist, I also hosted many conferences for Federal Reserve and Treasury officials. Both tasks made it easy for me to convert their gobbledygook into plain language. So, listen in as I try to capture an odd exchange among central bankers (Cent 1, Cent 2, etc.) of the major oil importing nations in 1973-74.

> **Cent 1**: The big oil exporters are ganging up on us. They control production and pricing of most of the oil produced around the world. Each of us is a heavy importer of oil. We have no immediate substitute for oil. What can we do?

> **Cent 2**: We have to import oil to survive, to run our factories, heat our homes, and propel our trucks and buses and automobiles. We can try to reduce our consumption of oil, but we can only go so far. Even if we cut the barrels of oil we import by ten percent or twenty percent, a price boost of one hundred percent would still mean soaring oil bills. Our import bill in dollars would skyrocket. That means a big trade deficit with oil exporters and OPEC.

> **Cent 3**: Yes, the demand for oil is inelastic and relatively insensitive to prices in the short run. We can't cut oil consumption enough to offset the rise in prices. Over time we can conserve oil and find new sources. We need time.

Cent 4: We don't have time. Oil is priced in world markets in dollars and paid for in dollars. We must get dollars to buy oil, but we are short of dollars.

Cent 5: Gentlemen, let me summarize. We must tighten monetary policy immediately. We have to restrict money growth, raise interest rates, restrain domestic spending, slow down our economies, cool internal inflation, become more competitive, stimulate our exports, and earn more foreign exchange to get the dollars to buy the oil to keep our economies humming.

Cent 6: Yes, we must constrict. We must constrict. We must deflate before it's too late. We must cool internally to export externally, to earn the mark, the franc, the pound, to get the dollars, to get the oil, to keep us sound.

All: We must constrict. We must constrict. We must deflate before it's too late.

All: Yes, we must constrict. Indeed, we must constrict before it's too late.

This insane dialogue is also linked to the fallacy of composition. It means that what may be true for one may backfire to prove false for all. It's insane in yet another way. Suppose that all major oil-importing nations shift to severe monetary constriction. In that case constriction would dry up money and credit and initially raise interest rates, which could and did produce recession even as inflation soared. We quickly experienced a deadly combination of collapsing incomes, rising inflation, reduced borrowing, lower industrial output, fewer jobs, and higher interest rates.

The policy blunders of 1973-74 signaled a major recession lasting many months. Could monetary-fiscal blunders and the Military, Industrial, and Big-Oil Complex again produce a blockbuster recession starting in 2008 and lasting four or five years? Can we find specific parallels today with the developments in 1973-74? The answer is yes. A brief analysis of the Military, Industrial, and Big-Oil Complex can help to explain why.

The Military, Industrial, and Big-Oil Complex

President Dwight D. Eisenhower warned of the "Military and Industrial Complex." Still, oil cartel power is now stronger today than ever before. We are faced now with an even more destructive crowd, namely, the powerful Military, Industrial, and *Big-Oil* Complex. Many in the Congress, the Treasury, the Federal Reserve, the Supreme Court, and in White House administrations still preach an intense laissez faire doctrine that allows cartels to grow strong enough to strangle the economy.

Before we compare 1973-74 to 2008, let's first hear what Eisenhower had to say. President Eisenhower, a former commanding general of the US Army, made his farewell address to the United States on January 17, 1961. Here are his exact words.

The conjunction of an immense military establishment and large arms industry is new in American experience. The total influence—economic, political, even spiritual—is felt in every city, every statehouse, and every office of the federal government. We recognize the imperative need for this development. Yet we must not fail to comprehend its grave implications. Our toil, resources, and livelihood are all involved, as is the very structure of society.

In the councils of government, we must guard against the acquisition of unwarranted influence, whether sought or unsought by the military-industrial complex. The potential for the disastrous rise of misplaced power exists and will persist. We must never let the weight of this combination endanger our liberties or democratic processes. We should take nothing for granted. Only an alert and knowledgeable citizenry can compel the proper meshing of the huge industrial and military machinery of defense with our peaceful methods and goals so that liberty and security may prosper together.[16]

I don't believe I have every read or heard a better speech on the constant need to fight the arrogance of "misplaced power" that can destroy "peaceful methods and goals" so that "liberty and prosperity could prosper together." Ugly capitalism has replaced peaceful methods and diplomacy with preemptive first-strike military attacks and a wide array of programs and policies that not only kill liberty and security but also often lead to needless suffering and death across America. What would Eisenhower have said about America under the Bush administration? I suspect he would be alarmed and disgusted.

Parallels: Fiscal-Monetary Policy Blunders 2007-2008 and 1973-1974[17]

Let's return now to the parallels of 1973-74 and recently. One that makes sense is blundering policymakers. In 1973-74 it was extreme and deadly constriction by the Federal Reserve. Today it is the lagging backlash of extreme and long-sustained fiscal and monetary expansion that now leads to severe slump and possibly intractable deflation.

You may recall that Gerald Ford became president in 1974. Arthur Burns was then chairman of the Federal Reserve. Now, have you ever wondered where President Ford got his key policy suggestions? He got them from Burns, and from what I dubbed at the time "the classical preachers." The preachers included Alan Greenspan, then chairman of the Council of Economic Advisers; L. William Seidman, Ford's political and economic adviser; and Secretary of the Treasury William Simon. Thanks to the classical preachers and their extremely constrictive policies in 1973-74, I started worrying in print about recession as early as November 1973. I became progressively more bearish in the spring and summer of 1974 with an admittedly irreverent attack on September 16, 1974. I then wrote:

Mr. Ford [should] pay more attention to the weakening forward indicators of demand and less attention to his new economic advisers. I wonder if Mr. Ford, Mr. Simon, and Mr. Greenspan are not gearing policy to fight the wrong economic war with the wrong weapons at the wrong time. [18]

How Monetary Overkill Begets Severe Recession[19]

While I omitted including L. William Seidman in that release, I (RH) more than made up for it by hosting a forum for Mr. Seidman (WS) and thirty-five institutional investment officers in the fall of 1974 in Boston. What follows are key excerpts from the meeting:

RH: Thank you for an excellent presentation. As host, I get the first question. The Ford administration has a legitimate concern, of course, in getting high inflation down. You have passed out WIN buttons, an acronym for Whip Inflation Now.[20] Your objective is to get consumption spending down. You ask consumers to tighten their belts. My question has to do with timing. Are you not worried that the WIN program is being introduced too late? The fall of the economy now underway makes clear that demand is evaporating fast.

WS: Look, our problem is inflation. We have to get inflation under control. We have to cut government spending, but the public must do their share, too. The public has to consume less and save and invest more from their salaries and wages. Yes, they must tighten their belts. This will slow inflation, get interest rates down, and generate the private saving to finance new investment in plant, equipment, and new technology. Our goal is to get production up and inflation and interest rates down. We must beat inflation here and now. That's WIN.

RH: But you have three depressants all working at once. The Federal Reserve is squeezing the lifeblood from the economy.

Commodity inflation is zapping buying power. WIN would further depress consumer spending, which is already heading downhill. Total spending is falling even as we hold this meeting. Aren't you, Alan Greenspan, and President Ford pursuing policies that would make the ongoing recession deeper and longer? It is already the worst recession since the Great Depression.

WS: What recession? Let me be perfectly plain. This is your view, not ours!

It was mind-boggling to witness Mr. Seidman and the resuscitated classical economist, Alan Greenspan, ignore one of their own. I have in mind the great economic neoclassicist Alfred Marshall (1842-1924). Marshall warned in his *Principles of Economics* (1890) that if you kill *final* consumer demand you risk killing *derived* investment demand. If you depress the demand for automobiles and other consumer goods, you then depress the derived (associated) demand for machine tools, equipment, and the assembly plants necessary to produce these goods. You also depress the derived demand for rubber, steel, and plate glass necessary to produce automobiles or TV sets. You depress the derived demand for engineers, designers, computer experts, and even economists. If you constrict consumption in a falling economy you also kill investment.

More Bumbling Characters on Whip Inflation Now (WIN)

Now consider this list of bad oligopolistic characters. I (RH) named them **Misled** and **Stink Oil**. Their names are imaginary but each one reflects the constant nonsense I heard from the Ford administration in the recession of 1973-74.

Misled: RH, you are way off base. We used WIN to kill inflation. Stagflation was killing the economy with record oil prices that led to extreme inflation. We succeeded.

RH: Yes, you finally succeeded at the cost of a terrible recession. You began your constrictive WIN program at the very time the economy was already tumbling into recession. You brought with WIN the worst recession since the Depression. You call that blundering and fumbling policy a success?

Stink Oil: You are nothing but a troublemaker. You can't even think straight. Both the Treasury and the Federal Reserve applauded our acts of constriction under WIN.

RH: The Treasury and the Federal Reserve failed to understand that America had already fallen into a terrible slump. They continued to constrict for a long time *after* the economy had plunged into a severe recession.

Refusing to Wear the WIN Button

On another matter, as chief economist of Blyth Eastman Dillon I refused to wear the WIN button. Senior officers of the firm were annoyed, but I warned them it would be the height of hypocrisy for me to wear a WIN button when I was convinced that the economy was already in recession. Their annoyance with my refusal disappeared once the 1973-74 "minidepression" struck with its full fury.

A Chat with Dr. Arthur Burns, Former Federal Reserve Chairman

I had countless meetings with investment groups in the wild 1973-74 years. One was with the Federal Reserve Chairman, Dr. Arthur Burns. I always had great respect for Dr. Burns, especially his studies in business cycles. At one time he offered me a post as executive director of the National Bureau of Economic Research (NBER). I decided not to accept because I worried, as you might guess, that his authority might clash with my unbridled skepticism of authorities in power.

I brought with me three investment officers. We met with Dr. Burns (AB) in late 1974, very late in the recession that was underway. Here is an excerpt from the short exchange:

RH: Dr. Burns, we understand why you are so concerned with curbing inflation. But it seems to us that continued Federal Reserve constriction runs the highest risk of turning this recession into an outright depression.

AB: Robert, you have three problems. The first is interpreting the past. The second is analyzing the present. The third is forecasting the future.[21]

A Powerful Option: Sue OPEC?

Thomas W. Evans was an adviser to presidents Ronald Reagan and George H. W. Bush, (George W. Bush's father).[22] He says now that the United States has the power to destroy OPEC. He says it is an illegal cartel that drove the price of oil to a record high inflation-adjusted $150 per barrel in June 2008. A suit could be filed, he said, without any invasion or bombing, and no special legislation would be needed. All that is required is for the US president to take the suit to the Supreme Court, making clear that OPEC is in violation of the antitrust laws.

He writes that even if actions of individual citizens fail, a seldom used Article III of the US Constitution grants original jurisdiction to the Supreme Court over "lawsuits brought by U.S. states against foreign states as expanded by the United States code over aliens." He encouraged the attorneys general of the various states to sue OPEC as an alien, or alternatively as a foreign state. Further, Mr. Evans said that a joint action by the attorneys general has already been used to sue tobacco companies, Microsoft, and health maintenance organizations. So, why is there any hesitation to sue OPEC?

I do hope Mr. Evans is correct. Given the terrible problems of air pollution, oil spills, and destructive oil drilling, Americans do need the help of the Congress and the courts. I will just note here four of the oil problems that have made headline news.

1) *The Oil Spill on the Mississippi River*[23]

In 2008 a layer of oil coated the Mississippi River for nearly 100 miles from the center of the city of New Orleans (my home town) to the Gulf of Mexico. This was the worst oil spill in nearly a decade. A fuel-ladened barge collided with a heavy tanker, and the thick industrial fuel pouring from the barge could be smelled for miles in city neighborhoods up and down the river. Hundreds of cleanup workers struggled to contain the hundreds of thousands of gallons of oil spilling into the river. Some environmentalists worried about reports of fish and birds killed in sensitive marsh areas downstream.

The Mississippi remained closed to all boat traffic—an action that stranded some sixty vessels. The city's port authority estimated that the shutdown would mean an economic loss of at least $100,000 per day. As the oil slick moved downstream, officials remained concerned about the impact on the Delta National Wildlife Refuge at the mouth of the Mississippi. The oil flowing down to areas not protected by levees, would damage the ecology of the swamps, according to the Louisiana Environmental Action Network.

In 2010 the deadly explosion on a British Petroleum (BP) oil rig in the Gulf of Mexico and the millions of gallons of oil that gushed into the gulf have caused untold economic and environmental damage. It will take many months, if not years, to ascertain the long-term consequences of such a disaster.

2) *Drilling for Oil in the Arctic*[24]

The Arctic may hold as much as 90 billion barrels of undiscovered oil reserves and 1,670 trillion cubic feet of natural gas. This would amount to about thirteen percent of the world's total undiscovered oil and thirty percent of undiscovered natural gas. While the findings contain some uncertainty, they confirm an *oil industry belief and hope* that the Arctic may be the next frontier for global oil exploration. I hope their beliefs are wrong.

It's no wonder Arizona Senator John McCain wants to drill for oil. It's a quick fix to our energy needs and scores political points with those who can expand his power base in the Republican Party. But if he gets his way, which I believe he won't, one can expect to see further degradation and destruction of the environment. Since oil spills and oil pollution sicken and kill people, I cannot think of a worse option than more oil drilling, especially in the Arctic region. We must curb oil and gas drilling and polluting cars and factories before these noxious and toxic poisons kill many more people. New drilling would, of course, increase the prospect that polar bears would also become one of the first beautiful and wild animals to become extinct.

As a result of the BP oil rig disaster, the federal government has sought to stop further deep water drilling in the gulf and other off-shore areas until safety measures are firmly in place to prevent future oil spills. Legal challenges have been filed to stop this government action, and at least one federal court has ruled against the US government restrictions on future drilling. But federal regulators continue to insist that the restrictions are legal and necessary.

3) *Flaring Up Again: The Painful End of Oil Self-Sufficiency in Britain*[25]

The last time oil prices were as high in real terms as they are today—in the dark days of the 1970s—the British had one reason to be cheerful. The discovery of large dollops of oil and gas beneath the North Sea transformed their country from an importer of energy into an exporter. This held promise of a big economic windfall and insulation from wildly gyrating oil prices.

Today that cushion is gone. British output from the North Sea is well past its prime. Production peaked in 1999 and has declined rapidly ever since. So Britain is once again a net importer of both oil and natural gas. Worse, the cut in output coincided with the surge in oil prices. Since international gas prices correlate closely with oil prices, British consumers look now for a ghastly shock when they get their winter energy bills.

One energy firm, Centrica, estimates that gas bills will rise by two thirds over the coming months and stay high for the foreseeable future. As domestic supplies dwindle, Britain must make up for the shortfall from overseas, either through pipelines from Europe or by buying tanks of liquefied natural gas (LNG) on the global market. Consumers have already discovered how vulnerable they are now that Britain is no longer self-sufficient. In the midst of the coldest winter in years, gas prices in November 2005 quadrupled in just a few days. Did global warming end after November 2005? No.

4) The Puzzle of Oil Production[26]

The *Economist*, one of my favorite publications, explains why the Saudis may be worried over the record high prices of oil. Oil prices peaked at about $145 a barrel in July of 2008. That meant Saudi Arabia stood to receive a windfall in 2008 of up to $400 billion, double what it earned from selling oil in 2007. So, why are they worried? Should they not be dancing with joy as a tsunami wave of dollars flooded their strongboxes?

For one thing, no one in the Saudi oil ministry has forgotten what happened *after* the oil shock in the 1970s. The Arab boycott of 1973 was a protest against the Western backing of Israel. Meanwhile, oil prices tripled. But the boycott also prompted oil exploration in tricky places such as the North Sea. In addition, conservation measures reduced demand. The result was a long-term slump in crude oil prices and a drop in the Saudis' market share. The Saudis now fear that an intensified search by the West for alternative energy will result in the same thing happening again.

But the more immediate worry is that high oil prices may slow not just America's but the whole world's economy. That would trigger a sharp fall in the demand for Saudi oil. Just as bad, a sharp global slump would likely slash the value of the kingdom's hundreds of billions of dollars in overseas holdings, especially in America. As already noted, bubble oil prices have already fallen hard in response to a global economic slump.

Oligopolies Lose Power in Recessions

The Saudi fears are genuine. The minidepression I forecasted in 1973-74 for America meant a collapse in the economy, reduced credit demand, and rising inflation, including oil inflation. Oligopolistic power, unlike in 1973-74, typically evaporates in sustained and major economic downturns. That's why my forecast for 2008 included a worsening financial meltdown that would trigger a major and sustained recession; a collapse in credit demands; a stock market rout; plunging prices of gold, grains, wholesale and retail prices, and oil and gas prices. Market interest rates would also nosedive (which could send prices of thirteen-year-duration TIPS [Treasury Inflation Protected Securities] soaring).

Oil Contagion and the International Scene

What about the dollar in a global recession? It will likely fall against several key currencies, but then rebound. The notion that foreign currencies can decouple and not suffer major price declines is false. When the United States runs off the track, you can be sure foreign nations will also run off the track. When the largest national economy in the world falters, the rest of the world will falter as well. That's the elementary economics of contagion on an international scale.

Oil Subsidies Backfire to Push Oil Prices Higher[27]

Governments in Mexico, China, India, Indonesia, and in other desperate countries heavily subsidize energy industries so they can sell their commodities at artificially low prices relative to the actual market price. Their intentions are good (i.e., affordable energy for their people) but the result is often to ignite a self-generating upward spiral in oil and gas prices. What do I mean by spiral? Well, soaring oil prices can bring with them protests and riots, which encourage governments to subsidize oil and gas, which increases even more the demand for oil and gas, which raises energy prices even higher, which fosters more rioting and violence, which encourages. . . . The oil company British Petroleum (BP), viewed as reliable for its statistical and economic analysis of energy markets, estimates that, "countries with subsidies accounted for ninety-six percent of the world's oil use last year (2007)—growth that has helped drive [energy] prices to record levels."

In a statistical chart, BP concludes: "Fuel consumption has grown more in countries that subsidize it than those that tax it." The chart showed that the change for fuel consumption in 2007 was six hundred and eight thousand barrels a day for countries with moderate fuel subsidies. Countries that taxed oil heavily cut fuel consumption absolutely by over two hundred thousand barrels a day.

I am no expert on oil, and I found some of the BP statistical work puzzling. Still, I would draw three important conclusions about sensible government policies on energy, regardless of whether or not the BP analysis is entirely valid. First, fuel subsidies play a big role in the overflowing coffers and profits of the oil oligopolists at the expense of oil consumers globally. Second, oil subsidies perpetuate the world's reliance on oil. Third, oil subsidies fuel further degradation, destruction, and toxic pollution that sicken and kill millions of people globally.

The third conclusion should be obvious. To help consumers and industries end their reliance on oil, governments should subsidize in other ways. They could subsidize companies that seek new technology and alternative fuels that do not pollute and kill. They could subsidize farmers and companies worldwide to develop new technology to multiply the productivity and output of farmers everywhere. Such actions could produce a bounty of good food even as farmers cut their dependence on oil.

Governments could subsidize a further exploration of space and our moon. Given the present continued destruction on Earth, maybe the

Moon could some day become a refuge for people to live and prosper. Who knows? In any case, we should not now or later subsidize the oil industry! As I have noted repeatedly, the most important task for government now is to ward off a major recession or worse. As with the Reconstruction Finance Corporation in the Depression, we must create jobs and incomes for the unemployed via major public works programs. The Treasury should award contracts to companies on a competitive bid basis, and the Federal Reserve should make certain that the work programs are fully funded. These programs could be intended to meet both immediate needs and to develop future projects that hold the promise of energy savings, alternative sources of energy, and creative resource development.

Federal Power and Will: Both Needed to Create Jobs

Together the Treasury and the Federal Reserve have the power to put people to work. All they lack is the will, a will destroyed by extreme right-wing ideological nonsense. After all, the United States enjoyed enormous success in conquering space in its journey to the Moon. We should surely be able to block destructive ideology and thereby put people back to work. A good first step in any successful funding of public works would be to terminate US military spending in the trillions of dollars for lost wars in Iraq and Afghanistan. Diplomacy must crowd out war and war spending if the United States is to succeed in warding off a devastating and sustained economic slump.

Headlines on Failed Catastrophic Forecasts[28]

Volatile times have also brought a flood of brash pronouncements as the cassandras of the financial set try to outdo themselves with increasingly outlandish predictions. Edward Yardeni, one of my favorite economists, said: "These are volatile times. There are a lot of moving parts here, and nobody can quite figure out how they all mesh. You're hearing a lot of catastrophic predictions." Yardeni is right. But I would add that Wall

Street is always glued to the positive side regardless of whether the outlook is dark or bright. Also, as spelled out briefly in the preface, Wall Street relies far too much on the coincident indicators such as gross domestic product, industrial production, and wholesale and retail sales. None are useful for gauging the future course of the economy. It's worth repeating that "rear-view mirror indicators" tell you where you have been, not where you are going. Relying on the rear-view mirror as a driver will soon find you in a crash. That simple analogy also applies to coincident indicators, the most popular but the most useless of economic forecasting tools.

Even more devastating for forecasters is their failure to rely on a wide range of forward indicators, especially the initial and lagging effects of monetary, fiscal, and international financial policies. Just a cursory glance of the chapters in this work should remind readers of the enormous importance of government policies. Incredibly, both the Treasury and the Federal Reserve seldom track the lagging results of their own failed policies.[29] Nor do they admit policy errors, even those that prove to be disastrous.

Pollution, Smog, and China's Olympic Games?[30]

Bogus predictions now show up as harsh reality in many nations. China, for example, frantically tried to clean up poisonous pollution, though for years it denied that pollution was even a problem. Like the United States, China often lies, which good photographs can confirm. The *New York Times* of July 29, 2008, for example, printed a front-page photograph of Beijing's central business district. It showed a frightening and choked up area mired in a dark gray haze of toxic smog.

China's own pollution readings exceeded safe levels shortly before the 2008 Olympics were scheduled to start. With the prospect of international embarrassment, Chinese officials considered even tougher measures. These included shutting more factories and banning as many as 90 percent of Beijing's private vehicles on especially bad days during the games. Would these desperate actions solve the problem of toxic smog that sickened and killed its people? No. At best, it might help a little for a short time. Still, the world would continue on the road to global warming.

Is It Soon Time for Gas Masks?

Currently, a unified effort by major nations, through international ecology summits and the like, to replace oil with safe energy sources looks unlikely, though many nations are looking at possibilities on their own. The most recent world summit in Copenhagen showed the fractured state of international commitment to improved emission standards. Meanwhile, strong air currents carry China's toxic smog across the Pacific Ocean to California. Is it almost time for people everywhere to get gas masks, especially for the elderly and little children?[31] Time marches on while nations remain frozen in apathy.

There surely is a triple threat currently confronting us: (1) global warming, (2) war, and (3) the increasing oil prices by the Military, Industrial, and Big-Oil Complex. I earlier cited the dire forecasts of global warming by the Military Advisory Board.[32] Yet another specialist is Thomas Homer-Dixon of the Trudeau Center for Peace and Conflict Studies at the University of Toronto. He fears that within our children's lifetimes, droughts, storms, and heat waves could rip societies apart.[33] Climate stress, he concludes, could be just as dangerous as the earlier arms race between the United States and the Soviet Union, or the current proliferation of nuclear weapons among rouge states.

Macho Mad Global Leaders with WMD

Rogue states are hardly our only risk. Huge challenges also rest with the great powers, including America, who have within their boundaries potential ascetics who would like nothing better than to go to war with weapons of mass destruction in the name of their respective causes. Ascetics at war? Yes. It's true that most people think of "hedonists," not ascetics, as the bad guys. That's no longer true. Extreme self-designated-do-good ascetics are far more dangerous. These are the inflamed politicians or religious leaders who claim falsely to help society. Enraged political or religious ascetics willing to go to war using lethal weapons declare that they will fight as "heroes" to their deaths (and ours) for their country, their political convictions, or their special god.

Many highly educated ascetics will sacrifice their lives for their special beliefs. In contrast, a hedonist would not likely sacrifice anything that would get in the way of his or her own pleasure and health. So who is the more dangerous, the hedonist or the extreme ascetic? Anger- and hate-gorged political or religious ascetics armed with massively destructive weaponry are the most dangerous humans on Earth. They pose a huge risk to all humankind.

We will try to show why this is the case in the next chapter. My goal is to find ways to persuade humanity to destroy these weapons and work for peace and happiness for all people. I have no assurance that anything I might propose can help. But I will make clear that the same fears I hold are shared by many of the world's best scholars.

Chapter 9

THE DANGERS OF GLOBAL ASCETICS AT WAR WITH WMD

Some say the world will end in fire,
Some say in ice.
From what I've tasted of desire
I hold with those who favor fire.
But if it had to perish twice,
I think I know enough of hate
To say that for destruction ice
Is also great
And would suffice.

—Robert Frost, "Fire and Ice,"
Harper's magazine, December 1920

Who knows how the world will end. Will it be by fire? Many scientists appear to agree with Frost. They predict that, billions of years from now, our sun will die. As our solar system's sun approaches its own death, it will swell immensely to send scorching heat rays to Earth. Then our world and all its inhabitants will presumably be blown to bits in a big fireball. In that scenario our relatively small solar system within our vast galaxy would end quite abruptly, very much the way the much larger universe began—with a big bang. I doubt, however, that the poet T. S. Eliot would buy the death-by-fire thesis. In his poem, "The Hollow Men,"[1] he foresees our world ending "Not with a bang but a whimper."

Are there other final endings possible for our planet, our solar system, our universe? Of course: What if an extra-large asteroid smashed into the

227

Earth? That would probably suffice to obliterate our planet. What if mad and enraged ascetics, armed with weapons of mass destruction, seek to obliterate their enemies or attempt to convert others to their specific views or beliefs by unleashing a global nuclear war? That could certainly end our world as we know it.

Crazed Warring Ascetics

Not unlike the war dogs of chapter 2, mad ascetics pose some of the very highest risks to humankind here and now, not millions of years from now. The fallacy of composition tells us that. It warns that the mix of hate, rage, anthrax, the proliferation of massively destructive weaponry, and highly motivated ascetics would suffice to end our world. Bertrand Russell has told us this. As I noted in chapter 2, Russell said many years ago that nations could fatally stumble into a global nuclear war through "accident, miscalculation, or design."

Many world-renowned physical and social scientists and other scholars warn that if these destructive weapons are not eliminated or their numbers at least significantly reduced, a terrorist act or a rogue state could start a chain of events that might well result in humankind as we know it disappearing in the present century. As I'll shortly document, angry political and religious zealots now have access to the doomsday weapons to blow up themselves and everything else on Earth in the twinkling of an eye. I'll focus first on the scholars and other notables who speak of the huge risks of a global nuclear war. I tried to pick the best of them, whether still living or long since dead. Here are some of their statements that can serve as a preview to this chapter.

> **Dr. Stephen Hawking** warns that a nuclear war could end all life on Earth. He says that humanity's ultimate survival depends on colonizing the solar system and beyond.[2]

> **Dr. Martin Rees** in *Our Final Hour* says humans have no more than a fifty percent chance of surviving until the year 2100.[3]

Robert Frost declares that widespread hate could destroy the world.[4] Yes, hate plus chemical, nuclear, and biological bombs dropped from the sky could destroy all of us.

Milan Kundera in his *Art of the Novel* says there is no escape for anybody in a global war using weapons of mass destruction such as nuclear or biological bombs.[5]

Edgar Allan Poe in his *Masque of the Red Death* says that walls can't keep out mass death.[6] Poe added that reality and truth will, sooner or later, break through any strong lockbox, safe, wall, fence, or even a heavily defended grand castle. Remember his Prince Prospero?

Sir William Gilbert writes of how angry liberals and conservatives can spark wars.[7]

The fourteen apostles of science and truth, who were discussed in chapter 3, counsel us on the horrors of political or religious superstition, torture, brutality, genocide, marauding crusades, and global nuclear war. I have already expanded on the thinking of these celebrated figures in imagined discussions.

The Parallel of Sick Rats and Crazed Humans

Sick rats act like war-crazed humans. Let me explain. Long ago in the fourteenth century the deadly bubonic plague struck China. Some people called it the Black Death. The plague turned its victims' skin red first, and then black. Edgar Allan Poe called it the Red Death because of the profuse bleeding that quickly killed.[8] Fleas would bite diseased rats piled high in the streets, in garbage cans, and in offices and homes. The fleas then bit people to spread the contagion. The Black Death spread quickly by merchant ships and other means to other countries and to millions of people. In just five years this bubonic plague killed one third of Europe's population, roughly twenty-five million people. The novelist Albert Camus also wrote of dead rats and humans in his work *The Plague*.[9] The rats, Camus wrote, ran into the streets to die in batches, blood spurting from their mouths onto humans who also lay in the streets. Frantic rats ran up stairways to the attics. Rats ran and died everywhere.

Rats and humans were both victims of the Black Plague. Today, we have a new plague, one that threatens to wipe out the entire human population. It comes to us in the form of war dogs, terrorists, and ascetics, many of whom are fully armed with destructive weapons and more than willing to use them to achieve their ends. Today, faced with the lethal potential of these groups, humanity faces a horror far greater than any plague. Global nuclear war could forever wipe out life on the planet.

The world now faces many terrors. Global warming is one, while the sinister actions of the Military, Industrial, and Big-Oil Complex is yet another. The risk of accelerating wars with chemical, biological, and nuclear weapons is still another. Like rats, we humans carry around with us the possibility of creating our own black plague. Daily headlines scream of wars, genocide, suicide bombings, and massive death.

Good and Bad Ascetics

I noted earlier in chapter 2 the risks of warring ascetics. Some people still tell me that ascetics are supposed to be good people who deny themselves many of the things that make the rest of us happy because they are devoted to their respective causes or religious beliefs. Well, that proposition is sometimes correct; but all too often it is wrong—dead wrong. Let's start with the good ascetics. Any dictionary tells us that ascetics are those who practice self-denial as a form of personal discipline. For example, hermits, monks, and nuns are viewed as ascetics. They are usually stern and simple in appearance, manner, and dress. Some avoid the normal pleasures of life such as fine food, marriage or having a family, or recreational outings. Extreme but deeply religious ascetics may humiliate or injure themselves on purpose to demonstrate faith to their special god. As a rule, ascetics don't seek to have beautiful clothes, expensive cars, and mansions. They may trade bliss and pleasure on Earth for a perceived paradise in what they believe to be a life after death.

Who are the bad ascetics? These are the self-declared asocial types who are so often engorged with such hate and rage that they will sacrifice their own lives (and the lives of as many others as possible) for their beliefs. Some commit suicide with bombs strapped to their bodies to deliberately kill those they perceive as their enemies. Others set off roadside bombs that kill or cripple hundreds of innocent people who are shopping for food, or who just happen to be passing by.

The Greater Risk: The Hedonist or the Self-Appointed Ascetic?

I worry far more about self-styled ascetics than hedonists. A hedonist would not likely set off a bomb that he new would kill others and himself. The reason being that the hedonist, by definition, is a pleasure-seeking person. He looks to maximize happiness and health. Since one of the greatest pleasures is life itself, the hedonist would seek to preserve his own life, which rules out being a martyr. Thus, being an advocate of self-preservation, he has no interest in taking any personal risk with guns, bombs, or other lethal agents.

In contrast to our hedonist, extreme ascetics willingly forfeit their lives as suicide bombers. They consider themselves valiant do-gooders for society. That's why extreme ascetics, armed with WMD, present a huge threat to human survival everywhere. Death at the hands of ascetics is already well underway globally. Human madness coupled with popular apathy is mainly responsible for the perils of global warming and the fighting and killing sparked by the military, industrial, and big-oil oligopolists. These forces multiply the threat to human survival.

As just noted, huge risks to humankind cannot be explained solely by selfish human beings—overzealous, avaricious, laissez faire, no holds barred types, on the one hand, and single-minded, overzealous, ultra-believer ascetics, on the other. No, the problem stems mainly from the apathetic masses, the I-don't-want-to-get-involved crowd. To repeat, we waste time in trying to determine how selfish or unselfish humans are. David Hume has a useful point to make about the conflicting forces governing human beings:

> We're not even close to calculating the proportions of the dove in man versus the wolf and serpent in him. That's a sterile exercise.[10]

Suicide Bombings: The Quintessence of Evil

Far more dangerous than the hedonist is the fired-up ascetic who is willing to kill himself and many of us in the furtherance of his beliefs. Moreover, suicide attacks are one of the worst of cruel behaviors because many innocent adults and children are also killed or maimed for life.

No reputable scholar would assert that any god is on the side of suicide terrorists, or on your side, or on my side. God, however one interprets that term, does not take sides. To say that God takes sides, whether on economic, political, or religious grounds, is one of the most dimwitted and terrifying superstitions humans have ever held. I learned from serious students of human nature, whether scientists or poets, to fear the ravings of ascetic heroes, whether on the economic left or right, whether from the liberal or the conservative camp. Listen to Sir William Gilbert's view on the constant struggle between liberals and conservatives:

> I often think it's *comical* how nature always does contrive.
> That every boy and every gal that's born into this world alive,
> Is either a little liberal, or else a little conservative.[11]

Comical? I am not amused but instead frightened by warring ascetics, whether on the political left or right, liberal or conservative. We have seen how ultraconservative Republicans are now consumed with hate and rage against liberals. Extreme ascetics demean science and truth. Angry ascetics with "noble causes" and nuclear bombs can kill all of us. My fear is that warring ascetics could annihilate themselves and all of humanity over some superstition-laden dispute. True, risks abound in the struggles of hedonist versus hedonist, or hedonist versus ascetic. But the greatest peril comes from warring ascetics. They are the ones who would risk human extinction, political institutions, even such a revered social and economic foundation as capitalism itself, to advance a political ideology, avenge some slight to their territorial integrity, settle a matter of doctrine among factions of their own faith, or achieve some reward in the afterlife promised by their one-and-only god.

The Awesome Horrors of a Global Nuclear War[12]

To allude to the horrors of nuclear war is not enough. I decided, therefore, to set forth the frightening words of famed experts on the hideous damage and death of a nuclear war. I caution readers that the quotes I have chosen are terrifying. Still, maybe they can help to prod nations, including the United States, to rid themselves of their nuclear arsenals. See especially quotes (9) and (10) on Japan's calm reaction to America's horrifying nuclear bombardment of Hiroshima and Nagasaki.

1) "If the radiance of a thousand suns were to burst forth at once in the sky, that would be like the splendor of the Mighty One. . . . I am become Death, the shatterer of worlds." *Bhavagavad Gita, the sacred Hindu epic recalled by J. Robert Oppenheimer while viewing the first nuclear explosion at Alamogordo, New Mexico, July 16, 1945.*

2) "We can sum it up in one sentence: Our technical civilization has just reached its greatest level of savagery. We will have to choose . . . between collective suicide and the intelligent use of our scientific conquests. . . . Before the terrifying prospects now available to mankind, we see even more clearly that peace is the only goal worth struggling for. This is . . . a demand to be made by

all peoples to their governments—a demand to choose definitively between hell and reason." *Albert Camus, in the newspaper* Combat, *August 8, 1945.*

3) "We are here to make a choice between the quick and the dead. That is our business. Behind the black portent of the new atomic age lies a hope which can work out to our salvation. If we fail, then we have damned every man to be the slave to fear. Let us not deceive ourselves: we must elect world peace or world destruction." *Bernard Baruch, Speech to the UN General Assembly, 1952.*

4) "There are plenty of problems in the world, many of them inter-connected. But there is no problem which compares with this central, universal problem of saving the human race from extinction." *John Foster Dulles, Speech to the UN General Assembly, 1952.*

5) "The survivors would envy the dead." *Nikita Khrushchev on the likely result of a nuclear war,* Pravda, *July 20, 1963.*

6) "A full-scale nuclear exchange lasting less than 60 minutes . . . could wipe out more than 300 million Americans, Europeans, and Russians as well as untold numbers elsewhere. The survivors . . . would inherit a world so devastated by explosions and poison and fire that today we cannot conceive of its horrors." *President John F. Kennedy, address to the nation on the Nuclear Test Ban Treaty, July 26, 1963.*

7) "In an all-out nuclear war, more destructive power than in all of World War II would be unleashed every second during the long afternoon it would take for all the missiles and bombs to fall. More people would be killed in the first few hours than all the wars of history put together. The survivors, if any, would live in despair amid the poisoned ruins of a civilization that had committed suicide." *President Jimmy Carter, Farewell Address to the American People, January 14, 1981.*

8) "From now on it is only through a conscious choice and through deliberate policy that humanity can survive." *Pope John Paul II, Address in Hiroshima, 1981.*

9) "Humankind continues to face the threat of nuclear annihilation. Today's hesitation leads to tomorrow's destruction. The fates of all of us are bound together here on Earth. There can be no survival for anyone without peaceful coexistence for all." *Takashi Araki, Mayor of Hiroshima, August 6, 1995.*

10) "The human race cannot coexist with nuclear weapons." *Iccho Itoh, Mayor of Nagasaki, Nagasaki Peace Declaration, August 9, 1995.*

The Many Facets of Terrorism and Mass Death

I investigated countless books, the media, and the Internet to find how many ways civilization could commit grand suicide. There are literally dozens of ways to kill the civilized and the uncivilized alike. I tracked many of the worst ones in earlier chapters. In the next chapter I'll set forth ways that we may help to block cataclysmic evils.

Cataclysmic. Catastrophic. Call it what you will, I focus in this chapter on identifying three deadly forces demanding attention here and now. They are threats of (1) the multiple and simultaneous bioterrorism attacks on major cities and rural areas that could kill millions of people, (2) the militarization of space that could destroy our small planetary part of the heavens, and (3) the global nuclear wars that could destroy everything. Neither the United States nor any other nation can protect itself from these three horrors. I have repeatedly said that the reason lies in the fallacy of composition. No matter what kind of offensive or defensive systems a nation builds, whether in space or on Earth, no one can be sure that others will not do the same and with even more firepower. First one nation declares that it must develop and possess such weaponry for its own defense. But what is seen as a defensive measure by one country is viewed by others as a means to undermine the defenses of all nations. What is mistakenly taken as truth for one is shattered when it is falsely applied to all. The race to own weapons of mass destruction begets proliferation of WMD to put all at risk of attack and war.

If Bertrand Russell were alive today, I believe he would say that the three deadly forces I list complement the three quite different risks he outlined: "accident, miscalculation, or design." Yes, bioterrorist military attacks, star-war-style conflicts in space, or global nuclear war could devastate our little part of the universe through our own accidents, miscalculations, or deliberate design.

I have already documented the unspeakable horror of nuclear war. Let's turn next to the potential cataclysmic destruction of bioterrorist attacks on major cities, and then to the destructive wars in space with the most ghastly WMD ever created by bellicose humans.

Anthrax, Biodefense Scientists, and Bioterrorist Attacks[13]

Many years have passed since I first wrote of anthrax sent through the mail designed to kill the recipients. The anthrax attacks took place in 2001, but it was during the publication of *Unlocking the Secrets of Wall Street* in 1998 that I first noted the dangers of anthrax.[14] In August 2008 anthrax again became headline news. Until the 2001 attacks, Dr. Bruce Ivins was "one of just a few dozen American bioterrorism researchers. He studied the most lethal biological pathogens in high-security military laboratories. But Dr. Ivins committed suicide after he learned that FBI investigators began to suspect him for the anthrax attacks."[15] Perhaps Dr. Ivins feared that he would be indicted for murder, but nobody is sure of that.

The problem this time seems to be in the sharp rise of bioterrorist research labs. Today there are hundreds of bioterrorist researchers in university laboratories and other research centers in the United States. This has reignited fears that the unprecedented expansion of biodefense research has made the country far less secure. The considerably larger number of places and people with access to dangerous germs, bacteria, and viruses is itself a form of proliferation. It signals a heightened risk that bioterrorist attacks will be undertaken, an exact parallel with nuclear warhead proliferation.

In the years since letters laced with anthrax were sent to members of the Congress and news organizations in late 2001, killing five people, the federal government has spent some $50 billion to build new laboratories to develop vaccines and drugs to deal with any future cases of anthrax attacks. At the same time, the FBI has long speculated over the motives for the attacks. News investigators Eric Lipton and Scott Shane of the *New York Times* conclude that, "the motive for the attacks, if carried out by a biodefense insider like Dr. Ivins, might have been to draw public attention to a dire threat, thus attracting money and prestige to a once-obscure field."[16] If that was in fact the motive, say Lipton and Shane, it succeeded.

That may well be, but nobody is sure about the motive. One thing is certain: we will never learn what happened from the deceased Dr. Ivins's own lips. Nevertheless, investigators are still combing through computer, e-mails, letters, and phone calls to uncover his behavior and plans. Modern technology means the truth can break out into the open for anyone suspected of a crime, even those who are now deceased.

Bad News: Identifying Pathogens and Treating Poisoned People

The problems in detecting and confirming pathogens are many, and often intractable. For example, the BioWatch System tracks and ideally identifies poisons that can kill or injure millions of people. According to BWS, it takes up to thirty-four hours to detect and then to confirm a pathogen. Other experts say that the nation's ability to detect biological weapons is still inadequate in most locales, as is its ability to distribute drugs to the population once the lethal agents have been identified. Hospitals warn that the volume of casualties from an attack would overwhelm their facilities. Millions would die.[17] As I write this I also hear ear-splitting sirens as a test for a nuclear plant in Westchester, New York. Now the sirens are quiet. It seems no leaking poison gas was detected, at least for today. But it's tomorrow that I worry about, all the tomorrows.

The US Government's Mad Scientist Theory

Most disturbing but always suspected, the Bush administration may have suppressed or twisted the truth. Apparently, all we really know about the case against Dr. Ivins has been leaked by the Justice Department. That's not unusual. This is the way the department has behaved for the whole of the Bush presidency. Much of what was previously leaked turned out to be false.[18] For example, in June 2008, the Justice Department agreed to pay $5.8 million to scientist, Steven Hatfill who worked for the federal government. The payment was for wrongfully charging him as an anthrax suspect and for pursuing him literally everywhere for years.

Dr. Ivin's attorney says Ivins was innocent, and blames his client's suicide on the government's relentless pursuit. It cost Ivins his lab access and he felt besieged. Other anthrax experts—notably former biodefense official and UN inspector Richard Spertzel, who knew Ivins—also doubted that Ivins could have been able to turn laboratory anthrax into the small spores that proved so deadly.[19]

Further, the two defenders of Dr. Ivins dismissed information leaked by the government that he might have had a financial interest. Dr. Ivins had two patents that might have earned royalties from the development of an anthrax vaccine to save lives. In short, the FBI may have invested its credibility in promoting the mad scientist theory to fit what it knew about Dr. Ivins.

A *New York Times* editorial concluded that then FBI Director Robert Mueller should have reassured Americans that his agents wouldn't target another innocent man because he fit an FBI psychological profile. Further, the editorial insisted that Congress hold hearings to explore how the FBI pursued the case from the very beginning. It said that the FBI cannot be allowed to close the case and declare victory. It also asked why it took the FBI seven years to supposedly "solve" this case.

The Great Unsolved Mystery of Dr. Ivins

Not many people believe that the Ivins case is solved. The *New York Times* and the *Wall Street Journal* posted front-page headlines on new developments in the case. Both painted chilling portraits of Dr. Ivins, but in the same articles they make clear that many experts think Ivins is innocent.[20] Who knows? Maybe we should get an independent investigator on the case. How can one have any confidence now in the FBI or the Justice Department? For the eight years of the Bush administration these bumblers and fumblers have lied and deceived. Predictably, their credibility has evaporated to match the low esteem of their commander-in-chief. But there is nothing new in the current failures of government. History makes that clear with the many and repeated first-strike wars unleashed by the United States against many other countries, as I noted in the preface.

A Brief History of US Military Violence[21]

In preparing documentation for this work I spent long hours reading and studying *A People's History of the United States* by the renowned historian and social activist Dr. Howard Zinn. Here are a few valuable quotes and my comments from his work:

> Would the behavior of the United States during war, in military action abroad, and in treatment of minorities at home . . . respect the rights of ordinary people everywhere to life, liberty, and the pursuit of happiness? [Can] the United States [honestly] step forward as a defender of helpless countries to match its image in American high school textbooks? Would its policies at home and overseas exemplify the values for which the war was supposed to have been fought?

> The United States opposed the Haitian revolution for independence from France at the start of the nineteenth century; instigated a war with Mexico and took half of the country; pretended to help Cuba win freedom from Spain and then planted itself in Cuba with a military base, investments, and rights of intervention; seized Hawaii, Puerto Rico, and Guam; fought a brutal war to subjugate the Filipinos; "opened" Japan to trade with gunboats and

threats; declared an Open Door Policy in China to insure that the United States would have imperial powers to exploit China; sent troops to Peking to . . . assert Western supremacy in China and kept them there for thirty years; insisted under the Monroe Doctrine and U.S. intervention on a Closed Door in Latin America— that is, closed to everyone but the United States; engineered a revolution against Columbia; created the independent state of Panama in order to build and control the canal.

It sent five thousand U.S. marines to Nicaragua in 1926 to counter a revolution and kept them there for seven years; intervened in the Dominican Republic for the fourth time in 1916, and kept troops there for eight years; and intervened time and time again in Haiti, Cuba, Panama, Guatemala, and Honduras. By 1924 the finances of half of the twenty Latin American states were [largely] under U.S. control. By 1935 over half of U.S. steel and cotton exports were sold in Latin America.

Whether you agree or not with all that Dr. Zinn says, you must admit that he is determined to be thorough in his accounting of the US attacks on and occupation of foreign nations. But these brief excerpts do not include his detailed study of America's lying and bullying in the Vietnam War; the Gulf of Tonkin fake reports that precipitated war with North Vietnam; and the cruelty, brutality, and enslavement of America's Indians, among other foul US acts. As brutal as this US history is, the present status of the United States is far worse. I have in mind the risk of nuclear war sparked by US arrogance and power.

Other US Armed Attacks Overseas

In 1962 Secretary of State Dean Rusk testified before a Senate committee on "Instances of the Use of United States Armed Forces 1798-1945" in which he cited 103 US interventions that took place in other countries during this period.[22] Here are excerpts and my comments with the "exact" descriptions given by the State Department:

✓ 1852-1853 Argentina: marines landed and stayed in Buenos Aires to protect American interests during a revolution.

✓ 1853 Nicaragua: to protect American lives and interests during political disturbances.

✓ 1853-1854 Japan: the opening of Japan and the Perry Expedition. [The State Department does not give more details but this involved the use of US warships to force Japan to open its port to the United States.]

✓ 1853-1854 Ryuku and Bonin Islands: Commodore Perry, on three visits before going to Japan and while waiting for a reply from Japan, made a naval demonstration, landing marines, and secured a coal concession from the ruler of Naba in Okinawa. He also demonstrated in the Bonin Islands, all to secure facilities for commerce.

✓ 1854 Nicaragua: San Juan del Norte (Georgetown) was destroyed to avenge an insult to the American minister to Nicaragua.

✓ 1855 Uruguay: US and European naval forces landed to protect American interests during an attempted revolution in Montevideo.

✓ 1859 China: for the protection of American interests in Shanghai.

✓ 1860 Angola, Portuguese West Africa: to protect American lives and property at Kissembo when the natives became troublesome.

✓ 1893 Hawaii: ostensibly to protect American lives and property; actually to promote a provisional government under Sanford B. Dole. This action was disavowed by the United States.

✓ 1894 Nicaragua: to protect American interests at Bluefields in a revolution.

Again and again, these statements call for protecting American lives and "interests." Even a quick study of this euphemistic language shows one how to hide cruelty within the guise of jargon. Replace the word "interests" with "plunder" to get an "exact" reading. We turn now to far greater dangers than conventional ground wars. Here I mean suicidal wars in space with weapons of mass destruction. I can't imagine any peril more deadly than global space wars in which the combatants are armed with WMD.

Dangerous Driving in the Heavens[23]

This caption is the title of a most fascinating but sad period in human history. The *Economist* in an unsigned article makes the point that humankind has invented sensible rules at sea and in the air to avoid accidents. But in space a free-for-all prevails. On a bad day it looks more like road rage in space, the article concludes. Relevant here, America fumed when China tested a missile by shooting down one of its own satellites. One thing that made the test look dangerous is that it created the worst-ever cloud of man-made debris in the sky. At orbital speeds space satellites colliding with an object the size of a pebble can destroy a multibillion-dollar media signal relay device or some military spy hardware.

By using a missile to blow apart one of its own satellites, China demonstrated that it had the power to destroy the spy and navigation satellites on which America's armed forces depend. Of course, those who drive cars and trucks on Earth would also face great loss. They would no longer be able to use their global positioning systems (GPS) once American satellites are hit and destroyed.

The clear dangers of a clash in space and the extent to which military and civilian uses of space have joined are not open to question. So, why have the major powers so far failed to negotiate either arms-control agreements or even simple rules to manage satellites in space, as they have with maritime laws and air space regulations here on Earth? Russia and China have agreed to negotiate a treaty banning space weapons, but America still says no. America obfuscates, procrastinates, and sets forth arguments that are senseless and bound to backfire. As we have seen with other situations, whether it be earthbound nuclear, conventional, or biological weapons systems, any such weapons a nation might decide to put into space will immediately be viewed as a threat to its neighbors, who will feel obliged to do likewise, which raises the ugly specter of proliferation and exacerbates international tensions.

About the strangest argument put forth by the government is one that relates to definition. The American government has said that it cannot even define what a space weapon is. In fact, though, this claim is a ruse to justify the development of an antimissile system in space and on the ground—what has long been called the Strategic Defense Initiative (SDI) since the Reagan days. This is hardly new. Obstruction, hollow talk, and treaty breaking are all old news for those who observe American policy. Our government's refusal even to begin talks on banning space weapons is a surefire way to speed up the race for them. The *Economist* writes that America is "unduly rigid," but the phrase is a weak euphemism for doing nothing. In reality, US actions strike me more as a cesspool of arrogance and dishonesty that speeds the potential for terrible warfare in space. It is a bad mistake for anyone to take lightly the risk of extraterrestrial warfare, including highly respected publications like the *Economist*.

Earth-Shattering Space Warfare:
Causes and Effects

Any minor incident can trigger a war in space through miscalculation, accident, or design. That would include retaliation for a believable but entirely false official alert that nuclear missiles will hit New York City in a matter of minutes. A deranged government official could well be the one who might issue any such alert. In any case, it would be too late for any protection. Further, if such an incident occurred, retaliation by the party attacked would likely beget a counterattack, thus beginning a full-scale nuclear conflagration. The accidental firing by India of a nuclear projectile that subsequently destroys an alleged Pakistani missile instillation in the Kashmir region could easily provoke instant retaliation. A deliberate US preemptive military attack on Iran's nuclear facilities could quickly ignite a nuclear war. One need only look to Israel's 2007 air strike on a suspected Syrian nuclear missile site for proof that such a possibility remains a major concern.[24]

I have no faith that White House administrations like that of former President Bush or the Pentagon under such administrations would refrain from future preemptive attacks. White House talk and promises lost their credibility under Bush. President Obama has already stated that the

United States and Russia have agreed to cut their arsenals of nuclear weapons to set an example for other countries. This proposal is already under attack by Republicans. The point is that the world still fears the United States but no longer trusts America's leaders.

What would then be the likely effects of a nuclear attack on the United States? First, invading missiles might well target US space-based communications and offensive/defensive weapons-related satellites. These antisatellite weapons would instantly paralyze American troops, ships, and planes across the world since contact among military forces would be interrupted or destroyed. Space itself would be polluted with debris for decades, and made unusable for future satellites, assuming that there is a civilization left to create and deploy them. The global economic system would collapse, including air travel and the ability to send messages to reach others in desperate need.

What about cell phones and the latest GPS navigation systems installed in your car? They won't work either. If you can no longer reach your family or business, then you cannot help them. What about the US military might? It would most likely prove to be impotent: a communications apparatus that cannot contact its own troops would hardly be in a position to contact the enemy to negotiate an end to hostilities.

The end result of a nuclear war would be "tremendous," said Daryl Kimball, executive director of the Arms Control Association in Washington. The consequences of war in space are in fact so cataclysmic that arms control advocates like Mr. Kimball would like simply to prohibit the use of all weapons beyond the Earth's atmosphere.[25]

Yes, we should block war in space no matter what the provocation, but we have not done a thing. We have not even joined other nations to talk about solutions, even though the fallout itself from a nuclear exchange could quickly kill millions.

Too Late for Preventing Wars in Space?

The ironic tragedy is that what makes people insistent on banning the militarization of space is just what keeps the US military busy preparing for war. The Pentagon, the arms industry, and the oil industry must surely be celebrating together. Yes, many administrations have made sure that the Military, Industrial, and Big Oil Complex will now reap many more billions of dollars with the huge and extremely expensive plan to create the most powerful capacity anywhere to wage war in space, on the crazy logic that we need it for *defense*.

The logic is mad because it collapses for the group. We now witness the most deadly example in history of how the fallacy of composition can bring our universe to an inglorious end. Relevant here is the US rocket that crashed into an out-of-control US satellite over the Pacific Ocean. That accident led many officials and experts to give up their efforts to block space war lunacy. They say that the United States has already decided to build the capacity to wage war in space. Further, advocates of extraterrestrial war will insist that they need nuclear arms for defense. Such crazed logic signals disaster for all of us.

White House Opposition to Banning Space War

The Bush administration repeatedly opposed any treaty banning weapons in space. Mr. Bush's press secretary, Dana Perino, said it would be unenforceable. "Even a benign object put into orbit could become a weapon if it rammed another satellite."[26] How this argument could possibly negate the need for controls is beyond me. It sounds more like an argument for implementing controls to prevent debris and arms from cluttering up space.

In any case, US research moves forward on how to protect American satellites, and how to deny the use of space to other nations. The research includes, "work on lasers, and whiz-bang stuff like cylinders of hardened material that could be hurled down from space to targets on the ground. They are called 'Rods from God.'"[27] I always wondered when George Bush would once again insert God into his plans for space war. Now we know. Let's hope that President Obama will see war in space as just another foolish notion that would put all Americans at high risk. Perhaps one of Obama's decisions might be to replace any Bush cronies who favor "Rods from God." That would be glorious.

Mike Moore is the author of the book, *Twilight War: The Folly of U.S. Space Dominance*.[28] He argues that the space plan is "misguided." The belief that the United States can or should dominate space, he says, only prods others to respond the same way. Why trigger an arms race, he asks. I am glad that Mr. Moore agrees with me, but I have one suggestion for a change. Simply replace the word "misguided" with "mad" or "idiotic."

Evil Women in a Macho Male World

I have frequently used the term "macho man," often to refer to arrogant and cruel people. Still, I don't mean to imply that men are the only villains. Some women are also violent and murderous. Some kill their husbands or boyfriends. Others lie, steal, and poison their mates. Literature is replete with such evil women. Shakespeare's avenging murderess Lady Macbeth comes to mind. Evil women through the ages kill for money, jealousy, rage, position, or political and social power. Some turn into serial killers. Some kill their children. Some are as abusive as dictators. I could cite many other instances but women are not the world's worst villains. The worst are still the macho men.

Even so, women have made great strides. Until recently there was widespread speculation that the next US president would likely be a woman, namely, Hillary Clinton. She is now our secretary of state, a highly prestigious and potentially powerful post. So now we have a black man as president and a white woman as secretary of state. I look upon this magical duet as one of the most important and positive changes in a long time for America. But the change is only just starting.

For example, American women college graduates now exceed male college graduates. Many of our best colleges currently have a woman as president. Things look better for women even as the unbridled power of machos weakens. But better is not good enough. Women still have a long way to go before they can fully overcome the long and deadly road of macho domination and cruelty. And it is wonderful also to envisage just how a black president might work to improve the life and status of blacks everywhere. We have left the dark age of suppression of rights under George W. Bush.

Employing a broader perspective, I investigated long ago the bright side and the dark side of humankind.[29] On the bright side, I noted how classical economists viewed competitive markets as a powerful force in increasing the wealth of society. Later economists claimed they found freedom, progress, wealth, and equality in their models. Yes, but with machos in control of the planet, the dark side shows up time and time again. Macho bullies run mad over human rights. In other works I made note of a succession of crises and catastrophes that ran through two world wars, the Great Depression of the thirties, the recession on top of depression in 1937, ethnic and religious fighting, the Holocaust in Germany, sectarian and civil wars across the planet, and recurrent recessions. Poverty and joblessness now hit eastern Europe, Latin America, Africa, and the Middle East, as well as many other parts of the globe. Daily headlines on rape, murder, genocide, bombings, and war seem never-ending.

The Unity of Humankind

Widespread horror takes me now to the famed novelist Milan Kundera. He appears to have worried as much as I have over the threat of global destruction. In his work titled *The Art of the Novel*, Kundera says the risk of global destruction has unified humankind. He writes:

> The modern era has nurtured a dream in which mankind . . . would someday come together in unity and everlasting peace. Today the planet has finally become one indivisible whole, but it is war that embodies and guarantees this long-desired unity of mankind. Unity of mankind means: No escape for anyone anywhere.[30]

Kundera's outlook seems bleak with no escape for any of us. Still, I would put the risks a bit differently. First, guarantees don't exist in this world or in any after-death, imaginary world. It's true that people have carried signs for centuries warning, "The end is near." They were wrong and often dismissed as crackpots. How about today? Well, it's folly to dismiss the warnings of our best scientists, not in this brand new age of powerful lethal weapons.

We cannot know the exact probability that ascetics at war may destroy the human race.[31] I just don't know. Kundera doesn't know. Nobody knows. I fear, though, that what I dub the ascetic risk poses by far the greatest risk to humanity. The *Economist* worries that such a risk may lay in "the fundamental fear," in other words, war between Islam and the West. Maybe, but I count some seventy wars, revolutions, insurrections, and civil conflicts across the globe.[32] That's quite enough to frighten any probability theorist over the risk of war with weapons of mass destruction. I am far more frightened of warring ascetics than I am of killer asteroids or global warming, though any of these threats could smash the Earth and all of us with it.

A Seven-Point Plan to Regain Trust in America

I still can only guess what's going to happen in Iraq. It's always on my mind. All I am sure of is that the previous administration betrayed America and the world. It justified its unilateral first-strike military attack on Iraq on a pack of lies. Over five thousand US soldiers and many more thousands of Iraqi civilians now lie dead.

Now the deaths of American soldiers in Afghanistan number well over 1,100. In 2008 the *New York Times* posted small photographs of the 500 dead (at that point) that covered over two full pages.[33] How sad it was to look at each face one by one. June 2008 was the second deadliest month to date for the US military in Afghanistan since the war began in October 2001. In the face of an expanding threat from the Taliban the conflict became more violent for American troops, as deployment levels increased, and more troops were sent on President Obama's orders. Foreign nations and many Americans now question the integrity and honesty of the United States. So, what can America do to win back its lost trust? For a start, consider these eight suggestions:

1) Apologize to Iraq for our immoral and illegal military attack and occupation.

2) Declare that all American troops will return home from Iraq and Afghanistan in 2011.[34]

3) Create a new Marshall plan to rebuild Iraq with mainly American funding.

4) Provide jobs for the Iraqis in rebuilding everything from lost homes to factories.

5) Compensate Iraqi families for losses, including deaths from the US invasion.

6) Join an international program to reduce and destroy weapons of mass destruction wherever they exist.

7) Join international treaties to curb wars and fight poverty wherever they exist.

8) Make sure that any oil profits of Iraq are not stolen by occupying countries.[35]

Maybe these eight steps could help the United States to be a leader in a new and novel race for peace. Maybe then we could begin to erase the shame we have brought on ourselves internationally.

Chapter 10

CAN SCIENCE AND NEW LIBERAL LEADERS SAVE CAPITALISM?

The Huge Potential of Science for Bettering Humankind

In preparation for this chapter I studied more than some fifty breakthroughs in science, but I chose to review eight in depth because they bear directly on the future prospects for humankind in general and capitalism in particular. They include (1) how evolutionary science has finally destroyed the chief tenets of religious superstition called "creationism," (2) how humankind learned to regenerate perfect human body parts exactly like those original parts lost or diseased, (3) how nanotechnology is speeding human productivity and health, (4) how improvements in science can help us identify the wrong as well as the right ways to fight global warming, and (5) how the doping dilemma in sports and the "prisoner's dilemma game" can solve problems in economics and finance.

In addition, I tracked (6) "the rulers of light," which multiply the productivity and new technology of many scientists to create new products like atomic watches that we will someday wear and (7) why right-wing economists have no substance since they have not been supported theoretically and empirically over the centuries.

1) Evolutionary Science Destroys Creationism[1]

Let's address each of these breakthroughs individually starting with the nonsense of creationism. On this score we have good news. Science has identified one of the great falsehoods creationists publicize in their attack on evolution. The creationists shout constantly that nobody can see evolution in action here and now. On the macro level, this may indeed appear to be the case. But for many micro-organisms such a claim is obviously untrue. The evolution of relatively new viral diseases such as AIDS has brought with it antibiotic-resistant bacteria. Still, bacteria and viruses breed and mutate fast to adapt to their environments and thus survive, which is the point of evolution—those organisms that can adapt to new environments survive, those that can't will die out. This means natural selection can be seen within the span of a human lifetime, and it can show us the way to defeat bacteria and viruses that survive our attempts to eradicate them.

A startling example just showed up in a publication logically named *Evolution*. It is all about Horned Beetles and written by Indiana University scientists Harold Parzer and Armin Moczek on the *Onthophagus Taurus* (OT).[2] As you guessed correctly, OT is my nickname for the Horned Beetle. It is both hilarious and a major contribution to the science of evolution. The article clearly identified OT's primary and secondary sexual characteristics, namely, its penis and horns. The researchers' hypothesis was that the bigger the horns, the smaller the penis, and vice versa; and, as they predicted, the researchers found precisely this to be the case, with no exceptions.

An OT uses its horns to fight another OT over females. The OT that loses such a fight does not get to mate with its chosen females. On the other hand, if a particular male does get to mate, having big sexual organs would likely increase the chance that it will be his sperm rather than some other OT's that fertilize the female's eggs. The more fighting the OT has to do, the more strength its horns will require and the less strength will be left for his penis. Horn size determines penis size. Penis size then dictates the female's vagina size. These requirements stop cross breeding between groups and opens up the reproductive isolation that leads to the evolution of other species of OT. From the variations resulting in a single species, we now have 2,400 species, which is more than any other species in the animal kingdom. It is known (a) when these new populations were introduced and (b) that none is older than fifty years. Presto! Evolution has done its work for all to see, including religious creationists, within their normal lifetimes. The unsigned author of the OT article in the *Economist* writes that, "Darwin, no doubt, would have been delighted."

Darwin might well have been delighted but surely not surprised. He was fully aware of his own discovery, namely, the science of change and evolution in species over time via natural selection. Darwin's evolution will remain a final truth for all time. Religious creationism must be recognized as one of the most unenlightened and dangerous doctrines of all time because, if followed, it would undermine science rather than enhancing it, and that would be to the detriment of all of us.

I forecast that increased education and scientific awareness will spell the death of religious creationism in this century, but only under the premise that humankind does not first blow itself and the planet into tiny, blistered pieces. With that premise firmly in place let's now address several other remarkable scientific discoveries that could radically change humans from warring beasts to happy, productive, and peaceful beings. The first is progress in regenerating (re-growing) major body parts much like the salamander does.

2) Science Learns from the Salamanders[3]

The scientists Ken Muneoka, Manjong Han, and David M. Gardiner are part of a multidisciplinary research team funded by a multimillion-dollar research grant from the Defense Advanced Research Project and focused on human limb regeneration. Muneoka and Han are professors of cell and molecular biology at Tulane University, and Gardiner is a researcher in cell and molecular biology at the University of California, Irvine.

Let's explain briefly step-by-step what is involved. You may already know that a salamander's limbs are small and somewhat slimy. A loose arrangement of cells called fibroblasts holds all these internal tissues together, and gives the limb its shape. Yet a salamander's limb is unique in the world of vertebrates. It can regenerate a lost arm or leg over and over again, no matter how often the limb is amputated. "The salamander is the only vertebrate able to *re-grow complex but perfect replacement parts throughout its lifetime*" (emphasis added).

But how do salamanders pull off this great feat? As with humans, why doesn't the skin at the stump form a scar to seal off the wound? Human amputation leaves scars and blocks any regeneration. Again, how does the salamander do it? Let's follow this step-by-step with amputation of a leg. When a salamander's leg is amputated, blood vessels in the remaining stump contract quickly, bleeding is limited, and a layer of skin cells rapidly covers the surface of the amputation site. Next, in the first few days after amputation, the wound's epidermal area transforms into a layer of signaling cells that are indispensable for successful regeneration.

At the same time, tissue fibers break free from the connective tissue of the wound. These fibers move across the amputation surface to meet at the center of the wound. Finally, the fibers increase in number to form a clump of stem-like cells that serve as the beginning for the new limb.

In summary, the wound closure is followed by healing processes that guide the behavior of other cells and the movement of the tissue fibers and muscle cells toward the wound site, which results in the creation of a mass of cells that then take shape and emerge through lengthening and stretching into the regenerated limb.[4]

Potential for Limb Growth at Our Fingertips

I should make clear that the perfect re-growth of major limbs could be just a decade away. Imagine how important that could be for athletes, soldiers, or anyone else who loses their arms or legs or fingers. What we already know about limb re-growth is at our very fingertips, literally. The evidence is here that our fingertips already have an intrinsic ability to regenerate. This observation was first made in young children more than thirty years ago, but since then similar findings have been reported for teenagers and adults.

Fostering regeneration is apparently as simple as cleaning the wound and covering it with a dressing. If allowed to heal naturally, the fingertip restores its contour, fingerprint, and sensation, and undergoes varying degrees of lengthening. The success of this ultraconservative treatment of fingertip amputation has been documented in medical journals thousands of times. The alternative practice for such injuries typically includes operating to sew a skin flap over the amputation wound. But we now know that this alternative treatment will in fact inhibit regeneration even in the salamander. Why? Simply put, it blocks the formation of the wound epidermis, one of the steps we tracked.

The profound message in these scientific studies on regeneration is that human beings have inherent re-growth capabilities that, sadly, have been suppressed by our own traditional but now outdated medical practices. Of course, we cannot go around amputating human fingers to prove our case for human limb regeneration. But we do have a widely documented history of animals such as small mice and huge alligators that re-grow their tails.

Keep Listening to the Salamanders

To be sure, to re-grow an adult limb may take as long as it took the first time. But for salamanders, a poorly understood phenomenon known as "catch up" allows the regenerating limb to go through a phase of rapid growth with the limb appropriately scaled to the rest of the animal. Great! We still have a lot to learn from salamanders. We also have much to learn from the huge potential for human achievement already developed by physicists. They are nanotechnology and the miracle of graphene.

3) *Physics, Nanotechnology, and the Huge Potential of Graphene*

You have never heard of graphene? Well, every time you write with a lead pencil, the resulting script mark includes "bits of the hottest new material in physics and nanotechnology: graphene."[5] Graphene comes from graphite, just like the lead in a pencil. It is a kind of pure carbon formed from flat and stacked layers of atoms. Physicists have only recently isolated graphene, but its potential application for benefiting humankind is vast:

- ✓ The pure, flawless crystal of graphene conducts electricity faster at room temperature than any other material scientists know about.

- ✓ Engineers envision a range of products made from graphene such as ultra-high-speed transistors and films thin enough to be optically transparent.

- ✓ Physicists say graphene enables them to test exotic theories once thought to be observable only in black holes and high-energy particle accelerators.[6]

For many years, however, all attempts to make graphene ended in failure. One popular approach was to insert various molecules between the atomic planes of graphite to wedge the planes apart, a technique called chemical exfoliation. It didn't work. The final product emerged as an odd combination of graphite particles, much like wet soot. Later experimenters split graphene crystals into progressively thinner ones by scrubbing them against another surface.

The Nanopencil Invention

Scientist Philip Kim, working with Yuanbo Zhang of Columbia University, refined this scrubbing method called micromechanical cleavage. Together they invented a high-tech version of the pencil, a nanopencil. Writing with the nanopencil yielded slices of graphite just a bare fraction of an atomic layer thick. Still, the resulting material was ultrathin graphite, not graphene. Nobody expected that such a material could even exist in nature.

The experimental discovery of graphene led to a deluge of international research interest. Not only is graphene the thinnest of all possible materials, but it is also extremely strong and stiff. Moreover, as was noted above, graphene in its pure form conducts electrons at room temperature faster than any other material. Engineers at laboratories around the world are currently examining graphene to see if it can be fabricated into super-tough composites, incorporated into new displays, formulated into ultra-fast transistors, and new computer chips, among other products.

Perhaps most exciting, physicists can now investigate some of the most exotic forces in nature right in their own laboratories. Thanks to graphene, they can test in their own workshops the predictions of relativistic quantum mechanics. Up until now, such research was limited to astrophysicists and high-energy particle physicists working with multi-million-dollar telescopes or multibillion-dollar particle accelerators. No more.

You have only to imagine how graphene can speed new discoveries, inventions, economic productivity, and new and improved business and consumer products not only in the years ahead but far into the current millennium. Darwin would be thrilled by the huge potential graphene possesses for the future of humankind (just as he would be distressed by the turtle-like speed of our efforts to ban all weapons of mass destruction).

In chapter 7 we discussed the devastating effects of global warming and humankind's "carbon footprint." Our introduction to graphene now takes us logically (a) to a related update on the critical need for climate protection and (b) to my even more caustic critique of why so many proposals, including those of presidential contenders, backfire to speed the scorching of our Earth and to spew forth poisonous gases that sicken and kill people.

4) *"Keys to Climate Protection"*[7]

Jeffrey D. Sachs, director of the Earth Institute of Columbia University, writes, "Immediate commitment to nurturing new technologies is essential to averting disastrous global warming." Sachs adds, "Even with a cutback in wasteful energy spending, current technologies cannot support both a decline in carbon dioxide emissions and an expanding global economy." Then he proceeds to attack the suggestion of putting a price on carbon emissions through tradable permits or a carbon tax, or both, because he does not believe either of these will have enough of an effect to cut back on poisonous emissions. His list of negatives includes the following points that I have simplified a bit with straight prose. Brackets include my own words.

1) Europe's carbon trading system and carbon taxes have not shown much success in sparking rapid breakthrough technology for alternative and safe fuels.

2) A trading system will only marginally influence the choice between coal and gas plants or speed the development of solar and wind power [even as they enrich those who trade in them].

3) The much-touted and alternative low emissions technology of (a) carbon capture and sequestration (CCS), (b) plug-in hybrid automobiles, and (c) concentrated solar–thermal generation and transmission of electricity are extremely costly and troubling.

Extremely costly and troubling? Well, Sachs argues that a vast network of carbon dioxide pipelines to keep the lethal gas from escaping into the atmosphere would require major regulatory and policy support that would likely conflict with the property rights of those whose land the pipelines would traverse as well as environmental standards set by various layers of government. The ability to capture and hold carbon dioxide on a large scale must first be proved and then carefully monitored and environmentally regulated. Early experimental projects are likely to be far more costly than later ones. Moreover, government support will be crucial to success. In fact the government has failed to get even one CCS power plant off the ground.

Plug-In Electric Vehicles

You have probably read the hype on plug-in hybrid automobiles. On this point Sachs brings up questions about the safety, reliability, and durability of the batteries these vehicles would require and the need for extra investment in the world's electric power grids in an effort to support them. Solar thermal power, which uses concentrated solar radiation in desert locations to boil water for the steam turbine generation of electricity, also suffers when attempting to solve a host of production and delivery problems.

These scientific challenges include the nighttime storage of solar power, the regulatory and financial obstacles to installing new high-voltage transformers, and the direct current transmission facilities needed to carry power over long distances from the desert and other solar sources to those who need the power. Dr. Sachs sees many problems ahead. I do too. One is the drilling mania of politicians. Their proposals to drill, drill, drill to get oil is simply not a solution to the dangers of global warming. They quickly retreat from their loftier goals of developing safe and less costly alternative energy sources. President Obama said in a speech that drilling "is not a long run solution." Even in the short run, drilling for oil weakens the fight against global warming. Successful drilling and increased oil supplies leads to lower-cost fossil fuel prices and a misperception by the public that the need for energy alternatives is not urgent.

It is vital to emphasize over and over again that cutting oil consumption and fighting global warming demands that we tax heavily the use of oil and gas for both businesses and consumers. Why are not both Democrats and Republicans demanding in the strongest possible terms an early end to our wars in Iraq and Afghanistan? Why were the Democrat majority leaders in Congress doing so little to bring senior government and corporate executives to stand trial under oath? I have answered all three questions. My answers bear directly on why I forecast the coming demise of US capitalism. We have the power and resources to cure ugly capitalism, but we lack the resolve to do so. Is America unable to escape from its past? Is it trapped in a prison of its own making? As in the "prisoner's dilemma game," will America's leaders cooperate or betray our nation's great heritage?

5) Prisoner's Dilemma and the Doping Dilemma[8]

Doping is a terrible problem in sports and its history is a long one. For example, some athletes on the 1984 US Olympic team took drugs before their events. Many also injected themselves with extra blood before competing, either their own blood or that of someone else with the same blood type. "Blood Doping," as the practice is called, was not banned at the time. On a sliding moral scale doping, at that time, seemed only marginally different from training at high altitudes. Either way, the athletes increased the number of oxygen-carrying red blood cells in their bodies.

Many athletes felt they had no alternative to doping if they were to remain competitive. They had witnessed far too many competitors who had to drop out of events because they became physically exhausted, often suddenly, just before the end of an event. Indeed, an alarming number of sports—baseball, football, track and field, and especially cycling—have been shaken by doping scandals in recent years. Among the many banned drugs in cycling, the most effective is one called recombinant erythropoietin (r-EPO) that stimulates the production of red blood cells, thereby delivering more oxygen to the muscles.

Game Theory in Sports, Finance, Investment, and War

Game theory is the study of how players in a game setting choose strategies that will maximize their return (or profits in the case of capitalism) in anticipation of the strategies of the other players. Game theory is widespread in sports, poker, gambling of all sorts, and even deadly choices when people agonize over military decisions and national diplomatic strategies. What they all have in common is that each player's moves are analyzed according to the multiple options open to other competing players.

Classic Game Theory: The Prisoner's Dilemma

Ask yourself how the "Prisoner's Dilemma" may apply to the bungling, fumbling, and failures of major industries, huge corporations, consumers, and especially a US government's misguided choices that helped me to forecast dire results for finance and the economy in every chapter of this book. The concept of the Prisoner's Dilemma was originally framed by Merrill Flood and Melvin Dresher, both of whom worked at the Rand Corporation in 1950. Here is their classic example of the dilemma.[9]

Two suspects are arrested by the police. The police are aware that they have insufficient evidence for a conviction. They separate the two prisoners and question them individually, offering the same deal to each. If one turns the other in then the prisoner who talks will go free while the silent prisoner will get a stiff jail sentence. If both prisoners remain silent, both will be sentenced to only a short jail term. If each betrays the other, each receives a shorter sentence than would be the case if each had been silent while his fellow prisoner betrayed him. Each prisoner is assured that the other would not know about the betrayal before the end of the investigation. How should the prisoners act?

What was your answer? According to Flood and Dresher, the best thing both prisoners can do under the circumstances and to improve their situation is to betray their partner. It is believed that in the situation as described, betrayal is always better than risking silence and a much lengthier sentence. In repeated instances of the dilemma with the same players, soon they see that it is to their mutual advantage to cooperate and remain silent.

I sincerely believe that the scourge of doping can and should be eliminated. Would that not be a tremendously positive advance for sports in particular and humankind in general? One reason I took the time to set forth the prisoner's dilemma is to point out its potential positive applications in other fields. I'll return shortly to this theme. But first let's explore a beautiful scientific finding that meshes with the positive side of human evolution and happiness.

6) The Rulers of Light[10]

I mistakenly thought I knew a lot about light and laser beams. It turns out that another light has for many years caught the attention of scientists. It's a revolutionary kind of highly stable laser dubbed an "optical frequency comb." I leaned hard on three scientists to learn about this magic comb: John Hall, a Nobel Prize winner in physics, Steven Cuniff, and Jun Ye. All three are fellows at JILA, a joint institute between the National Institute of Standards and Technology and the University of Colorado at Boulder. The list of applications of comb technologies is considerable:

1) **Optical Atomic Clocks**: The most accurate and precise clocks ever made, optical atomic clocks, have already surpassed the microwave-based systems that have been the standard since 1957. Atomic clocks play a key role in space travel, communication among satellites, and in assuring accurate empirical findings.

2) **Chemical Sensors**: Researchers have demonstrated ultrasensitive chemical detectors based on optical combs. Comb-based sensors will let security screeners rapidly identify hazards such as explosives or dangerous pathogens (poisons). Doctors will diagnose illnesses by detecting chemicals in a patient's breath.

3) **Super Lasers:** With frequency combs, the outputs of many lasers can be stitched together to form a single stream of pulses whose light is organized ("coherent") as light from a single laser. Eventually, it should be possible to control the electromagnetic spectrum coherently from radio waves to x-rays.

4) **Telecommunications**: Optical combs will multiply the number of signals that can be sent down a single optical fiber (line), and require only one comb instead of many individual lasers. Interference between the channels will be reduced. Secure and confidential communications will benefit from the use of combs.

5) **Designer Chemistry**: Scientists are already investigating how to use the coherent light of lasers to control chemical reactions. Optical combs will make this technique more predictable and reliable and help in developing a new class of so-called ultracold chemical reactions. One day the combs will manipulate biological reactions, which are more complicated than other chemical reactions.

6) **Lidar**: The word stands for "laser radar" (light detection and ranging) to determine the position, velocity, and structure of distant objects. By generating wave forms with custom-designed shapes, optical frequency combs are expected to multiply many times lidar's sensitivity and range of view of far distant objects.

I forecast that within roughly ten years the demand for optical clocks and watches, as well as the many other benefits of optical combs, will soar. They will make you more productive but weaken any excuses for being late.

My attention now turns to a theme I stressed in every chapter: Why are unscientific assumptions in economic theory blocking efforts to solve key problems?

7) *The Right-Wing Economist Has No Clothes*

To pass off right-wing twisted ideology as science is both destructive and immoral. In this work, starting with the introduction, I have warned of the selfish and dishonest pitches of neoclassical economists. I also faulted the resuscitated classical economists, including former Federal Reserve Chairman Alan Greenspan and his successor, Benjamin Bernanke. Further, I cited the ultraright Supreme Court Chief Justice Roberts and a wide range of Republican executive robots who followed without question the malevolent orders of former President George W. Bush and former Vice-President Dick Cheney.

All are powerful but cruel titans of America. Many economists were also so far right of center that they were blinded by what really constitutes truth and science. As one critical and liberal economist put it, "The strategy the right-wing economists used was as simple as it was absurd."[11] What is not widely known is that many legendary economists such as William Stanley Jevons, Leon Walras, Maria Edgeworth, Vilfredo Pareto, Milton Friedman, Beryl Sprinkel, and most economists of the Chicago School are right-wing ideologists who pass off their ideology as science.

As I noted earlier, economist Raymond T. Bye constantly demanded that true economists had to leave politics and ethics out of their thinking. That was the equivalent of asking me to put truth and science last and religious superstition and myths first. Bye's dictate was the quintessence of absurdity for anyone seeking science and truth. That included me as a highly skeptical student at the Wharton School of Business working on his PhD. What exactly did these legendary economists do that reminds me now of the present-day supply-side theorists? They created "indifference curves." They derived demand and supply schedules from these curves and pretended to measure and even aggregate utilities that measured pleasure and disutilities measuring pain. They plotted demand and supply curves and insisted that they had transformed economics into a rigorous mathematical science.

Economist Robert Nadeau made a list of unscientific assumptions that had long been revered in neoclassical and classical economic theory. His point was to show how absurd these assumptions are in an international economy facing, for example, environmental problems. Here is his list that I have put in simpler prose with my comments in brackets.

- ✓ The market system is a closed circular flow between production and consumption for any nation, with no inlets or outlets. [This is absurd if one believes that most economies are international in nature and therefore frequently affect one another.]

- ✓ Natural resources [land, labor, and capital] exist in a domain that is separate and distinct from a closed market system, and the economic value of these resources is determined only by the dynamics within the system. [One need only look at major international commodity markets to see how bizarre this position is.]

- ✓ The costs of damage to the external natural environment by economic activities must be treated as costs that cannot be included in the pricing mechanism within the system. [Obviously those who believe this assumption have never heard of gasoline taxes, utility taxes, or toll roads.]

- ✓ The external resources of nature are largely inexhaustible. [What nonsense!]

Nonsense? Yes. In general, how does one explain the exceedingly poor record of economic forecasters, both in the United States and abroad? Two additional reasons bear on the thrust of this chapter. As was documented in chapter 4, the first reason is that forecasters fail utterly to focus on the right data. Most damaging to their abysmal performance, forecasters simply do not focus first and foremost on the leading indicators, especially the initial and lagging effects of monetary, fiscal, and international financial policies in forecasting major cyclical and secular swings and their easily predictable catastrophic results.[12]

Instead, most economists remain glued to the coincident indicators such as production, income, retail and wholesale revenue, and the quintessential but useless gross domestic product (GDP) for forecasting purposes. These "rear view coincidence indicators" cannot signal where the economy is heading but only where it has been. If you don't focus on the road ahead, you will surely crash. The mistaken emphasis on the coincident indicators explains why investors, economists, and monetary, fiscal, and international policy makers almost always fail to see bubbles until *after* they have burst or major recessions until *after* they have blown away jobs, incomes, savings, the financial markets, as well as millions of people's hopes and dreams.

The second reason that economic forecasters get it wrong so often is their use of defective theory. As I have just argued, throughout history right-wing, ultraconservative ideology has crowded out economic science. Except for David Ricardo, Thomas Malthus, and a few other classical theorists, rewards and costs of environmental problems were absent from classical analysis. Any limits to economic growth were seldom mentioned. Instead, except for Alfred Marshall, the classicists argued that it was impossible in a free market economy to suffer recession, and that any temporary slump would quickly generate the automatic forces for early and full recovery.

The resuscitated free market classicists did no better. They first showed up in the Reagan administration, which persuaded me in the 1980s to forecast the worst recession since the Great Depression. These same economists were back again with George W. Bush's administrations, which led me to forecast the collapse of the overinvestment boom, bursting stock gauges in 2002, the biggest housing bust in US history, and now a financial nightmare and high risk of a deep, deep recession that could easily surpass the 1981-82 slump that lasted sixteen dreadful months.

As a corollary, resuscitated classical theorists and ultraconservative

Republicans block efforts to fight climate change and other severe threats to our planet. When they are not destroying the economy and the Earth, Republican conservatives spend a lot of time ridiculing what they dub as the "liberal press."

Marvels of the Liberal Press in Exposing Abuse and Dishonesty

In fact, it is the liberal press more than anything else that exposed ultra-conservative corruption in financial markets, fake reasons for the military attack on Iraq, and lying about America's use of torture and illegal imprisonment. We should thank Alan Abelson of *Barron's*; Gretchen Morgenson, Paul Krugman, and Bob Herbert at the *New York Times*; David Francis of the *Christian Science Monitor*; and the investigative reporters (but not the editorial writers of the *Wall Street Journal*), among many others for publishing the truth about White House corruption, deception, and its constant attacks on science and truth.

Now is the time for liberals to shout out loud the severe and long-term damage Republicans have inflicted on Americans and the world. It is also the time for liberals to make clear that their philosophy of life and of human values is far superior to the ultraright Republican TV and Internet advertisements that ridicule liberals as unenlightened pussycats who are blind to the dangers of foreign enemies.

Blossoming Science in a Self-Destructive Economy

The several examples I cited of the spectacular and positive findings of science contrast sharply with the Bush administration's suppression and distortion of science and truth.

Yet science is resilient. It can move positively to promote change even in the least conducive environments. But to succeed we must first have the power and the resolve to block government and business policies that trample on justice, mercy, compassion, and economic and educational opportunity for all. America is still light years away from that far better world. With this fundamental caveat, consider these additional examples of how science may restructure capitalism for the better.[13]

> Liquid cooling could improve the performance of computers, allow waste to be recycled, and make solar cells more efficient. Generating electricity directly from wasted heat is becoming more practical for both vehicles and buildings. Image processing software may help to identify artists by their characteristic brush strokes to spot forgeries. Robots with visual systems that combine digital cameras with image-processing software allow them to plot their own course, to work out what they are looking for, and to decide what to do next. The robotic rovers sent to Mars did that. Look for them next in peoples' homes.
>
> There's much more. A new way of corralling cattle with satellite tracking and warning signals could rule out any need for fences or walls in favor of virtual fencing. Archaeologists now use free satellite imagery from Google to scan Earth to aid them in making discoveries, refine theories, and plan new research. In biomedicine, tiny nanotech medical robots could perform surgery inside patients with greater precision than current procedures provide. Advances in camouflage, concealment, and deception show attackers how to disappear, which could be good for honest governments but might well lead to more deception, lying, and preemptive military attacks by bellicose and dishonest governments.

The Liberal versus Conservative Creed

I earlier tracked the many preemptive US military attacks on other countries throughout our history, starting with the slaughter of American Indians and ending with the US attack and occupation of Iraq.[14] Pistol-toting Americans also have a culture all their own, which, as we have seen, can be quite murderous. I also quoted the liberal economist John

Maynard Keynes and Bob Herbert, a master writer of the *New York Times*. This is what Herbert said recently.[15]

> Ignorance must really be bliss. How else, over so many years, could the GOP get away with ridiculing all things liberal? Troglodytes on the right are no respecters of reality. They say the most absurd things and hardly anyone calls them on it. Evolution? Don't you believe it. Global warming? A figment of the imagination. Liberals have been so cowered by the pummeling they've taken from the right that they've tried to shed their own identity [by] calling themselves everything but liberal. Instead they present themselves as hyper-religious and lifelong lovers of rifles, handguns, or whatever.

The Liberal Creed

Bob Herbert further documents what liberals do, not what conservatives say they do. I became a liberal long ago in reaction to the superstition and discrimination I witnessed first hand against blacks and other minority groups in New Orleans and Virginia. I was not allowed to play with "the children who lived across the tracks." I did anyway and made great friends. Later, a Baptist minister in Virginia screamed at me, "You will blister forever in hell." Only eight years old, I never found out why the enraged preacher screamed or why he thought I would end up in hell. Still, to this day, that preacher's verbal outburst helped to sharpen my skeptical stance toward the bizarre and dangerous power of religious myth and superstition to block out justice, reason, and truth.[16] Herbert contends that we should judge people primarily by what they do, not what they say they do or by what others say they do.

Can we find love, compassion, and generosity in civil rights and women's rights? Liberals went to the mat for these movements time and again against ugly, vicious, and sometimes murderous opposition. The liberals gave us Social Security and unemployment insurance, both of which were in the original Social Security Act. Most conservatives despised the very idea of providing such assistance to struggling Americans. Republicans hated Social Security but most were afraid to give full throat to their opposition in public at the height of the Depression.

Liberals also gave us Medicare and Medicaid. Herbert asks, "How many of you or your loved ones are now benefitting mightily from these programs?" Republicans are proud of Ronald Reagan, who saw Medicare as "the advance wave of socialism." Reagan, according to Johnson biographer Robert Dallek, "predicted that Medicare would compel Americans to spend their sunset years telling their children what it was like in America when men were free. Under Reagan and later George W. Bush, I forecasted major recessions in both cases. Runaway and sustained tax cuts and explosive spending, I insisted, would fuel a giant overinvestment boom that would surely collapse, and bubble stock gauges that would surely burst.[17] We experienced all this plus a severe recession.

Liberals, including many Republicans who have mostly been drummed out of their party, ended legalized racial segregation and gender discrimination. Liberals gave America the children's Head Start program, legal services for the indigent, and the food stamps. They fought for cleaner air and cleaner water. There was a time when you could barely see Los Angeles through the air pollution and when some rivers in America actually caught fire because of the many chemicals that were dumped into our waterways. Liberals also fought to make food, clothing, toys, workplaces, and many other items safer.

Thanks to liberals the ability to go to college is manifestly easier. Thanks to the G.I. Bill of Rights, the federal government paid for my bachelor's degree in economics at Swarthmore College and my master's and PhD degrees in finance at the Wharton School. This book is largely the end product of a strong and sound liberal education.

It would take volumes, Herbert writes, to adequately cover the enhancements to the quality of American lives and the greatness of American society that have been wrought by people whose politics were unabashedly liberal. It is a record that deserves to be celebrated, not ridiculed or scorned. Herbert concludes, "Self-hatred is a terrible thing. Just ask that arch-conservative Clarence Thomas. Liberals need to get over it."

I repeat my conclusions of the March 18 and April 25, 2008 *Money and Capital Market* monitors: "The risk of recession soars. Recession could easily degenerate into deflation and depression. The slump will spread globally. The White House, the Fed, and the Treasury still have no policy in place to prevent an economic nightmare."

Chapter 11

SUMMARY AND DIRE CONCLUSIONS

*The world turns and the world changes, but one thing does not
change. . . . The Perpetual Struggle of Good and Evil.*

—T. S. Eliot
"The Rock" (1934)

Science does not accept final truths that are supposedly valid for all time. There are none. There are only claims that are warranted or stand true for a time until new evidence displaces them with new truths that hold for the time being. Maybe T. S. Eliot found an exception in the perpetual struggle between good and evil. Maybe not. The evidence is overwhelming that ugly capitalism brought with it the worst of social, political, and economic sins. As of the winter of 2009, for example, America had already suffered huge losses in its money and capital markets. In January 2009 the jobless rate jumped to its highest level in sixteen years. News headlines warned that the economy was "getting worse." New home sales continued to fall, housing prices continued to plunge, foreclosures continued to mount, and new factory orders continued down, down, and down.

The High Correlation of Bad Times with Crime

On a personal note, I have been unable to sell my apartment. After more than a year of waiting for zero buyers, I finally got one offer in January of 2009. I immediately asked my agent if the excited buyer had cash. I was told that the supposed buyer first had to sell his own apartment to get the cash to buy mine. Unfortunately, the deal fell through, but I did finally sell the apartment in the summer of 2010. My plight is just one of many suffered by millions of people both in the United States and abroad. Significant numbers of individuals have far greater woes than mine: Yes, if you can't sell, you can't buy. Worse, if your house is now valued at less than your mortgage (if you're "under water" as financial types say), then beware the army of scam artists who promise to refinance your home at *unbelievably* low interest rates. They target mainly desperate and depressed people. Don't believe them, for the goal of scam artists is to take your up-front money to secure the loan and then skip town leaving you in the lurch.

I asked in the introduction and elsewhere in this work whether the present major financial meltdown could degenerate into a second Great Depression. For many reasons, which I have detailed chapter-by-chapter, I came up with the same answer. Yes, despite the denials of policymakers and the always-positive consensus of economists, we could fall into a depression. Why am I more gloomy now than ever before? I simply believe it is too late now to ward off a deep and long depression. We have already run out of time.

As I have documented, the awesome power of runaway deflation has already sunk its teeth into our collapsing economy. We waited too long to put bottoms-up stimulus to work in creating vast public works projects that would bring much-needed jobs to many in our country. Obama offered hope for recovery with what he said were "vast" jobs programs. Well, the dollar numbers he cited were not nearly enough to turn the economy around and to support a satisfactory recovery. Moreover, the president is already facing stiff resistance from right-wing ideologues to any efforts he might wish to implement, even a semblance of a public works program. Many other forces are still at work to destroy capitalism. How serious are they? As I have said in prior chapters, potentially cataclysmic forces are at work.

Call my fears what you will, I tracked four especially deadly forces demanding attention here and now. They are threats of (1) multiple and simultaneous bioterrorism attacks on major cities and rural areas that could kill millions of people, (2) the militarization of space to wage warfare that could destroy the heavens and Earth, (3) global nuclear war that could destroy all life on our planet, and (4) global warming that could cause massive heat waves and drought, or it could drown coastal regions as a result of glacial run off. Many scientists warn us of these cataclysmic risks.

Hope and Reality versus Science

I had earlier planned in this summary chapter to find solutions to a number of the problems that plague humanity. But my own analysis in chapter 9 and elsewhere squashed my hopes of any sound findings. On the contrary, in reviewing each chapter, I find precious little evidence that US capitalism would or could change for the better. Here I'll document why.

One of my early readers constantly looked for solutions, compromise, common ground, and happy union and agreement. But my job as a writer is to document, both theoretically and empirically, the major horrors that face us. My goal is to spot problems in advance so that all of us can seek solutions. Most important, the villains we met in previous chapters have little desire to compromise or change their bellicose ways.

Destructive Backlash: Risk-Prone Lenders Turn Extremely Risk Averse

The key question at this juncture is whether capitalism can or even should be saved. I'll get to that all-important question shortly, but only after we fully review how we got into this terrible mess. One reason for the financial disorder is that lenders early on made low teaser loans at adjustable interest rates (e.g., they offered large home loans at small initial interest rates that ballooned to much larger rates a few years down the road), required little or no money down, and hardly bothered to conduct thorough credit checks. Lenders encouraged homeowners to tap into their home equity and borrow to the limit. Citigroup, for example, paid a billion dollars for an ad campaign from 2001 to 2006. It urged borrowers to, "Live Richly."[1] Lenders were then eager to take risks. They practically gave their money away.

The manic-style marketing pitch succeeded and then backfired causing bankruptcies for homeowners and lenders. Even the federally controlled lenders Fanny Mae and Freddie Mac suffered huge losses, and now face bankruptcy without help from the Fed. In reaction to the unstable financial climate banks turned completely around becoming risk averse and reluctant to offer loans to anyone. They sought lenders with substantial, high-value assets to secure a loan. Banks and other lenders are now desperate to raise new capital. They fear that rating agencies, which attempt to assess a value for assets of all kinds, will downgrade their loans to junk status. The downgrading of assets and the major economic implosion now signal an acceleration of huge bankruptcies across the country. The banking and finance funnel of loans to consumers and business has frozen solid. Even TARP monies wouldn't thaw it. Instead, the banks used the money as a cushion to prop up their capital reserves and improve their balance sheets.

Could my dire forecasts of even greater economic self-destruction prove to be wrong? That very question parallels the ones I often used when evaluating economists who sought to work for me. I would say to applicants: "Please use my computer to write in just one page where you believe market values will stand at the end of this year, and explain why in each case. Support your answers theoretically and empirically. The values to be assessed are (1) the thirty-year Treasury bond yield, (2) the price of the Japanese yen in dollars, (3) the Dow Jones Industrials and (4) core inflation. Clarify why others may disagree with you."

A Life-and-Death Question in Search of Answers

I'll provide my answers to these questions at the end of the chapter. But for now I face a more important question: What are the forces that may continue to cripple and destroy capitalism? In seeking answers, I posted a far more detailed question on the Internet:

> Can the physical and social sciences under capitalism ever replace with some measure of success human greed with generosity; hate with love and compassion; ignorance with wisdom; and war with peace? And, most important, can science ward off the specter of human extinction?

What did I find? In checking the Internet first, the most common response was to pray to Jesus Christ. An attached advertisement showed me how to order immediately a book on Christian prayer and God. Competing sales pitches for competing gods popped up. But I found little on how science could avoid extinction, except from scientists.

A large secular majority declared confidently without evidence that the end of humankind draws near; that extinction is God's revenge; that humans must accept without fear the final judgment day; that hell awaited sinners; that heaven rewarded those who accepted God as their savior; and that destiny is not a human option but a supernatural one.

The Sensible Creed of the Atheists

I am a veteran Wall Street forecaster. I cannot accept a notion that the future is not in our own hands. We can see a little into the future once we lean on good theory and the relevant data.[2] Except for the creed of the atheists, I found few responses that answered my question on the role of science. That figures, for as I wrote in chapter 3, almost all the famed scientists have been atheists. They say we should judge people not by their faith in any make-believe future world of heaven or hell or a person's conformity to commandments of conduct. Instead, atheists declare that we should focus on the here and now and on the good and bad deeds people perform on this Earth based upon shared human values that govern our behavior.

The Extraordinary Union of the Secular and the Scientific

Atheists offer many good ideas on how science might ward off human extinction.[3] Out of curiosity, I then perused over one hundred articles by lay writers, none of whom were scientists. What I found was a surprising and wonderful union.

Most of the sectarian responses dogmatically looked for human extinction but offered no compelling evidence. Instead, they cited religious tracts and their faith in God to support their desire for the coming judgment day when their God would seal the fate of believers and non-believers alike. In contrast, scientists cite the commanding theoretical and empirical evidence pointing to extinction, with no reference to religion or a god. What astounded me was the unusually hard agreement of religion with science, that on its current path humanity is doomed.

Highly Correlated: Human Apathy, Ignorance, and Mass Extinction

I know that arguments and counterarguments abound on global warming, but not on humankind's final fate. I find this fact to be quite startling. Is this dramatically increased level of pessimism explained by a global society that is collectively experiencing pain and anguish? To some extent yes. But the truth is that most people don't even get involved in the salient question of this century: Will human civilization blossom or die by its own hand?

In this chapter, I'll focus first on the long history of "mass extinctions" of many species, including humans. It's a terrifying tale. Then I'll review the discoveries made by science that could prove my expectations for the future to be perhaps a bit too pessimistic. Still, are we humans taking care to assure our own survival? I don't know for sure. I hold no final and absolute views on anything, including the fate of capitalism and life itself. But I worry that unless we humans change radically, the probability is high that our species is facing its demise.

Mass Extinctions Historically

Before the dispersion of humans across the continents, extinction still took place but at a much lower rate relative to the population. Mass extinctions of humans were then a rare event. Recently (in geological time), there have been five mass extinctions of life on Earth. In the last 3.5 billion years many species disappeared. This is a relatively short period of time as scientists measure Earth's history. The most recent was the Cretaccous –Tertiary extinction 65 million years ago at the end of the Cretaceous period. It was probably one of the most famous extinctions. Except for prehistoric birds, all land and water dinosaurs disappeared.

Modern Mass Extinctions

According to a 1998 survey of 400 biologists conducted by the American Museum of Natural History, almost seventy percent believed that we are presently in the early stages of a human-caused mass extinction,[4] generally known as the Holocene extinction. In one survey made in 2008, the respondents concluded that twenty percent of all living humans could become extinct within thirty years.

Another scientist, noted biologist E. O. Wilson, wrote in 2002, "If the current rates of human destruction of the biosphere continues, one-half of all living species of life on Earth would become extinct in one hundred years." Two other scientists, J. H. Lawton and R. M. May, concluded, "The rate of species extinction at present is estimated at 100 to 1000 times the average extinction rates in the evolutionary time scale of planet Earth."[5]

The Positive Side of Science and Discovery

Writing day after day about the dark side of capitalism can become very bleak and sad. I grow even more disheartened as I write about humanity's suicidal path to oblivion. We'll turn now to the brighter prospects for our collective future, especially the many new scientific discoveries. Hope remains that these breakthroughs could help our species regain some control of our fate, but for now our future is wildly out of control.

I frankly don't have much confidence that new discoveries will be developed in time to change in any radical way our bellicose and brutal ways. Still, let's look at the bright side first. Doing so might just restore a little confidence to offset my caustic and negative forecasts. I'll track for you several of these major advances in science.

Insect Birth Control[6]

Reporter Gautam Naik writes that an army of genetically altered mosquitoes are "on a mission to kill off their brethren with the most potent of weapons: sex." Thanks to the genetic tweaking of male mosquitoes, these insects can be born sterile. When they mate, their offspring inherit the defect and, presto, they die at the larval stage. If enough of the sterile males are released into the wild, they could overtake fertile males in the battle for female mosquitoe mates. The result would be a huge collapse of the mosquito population. Indeed, the extinction of mosquitoes would be a great blessing for all those humans who suffer from mosquito-borne diseases such as malaria.

The Peril of Dengue Fever

The aim is to use these sterile males to destroy the dreaded dengue fever, whose deadly reach has killed millions in recent decades. Dengue fever is also called "break bond fever." It's a flu-like fever that brings with it severe joint and muscle pains. A rare form of the disease can be fatal. The World Health Organization estimates that there are 50 million dengue infections each year that put 2.5 billion men, women, and children at risk of death. The effort to develop insect birth control via the sterile male mosquito is surely worthwhile.

Naik cautions that to conquer dengue fever is still "a hope." Well, I hope that science will be victorious. Still, will female mosquitoes be attracted to genetically engineered sterile males? I don't know and researchers are not sure. One way or another, science will eventually discover the right approach that will kill these insects that threaten human life.

Guiding Light: Another Way to Turn Sunlight into Power

The *Economist*,[7] in one of its usual unsigned articles, writes, "The main objection to the widespread use of solar power is the cost of the silicon cells that convert the rays of the sun into electricity." Thus, to keep costs down scientists now look for ways to minimize the size of solar panels relative to the amount of light they can absorb. An alternative now being tested is the luminescent solar concentrator (LSC). Instead of focusing the sun's rays on a solar cell, an LSC first traps the rays wherever they come from. It then delivers the trapped sunlight to the cell with what's dubbed a waveguide.

A standard LSC is made of a sheet of plastic containing molecules of dye stretched within a frame that, in effect, is a single and long, thin solar cell. But this approach has its own problem. Some of the light is reabsorbed as it bounces, and is lost as heat. Dr. Michael Currie and Dr. Jonathan Mapel of the Massachusetts Institute of Technology believe they have a better method. They would reject the plastic sheet in favor of spraying a sheet of glass with a mixture of dyes combined with another chemical substance. The dyes and the glass act as a waveguide to keep the light from escaping.

Yet another twist of these experts is to place a second "sandwich of dye and glass over the first." The upper layer of dye intercepts high-energy light such as ultraviolet. The lower one captures longer wavelengths. Together the two convert ten times more of the sunlight than a conventional solar cell. This is yet another entry in the increasingly crowded race to replace old-fashioned power generation with electricity that is "harvested" directly from the sun and then distributed when needed for power.

The Death Plague from Nicotine Addiction[8]

Bill Gates, the multibillionaire former head of Microsoft®, now devotes his time to running a huge charitable foundation. He and billionaire Mayor Michael Bloomberg of New York City have joined forces to stamp out smoking. Despite a decades-long struggle by health organizations to rein in smoking, it remains a systemic killer. I dubbed the tobacco industry a vicious predator in chapter 5. How vicious? Consider this short summary of horror.

> Smoking kills up to one half of those who fail to quit puffing on cigarettes. It cuts their life spans by an average of ten to fifteen years. The World Health Organization (WHO) concludes that five million people a year die a premature death from both the direct and the indirect (second hand smoke) effects of tobacco. The tobacco deaths of five million annually exceeds the combined toll of deaths from HIV/AIDS, tuberculosis, and malaria.

Since other efforts have failed, how might the present campaign succeed? There are three factors at work, namely, money, methods, and motivation. Methods interest me the most. In the past most antismoking money has been channeled through several large bureaucracies. But Gates and Bloomberg say they want to let, "a thousand flowers boom." They mean to employ many initiatives, public and private, to see what works. They would also fund grant programs for poor countries where the tobacco habit has taken a stranglehold. Their hope is that other donors and workers will join the fight against tobacco use.

Stranglehold of Nicotine Addiction: Money and Profits

What will work? I know one thing that works, at least for a short time. When I meet with students in the very first class of any course I teach, I ask whether anyone in the group smokes cigarettes. Usually about three students out of twenty-five will raise their hands. Then I point to a photograph of my son, a head and neck surgeon, all decked out in his surgical gown and mask. I then remind those students that he often has to operate on young people, mostly in their early twenties. He may have to cut out parts of the nose, the cheeks, the tongue, or even the voice box in his effort is to contain the spread of cancer before it attacks other organs. Often, the disease spreads to vital organs and kills anyway. Believe it or not, once they hear about the voice box, many of these smokers abruptly quit. But does their addiction snare them again? I don't know. Science tells us that the tobacco industry lies about the content of their product in order to promote addiction. Why? That's where the profits are, in long-term tobacco addiction.

The War against AIDS[9]

Like tobacco addiction, the war against AIDS is far from won. But the Sixteenth International Aids Conference offers some new hope. It points out three ways we might eventually win the war that now kills many millions of people each year. One possible way, "has been sitting under people's noses for years." It is antiretrovirals (ARVS). These are drugs used to treat AIDS by stopping the breeding of HIV (the virus that causes AIDS). It's a big job since total worldwide deaths due to AIDS jumped dramatically between 1990 and 2007. The increase was greater, almost threefold, for people not receiving antiretroviral drugs in low- and middle-income countries.

These drugs work by stopping HIV from breeding. They do not cure, because there are still places in the body where the virus can hide. The good news is that by taking the drugs on a regular basis, the virus almost always disappears from the blood stream. These observations have led to three avenues of research. The first is to give ARVS to uninfected people to destroy any new infection before it starts. The second is to use ARVS as a microbiocide. For women, ARVS placed in the vagina would stop the AIDS virus from breeding before it could reach other areas of the body. The third approach is the most intriguing. It is to do nothing more than to press ahead faster with present treatment programs. Studies in Taiwan and British Columbia show a big decline in transmission rates of the disease with the use of ARVS.

Behavioral Change Is Prevention's Orphan

Yet another way to fight AIDS is as old as the hills, but often ignored. Hidden somewhere in the long article in the *Economist*[10] was a prophetic phrase: "Behavioral change is, in some ways, prevention's orphan." The reporter cites the chiding voice that says (a) use a condom or (b) don't have sex with anyone but your regular partner. This is not what young people want to hear yet such a simple change in behavior has gone a long way in stamping out the human history of AIDS. Still, Helen Gayle of the Global HIV Prevention Group says, "No epidemic of AIDS has been controlled without it." I don't believe that sexual abstinence by itself can work to prevent AIDS, yet it seems only logical that every tool we can find should be used to fight the horror of this disease.

Other Important Steps
for a Safer and Happier Life

I have put together a collection of articles from countless magazines, books, and news stories that speak to the bright side of a better world. I have noted the beauty of insect control to prevent diseases such as malaria, the huge potential for obtaining electricity from the sun to cut the worldwide dependence on coal and oil, the war we must win against the fiendish tobacco industry, and the parallel war to eradicate AIDS. Still, there are many other important battles we can confront and win to protect humans. I'll list a few more here.

- ✓ Biomimicry (imitating natural's efficiencies in manufacturing processes) and robots, both large and nanotech small, that dramatically ease workloads and conquer disease.

✓ Fuel cells of hydrogen and oxygen that beget electricity with zero pollution.

✓ Plants that absorb more light, produce energy, consume more carbon dioxide, and give off more oxygen.

✓ Groups of scientists tasked with tapping subterranean energy and heat reserves from Earth's geothermal core.

✓ Pills that mimic exercise and build muscle to fight obesity and deadly diseases.

✓ Genetic science that fights aging and doubles life spans, health, and happiness.

Danger: Superbugs in Hospital Intensive Care Units[11]

I do not mean to imply that all medical or genetic discoveries are likely to save us. As recent history has shown, many heavily marketed drugs can backfire with serious effects, even death. Also, many antibiotic drugs can, over time, turn out to be worthless in preventing infection. In thinking how to proceed, I accidently stumbled on a name I recognized. In the very first sentence of a medical dispatch, New York University's Tisch Hospital popped up. The name Tisch caught my attention. For many years Larry Tisch, now deceased, was one of my favorite investment clients.

I devoured all ten pages of this medical report written by Jerome Groopman. His long article also cited in its first sentence Dr. Roger Wetherbee, an infectious-disease expert at Tisch Hospital. Coincidentally, I was at the time doing a lot of research and reading on the same subject of infection outbreaks in hospitals. In August 2000, Dr. Wetherbee was in charge of handling outbreaks of dangerous microbes in the hospital. The laboratory had isolated a bacterium called *Klebsiella pneumonia* from a patient in the intensive care unit. It proved to be resistant to every meaningful antibiotic the hospital possessed.

Dr. Wetherbee said, "My God, this is an organism that basically we can't treat." After all, this was the first major outbreak of a multidrug resistant strain of klebsiella in the United States. Dr. Wetherbee worried that the bacterium had become extremely well adapted to the intensive care units. As a result, it could not be killed with the usual ammonia and phenol disinfectants.

Wetherbee and his team then gave orders that doctors, nurses, and custodial staff had to perform meticulous hand washing and wear gowns and gloves when taking care of infected patients, and that strict rules had to be followed to change gloves and wash hands vigorously to disinfect them before attending subsequent infected patients, or after handling tubing on each patient's ventilator. Spray bottles were installed in all the ICUs, and surfaces and equipment had to be cleaned several times a day. Even with all of these precautions, as the months passed, klebsiella infected more than a dozen patients.

Hospital Crisis: Ninety Thousand Deaths Annually

Ten years ago the Institute of Medicine of the National Academy of Sciences assessed the economic cost of resistant microbes at some five billion dollars, but now experts believe that estimate to be too low. In July 2004, the Infectious Disease Society of America released a white paper titled, "Bad Bugs, No Drugs: Antibiotic Discovery Stagnates, a Public Health Crisis Brews." The Center for Disease Control and Prevention (CDC) found more than a hundred thousand cases of antibiotic-resistant bacteria. It also concluded that about twenty percent of the hospitals examined included patients with infections acquired while being hospitalized. Researchers and doctors fear that dangerous bacteria may become entrenched in hospitals and thereby threaten any patient who has "health issues." Dr. Louis Rice, an expert on antibiotic resistance at Louis Stokes Cleveland VA Medical Center says, "The problem is that any of us could be an ICU patient tomorrow."

Science, the Future of Capitalism, and the Future of Humankind

As I argued in chapter 7, we have many serious problems with the degraders and destroyers of our Earth. The situation has worsened since Presidential Obama and Senator McCain shifted from their earlier positions toward the environment and energy when they were candidates vying for the White House. Both would now drill for more oil, though Obama adds the cautionary note that drilling is no long-term solution. Still, they both claim that drilling would help to solve the short-term shortage of gas and oil and maintain consumer prices at a lower level. In fact, their plans for the longer term are perfect prescriptions for environmental disaster. In any case, prices have already fallen sharply from their highest levels. The federal government's recent effort to stop additional offshore drilling in the Gulf of Mexico, as a result of the British Petroleum oil spill, is not likely to keep drilling at bay for very long. Bumbling government policymakers now have the almost impossible job of blocking a full-blown deflationary depression.

The Big Battles Ahead for President Obama

President Obama must be given a national mandate to fight hard against those who still belittle the threat of global warming; to counter the cultural, sexual, and racial predators that stain America; to exert control over what I have dubbed the Military, Industrial and Big Oil complex; to make clear just how we can ward off a devastating recession or worse; and, most important of all, to find ways to diminish the risks of a global war launched with WMD.

The Moral Mess That Is Immigration

I have tried to expose and confront many forms of rage, hate, and discrimination. I am more dismayed and disgusted than ever over the cur-

rent forced deportation of hard-working immigrants by those who hope
to chase them out of America. Undocumented mothers and fathers are
forced to return to their native countries, separated by force from their US
citizen children who were born here. That is despicable treatment perpetrated by a government that claims to honor family values. Like the beg-
gars throughout history, US immigrants are now humiliated, spat upon,
and forced out of town.[12]

> Some people gave them white bread.
> Some people gave them brown.
> And some gave them a good horsewhip,
> And sent them out of town.

For years immigrants were mistreated by the Congress and, more
recently, by the now defunct and disgraced Bush administration. To this
day they remain exploited and abused in this the land of the free and
home of the brave. To be sure, a recent proposed Senate bill would supposedly permit illegal immigrants to become legal residents. But the bill
has hurdles that poor immigrants can't jump over. It requires them to pay
a $5,000 fine for being in the United States illegally, which few can
afford. It demands that they return home to their native countries and possibly wait for years, if ever, to return with the proper documentation. The
Senate bill would disallow visas to close family members, and those that
are provided are only temporary. The bill "cherry picks" those who will
be granted visas to favor the educated and the skilled.[13] In its present
form the bill is an insult to all immigrants who risked so much to come
to America for a better life. Cruel immigration policies now shame
America throughout the world. Former TV commentator Lou Dobbs and
extreme Republican conservatives applaud this wretched bill. They
would like nothing better than to have iron gates to block entry to all who
are desperate for a better life.

The Close Correlation of Religion and Crime

I have praised science while warning constantly against being swayed by superstition and myths. That was the point of chapter 3 on the religious assault on science. I neglected, however, to write of the sexual crimes perpetrated by Catholic priests. Such abuse has found its way into the headlines both here and abroad. Still, the Catholic Church is not alone as a source of predatory sex offenders. Sexual abuse charges have also been directed against camp counselors, schoolteachers and aides, healthcare workers, and clergy of many faiths.

And sex crimes are certainly not confined to the religious community. Regrettably, these cruel acts can also be found in business offices, hospitals, nursing homes, all branches of the military, childcare centers, summer vacation camps, and in the homes of macho men who abuse their own wives. Sexual predators remain a constant threat.

The Road to Capitalist Crisis and Self-Destruction

The road to crisis has many blundering twists and turns, according to former vice chairman of the Federal Reserve Alan Blinder:

> Recognizing and understanding our errors can help us to "fix" capitalism so that it doesn't malfunction badly again. Our capitalistic system did not condemn us to this fate. It was a series of avoidable—yes, avoidable—human errors.[14]

Were they really avoidable human errors? Not as far as I can tell. The actions taken were for the most part deliberate and planned far in advance. They predictably resulted in huge damage, suffering, and, all too often, needless sickness and death. Both the private sector, especially Wall Street and the broader financial community, and the federal government were heavily involved.

Blinder lists only six blunders. None were simple errors. My list, which can be found throughout this work, is a far more realistic and deadly account of the private and government policies that have spun our economy, and capitalism in general, far out of control and have left it in its current sick and debilitated condition.

Wars without End

It is fitting to start with the US government's preemptive military attacks and occupation of other countries on false or questional grounds. The most recent are the attack on Iraq to remove Saddam Hussein and our ongoing military involvement in Afghanistan. Are we to have wars without end? I have already argued that war has hollowed out the US economy even as it has led to a growing death toll of American soldiers, and innocent civilians. One of the most tragic elements of war now shows up in the suicides of American soldiers either while they are still in the theater of action or after they have returned home with serious physical or emotional injuries.

Even worse, our bellicose stance in these and other regions of the world increases the risk that other nations whose governments fear similar military actions against them, insurgents who hope to gain support for their particular political cause, or religious ascetics who want to further their particular religious beliefs will make use of nuclear weapons to start a regional war that will inevitably escalate into a worldwide conflagration from which few will survive. Without relative peace on a global scale there can be no rebirth of capitalism in the United States or anywhere else.

"Suicides Reach New High"[15]

The above caption is one of many similar reports in the late January 2009 and even current newspapers as well as other publications. The tragic surge of suicides has taken place both on the battlefield and when soldiers are sent back home, often seriously injured. Fifteen-month deployments to the war zones with only short furloughs at home before being redeployed offers combat personnel little time to recuperate physically or to reach out for emotional support. All too often this approach to conducting military actions results in post-traumatic stress disorder (PTSD), depression, alcohol abuse, and family problems. Thirty percent of the suicides in the last four years took place in the battle zones while another thirty-five percent occurred after the solders returned from the battle lines to safer areas controlled by our own forces. The huge remaining thirty-five percent who had never been in battle also chose to kill themselves. The most common factors in these suicides by soldiers returning home were fatigue, depression, personal and legal problems, and the inability to find good jobs (or any jobs). In 2006 the rate of military suicides exceeded the civilian rate.

Comments by high-ranking military officers lament the many lives that have been lost to suicide. They declare that we have to move quickly to reverse the trend. I have two questions for our military higher echelons: How can you meet this goal in the absence of peace? Second, why did it take so long to recognize this tragic situation? I'll answer my own questions. Maybe President Obama can succeed in ending these wars and bringing peace to America once again. But to succeed he must first tame and subdue the stranglehold of the Military, Industrial, and Big Oil Complex. That's unlikely.

The Perversion of Simple Keynesian Truths

I list as a second destructive force the present right-wing attacks on Keynesian doctrine by Republicans and other extreme laissez faire ideologues. One reason the economy continues to plunge closer and closer to outright depression is the failure to unleash here and now vast public works programs to provide millions of the unemployed with jobs and incomes to repair and rebuild America. Angry right-wingers are still consumed with rage for having lost the 2008 election. That's one reason why they remain firmly opposed to bold government action and instead spew out false arguments claiming that such public works programs cannot solve our problems. They say it takes too long to get public works developed and running at full speed and by the time these projects are ready to commence, the economy will be on the mend again. But their real reason for dragging their feet and being obstructionist is that they have no interest in public works to create jobs. They contend that such actions by government will supplant free markets and destroy capitalism. But hasn't that already happened? The bumbling and failed government interventionist monetary policies now replace those minimalist or nonexistent policies suggested by private laissez faire advocates. Obama should show the door to both the government bunglers and the extreme right ideologues. He should run them all out of Washington.

The Same Spurious Right-Wing Pitch

The opponents of "big government" today offer up the same nonsense that was urged decades ago during the Great Depression of the 1930s. Among the fallacious arguments getting attention once again is the view that Keynesian efforts did not work in the thirties and cannot work today. They cite the fact that Roosevelt never met Keynes until 1934. According to his labor secretary, Francis Perkins, Roosevelt declared that Keynes "left him a rigmarole of figures, that he must be a mathematician, not a political scientist."[16] That may be true, but it's irrelevant. The relevant point is that in 1934 Roosevelt brought the panic under control. He stabilized the banking system, provided bank deposit insurance, invested federal money in banks, and imposed restrictions on banking practices. The run on banks was over, thanks to Roosevelt and Keynes. To buy more time to shore up the banking system, Roosevelt broadcasted his regular "fireside chat" radio addresses to calm the nation and offer them aid and hope.

Most important, Keynes provided the theoretical keys to foster sustained economic recovery in his *General Theory of Employment, Interest and Money* (1936). In his second masterwork *How to Pay for the War*

(1942), Keynes gave us the best-financed war—World War II—in our entire history. Strict controls and the war bond campaign kept inflation down while generating the buying power to spark the postwar economic recovery. Enraged Republicans and other right-wing ideologues have yet to admit the monumental Keynesian success.

"United States Infrastructure Is in Dire Straits"[17]

I titled this chapter "Summary and Dire Conclusions," but was surprised to spot the same word "dire" in the press headline quoted above. This hollowed out economy of ours is worse than I had imagined. Call it dire, dreadful, horrible, for it's all of these terrible things and more. The American Society of Civil Engineers (ASCE) assigned a D grade to the state of our overall infrastructure. This group warns that it would take $2.2 trillion of investment by government over the next five years to repair the current damage, much less build modern up-to-date roads, bridges, water and sewage systems, and the like. A Congressional Budget Office analysis was more depressing. It concluded, "Only 64 percent of [any infrastructure] bill's spending could be completed in 19 months, and spending on construction projects will take a yet longer time to complete." How far into 2011 must we go to get emergency spending and aid in place? Are we already too late to be of any lasting benefit to the general economic recovery?

Are We Running Out of Time to Block Depression?

Have we already run out of time to block an impending depression? By the way, "depression" is a word seldom used by the press, Wall Street analysts, or the great consensus of economists to describe what we could be facing. Instead, they argue that the present recession could easily turn into a slump, a decline, a downturn, or whatever. Well, there is a colossal difference between a slump and a depression. Consider this long list of unresolved problems that still face us.

Those civil engineers we mentioned in the previous section warn that a quarter of our bridges are structurally deficient or obsolete, that leaky pipes lose an estimated seven billion gallons of drinking water daily, and that sewage systems send billions of gallons of untreated waste water into our waterways each year. Further, crumbling infrastructure, they warn, has a direct impact on our personal and economic health, and endangers our future prosperity. If done responsibly, investment in infrastructure would provide tangible benefits to the American people in reduced traffic congestion, improved air quality, and clean and abundant water supplies, and all the while creating good-paying jobs that would benefit the overall economy.

Despite these urgent needs, the almost $900 billion stimulus bill of the Obama administration and the Congress would allocate less than a third of the amount for infrastructure, and less for traditional concrete-and-steel projects like roads and public transit systems. I fear that even with this limp approach to repairing our cities and basic structures most of these programs will come too late to block a second great depression.

Playing Right-Wing Fiddles as America Crashes

So, who is celebrating? In my view, it would be groups like the American Enterprise Institute, the Heritage Foundation, the National Bureau of Economic Research, and other right-wing think tanks I addressed at length in this work. These beltway conservatives embody the antithesis of honest social science. They preach sun and cheer, forecast always to the bright side, and constantly identify extreme economic freedom without controls as their ideal. As strong supporters of the disgraced George W. Bush, the so-called research of these think tanks is still funded largely by major corporations who have something to sell us, including extreme free market ideology. They produce "research" to please their corporate masters who hate effective regulation and control. They tout fairness, compassion, and science yet all the while they betray these ideals and destroy US capitalism.

Bumbling and Fumbling Laissez-Faire Ideologues

Who would you include as the most misguided right-wing economists who forever pass off their ideology as economic science? I would put Milton Friedman at the top of the list. Much of the modern laissez faire doctrine can be traced to Friedman and the so-called Chicago School of economics. Their cry has always been pure freedom without controls. But as we all know, market freedom without sensible regulation and control now leaves us with out-of-control capitalism that courts its own destruction. I believe that Friedman's pure laissez faire doctrine is now quite dead.

Second in disgrace are the Wall Street types and the wide array of banks, mortgage companies, private investment firms, brokers, and dealers, small and giant corporations, and others that practiced to deceive. Together their selfishness was at the center of the easily predictable freezing up of the financial markets and the severe plunge in our economy. I wrote earlier that financial economists attempted to carve out for themselves a separate niche distinct from that of the queen of the social sciences, economics. They failed. Instead they invented false concepts that cost Americans their jobs, their homes, and their hopes.

Seven Roads to Major Crisis and a Deepening Slump

Extreme laissez faire views have been linked to (1) extreme leveraging (reckless borrowing); (2) an unregulated market for investment derivatives that predictably collapsed; (3) a subprime mortgage boom with teaser variable rates that burst and spread to phony AAA-rated mortgages and bonds; (4) specious credit default insurance with zero collateral or cash to pay off these contracts that led to widespread bankruptcies; (5) soaring foreclosures as the housing boom collapsed while the Treasury, the Fed, and Congress did little to stop the carnage; (6) the bumbling of the Troubled Asset Recovery Program (TARP); and (7) the absurd decision to ask many Wall Street executives to clean up the mess they themselves made.

The Most Damaging Financial Inventions

In the category of "most damaging financial inventions" I would list collateralized mortgage bonds and credit default insurance swaps as the most dangerous to America and to the world. Both were frauds. Banks made many very iffy mortgage loans, and then bundled them together into separate contracts or mortgage-backed securities. They then sold the contracts labeled as collateralized mortgage bonds to investors. Some of these groups of related securities contracts (collectively called tranches) were supposedly high grade and rated AAA to appeal to risk-averse investors. Other tranches would receive lower grades that were supposedly attractive to the risk-prone investors who raced after higher yields.

But the economy plunged into recession, interest rates rose, and most of these contracts fell sharply in price. Millions of homeowners could no longer pay the higher interest on their mortgages that they owed to bond holders. Owned all over the world, these mortgage-backed securities are now priced far below their initial values. Defaults, bankruptcies, and foreclosures followed in America and abroad making the bonds "toxic" because creditors couldn't collect on them and their values were in limbo since with so many defaults no one could determine their actual value in the marketplace. Many of these contracts are now worthless.

Credit Default Swaps

Credit default swaps are simple to understand. If you have property, either a house or business property, you would most likely have insurance on that property to protect you from major losses resulting from fire or other damage. Credit default swaps are in that vein, but again most turned out to be fraudulent.

You might, for example, buy insurance on your house to protect yourself if you should lose your job and income and not be able to make your monthly mortgage payment. The insurance company would presumably then pay you the amount agreed on, which would be sufficient to meet your mortgage payments for both interest and principal, and perhaps your other living expenses. As it turned out, many people also bought insurance on properties (securities) they did not own or live in. They did that for purely speculative reasons. They bought insurance on the securities they purchased. If the mortgage holders defaulted on their payments the insurance would pay the security holder what was owed. Then the crash came and these contracts were not honored because the insurance brokers didn't have enough money to cover the commitments they made, which rendering the insurance worthless. Those who held securities were not paid by those who owed on their mortgages, which meant that these securities were as worthless as the mortgages upon which they were based. The classic case of the American International Group (AIG), a giant and unstable insurance company hit the headlines. It had no reserves in cash to pay off those who bought insurance contracts. Indeed, the total number of contracts outstanding exceeded by far those purchased to protect the value of properties (securities). Most of the outstanding and worthless contracts were purchased for speculative purposes to get rich fast. Instead, the fraudulent contracts made their owners poor even faster.

The Worst and the Best Case Scenario for Capitalism

So far I have advanced my worst-case scenario. I now envision a seventy percent probability of a terrible depression of three to seven years. Over three years ago, my judgment was that of a sixty percent probability of depression. Actually, capitalism is now half dead. We have already run out of time and resolve to ward off a depression that could easily exceed that of the Great Depression of the Thirties.

The Best Case Scenario

The best-case scenario would be a twenty percent probability or less that US capitalism will shed its evil and bellicose ways. Our overriding goal should be to end war and gain peace. Is that likely in this twenty-first century? Several of the scholars I tracked in chapter 9 predicted that the human race would become extinct before the twenty-first century ends. In that same chapter I quoted Iccho Itoh in his Nagasaki Peace Declaration of August 9, 1995. His statement is worth repeating. I view it as both precise and extremely relevant to human life. He said: "The human race cannot coexist with nuclear weapons." I consider this to be one of the single most important quotes in this entire volume.

Answers to Questions Posed Earlier

I promised to answer the questions I posted on the Internet. They included the values for (1) the thirty-year Treasury bond yield; (2) the price of the Japanese yen in dollars; (3) the Dow Jones Industrials; and (4) core inflation. Clarify why others may disagree with you.

My answers rest with the fact that the major recession we are experiencing gets worse day by day even though there may be the occasional bright spot. A huge recession will bring with it a collapse in credit demands, the stock market, and inflation. Ugly deflation, or the rapid lowering of prices for goods and services, will quickly replace inflation in the core index of prices. Deflation will also hit food, energy, commodities, oil, and property prices. It's anyone's guess what will happen to the price of the Japanese yen in dollars. Both countries will run off the track into major slumps.

Here is my last question: What does turmoil, unemployment, poverty, loss of shelter, incomes, and savings, and a global recession coming on top of a hollowed out economy imply for humankind? Cataclysmic economic failures raise the risks of riots, genocide, suicide, sectarian and religious fighting, violent disputes within families, global nuclear war, and the end of ugly capitalism. Given this dire economic and financial environment, my forecast focuses on Treasurey bonds, the only nontoxic investment available. It comes as no surprise to me that TIPs (Treasury Inflation Protected bonds) continue to rise. As depression strikes with full force, TIPs will soar in price. They are the only inflation-protected securitios rated AAA the world over.

The Liberal Tone of the End of Capitalism

You probably are aware of Bernard L. Madoff's $50 billion systemic fraud. It was the biggest Ponzi scheme ever, according to prosecutors. They demanded that Madoff be removed from his penthouse apartment and jailed immediately for having violated the terms of his bail.[18] He is now serving a lengthy prison term that will last the rest of his life. Madoff had earlier written a letter of apology to his neighbors that reads:

> Dear Neighbors,
>
> Please accept my profound apologies for the terrible inconvenience that I have caused over the past weeks. Ruth and I appreciate the support we have received.
>
> Best Regards, Bernard Madoff

Reporter Susan Dominus wrote, "Madoff's short note had a familiar and reasonable tone to it, as if the person who wrote it is still clinging to the belief that he's basically a decent guy, just a good neighbor and citizen who made a few bad decisions." I cite the Madoff case as a liberal writer. The entire tone of my work is that Madoff and others who have stolen and harmed innocent people need to be exposed, prosecuted, and jailed. That's the tone or consistent theme that shows up in every chapter of this book.

The Curse of Acting Too Late with Too Little

Maybe the scientific advances I cited will help humankind to advance over the long run. In any case, the short run is already lost. We simply acted too late to counter the destructive forces of an economy out of control. Capitalism as we know it is already half dead. Gloom and decline will now exercise dominion in the United States and globally for at least four or five years. Later, any credible recovery would still require a full reconstruction of capitalism to expel its poisonous elements. That's possible but improbable, and would also take a long time.

Epilogue

THE LAST DAYS OF CAPITALISM?

Psychological hedonism [is] the simple and naïve view, so pop-
ular in the nineteenth century, [that] man always seeks to
achieve pleasure and avoid pain. [But] under the influence of
the ascetic motive, [man] might just as truthfully be called a
pain seeking as a pleasure seeking animal.
                    —J. C. Flugel, *Man, Morals, and Society* (1945)

I earlier had quoted these remarks by Flugel in *Unlocking the Secrets of Wall Street*.[1] Flugel was adamant in attacking the idea that individuals, seeking their own best interest and pleasure, would produce social harmony. I made the same argument in *Unlocking* and I trust I have furthered the case in this volume. In every chapter of both works have I set forth my sincerest conviction that when extreme laissez faire capitalism is permitted to proceed virtually unchecked, with pitifully weak controls, a dangerous outcome will result. This poisonous concoction now leaves America in the grip of a self-destructing economy.

Numerous people who have read this manuscript have applauded my stinging attack on the selfish and abusive practices of capitalism. Yet, surprisingly, none of the readers asked me how the role of science might turn capitalism into a better system. My answer is that science could radically change capitalism's prospects for the better, a matter I addressed in chapter 10. However, a first big hurdle would surely be to change the very nature of the self-involved human being, a subject I will now address. But first I'll try to answer briefly but directly several questions posed by those who read earlier drafts of this work.

1) Is there a contradiction between the defining characteristics of capitalism and doing good for others? Yes. Karl Marx (1818-1883) was the economic theorist to spell out in detail that hedonistic capitalism would "implode" (self destruct) as a result of its inherently bellicose and selfish contradictions. Capitalism has long glorified human self-interest and self-love as a virtue. Even Adam Smith borrowed a bit from Bernard de Mandeville's adoration of greed. Far worse, the modern right-wing supply-side theorists revel in selfishness and greed.

Nobody ever put the ultraright-wing hedonistic rationale more forcefully than Bernard de Mandeville when he wrote, "Thus every part was full of vice, yet the whole world a Paradise." I can only say that the word master de Mandeville is wrong. My entire point in this book has been to expose corrupt and selfish capitalism and to denounce the damage it has done and continues to do to markets, institutions, and individuals. This compels me to rewrite de Mandeville as follows: "Thus every part was full of vice and too much of the world a blazing hell."

2) What would it take to turn capitalism around and improve the lot of humankind while at the same time promoting a blossoming of wealth, prosperity, growth, and progress? As has already been noted in chapter 10, the question can be turned around to read: "Can the physical and social sciences under capitalism replace, with some measure of success, human greed with generosity, hate with love and compassion, ignorance with wisdom, and war with peace?

I have tried to answer this second question in chapter 10 and throughout this volume by emphasizing that new scientific findings and better economic decision making can multiply our power to benefit all people. But yet another question worries me: Do we have the resolve and necessary controls within capitalism to make desperately needed changes to promote a blossoming society and an ethical and loving human community? Again, time is against us. The destructive forces now at work, from economic collapse to global war, could undermine if not completely kill off our self-control and resolve. Without the individuals needed to see them through, the promises of science are put at considerable risk.[2]

3) How could trickle-down theory properly implemented actually work for the welfare of humanity? It cannot. Trickle-down theory is inseparable from right-wing policies that are deliberately designed to benefit the wealthy through tax cuts, tax avoidance, and tax evasion. The well-known right-wing economists and think tanks—for example, Martin Feldstein and the American Enterprise Institute—have long publicized fallacious views on who pays taxes. The alternative to unworkable trickle-down theory, is trickle-up theory, which does work. Trickle-up theory, also known as bottoms-up stimulus, argues that to ward off a major recession the Treasury must issue large contracts for public works on a competitive bid basis to give people jobs and incomes, with the funding fully assumed by the Federal Reserve, which has unlimited ability to create credit and money.

The Ultraright-Wing Hatred of John Maynard Keynes

Will such a trickle-up policy be put into effect? Not likely. Conservatives generally and the right wing in particular stridently opposed Keynesian economics to end the Great Depression. These same groups now oppose our taking the necessary steps to fight full recession. It has always objected to big government involving itself when attempting to solve big problems. But why? A quick answer is that Republicans hate anything liberal. That includes the counsel of one of the greatest liberals in economic history, John Maynard Keynes.

Also, we cannot simply rule out the specter of a deflationary depression lasting many years. In such a scenario prices fall to attract buyers, but buyers wait to spend because they expect prices to fall even lower. What makes prospects even worse is that any major slump will now come on top of a hollowed out economy brought on by the high costs and increased government borrowing during a period when we are fighting wars on two fronts. The colossal Treasury debt load from war will roughly double if one includes government guarantees of the collapsed securities of bankrupt investment banks and mortgage companies Fanny Mae and Freddy Mac. All the while, tax evasion and tax avoidance still account for pitifully low Treasury revenues, even though efforts are being made to recover taxable revenue from off-shore tax havens in the Caribbean and in Europe. If my forecasts of a major and sustained recession are only half right, tax revenues will shrink to create record deficits reminiscent of the Great Depression.

Economic Humans versus Ascetic Humans

It is never easy to focus on the long-run evolution of humankind in the twenty-first century. Of course, I cannot forecast one hundred years ahead. It will take me the rest of this epilogue to answer the questions I posed at its beginning. In formulating my answers, I must include the most recent evidence of the US economy sinking deeper and deeper into recession, a spreading of the subprime depressed market to prime lenders, and a wide array of forward-looking economic indicators that signal far more trouble ahead for the bond market, the stock market, and major industries.

This entire work has been a stinging indictment of the ugly capitalism that has brought with it the worst financial meltdown since the 1930s. The economy gets worse every day as bankruptcies soar.[3] Still, I see no evidence that we will take the necessary steps to prevent a slump that could easily exceed the 1981-82 blockbuster recession of sixteen dreadful months that almost turned into a full depression.

Recall our earlier review of the ascetic as a self-sacrificing person who denies himself the usual pleasures of life for the good of others. With the major exception of the suicide-bombing terrorists, our list of "good" ascetics could include doctors, lawyers, soldiers, nurses, educators, ministers, writers, athletes, explorers, revolutionaries, politicians, businessmen, and countless others. Psychologists often argue their case from the history of human development and from psychoanalytical research and experiment. Most important, they say they can find no scientific evidence supporting the economist's notion of a fixed, unchangeable, and innately self-interested human being. Psychologist Erich Fromm has been the most direct. Consider this stinging barb in his *Anatomy of Human Destructiveness*.[4]

> The assumption of a fixed human nature...has so often been abused as a shield behind which the most inhuman acts are committed. In the name of human nature, for example, Aristotle and most thinkers up to the eighteenth century defended slavery. Or in order to prove the rationality and the necessity of the capitalistic form of society, scholars tried to make a case for acquisitiveness, competitiveness, and selfishness as innate human traits.

The Abuses of Positive versus Normative Economics[5]

I believe that Erich Fromm is correct and that the great majority of my fellow economists are wrong. This is not a new conviction. I held the same views during my doctoral studies at the Wharton School of the University of Pennsylvania, where bestselling author and economist Dr. Raymond T. Bye insisted that the job of the economist was to explain how one can reach economic goals theoretically. Leave out politics or ethics, he proclaimed. Don't get sidetracked, he insisted. I could never agree. Once the United States dropped a nuclear bomb on Hiroshima, any artificial separation of science from ethics and politics was neither possible nor desirable.

Economists have yet another defense for their views on the selfish character that they say is permanently built into the human being. They tell us they deal in positive economics—i.e., how economics is actually conducted. They tell us to distinguish this from normative economics— what economics ought to be. They infer from all of this that they are strictly scientific. "We'll leave the normative economics, the ethics, to you," they seem to say. "We just describe what we see."

Nonsense! All economists, whether consciously or unconsciously, put ethics directly into the models they build. As I have repeatedly argued, the extreme free market economists are a case in point with their innately self-interested economic man. When it comes to income distribution theory, economists of all persuasions have their private ethical agenda, whether they are classical, neoclassical, Marxian, Keynesian, neo-Keynesian, monetarist, or supply-sider. You name it—they all bastardize science in the name of ethics. Whether on the left or the right, professional economists hold the strangest notions about eternal and fixed natural laws. For example, note here American philosopher John Dewey's devastating attack on Marx's notion of class conflict as natural law.[6]

> Marx reached the conclusion that all social development comes from conflict between classes, and that class warfare is to be cultivated. Hence a supposedly scientific form of the doctrine of social evolution preaches social hostility as the road to harmony. It would be difficult to find a more striking instance of what happens when natural events are given a social and practical sanctification.

Taking my cue from Dewey's assault on Marx, and using Dewey's very words, I could turn natural law against the father of capitalism, Adam Smith. I could write:

> Smith reached the conclusion that economic harmony for society as a whole comes from competition among individuals, and that competition is to be cultivated. Hence a supposedly scientific form of the doctrine of social evolution preaches individual selfishness as the road to social harmony. It would be difficult to find a more striking example of what happens when natural events are given a social and practical sanctification.

I doubt that Dewey, who writes of "the exaggeration of harmony attributed to nature," would have objected to my restatement. On the contrary, I believe Dewey would have shouted that whenever natural law enters into argument over political and social systems, the disputants are forced into interminable and sterile debate. Let's put it this way: When the Law of Nature walks into economic and ethical controversy, science walks out.

Naturalists on Economic Beings

Who are the most influential of all scientists on our nature as economic beings? They are, I would certainly argue, those versed in natural history. Let's proceed with our inquiry on evolution in this century by citing the best of the lot, Charles Darwin. Consider here Darwin's words in his *Descent of Man.*[1]

> The more important elements of man are love and the distinct passion of sympathy. The fact that man is the one being who certainly deserves this designation is the greatest of all distinctions between him and the lower animals.

Love and sympathy? Yes, Darwin used these two words to describe the chief attributes of humans. That hardly sounds hedonistic. What about our allegedly fixed nature? Darwin's answer is in his "main conclusion." There he presented his earth-shaking finding:

> The main conclusion that man is descended from some lowly organized form will, I regret to think, be highly distasteful to many.

Darwin's main conclusion may go down as the understatement of all time. Thus humankind's nature is not fixed but forever changing, evolving. From what I can see, warring economists, beset and bedeviled by submerged ideological convictions, have yet to incorporate Darwin's *positive* outlook on humanity into their own thinking. Instead, they have misinterpreted and bastardized his core views. They took "survival of the fittest" to mean an innately selfish being. Darwin reached no such conclusion. It was social philosopher Herbert Spencer (1820-1903), not Darwin, who coined the phrase "survival of the fittest."

Anthropologist Ernest Becker on Economic Man

Just as was the case a century ago under unbridled hedonistic theory, professional economists and religious zealots twist beyond all recognition Darwinian science on the nature of humankind. Ernest Becker put it precisely in his work *The Structure of Evil*: "To use simple hedonism for deductive prediction was bound to err [since] it is based on the shallowest of understanding of the complexity of human behavior."[8] Five years after Becker published the *Structure of Evil* he produced his masterwork *The Denial of Death*.[9] Becker concluded that the absolute certainty of death was a mainspring of human motivation, a positive force for progress. Here are Becker's words:

> The idea of death, the fear of it, haunts the human animal like nothing else. It is a mainspring of human activity—activity designed largely to avoid the finality of death, to overcome it by denying in some way the final destiny of man.

The Paradox of Selfish Man versus Heroic Man

A mainspring? Yes, a noble mainspring for most of society, argues Becker. This places us in a paradox. On the one hand, says Becker, we are narcissistic. That human beings love themselves, often above all else, cannot be argued away. Relevant here, Becker cites Aristotle's quip that luck is when the guy next to you gets hit with the arrow. That's self-love, hedonism, narcissism. Call it what you will, this self-directed love of human beings for themselves is understandable, for we are determined to survive. On the other hand, Becker writes that we humans are heroic. We want to be heroic for society even at the cost of our own lives. Consider this from Becker's *Denial of Death*:

We mentioned the meaner side [of] narcissism, but there is obviously the noble side of man as well. Man will lay down his life for his country, his society, his family. He will choose to throw himself on a grenade to save his comrades. He is capable of the highest generosity and self-sacrifice. But he has to feel and believe that what he is doing is truly heroic.

So, Becker the anthropologist and Flugel the psychologist see eye-to-eye. I have coupled their views into one sentence: Man is also the ascetic, the seeker of pain and strife, who strives to be a hero for society. In pointing up the mainsprings of human motivation—sacrifice, love, sympathy, cooperation, and the *excitement* of tireless research and discovery—our physical scientists, social scientists, poets, novelists, and nonfiction writers help to make life worth living. Note that I have highlighted *excitement*. That's my way of paying tribute to bacteriologist Hans Zinsser, who so beautifully but unintentionally documented the thrill of discovery as a powerful force in human beings.

Zinsser makes mincemeat of the economists' models of selfish man loaded with utils, disutils, and indifference curves.[10] I focused in chapter 10 on whether science and new leaders can save capitalism. My focus was on the huge and positive potential of science. Here I repeat that there are no strong forces currently at work to "save" capitalism from an early death.

The End of Capitalism in the Twenty-First Century?

Humans can look forward to better days. But the question I asked at the beginning of this epilogue must first be answered before we can make any firm judgments on the evolution of humanity in this century or in the third millennium. It's worth repeating the question:

Can the physical and social sciences under capitalism ever replace, with some measure of success, human greed with generosity and compassion, hate with love and tolerance, ignorance with wisdom, and war with peace?

I still don't know the answer to this question. All I do know is that the speed at which new technology is being created may multiply exponentially. If the three futurologists I tracked in chapter 10 are correct, then the creation of new and potentially cataclysmic weapons of mass destruction for global war on Earth or in space may also accelerate at an exponential rate. Ron Suskind's book *The Way of the World*[11] raises similar questions. Specifically, Suskind criticizes the Bush administration's malfeasance at home and at war. One reviewer of Suskind's book wrote the following:

> At the heart of Suskind's story is a potentially existential threat to the United States in the here and now. Suskind warns of what may be humanity's last great race between civilized governments and radical terrorists, with the prize being a mushroom cloud in an American city, or its merciful absence.[12]

The Data Signal an Accelerated Downturn for the US and Global Economies

Iccho Itoh, a first spectator of nuclear destruction in Nagasaki, was precise and succinct in his sobering comment that peace and nuclear weapons cannot exist side by side. But we must also track carefully what the current data tells us. As of May 2010 the data signal, nothing but more trouble ahead. First, in contrast with those who see inflation ahead, namely, the extreme right-wing ideologues who incessantly claim that deficit spending will cause future inflation that we must combat now by curtailing federal spending, the data make clear country by country that deflation has in fact sunk its sharp teeth into the world's economies. Britain's *Economist*[13] estimates that the dollar price index as of June 2009 for all commodities is down 30.5% year over year. Year-over-year food prices are down 25.2%, all industrial materials are down 37.9%, and metals are down 37.8%. Priced in pounds sterling, the Euro index for all prices is down 22.4%. West Texas Intermediate oil prices in dollars are down year over year 47.3%. My sense is that the scourge of deflation is here to stay, and it will grow far worse as global economies continue to tumble or at least remain flat.

In fact deflation is far stronger than would show up in commodity prices alone. Deflation has also struck housing, with prices now far below what the current owners paid. Many homeowners now are troubled that their total debt far and away exceeds the market value of their house or apartment. They worry every day that their lender will either raise the interest rate on their mortgage or institute foreclosure proceedings if they are late on mortgage payments. Deflation has even struck many landlords who are so burdened with debt, sharply higher interest rates, and falling revenues from delinquent renters or vacant properties that they cannot meet their own mortgage bills. Deflation has also struck commercial buildings, corporate bonds, stocks, and a wide range of retailers from clothing stores to restaurants. In such a deflationary market no one can improve their bottom line by raising prices without risking the loss of customers who are demanding ever lower prices before they will buy.

True, if you have cash you can buy property or goods at bargain prices. Cash is now king. But if one is short of cash, one is simply out of luck. Consider this example: homeowners find that they cannot sell their own house or apartment that has fallen sharply in price, and expected to fall still further. So they can't get the cash to buy another house. Unsold properties pile up and speed the pace of price declines and foreclosures. As prices decline more and more, expectations set in that prices will continue to fall. Thus many consumers will postpone buying or cut back sharply on their purchases to wait for lower prices. The net effect of lower consumer spending, of course, is merely to speed the pace of deflation—the further lowering of prices to attract buyers. Also, as consumption falls the investment or replacement cost of capital goods also decreases. A self-reinforcing downward cycle sends economic output down, down, and down. The gross domestic product sinks lower and lower at home and abroad.

The Frightening Slide in Gross Domestic Product (GDP)

What about gross domestic product? The "latest" data for May 2010 show declines across the global economy. Here are estimated percentage changes "on the previous quarter that are translated into annualized numbers" (for example, if output falls 1% in a given quarter, then the computed annualized rate would be four times 1%, or 4%). The annualized data say that the United States was down 5.7%, Japan down 14.2%, Britain down 7.4%, Canada down 5.4%, Euro Area nations as a whole down 9.7%, Austria down 10.6%, Belgium down 6.2%, France down 4.7%, Germany down 14.4%, Greece down 4.6%, Italy down 10.1%, Netherlands down 10.7%, Spain down 7.4%, Czech Republic down 12.9%, Denmark down 7.3%, Hungary down 9.6%, Norway down 1.8%, Russia unavailable (but the first quarter was down 9.5%), Sweden down 3.6%, Switzerland down 16%, Hong Kong down 16.1%, Singapore down 14.6%, Thailand down 7.3%, Mexico down 21.5%, Israel down 3.6%, and South Africa, down 6.4%. These are big and frightening declines as they relate to each specific national economy.

What do these data tell us? They warn that the United States and the global economy are at great risk of a continued slide in output coming on top of deflation. The same holds for industrial production. For example, the "latest" industrial production for the United States was down 13.4% in May 2010, Japan down 30.7% in May, and Britain down 12.3% in May. The biggest declines were in the Euro Area where the nations as a whole were down 21.6%, France down 18.8%, Germany down 21.6%, Spain down 28.6%, Sweden down 21.2%, and Pakistan down 20.6%. An exception to the low numbers was China's 8.9% rise in production in May.

What about country by country stock prices? The *Economist* lists the percentage changes in stock prices since December 30, 2008, and calculates the changes in local currencies, and in dollars. Most stock gauges are up over this period, and many newspapers and articles have argued that the worst is over for the stock market. Others celebrate what they believe will be higher stock prices ahead. Some look for a huge and sudden surge in stock prices. But what is so often omitted from these reports is the dismal data documenting that stock prices currently are still far below their earlier peaks before the global financial meltdown. That's why there are still many toxic assets (e.g., properties, highly leveraged securities, and the like) that few people want to buy, including the commercial banks, the investment banks, and a wide range of private equity institutions. Until these assets are actually given an initial value and placed on the market to see what they will bring based on who appears willing to purchase them, we will never really know their true worth or if they can ever be sold.

The Failures of Capitalism to Spur Recovery Signal a High Risk of Depression

There were many failures on many fronts as of June 2009 that signaled terrible times for US and global capitalism. The following list is long and detailed, failure by failure.[14]

War and Peace

I have repeatedly stated that no satisfactory economic recovery is possible (a) without peace and (b) an early and swift federal jobs program that would match or exceed in magnitude that of the Great Depression of the 1930s. But peace in Iraq still seems like an illusion despite many headlines that declare the worst is over. Yet headlines abound that terrorist bombings continue in areas throughout Iraq, even in locations originally thought to be relatively safe. US Marines have been steadily reducing their presence in Anbar Province, which includes the city of Falluja. Brigadier General Sadoun of the anti-insurgent militia police declared in 2008 that Falluja "was almost completely stabilized."[15] But, "seven months later it's getting worse and worse," General Sadoun said. Indeed, it has gotten a lot worse.

The attacks include the killing of three Americans who were in a convoy of eleven armored sport utility vehicles. Then on a Saturday a bomb hidden in a parked car near Karma blew up and killed three members of the Iraqi police patrol. Major General Tariq al-Youssef, the Anbar Province police commander arranged "a street-level tour for a reporter of the *New York Times*." But the walk was cut short after the general ordered troops to "clear the streets and rooftops." Late June 2009 headlines declared (a) that American soldiers will shortly depart from Iraq, which (b) has sparked Iraqi celebrations.

Is there a moral here? Yes. Don't accept without good theory and good data what the Pentagon and other US or Iraqi officials say. Track instead what officials do, not what they say they do. Double check the theory and the data to get to the truth.

Speaking of good data, they prove to be indispensable in seeking the truth. Good data now signal big trouble ahead. Most are serious and a couple are potentially catastrophic. I'll review them one by one, starting with the explosion in corporate defaults.

United States Corporate Defaults

My compliments again go to the *Economist* for its compilation of the data on corporate defaults. It has one chart on page 98 of its June 20, 2009 publication (already noted) that shows the number of defaults currently exceeding that of the year 2000, and significantly exceeding what I had forecasted and dubbed the "minidepression" of 1981-82, then the *worst recession* since the Great Depression that just barely escaped plunging into a full depression.[16]

Yes, elements of another recession *worse* than 1981-82 are already plainly visible. The comments that follow lean again on the *Economist*, though I paraphrased much of this to be succinct and simple. Note first that corporate defaults soared in the week of June 1, 2009, for seven firms, which meant total defaults of 209 companies as of that date, up 117% over 2008, and higher than in 2001 when the dotcom bubble burst. At the time I had forecasted wide corporate defaults and the bursting of "megabubble" stock gauges.

What economic forces currently brought about comparable bubble stock gauges slated to burst and an overinvestment boom destined to crash? The most important was the sustained and excessively loose policies of both the Treasury and the Federal Reserve. They fueled the overinvestment boom that predictably collapsed, megabubble stock gauges that predictably burst, and the mania-driven housing boom and the subprime boom with low teaser interest rates. They all collapsed together with the sudden climb in interest rates.

While runaway Treasury and Federal Reserve policies were at fault, what I found most disturbing was that none of our government policy makers or the Congress warned us of the financial crisis or of the major recession that loomed straight ahead. Isn't that their job? Instead, as I earlier noted, they were in denial that any problems even existed. They could not even see the folly of their own actions. Nothing was new here. In *Unlocking* I documented the grand folly and farce ingrained in governmental forecasting. I also summarized such folly in appendix I of that work.

But corporate managers were also at fault. They leveraged heavily with record issues of speculative-grade bonds and bought back their own stock shares with borrowed money. The wild mania-style overleveraging was crucial to my forecasts that all this would end up in a huge crash. Meanwhile, as the *Economist* stresses, "As troubling as the level of defaults is, Standard and Poor's says it is even worse. It declared that 43% of defaulting firms worldwide have a recovery rating of 6." That means creditors will probably recoup less than 10 percent of what they in fact paid for the bonds they purchased. What a double blow to recovery. Why? Those are toxic assets. That's why.

Yes, the subprime bonds are toxic, the better-graded bonds are toxic, the high-yield bonds are extraordinarily toxic, the housing and commercial mortgages are toxic, the financial securities held by commercial banks and Wall Street investment banks are toxic, and the investment holdings of many hedge funds and private equity groups are toxic. They are all still toxic, priced far below their purchase prices. That's one big reason the many programs of the Treasury and the Federal Reserve are not likely anytime soon to spark new and aggressive lending so crucial for economy recovery.

Indeed, without a huge jobs program, which we still don't have, nothing will work to stave off a worsening recession and the clear risk of depression. I am astonished that so few economists see this huge risk despite the ready availability of the data I have just reviewed. All they need to do is look at the figures.

Fredric S. Mishkin and His Fear of Inflation

Do you know who Fredric S. Mishkin is? He is an American economist, a professor at Columbia Business School, and was a member of the board of governors of the Federal Reserve System from 2006 to 2008. I have great respect for his writing, especially his *Monetary Policy Strategy*. But I am puzzled by his June 2009 *Wall Street Journal* article.[17] Here are his comments on "How to Get the Fed Out of Its Box."

> The Fed does not, and should not want to make it easy for the Treasury to sell its debt and thereby be an enabler of fiscal irresponsibility. Second, if the Fed loses its credibility to resist pressures to monetize the debt, it could cause inflation expectations to shift upward, thereby leading to serious problems down the road.

To be fair, I have also warned that any strong and unexpected recovery of the economy would surely send interest rates and inflation higher, especially if new data on war spending and Treasury debt turns out to be understated. Maybe that's what Mishkin means by "down the road." But his fears are not supported in the present (May 2010) setting of a deflationary recession spinning fast downhill and out of control.

Even a cursory study of prices documents that they are falling fast. That includes the detailed price statistics compiled by the *Economist*, which have been reviewed above. But to see full deflation at work one would also have to include the plunging prices of housing, commercial properties, corporations, major stock gauges, and the slide in prices of toxic mortgages, commercial banks, investment banks, and a wide range of hedge funds and private equity funds. Yes, the road we now travel includes ugly deflation, ugly toxic assets, and soaring and ugly unemployment. But the road just ahead is far more dangerous. It is the road to full depression, here and globally.

The Futility of Cutting Incomes and Saving

For many months now employers have tried to minimize the ravages of recession, falling profits, and job losses by cutting salaries, reducing the number of paid days in a week, or furloughing workers with the promise to rehire when the economy recovers. Meanwhile, the unemployed and those working for lower incomes are spending less and trying to save more. Hence retail sales fall. The slide in consumer spending then depresses investment spending. Worse, the fall in prices induces consumers to spend even less and try to save even more. These are the very forces that in past big recessions have produced a sustained cyclical slide. All this misery would be just fine if the recession should come to an early end, as many hope and pray.

But hopes, prayers, and saving more won't work to produce any economic recovery. On the contrary, the data across the board in the United States and globally rule out an early end to this recession. As I write these words in May 2010 the evidence is already here of the beginnings of a deep depression. Our government has already come too late with too little stimulus to ward of a major collapse. Part of this problem reflects extreme right-wing Republican ideological rejection of big government actions, and a turtle-like movement of Democrats to put into swift motion a full-blown jobs program.

"Not Enough Audacity"

The second part of the problem is one I have repeatedly stressed. It is the failed attempt to find bipartisan unity to ward off a depression. In my view it is ludicrous to ever expect right-wing Republicans and liberal Democrats to get together and solve big problems. On the contrary, I believe honest liberals should try to emulate Martin Luther King Jr., and now Paul Krugman. They shout out their rage over injustice and cruel acts and show the extreme conservatives the door. Relevant here, consider these words of the *New York Times* writer and Nobel laureate Krugman in his article, "Not Enough Audacity."[18]

> When it comes to domestic policy there are two Barack Obamas. On one side there is Barack the policy wonk, whose command of the issues and the ability to explain those issues in plain English– is a joy to behold. But on the other side is Barack the post-partisan, who searches for common ground when none exists, and is far too weak. If unemployment surpassed the administration's optimistic projections, Republicans wouldn't accept the need for more stimulus. They would declare the whole economic policy a failure.

"Welfare Cases Increase Sharply as Unemployment Pay Runs Out"[19]

A truly sad and new development is the surge in number of those who have no option except to go on welfare. Over many decades ultraright-wing Republicans railed against those on welfare, often blocking or cutting their benefits, and humiliated welfare recipients. They called the welfare recipients lazy (and many still do). But in checking the data historically, I found that unemployment and the welfare rolls both dropped whenever the economy enjoyed a strong and sustained economic recovery. So, did "lazy people" suddenly become energetic and productive? No. They never were lazy, despite Republican slurs.

What's happening now reminds me of the suffering of the Great Depression. Early in the present recession welfare rolls fell in many states. But now "twenty-three of the thirty largest states, which account for 88% of the nation's total population, report[ed] welfare cases above year-ago levels." The biggest jump in welfare cases were in states with some of the worst jobless rates. A map prepared by the *Wall Street Journal* and the Conference of State Legislatures shows that the percentage increase of welfare cases was thirty percent or higher in Washington, Oregon, California, Colorado, Ohio, South Carolina, Florida, and a part of Alaska.

What's your conclusion based on all these data? Mine is that higher unemployment, falling prices (deflation), higher bankruptcies, soaring foreclosures, higher suicide rates, higher crime rates, surging welfare rolls, toxic financial assets, right-wing depressants, and collapsing economies here and abroad confirm the beginnings of a second depression. To this list one can add, "Not Enough Audacity" and my "Ten Forecasting Sins of Capitalism" (see appendix G, especially [1] "The Missing Policy Stimulus").

Financial Reform in America[20]

Merton Miller, a Nobel Prize winning economist whom I have quoted frequently, along with Franco Modigliani, are known for their superb theoretical work in estimating the fundamental values of major stock gauges. They tackle the question of the many government programs being suggested to get America back on a solid economic track. Yes, we need financial reform and, more important, a huge jobs program. Then in June 2009 came President Obama's eighty-eight-page white paper on the subject of financial regulation. My own reading warns, at the risk of seeming like a broken record, that Obama's white paper is not strong enough to produce a satisfactory economic recovery. Again, time is against us. I just wonder (a) how many people will study and procrastinate over these pages and (b) whether any further effort to implement change will come too late, be too weak, and come across as too confused to do much good.

One problem may be in the complexity and the large number of regulators, with no one clearly in charge. The problems are many. How to supervise companies believed to be too big to let fail is certainly a major issue. Apparently that would be the job of the Federal Reserve. Another task is to make sure that the procedures to "wind down" any failed financial giant are in place. The goal is to be sure that officials will not again be forced to choose between a massive bailout versus an earthquake-style systemic destruction of the interlaced financial system.

Supervisory officials will also have to make sure that credit default loans and loan securitization does not once again suffer systemic collapse. The lender itself would be required to retain five percent of any securitized loans. That, in my view, would hardly be enough to ward off securitized fraud once again. Remember AIG? The supervisory officials will also have to make sure that grand fraud does not take place once again. Bernard Madoff and his Ponzi scheme cost investors upwards of $65 billion (much more than the earlier estimates of $50 billion). That cannot happen again. But I suspect it will with federal money floating everywhere.

Yet another challenge Obama faces deals with what the *Economist* called "a tangled web of regulators," including the Office of Thrift Supervision (OTS), which will be absorbed by another agency. Four federal bank regulators and state agencies will work with the OTS and other agencies yet to be named. Yet another agency in Obama's white paper is a new Consumer Protection Agency (CPA) with broad powers over mortgages, credit cards, Liar Loans (loans that borrowers got without documenting incomes and or their ability to repay) and ARMS (those high-risk mortgages that some dubbed radioactive). In July 2010 President Obama signed a Financial Regulation Bill into law that seeks to address many of these concerns. The skeptics are worried that it won't do nearly enough to control financial institutions or prevent future economic meltdowns,

Another part of the problem goes far beyond Obama's white paper. I mean the types of failures I documented in this volume. They include the failure to replace war with peace; the failure to set into motion a major jobs program; and the multiple failures to attack and correct the lying, grand theft, dishonesty, discrimination, exploitation, and physical harm I tracked in the previous chapters, let alone the wide array of financial abuses, dishonesty, frauds, and law breaking I tracked in *Unlocking the Secrets of Wall Street.*

It looks to me like humankind has yet to learn how to love and survive on this Earth. Maybe that's why so many of the scientists I tracked say humans will become extinct before this century ends. The good Earth will still be here, and maybe the ants. Superior beings from another planet may someday occupy and love our Earth as we once did. But how will we humans ever know anything of the future if we are gone? What bothers me most is that humans would then never be able to reflect on the beautiful and happy times they shared with parents, children, grandchildren, and friends. Why? Because humankind's demise would obliterate all our memories. Many of the insects would probably survive, but not us.

New Evidence on the Collapse of Capitalism

The evidence for a calamitous end of capitalism is overwhelming. To be succinct I will list briefly many of the most self-destructive forces at work. The list includes alarming developments I had not yet addressed: for example, the collapsing shipping industry. Other major industries will also face catastrophic collapse in a second great depression.

I raised the risk of depression to 90 percent in this epilogue from the 60 percent probability I had originally included in the introduction when I began this project. My list follows breaking news and hard evidence. The frightening evidence follows:

1) Reporter Landon Thomas Jr. of the *New York Times* writes of "Little Cargo, Loads of Debt: As European Shipping Slows, European Banks Fear Loan Defaults."[21] Yes, this is the old story of overbuilding of ships that now rest idle and of overborrowing to finance them. Shipping is down and the prices for ships are in a tailspin, thousands of unsold autos clutter US docks, and major losses signal that many dock workers will lose their jobs.

Does not this latest collapse remind us of the earlier subprime collapse of housing and the toxic mortgages and bank loans that are still priced far below their purchase prices? Actually, we don't know what prices these toxic instruments would command in the market. The owners won't say. Transparency—the ability to know what financial assets are worth—has evaporated. Government does not demand transparency, but without it the credit markets remain frozen.

Japan followed a similar path after the collapse of its economy and its stock market in 1990. Anemic growth and high unemployment plagued that once affluent country for ten years.[22] Could such an economic disaster be avoided in the United States? Yes, but it would require that we immediately create a huge program of job stimulus to repair and replace a rotting infrastructure.

2) Bellicose former President George W. Bush is now discredited. Still, enraged Republican supporters tried to block any liberal program for healthcare reform and creating jobs. Even President Obama, a revered liberal, has backtracked somewhat on his election rhetoric to create a huge "bottoms up" job program to give the unemployed work and incomes. The president must move immediately, and decisively, on a huge program to create new jobs. Any further delay risks a full depression that could strike at any time with dire consequences. President Obama, you are admired and have great power. Please exercise your power now.

3) The superb journalist Bob Herbert writes "What the Future May Hold."[23] He writes about job losses and infrastructure. His warnings are alarming but true.

In 20 years will today's toddlers be traveling on bridges that are in even worse shape than today? Will they endure mammoth traffic jams that start earlier and end later? Will their water supplies be clean and safe? Will the promise of clean energy visionaries be realized, or will we still be fouling the environment with carbon filth to benefit traditional energy conglomerates and foreign regimes? . . . You can't thrive as a nation while New Orleans is drowning, and Detroit is being beaten into oblivion decade after decade, and a bridge is collapsing into the Mississippi River, and cities in upstate New York and the rust belt are rotting from lack of employment.

4) Reporter Reed Abelson quotes Nancy-Ann De Parle, the director of the Office for Health Reform, as she rebuts what she believes are false statements by the health insurance industry on costs.[24] Ms. De Parle says, "Despite being roundly and thoroughly debunked, the [healthcare] industry lobby continues to release studies that push their bogus conclusions on how healthcare costs will greatly increase the cost of premiums."

My hat goes off to Ms. De Parle! As a veteran economist I once worked as research director for the Life Insurance Association of America (now the American Council of Life Insurance). There I learned a lot about how the life insurance and health insurance industries deceive, lie, and overcharge in order to bolster their profits. They do all that now by falsely overstating the costs of a government-run insurance program. I included my findings in chapter 5.

5) Reporter Alex Berenson of the *New York Times* wrote a story titled "A Year After a Cataclysm, Little Change on Wall Street. Progress Is Slow on Regulatory Overhaul, Posing Risk of Even Bigger Crisis."[25] Yes, a history of high-risk investments funded with huge debt is now signaling major bankruptcies on top of soaring unemployment. Recent alarming data on unemployment have sparked major crimes as well as family arguments that lead to murder, suicide, and runaway children who end up wards of the state or, worse still, prostitutes on our streets. Some children disappear. Others end up dead.

Any major "bottoms-up" jobs program is nowhere in sight, or even planned for that matter, despite the collapse of the state budgets in California, Texas, and many other states. Joblessness properly calculated is now at probably 30 percent, and for minority groups it's far higher when such figures include those who are seriously underemployed or who have simply stopped looking for work. Many other people work part time at poverty wages with zero benefits.

6) Leon Wieseltier of the *New Republic* writes: "Obama believes above all in common ground. His diplomacy consists in underestimating differences and overestimating similarities.[26] To be sure, this reporter makes a lot of sense. Trying to find common ground with right-wing and hate-filled Republicans is not possible. Nor does the Democratic Party need Republicans who will most certainly try to block every liberal program Obama supports, from job creation to a comprehensive and mandatory health insurance program that will cover all Americans, and ideally include immigrants. Surely immigrants should have a chance to become American citizens.

7) David Streitfeld of the *New York Times*, in an article titled "Housing Agency Cash Dwindling, Tightens Rules," explains what many of us already know, namely, that the shortage of cash is a result of "more borrowers defaulting on their mortgages."[27] Yes, given the absence of any major jobs programs, one would logically forecast that more sorrow and higher rates of foreclosure lie straight ahead. Yet many declare that the recession is over. Are some blue-sky reporters falling for the deception of Wall Street senior executives who always paint to the bright side?

8) Christopher Drew of the *New York Times* wrote a piece titled "High Costs Weigh on Troop Debate for Afghan War. At $1 Million a Year per G.I. the Cost Could Top Savings from Iraq."[28] These high expenditures represent a terrible opportunity cost in that the same dollars could be used for all types of spending to

help the poor, the sick, and the jobless, and to repair and modernize infrastructure for a sunnier future.

9) Elsewhere in this work I have addressed the huge opportunity costs of war, the dead soldiers and civilians, and our own returning soldiers who do not get adequate health services and who suffer terrible postwar traumatic physical and psychological injuries. Many soldiers now commit suicide and suffer terrible depression. Headlines scream of some American soldiers shooting their fellow soldiers in their own military camps. One terrible shooting incident is that of Army Major Nidal Malik Hasan who allegedly shot and killed thirteen people on the army base of Camp Hood, Texas. This new horror comes as no surprise to me (see chapter 1 on "The Plague of Gun Violence across America"). I had not expected to see the horror of guns explode on a US army base.

I also addressed in some depth what I dubbed the Military, Industrial, and Big-Oil Complex. I do believe (a) the secret links of the Pentagon to the corporations that provide arms; (b) the government's secret deals with arms producers; (c) the huge federal subsidies provided to both the arms, oil, and gas corporations; and (d) their links to the Congress together make up the biggest single risk to America and the world.

The *Economist* and Its Empirical Support[29]

Let's turn finally to toxic stocks, mortgages, hedge funds, and a wide array of derivatives that pose another huge danger to America. I direct my compliments to the November 14, 2009 issue of the *Economist* for their empirical work on stock prices, unemployment rates, and primary energy demands. They show that "by 2030 China and India together are expected to account for almost a third of global energy use. By then the world will consume 16.8 billion tons of oil equivalent. Coal will fuel the bulk of

China's increased energy use." Just imagine the "carbon imprint" and poisonous pollution that the winds will push across the Pacific Ocean to California. Just imagine the dangers of global warming, including home-lessness, tornadoes, massive floods, and widespread death.

The *Economist* also tracks unemployment rates for major cities. It lists unemployment rates for major countries as a percentage rate. It lists the US jobless figure at a 10.2% rate (although it is actually higher at 10.6%). As already noted, the rate properly calculated is closer to 30%, and much higher for minority groups. Japan is listed at 5.3%, China at 9.2%, Britain at 7.8%, Canada at 8.6 %, and France at 10%. Although unemployment rates have slowed their rise a bit in recent months, the fact is that they still rise. Unemployment is still an extreme problem globally and continues to increase.

What about current consumer prices? They are down or weak almost across the board. The same holds for interest rates. These statistics come as no surprise since we know that consumption is weak, incomes are weak or disappearing, and investment spending is down sharply even as unemployment further depresses spending and the outlook for future spending. Industrial production and the jobs that accompany it have also shown sharp declines with no early recovery in sight.

Perhaps most distressing is that there are no major bottoms-up jobs programs in sight. Yet we need desperately, here and now, such a program that must be in magnitude even larger than that of the Great Depression of the 1930s. Every week the *Economist* updates the data. It deserves all my thanks. Their judgment, however, that private markets with minimum controls are best for America is dead wrong. Markets with weak regulation and controls quickly become out of control. US capitalism with piti-fully weak controls is now out of control and headed for destruction.

Appendix A

THE DEBT WE OWE TO JOHN MAYNARD KEYNES

(Foreword to a reprint edition of Keynes's The End of Laissez-Faire *and* The Economic Consequences of the Peace *[2004])*

In *The End of Laissez-Faire* (here abbreviated *End*, 1926) and *The Economic Consequences of the Peace* (*CP*, 1919) John Maynard Keynes identified Adam Smith, John Stuart Mill, David Ricardo, and many others who richly deserved to be called professional economists. He noted that the best of the classical economists extolled competition, but *competition with limits*. For one example, Keynes made clear that a key role of government is that of regulation and control to assure that robber barons don't run free under 100 percent laissez-faire. Is there a parallel today with laissez faire style goals "to get government off the backs of the people"? Yes, corporate deception, accounting trickery in overstating profits, looting, and systemic fraud blossomed in the mania-driven, boom-to-bust cycle of 1995 to 2002, even as government restraint was irresponsibly weak. The classical economists, Keynes documents further, were acutely aware of government abuse, corruption, and monopoly business profits at the expense of society.

Indeed, in *End* Keynes faulted "semi-monopolistic" big business in generating great inequalities of wealth. Later, in his *General Theory of Employment, Interest, and Money* (1936), he, in fact, gave credit to Karl Marx for coining the term *classical economists*. It's odd, though, that Keynes did not mention in *End* the one economist who attacked "popularizers" with the very greatest fury. It was, of course, Marx. The "popularizers" equated individual selfishness under competition to group harmony without any qualifications whatsoever. Marx argued that any sanctification of individual self-love or selfishness led inexorably to domestic discord, even international war. Suffice it here to say that Keynes's critique of laissez-faire was mild, while Marx's attack was unforgiving and fierce. The war of ideas on whether individual selfishness is a glorious virtue or a fatal fault still rages. In *CP*, however, Keynes was unforgiving and caustic.

There he directed his anger and finely honed economic skills to attacking the Treaty of Versailles. He argued cogently that the huge weight of the reparations demanded of Germany and others would impoverish Europe and risk civil war. His "remedies" required a radical revision of the treaty, the cancellation of the enormous debts contracted in war funding, and internationally funded loans to the war-devastated nations of Europe. Incapacitating reparation payments had to be canceled, he insisted. (Does not Keynes's plan remind you of the Marshall Plan, following World War II?) Many of Keynes's former officers in the treasury, where he was an adviser, were furious. They classed Keynes's *CP* as a betrayal. At Cambridge, though, his reputation remained intact as a supremely brilliant and influential economist.

The two treatises, *End* and *CP*, help immensely to explain Keynes's later and far more influential works. They are *The General Theory of Employment, Interest, and Money* (1936) and *How to Pay for the War* (1940). In the *General Theory* Keynes renounced classical economics. That was a startling declaration, for he himself had been a classical economist. He documented theoretically and empirically that the classical doctrine of automatic recoveries from economic slumps was fatally flawed. Government intervention must replace laissez-faire to ward off a deepening depression, he insisted. To spur sustained economic recovery, he counseled, the government should *monetize* (create brand new money) to finance budget deficits for tax cuts and major spending for public works. We got all that, and it worked.

In 1940 Keynes declared that the best way to finance a huge war and avoid inflation was to tax as much as possible, to save as much as possible (through his forced savings plan), and to restrict borrowing mainly to *nonmonetized* (zero or little money creation) sales of Treasury obligations to the public at large. He was right again. Like the farmer, Keynes would irrigate in time of drought and drain in time of flood.

We are all indebted, not economists alone, to Keynes's genius. Still, the detractors of Keynes stereotype him as a wild deficit spender for all times. Many government officials and some economists do so despite the clear and convincing evidence in Keynes's principal works. Right-wing, supply-side ideologists counseling former President George W. Bush were in a real sense the new "popularizers and vulgarizers." Others as well continue to swap warped ideology for economic science. The dangers of confusing one with the other are greatly understated. Keynes so warned repeatedly in his revolutionary contributions to economic science and against their just-in-time applications to the major geopolitical problems of his era.

Appendix B

FORECASTS AND CONTROVERSY: THE DANGER OF CONSENSUS FORECASTING 1970 TO 2010

THE PROPHET: A Wizard, sitting in the marketplace, told the fortunes of the passersby. A person ran up in great haste, and announced to him that the doors of his house had been broken open, and that all his goods were being stolen. He sighed heavily, and hastened away as fast as he could run. A neighbor saw him running, and said, "Oh! You fellow there! You say you can foretell the fortunes of others; how is it you did not foresee your own?"
—Aesop (Sixth Century BCE)

The Danger of Consensus Forecasting

Do you know anybody who has prescience or knowledge of things before they happen or come into being? I don't. Still, all planning requires forecasting, whether it is sloppy or thorough. Being thorough means (a) that you must not only pay attention to sound theory but also actively look for new data and new developments that may contradict your most precious convictions; (b) that you must be skeptical of authorities in power, always checking what they say against relevant data and sound theory; (c) that you not rely on luck, a fickle ally; (d) that you be wary of projecting ahead based upon only the most recent experience, the equivalent of betting on the horse out front no matter how long the race; and, most important, (e) that you extract yourself from the consensus herd that seldom sees a financial bubble until it has burst. To be thorough is to be scientific. *Economic forecasting is hardly an exact science, but economists can at least try to be scientific. Many don't even try.*

A Wall Street economist must have a thick skin. He knows the press will track his errant ways. He knows that selective reporting can be highly entertaining. He knows that psychology cannot be separated from data and sound theory on the fundamentals. The year 1994 will go down as a classic case: Inflation fears fanned by wolf calls of the Federal Reserve itself suddenly sent interest rates higher even as the actual pace of inflation continued down. *There are few good market timers in the short run.*

The following are mainly direct quotes from the press and some (a few) other published reports such as my own *Money and Capital Markets Monitor.* Each of my forecasts is followed by an explanation of subsequent events. Assuming we can learn from our errors, I have tried to explain what I think went wrong with my worst projections. I did, though, manage to spot the developments listed here. Luck was my consort in spotting Black Monday; the Nikkei 225 crash; the fall of the yen; and the overinvestment, overcapacity, and gluts that struck with fury in 1997.

Here is a list of various publications that covered my economic forecasts over the years: I have assessed the forecasts to relate them directly to chapters in this volume, especially to the Epilogue. Also, these economic assessments document a superb forecasting record that is in sharp contrast to consensus forecasts that have been mostly wide of the mark.

FORECASTS

1. *The Commercial and Financial Chronicle*, January 22, 1970, p. 1.

"The economist for one of Wall Street's largest firms (Robert H. Parks, Francis I. duPont & Co.) foresees a significant decline taking place in interest rates, particularly in shorter maturities, and concludes some sort of recession is now underway (and that) a serious and prolonged recession should not be entirely overlooked."

Fact: The economy entered a serious recession and rates fell.

2. *Wharton Quarterly*, University of Pennsylvania, Fall 1971.

"With excess demand eliminated from the economy, with ample labor and capital resources, and with governmental policies designed to lift demand, the likelihood is that we shall see a vigorous recovery of the economy in the two to three years ahead."

Fact: The economy did enjoy a vigorous recovery until late 1973 when both inflation and interest rates started to climb rapidly.

3. *Wall Street Journal*, August 20, 1973, p. 1.

I was quoted as stating, "King Gold is dead."

Fact: My focus was not on the price of gold. I argued, rather, that we should not and would not revert to some kind of gold standard; that the merits of gold were more myth than fact. I still hold to that view.

4. *Times Picayune*, November 24, 1973.

"Robert H. Parks (Blyth Eastman Dillon) sums up: 'Even a fairly optimistic assumption on the Mideast and oil would require a revised forecast of minirecession.' "

Fact: The economy entered into what I characterized at the time as a maxirecession (minidepression). See (8) below.

5. "Curriculum, 24th Annual University for Presidents," Acapulco, Mexico, March 31–April 6, 1974, p. 22 (debate between Robert H. Parks

and Eliot Janeway, a well-known and very popular lecturer and economist at the time).

"According to Robert H. Parks, if neither happens (oil spigots turned back on or oil prices reduced), the United States is headed for recession, with corporate profits falling by 10–15%, unemployment advancing to 7%, and a zero growth in real GNP for 1974. The likelihood is that the United States will run surpluses in net trade and capital accounts."

Fact: We did fall into recession, but I grew progressively negative, as indicated in subsequent forecasts, especially forecast (8). The United States ran surpluses on its trade and current accounts in the 1973–75 recession.

6. *New York Post*, September 24, 1974.

"Robert H. Parks, chief economist of Advest Inc., an institutional services firm, maintains that 'the price boom for industrial materials has just about run its course.'"

Fact: Industrial prices continued downhill.

7. *Wall Street Journal*, September 30, 1974.

"Robert H. Parks, chief economist of Advest Co., is worried that 'the ongoing government restriction of demand may lead to economic overkill.'"

Fact: Government policy overkill pushed the economy into a major recession.

8. *Christian Science Monitor*, November 18, 1974.

"Mr. Parks expects that real gross national product will decline 1.5 to 2 percent (as opposed to a conventional prediction of a flat GNP) and that unemployment will rise to 8 percent or higher."

Fact: Real GNP fell 1.2% in 1975 and unemployment averaged 8.5% for the year.

9. *New York Post*, January 24, 1975.

"Calling it a minidepression, Robert H. Parks said it will be short-lived in contrast with the protracted economic earthquakes of the 1930s. Parks said his turn to guarded optimism is based on 'new governmental stimulus not yet announced and a slowing of inflation.'"

Fact: Government policy shifted from restraint to stimulus, and overall inflation topped out a few months later.

10. *Wall Street Journal*, May 23, 1975.

"Robert H. Parks, executive vice president of Advest Institutional Services, was even more outspoken: 'The financial markets can easily handle the upcoming Treasury financing provided (a) the Federal Reserve is sufficiently accommodative and (b) Treasury Secretary [William E.] Simon gets more professional counsel on elementary economic and financial matters.' "

Fact: Treasury secretary Simon was worried, prematurely, about Treasury borrowing pushing interest rates up. Interest rates in fact declined through 1976.

11. *Business Week*, April 12, 1976.

"The simple fact, as Robert H. Parks, chief economist of Advest, puts it, is that 'business is not yet in a borrowing mood,' and 'the inventory reductions last year and the profits surge in the last half permitted companies to rebuild their liquidity bases.' "

Fact: That helped to explain the fall in interest rates in 1976.

12. *Money*, August 1976.

"Another pessimist, Robert Parks, says: '[Economist] Gary Shilling and I are from different planets. I think he is on Mars.' Parks thinks inflation will be back up over the 7% level by the middle of next year or earlier."

Fact: I was early, because inflation did not climb that high until the first quarter of 1978.

13. *Wall Street Journal*, January 23, 1977.

"Robert Parks, executive vice president of Advest Co., believes the president's [Jimmy Carter's] proposal for a voluntary wage and price control program is 'a folly and a farce—it simply wouldn't work.' "

Fact: It didn't work.

14. *Wall Street Journal*, March 22, 1977.

"In the view of Robert H. Parks (Advest Co.), he sees Treasury bill yields rising almost two percentage points later this year."

Fact: Three-month bills rose from 5.3% at the end of 1977 to 7.2% at the end of 1978.

15. *Business Week*, April 11, 1978.

"Mr. Parks is in a good position to assess the new state of psychology. He runs a roundtable for money managers [and] listening to what they say has convinced him of two things, both of them bad. The first dark prospect is inflation controls. The second grim prospect is tightness of money to fight inflation."

Fact: We got both.

16. *Wall Street Journal*, August 22, 1978.

"The Federal Reserve has a tiger by the tail (fast money growth of its own making and fast inflation), and the probability that it can live with fast money growth will approach zero in the next six months," asserted Robert H. Parks (Advest).

Fact: In November the Federal Reserve shifted gears to a sharp reduction in money growth.

17. *Wall Street Journal*, October 18, 1978.

"Mr. Parks predicts that 'when the Federal Reserve finally tightens, you'll see interest rates soar; you could get an increase of 1.5 to 2 points while you're having lunch.' "

Fact. The prime rate rocketed from 10% on November 1 to 11.75% by year-end. Branch managers wanted me fired for my extremely pessimistic forecast.

18. *Wall Street Journal*, November 6, 1978.

"The voluntary [price restraint] program 'will self-destruct within three to five months,' contends Robert H. Parks, chief economist at Advest Co."

Fact: It did just that as inflation soared in 1979 to high double-digit land.

19. *New York Times*, February 9, 1979.

"This combination of inflationary devils should lift the inflation rate from 12 percent to 15 percent, possibly even higher."

Fact: The inflation rate referred to was the producer price index. The index was later reported for January at a 15.6% annual rate.

20. *Journal of Commerce*, May 9, 1979.

"'That's why we look for more headline news on emergency financial bailouts of the savings banks. First Pennsylvania, a commercial bank, is a mere prelude to the troubles ahead,' according to Robert H. Parks, who heads up Robert H. Parks and Associates."

Fact: That was one grand understatement.

21. *Wall Street Journal*, October 20, 1980.

"'Look for a post-election blow off in interest rates as the Fed is finally forced to restrict the explosive growth of money and credit,' said Robert H. Parks, head of Robert H. Parks & Associates. 'The delayed monetary restraint will collide head-on with an inflation-fired climb in credit demands. The result will be to abort recovery and produce a deepening recession in 1981.'"

Fact: All of this happened just as I expected.

22. *Portfolio Letter* (Institutional Investor Publication) April 27, 1981.

"To pave the way for long-run sustainable growth, Parks believes the monetarist quintet is willing to risk recession."

Fact: By monetarist quintet I meant Baryl Sprinkel, Jerome Roberts, Norman Ture, Larry Kudlow, and Jerry Jordan, all key Reagan administration officials. But it was the Fed's extreme monetary restriction colliding head-on with massive public and private borrowing that (a) pushed interest rates sharply higher, (b) crowded out private spending, and (c) produced recession.

23. *Bondweek* (Institutional Investor Publication) July 20, 1981. The following quote from the publication focused on my July 9, 1981 *Monitor* titled "In Recession."

"Parks told *Bondweek* that 'the four major interest-rate bears, including economists Philip Braverman, Chase Manhattan; Henry Kaufman, Salomon Bros.; Sam Nakagama, Kidder Peabody; and Albert Wojnilower, First Boston [were wrong].' The message to investors is clear, says Parks: Buy long, prime-quality bonds. The worldwide recession will represent the first crack in the stranglehold of the oil cartel."

Fact: Recession brought interest rates and oil prices down hard.

24. *The Wall Street Journal*, April 29, 1982.

"Disinflation and recession are now coming on top of a dangerously overborrowed economy. This . . . should produce a record post-World War II fall in profits."

Fact: Profits fell hard.

25. *Business Week*, July 25, 1983.

"Indeed, in recent issues of his letter, *The Money and Capital Markets Monitor*, Wall Street economist Robert H. Parks—who had been a steadfast bull on bonds before and after their advance—has switched sides. He says flatly that interest rates will go up."

Fact: Interest rates did climb later, but I overstated the rise.

26. *Wall Street Journal*, April 18, 1984.

"Robert H. Parks of Robert H. Parks & Associates agreed that the pace of recovery probably will slow, but he contended that this doesn't necessarily mean that interest rates will decline."

Fact: Interest rates had a little further to go up, but then peaked around midyear.

27. *New York Times*, April 27, 1984.

"But the market also listens to Robert H. Parks . . . who says 'Drs. Death, Doom, and Gloom are understating the likely rise in interest rates this year.' "

Fact: Interest rates rose rapidly from April for several months, and then turned down in the second half of 1984.

28. *Barron's*, November 5, 1984.

"Another reason for listening to some current contrarians is that they also went against the crowd three years ago—and won. Then, with interest rates at record highs, they beat the drums for bonds—something Dr. Doom [aka Henry Kaufman of Salomon Brothers] didn't get around to doing until almost a year later. Two notable voices among them: Fred D. Kalkstein . . . and Robert H. Parks."

Fact: That was a nice compliment, but the fact is that I should have turned bull once again, then and there, on bonds. As it turned out, I waited until the next spring, and missed part of the long-bond rally.

29. Standard & Poor's *CreditWeek*, April 29, 1985.

"Fed policy has been expansionary—extremely expansionary—all along. That's a key reason now for ruling out early recession."

Fact: No early recession materialized, but economic growth slowed.

30. *Bond Buyer*, May 25, 1985.

"Our own view is that Gramm-Rudman is a placebo, an unmedicated political pill given to the economic body merely to humor."

Fact: The Gramm-Rudman bill was a weak and ineffective piece of legislation that put in place a few budget cuts to allegedly tame inflation. It failed predictably because the budget-cutting requirements were largely circumvented via accounting smoke and mirrors.

31. *Money and Capital Markets Monitor*, October 9, 1985.

"Until the March 27, 1985 *Monitor* we had been a persistent bull on the dollar. But we then warned that King Dollar may yet imitate Humpty Dumpty in the second half of this year. We switched completely in the May 3 *Monitor*, titled "Sell King Dollar NOW.""

Fact: The dollar came down sharply.

32. Standard & Poor's *CreditWeek*, July 8, 1985.

"Coming on top of extreme fiscal and monetary stimulus already in place, this third stimulus (i.e., a lower dollar) would push up interest rates sharply during the second half of 1986 or later."

Fact: Interest rates went down in the second half of 1986, but did move up in the first half of 1987. I underestimated the weight of global excess supply and underestimated the extent of foreign competition as a continuing force working against inflation. Put another way, the United States is not a "closed economy" but operates in an open and intensely competitive international world.

33. Standard & Poor's *CreditWeek*, February 3, 1986.

"But, the strong domestic fiscal/monetary forces are currently being subjected to huge offsets. This accounts for the sluggish economy over the last year and more."

Fact: A high-priced dollar in world markets, intense international competition, restrictive governmental policies abroad, and worldwide gluts all contributed to a sluggish US economy.

34. *Business Week*, June 29, 1986.

"(Recession) will drive down interest rates on long-term Treasury bonds from the current 7.5% to 5% by spring."

Fact: There was no recession, and my forecast of rates was wrong. I overestimated government restraint.

35. *Market Chronicle*, February 26, 1987, p. 15.

"Stock market bulls could profit by reading Charles Mackay's classic treatise on speculation. The title: *Extraordinary Popular Delusions and the Madness of Crowds.*"

Fact: That was good advice because world stock markets did fall hard. The US stock market peaked in August and then suffered a record one-day decline on Black Monday, October 19, 1987.

36. Standard & Poor's *CreditWeek*, March 7, 1987.

"Developing economies are without the means to generate the income even to service their debts. Put another way: revulsion + austerity + debt drag = default."

Fact: Brazil's recent suspension of interest payments on commercial foreign debt is an example of true default. "Revulsion" means an abrupt cutback of lending by the industrial world to the third world. "Austerity" means a suppression of demand and spending and borrowing, a restrictive policy imposed on the third world by the International Monetary Fund acting for the industrial lenders (see forecasts 97, 99, and 103 for parallel problems of Asian nations in 1997).

37. *Barron's*, June 8, 1987, p. 1.

"Robert Parks, a certified practitioner of the dismal science, Wall Street division, remarks on [Federal Reserve Chairman] Mr. [Paul] Volcker's adrenaline-codeine prescription for monetary policy and notes that the Fed's attempt to repair the damage wrought by overkill in '81-'82 resulted in an enormous explosion in credit, from $500 billion in 1982 to over $1 trillion last year."

Fact: Volcker's godlike image is overdone, as I have argued.

38. *Barron's*, September 21, 1987, p. 79.

"On a similar tack, Robert H. Parks, director of the Moore & Schley research unit bearing his name, also concludes that bonds' huge advantage over stocks' earnings and dividend yields makes prime fixed-income instruments 'attractive in the extreme.'"

Fact: Yes, indeed. Bond prices and long CATS (long zero-coupon bonds) soared following the stock market crash of Black Monday, October 19, 1987.

39. *Barron's*, November 30, 1987, p. 73.

"Right after the stock market crumbled, economist Robert Parks proclaimed in these pages that the phantom of inflation was dead. But Bob should have known better. Phantoms, alas, never die."

Fact: Yes, I should have known better. I was wrong.

40. Standard & Poor's *CreditWeek*, November 30, 1987, p. 1.

"Investor irrationality in US and Japanese stock markets lies in the failure to heed basic stock market theory. Investors are ignoring [stock valuation models] and their three crucial variables: interest rates, corporate income and dividend trends, and the cost of capital [the required rate of return that would rationally compensate investors for holding stocks]."

Fact (and a warning): My contention was that the Japanese stock market was for gamblers, not prudent investors responsible for other peoples' money.

41. *New York Post*, February 9, 1988, p. 33.

"I have not written much about Bob Parks' ideas because of the extremely secretive, even furtive, manner he has developed. He has an exasperating habit of issuing press releases that tell about all his interesting and influential clients and advisers who are going to hold secret meetings the press cannot attend. I find this sort of posing extremely irritating, and an obnoxious form of boasting. Nevertheless, Bob's ideas are logical and forceful. He was for [a] long [time] a lonely voice (for which he has my sympathy) in stating that the 1987 stock market boom in America was an insane development and would leave much pain and disaster behind. He was right."

Fact: The *Post*'s economics editor, Maxwell Newton, wrote this. Was I obnoxious? Perhaps. But all meetings were advertised. Many (not all) were kept off the record for a good reason. With the press in attendance, government officials and investment heads tended to imitate clams. Max's death saddened me, and I'll always remember his irreverence to "the high and mighty." He had no patience for Parrots and regularly crucified Pros.

42. *Barron's*, February 15, 1988, p. 102.

"On this scale, [Parks] recently told clients, Tokyo is flashing 'red, red [serious potential danger].' Parks rated the US (stock market) red-and-yellow [caution to possible danger] on August 18, 1987, red-red on October 7."

Fact: The US stock market crashed as predicted. We had to wait until 1990 to get a major plunge in the Japanese market.

43. *Market Chronicle*, March 31, 1988, p. 6.

"Corporate comptrollers . . . had the opportunity to raise capital through stock financing prior to Black Monday at sky-high prices, at dirt cheap rates. They blew it."

Fact: Yes, they blew it. They overloaded themselves with debt, including junk bond financing.

44. Standard & Poor's *CreditWeek*, May 23, 1988, p. 45.

"A flight to quality has already begun. In the last quarter of 1987 individual investors abandoned their DOGS [dangerously overpriced gung-ho stocks] and fled to CATS [certificates of accrual on Treasury securities] and other fixed-income vehicles."

Fact: Individual investors did begin to lighten holdings prior to Black Monday but, like institutional investors, they failed to get out early enough. The flight to quality dollar-denominated bonds accelerated in 1989, as forecast below.

45. *Barron's*, July 4, 1988, p. 2.

Barron's noted that (a) my forecast of interest rates "was the lowest of a group of financial economists [it] polled [for its] July 4, 1988 issue [p. 52]," and (b) I was extremely positive on the stock market.

Fact: Long rates came down, and short rates went up. My switch to a bull on US stocks and bonds proved timely even though the stock market had already recovered somewhat from its Black Monday lows by July.

46. *Business Week*, September 12, 1988, p. 26.

"The consensus outlook these days is that the big improvements in the trade deficit this year lie behind us. Don't bet on it, advises economist Robert H. Parks of Moore & Schley."

Fact: The first quarter trade deficit for 1989 dropped sharply.

47. *Market Chronicle*, November 17, 1988, p. 1.

"Professor Martin Feldstein and other academics set off their own false alarms (on the dollar). A good case can be made that these alarm bells are false alarms."

Fact: They were false alarms; the dollar rose as forecast until mid–1989.

48. Standard & Poor's *Credit Week*, November 21, 1988, p. 1.

"Major and sustained cuts in the trade deficit will occur in 1989 in lagged response to the dollar's massive fall. . . . The improvement is likely to bring about a buying frenzy for the dollar."

Fact: The trade deficits fell sharply, but the dollar slumped in 1989, and did not rebound until 1990–91.

49. *New York Post*, January 17, 1989.

"The consensus of Wall Street firms, including several of the giants, is to diversify out of the dollar and into key foreign-denominated securities. This will prove to be one giant error for the New Year. The United States now represents a prime investment market."

Fact: US dollar-denominated securities outperformed most world markets.

50. *Market Chronicle*, February 23, 1989, p. 1.

"Stock Valuation Models Flash Amber to Bright Green: The Advance Strike Against Accelerating Inflation" (headline of the editor for an article of mine they requested).

Fact: It was all go. What a contrast with the "red, red" signals incorporated in the October 7 and 14, 1987 *Monitor* (see forecasts 35 and 40–43).

51. Standard & Poor's *CreditWeek*, May 8, 1989, p. 48.

"Tighter money since early 1988 will also have a lagged impact and show up in a pronounced slowing of economic growth and inflation in the second half of this year, with long US treasuries trading in the 8.0% to 8.5% range. The Fed should shout victory and ease, here and now."

Fact: Luck must have been my ally, for real GNP growth slowed to about 1 percent in the fourth quarter and long treasury yields declined to trade between roughly 8 percent and 8.5 percent. But real growth, inflation, and interest rates all climbed sharply in the first quarter of 1990 to the surprise of just about everybody, including this startled economist.

52. *Business Week*, June 5, 1989, p. 27.

"Late last summer, economist Robert H. Parks . . . began advising his clients that some surprising drops in the trade deficit laid ahead (*BW*— September 12). He also advised his clients that neither world central bank chiefs nor King Canute will be able to hold back the return of King Dollar, and that US securities markets would rally sharply over the next 12 months. So what does Parks see ahead now that his earlier predictions have apparently borne fruit? In four words, more of the same."

Fact: The results were a bit mixed. Interest rates fell, stock prices rose (but not "sharply,"), the dollar soared against the yen but fell against other key industrial currencies.

53. *Tampa Tribune Times*, August 20, 1989, p. 2E.

"This soft landing stuff . . . what they're talking about is 1 percent growth, and that is going to raise holy hell with a lot of nonfinancial corporations, corporations so overloaded with junk bonds that this is going to produce (for them) a hard landing."

Fact: With this forecast of a "growth recession," revenues and cash flow fell short of the funds required to pay interest on many junk bonds, with the result that defaults soared.

54. *Barron's*, September 18, 1989, p. 71.

"'The proceeds of Treasury and [Resolution Trust Corp.] borrowing siphons money from the credit stream, but puts it into the hands of depositors or new thrift managers, who then return it to the credit stream. That's a wash, a net zero for new money and credit growth,' Parks asserts."

Fact: That's the way it is, something not generally understood by the markets.

55. *Bond Week*, September 25, 1989, p. 8.

"Parks predicts the ascendance of 'King Dollar.' "

Fact: I turned from bear to bull in early 1988, and have kept that bullish stance ever since. The dollar fell against major currencies in 1989, then rose in 1990–91, but not as much as I had forecast.

56. *Bond Week*, November 6, 1989, pp. 10–11.

"The monetarists still scream recession, asserting that once again the Federal Reserve has pursued monetary overkill. The recession-depression bears could be right, of course, but I hardly think a case can be made on their monetary calculations."

Fact: The monetarists were wrong, again. They failed to recognize the defect in "total adjusted reserves," which went nowhere. This term refers to the total reserves of cash banks have available to lend, less any increase in reserve requirements mandated by the Fed. A big increase in reserve requirements means that the banks have to cut back on how much cash they can actually lend to borrowers. Such heavy cutbacks in potential loans can generate anemic economic growth, recession, or worse. In fact, however, we experienced a de facto cut in legal reserve requirements that was the basis for the rebound in money broadly defined as M2.

57. *Business Week*, December 25, 1989, p. 77. *Barron's*, December 25, 1989, p. 32.

In a poll of economists on the 1990 economic outlook, I forecasted generally higher real growth, lower interest rates, and less inflation than the consensus.

Fact: My inflation forecast and interest rate projections were far too low.

58. Standard & Poor's *CreditWeek*, January 29, 1990, "Cost of Capital Crossover," pp. 1, 39.

"Perceptions that the US suffers an intractable competitive disadvantage versus the Japanese from prohibitive capital costs are incorrect. Differential costs of debt are narrowing between the two countries as Japanese interest rates surge. Meanwhile, equity costs are converging, too, and they could cross at any time, especially if the Japanese stock market megabubble collapses. . . . [The Japanese] should run from yen to dollars."

Fact: A bull's eye hit on this bear forecast. The Japanese stock market collapsed and the yen simultaneously weakened.

59. *Bond Week*, March 19, 1990, p. 13.

"The Japanese, who have a money growth rate of 10–11%, are now in the catch–22 situation of tightening monetary policy and watching the stock market go down, perhaps even crash, or allowing inflation to run amok."

Fact: What's new? All bubbles burst, but who can know just when? My early warning (forecast 40) was followed by a still substantial climb in the Japanese stock market. So, you would have profited—as a reckless gambler, not a prudent investor—if you had stayed in the Japanese market until late 1989.

60. *Wall Street Journal,* October 10, 1990, p. A12.

"Robert H. Parks, an economic consultant in New York, believes that the Fed has been too slow to adopt an easier monetary policy and, as a result, he now fears a 'major recession' instead of the mild one he previously predicted."

Fact: The recession was characterized as mild. I should have stuck with my earlier forecast. However, the recovery from recession after March 1991 was unusually slow.

61. *Dow Jones News*, Ticker Tape Release 12 Noon, October 26, 1990, by Candace Cumberbatch.

"While Parks has a sunny forecast for the dollar, he sees very stormy times for global economies. . . . The economy is being strangled by influences including the Federal Reserve's reluctance to ease more forcefully, fiscal restrictiveness and the oil shock caused by the Mideast turmoil, Parks says, adding that any Fed easing done now will likely be too little and too late."

Fact: The Fed pursued overkill once again and pushed the economy into the 1990–91 recession, as in 1973–75 and 1981–82. The Fed seldom learns from its mistakes.

62. *Barron's*, November 12, 1990, p. 60.

"'The dollar will be hit again the moment we get a couple of interest rate cuts,' predicts economist Robert Parks. 'But the huge interest differentials between the US and its trading partners will be short-lived.' Parks thinks the dollar [is] extremely undervalued on the basis of purchasing power parity [and] once the economies of our trading partners start to sag, interest rate differentials will implode and bargain hunters will start snapping up dollar-denominated assets."

Fact: The dollar did rebound (see forecast 68).

63. *Business Week*, December 3, 1990, p. 24.

"'Once the gulf crisis is resolved,' Parks says, 'oil prices will collapse in the context of a worldwide cyclical decline. Ironically,' says Parks, 'the darkest economic times are often the most promising for the financial markets. I am advising my clients to purchase long bonds now, and the highest quality stocks in the months ahead, when the recession hits with full force.'"

Fact: The stock market climbed, far more than I had expected, oil prices fell, and interest rates declined. Luck was with me on this.

64. *Barron's*, January 21, 1991, p. 56.

"Economist Robert Parks, who recorded Kindleberger's prognostications in an interview published in the May 1978 Pace University *International Newsletter*, believes the three Rs have come back with a vengeance."

Fact: That was revelry (stock market overspeculation), revulsion (an abrupt cutback in lending and Fed monetary overkill), and restriction (protectionism) as signals for recession. I have reviewed Dr. Charles P. Kindleberger's views throughout on many occasions and have noted the forums and interviews I conducted for this most distinguished and pre-scient economist.

65. Standard & Poor's *CreditWeek*, January 28, 1991, page 1.

"Interest-rate targeting required the Fed to strip reserves from the finan-cial system to brake the decline in interest rates. That procyclical policy is akin to monetary overkill, which led me to shift my forecast from a mild recession to a major one."

Fact: I was wrong in that the recession was mild, but the recovery from that recession proved to be the slowest in post-World War II history.

66. *Christian Science Monitor*, February 7, 1991, p. 8.

"'If the Fed does not soon start pushing liquidity into the system, I may change my forecast from major recession to depression,' says Robert Parks, an economic consultant to institutional investors. 'It is a dangerous situation.'"

Fact: The Fed shifted to an easier stance, but too late to avoid recession and post-recession anemia.

67. *Business Week*, May 13, 1991, p. 20.

"The most important leading indicator for the economy, insists economic consultant Robert H. Parks, is real private domestic borrowing—that is, borrowing by consumers, businesses, and state and local governments. He points out that such credit fell in real terms in the fourth quarter for the first time since the Great Depression and appears to be still declining—indicating 'no letup in the recession.'"

Fact: The recession was officially over by spring 1991 (sooner than I had forecast) but subpar recovery followed.

68. *Wall Street Journal*, May 28, 1991, p. C10.

"Among factors working in the dollar's favor are the current 'ultracheap' dollar levels that will likely attract bargain hunters, the possibility of 'dramatic continued improvement' in the US trade performance, and the likelihood of diminishing US inflationary pressures, Mr. Parks says."

Fact: Despite trade gains and lower inflation, the dollar weakened after midyear.

69. *Christian Science Monitor*, May 31, 1991, p. 4.

"By contrast [to those expecting early economic recovery], New York economic consultant Robert Parks [said] 'We have yet to see the full impact of restrictive credit and monetary policies.'"

Fact: The economy moved from recession to "growth" recession (subpar growth).

70. *Business Week*, December 31, 1991, p. 63.

"What economists are predicting for 1992." Of fifty economists polled, I was one of the most pessimistic on the economy for 1992.

Fact: Far too pessimistic! I was way off base because I underestimated the decline in foreign countries and overstated US exports.

71. *Barron's*, December 30, 1991, pp. 36, 37.

"Adds Robert H. Parks, who heads his own consulting firm, lower rates in and of themselves merely cut one borrower's expense and one lender's income. The economic stimulus comes from expanding the supply of money and credit, which he contends [Fed Chairman Alan] Greenspan & Co. have not done."

Fact: The Fed was too tight.

72. *Christian Science Monitor*, January 28, 1992, pp. 1 and 2.

"Mr. Parks argues that the sharp decline in interest rates last year was the result of a declining demand for money, rather than an aggressively stimulative monetary policy. Don't confuse Fed leadership with Fed 'followship,' he says."

Fact: The Fed did follow rates down, and was far too restrictive.

73. Standard & Poor's *CreditWeek*, February 3, 1992, pp. 1, 4.

"An overly restrictive monetary policy has helped cause a severe recession, already the longest and potentially the meanest since the 1930s."

Fact: My forecast of the 1990–1991 recession was correct. It turned out to be a fairly mild slump but was followed by subpar growth in the years 1991 through 1995.

74. *Barron's*, June 29, 1992, p. 38.

It published a survey of twelve economists forecasting interest rates, with my numbers being among the lowest.

Fact: Rates fell but less than I had expected.

75. *Business Week*, July 20, 1992, p. 20.

"Economic consultant Robert H. Parks has long insisted the Fed has been far too cautious. . . . Increases in currency in circulation and required reserves over the past year have almost completely offset soaring reserve growth, leaving 'almost nothing' to support credit growth."

Fact: The Fed habitually swings from monetary overstimulus to overkill.

76. *Christian Science Monitor*, October 23, 1992, p. 8

"Robert Parks, a Wall Street economist, worries about a repeat next year of the 1981 situation . . . when the Federal Reserve kept a tight monetary policy, refusing to finance the deficit with new money."

Fact: Yes, I worried that huge *nonmonetized* Treasury borrowing would "crowd out" private borrowing and demand. This made for subpar growth.

77. *Barron's*, December 28, 1992, p. 31.

"Among the bond bulls in this survey, only Robert H. Parks, who heads a New York economic consultancy, doubts the economy is headed for a sustained expansion. Constrictive policies, combined with a global recession, will push Treasury yields lower, while the Fed's misplaced inflation fears will induce it to push short-term rates higher next year."

Fact: Growth occurred but it was the most anemic recovery since 1945.

78. Standard & Poor's *CreditWeek*, January 25, 1993, p. 1.

"What worries me the most is the conspicuous absence of inflation-adjusted private credit growth and broad money M2. The good news will show up in continued disinflation and much lower yields on long prime dollar-denominated corporate bonds and treasuries."

Fact: That bond-bull stance was on target for 1993.

79. *Business Week*, April 19, 1993, p. 22.

"'The broad weakness in the monetary aggregates is definitely clouding the near-term economic outlook,' warns Parks."

Fact: "Monetary aggregates" are mainly the total reserves held by the Federal Reserve plus any Fed purchases of Treasury bonds or, conversely, total reserves less any Treasury bonds that the Fed has sold. Yes, insufficient stimulus was signaling subpar growth.

80. *Christian Science Monitor*, April 9, 1993, p. 8.

"Parks asks whether the combination of tight money (falling money aggregates), government spending cuts, and higher taxes will choke off business, depress money velocity, and send the economy back down again."

Fact: Real GDP dropped to a minuscule 0.7% advance in the first quarter of 1993.

81. *Barron's*, July 5, 1993, pp. 58–59.

"The biggest bull on bonds is the most bearish on the economy. Parks sees higher unemployment and lower bond yields [resulting] from a wrongheaded Fed [and] constrictive fiscal policy."

Fact: I had forecast a 5.9 percent yield on long treasuries, the lowest of fifty-five economists polled by *Barron's* (and the *Wall Street Journal*). Yields in fact fell to about 5.8 percent. The consensus was far too high.

82. *Christian Science Monitor*, October 28, 1993, p. 9.

"Dr. Parks argues that US monetary and fiscal policy is overly restrictive and that interest rates will be forced to decline [reflecting] slow economic growth."

Fact: The economy spurted strongly in the fourth quarter. Despite a continued down trend in inflation, inflationary psychology dominated. Interest rates soared.

83. *Barron's*, December 6, 1993, p.15.

"'Proposed fiscal measures to boost the Japanese economy mean little because they won't take early action to speed money growth,' says Robert H. Parks."

Fact: Their economy and markets were still struggling as of early 1998 and continue to struggle to this day.

84. *Business Week*, December 27, 1993, p. 69; and *Barron's*, December 27, 1993, p. 38.

Parks is concerned over "the delayed impact of constrictive fiscal and monetary policies."

Fact: My low inflation forecast was on target but interest rates surged anyway. Fear dominated markets. Psychology lifted rates even as the eco nomic fundamentals kept disinflation (lower inflation) on track.

85. Standard & Poor's *CreditWeek*, January 29, 1994, p. 1.

"[The] yen [bubble will] burst."

Fact: It did.

86. *Institutional Investor*, January 1994, p. 66.

"Even if [projected] earnings and dividends were to exceed the historical norms, [US] stocks are overpriced now. . . . Money managers run in herds like buffalo, and they will be caught this time, too."

Fact: Stocks went just about nowhere in 1994 but rose sharply in 1995.

87. *Business Week*, June 20, 1994, p. 121.

Polled by *Business Week*, I forecast the slowest GDP growth for the first half of 1995.

Fact: It was too low.

88. *Barron's*, July 4, 1994, p. MW8.

"Parks . . . insists that tight money and fiscal policies assure [economic slowdown]."

Fact: The data by year-end 1994 signaled a slowing in autos and housing, and a disturbing pileup in inventories.

89. *Christian Science Monitor*, November 18, 1994.

"Parks, a Pace University professor who also advises forty major financial institutions, expects velocity to reverse, slowing down the economy."

Fact: The unheralded surge in interest rates in 1994, I argued, would slow velocity (the rate at which money money is spent), kill the bond funds, and slow the growth of stock funds—most of which happened.

90. *Wall Street Journal*, December 5, 1994, p. C2.

"The very forces that led to a massive buildup of stock funds . . . have reversed themselves. I expect to see a shift away from stocks into bond funds again. . . ."

Fact: Not much of a shift took place until 1997.

91. *Christian Science Monitor*, January 6, 1995, p. 13.

"That's why Wall Street economist Robert Parks terms the Republican promise a Contract 'on' America. 'If Newt Gingrich gets his way, big Al Greenspan will not sit idly by,' says Mr. Parks. '[Mr. Parks calls the budget estimates in the Contract] ideological screaming. It has nothing to do with economic science.'"

Fact: We saw this voodoo economics before in 1981–82 (see forecast 30).

92. Standard & Poor's *CreditWeek*, January 23, 1995, p. 1.

"Fed-manufactured inflation phantoms . . . will evaporate as long as treasury yields skid abruptly below 7 percent."

Fact: A bull's eye, thirty-year treasuries plunged from almost 8 percent in January to below 6.4 percent by October.

93. *Barron's*, March 17, 1995, p. 42.

"Manic thinking now rules crowd behavior. . . . The coming resurgence of the dollar and the descent of the yen will spark a boom in dollar-denominated long bonds."

Fact: US bond prices rose sharply and the yen descended abruptly against the dollar, as predicted. The dollar bought about 80 yen, its low in April 1995, but soared to 104 by September of that year. The hot-air mania supporting the yen reminded me of comparable mania preceding our forecasts of Black Monday and the Nikkei 225 crash.

94. *Christian Science Monitor*, November 3, 1995, p. 8.

"A decline in commercial bank reserves since the start of 1994 troubles Robert Parks, a New York economic consultant. Similar declines, he says, signaled previous post-World War II declines. This time falling reserves will result in either very slow growth in the economy or another recession, he predicts."

Fact: Fed constriction of "adjusted" reserves regularly precipitates economic slumps. Fed policy, though, turned out to be fairly expansionary in 1996 and 1997. What a refreshing contrast with its past history of chronic overkill.

95. *Barron's*, January 8, 1996, p. 5.

"Robert Parks, a seasoned economist who has made some very good calls over the years, sees a real risk of a combination of fiscal and monetary restraint [signaling] a growth recession (block that oxymoron!) or the real thing."

Fact: Neither growth recession nor recession took place in 1996 in the United States, but in 1997 serious overcapacity, deflation, gluts in key industries, and financial meltdowns in Southeast Asia warned about the possibility of global decline and deflation.

96. *Christian Science Monitor*, January 12, 1996, p. 9.

"Parks is definitely among a minority in their gloom. . . .When surveyed last month, only six [economists] guessed that a recession would begin sometime this year and 15 said by the end of 1997. . . . But should there be a recession, it would be 'good news for bonds, bad news for jobs and profits,' Parks says."

Fact: I was too early, one reason being soaring M2 velocity. Still, stocks came under pressure but interest rates continued down as bond prices advanced. A quickening in the "circuit velocity" of money (the circulation of money among financial institutions) kept the US economy moving ahead despite slow money and credit growth in 1991–95.

97. *Money and Capital Market Monitor*, January 23, 1997, and February 3, 1997.

"The surge in productive capacity [for industrial countries] speeds far ahead of final consumer demand, a signal for an old-fashioned overinvestment under-consumption cycle that historically has produced gluts and falling profits."

Fact: Excess capacity, gluts, and high unemployment hit industrial Europe, Russia, Japan, China, Indonesia, Thailand, South Korea, and Brazil, among others. As internecine and competitive exchange-rate devaluations spread and currencies fell like dominoes, the earnings growth of major export nations suffered. Once again, policymakers failed to understand that investment spending is a lagging indicator, not a reliable forward indicator of economic expansion.

98. *Barron's*, April 1, 1997, quote in "Market Watch"

"The stock market is said to be liquidity driven, a consequence largely of the biggest mutual stock fund boom in history. That's true, but liquidity driven markets tend to backfire and collapse."

Fact: The stock market continued to surge into 1997, but later that year it faltered. Stocks sporting sky-high price/earnings ratios were hit hard. The defective liquidity-driven argument for continued advances in stock prices preceded my forecast of Black Monday in the United States (see forecast 38) and the predicted collapse of the Nikkei 225 "megabubble." (see forecast 58). It seems that old stock market fallacies never die.

99. *Barron's*, May 19, 1997, quoted in "Market Watch"

"Fundamental stock values now lie far below market prices even assuming (1) a Goldilocks economy . . . and (2) fantasyland high projections of profits growth. . . . Bond prices will soar when stocks swoon."

Fact: Stocks did "swoon" but then recovered. Interest rates continued to decline (bond prices rose).

100. *Wall Street Journal*, July 9, 1997, p. 1.

"Notable and quotable: 'When it comes to taxes, the unconscious mind puts its bank balance upfront,' says Robert H. Parks, an economics and investment advisor. 'Ethics and economic science sit in the backseat.'"

Fact: Yes, but I should have added that the conscious mind also puts its bank balance upfront, deliberately.

101. *Christian Science Monitor*, July 10, 1997, p. B7.

"Robert Parks . . . had predicted a burst in the market 'bubble.' Last month he changed his mind. 'Extraordinary and in some cases brand new forces signal that (overpriced) stocks may head significantly higher this year and into 1998,' he wrote."

Fact: I did indeed list unprecedented economic "green lights" in the seventh year of economic expansion (for example, growth, disinflation, lower interest rates, and continued profits advance), but I also warned that "investors would be well advised to employ a defensive posture . . . to hold a high percentage of cash [and] long prime bonds, [and] to avoid by all means the celestial P/E stocks . . . with towering multiples (6/25/97 *Money and Capital Markets Monitor*)." Stocks did advance, and then faltered.

With the currency and securities markets meltdown in Southeast Asia and elsewhere, I warned also of an earnings slowdown for US multinational corporations whose exports represented a high percentage of total earnings. *Developing nations, I maintained, risked an overproduction-overinvestment-overcapacity-underconsumption cycle, the oldest and deadliest of business cycles.* Compounding the depressant of gluts and plunging dollar prices of Southeast Asian exports, competitive exchange-rate depreciation led to a marked slowdown in world trade and widespread declines in corporate profits. Because many corporations borrowed short and invested long on an unhedged currency basis, I found that forecasting widespread financial collapse was a fairly easy call. What's new? Nothing (see forecast 98).

102. *Business Week* year-end 1997 issue.

"Economic Forecast Survey for 1998" (reproduced in the 1/14/98 *Money and Capital Markets Monitor*).

"[I forecast] a 1.3% CPI [consumer price inflation] for1998, the lowest of fifty economists polled by *Business Week* in its year-end 1997 issue. . . . With fifty economists, though, you get fifty different forecasts. As the saw goes, if you lay economists end to end they still can't reach a conclusion."

Fact: I maintained that the great disinflation wave coupled with deflation in key sectors throughout most of the industrial world had by no means run its course.

103. *New York Times*, June 11, 1998, p. D8.

"'Japan is in depression,' said Robert H. Parks [Wall Street economist] and professor of finance at the Graduate School of Business at Pace University in New York. 'Japan must stimulate its economy by cutting taxes and spending more on public works projects that are not boondoggles,' Mr. Parks argued, [and] 'the central bank must finance these projects with money fresh off the printing press [to be successful in avoiding a deeper slump]. The yen is tumbling either way,' Mr. Parks said. 'There's no bottom to a currency in the middle of depression.'"

Fact: We saw before, many times, how dangerous and counterproductive fiscal policy can be when divorced from monetary policy. Poor fiscal and monetary theory, the mother of even worse government policies, largely explains Japan's tragic but needless plunge into a major slump lasting ten years.

104. *Money and Capital Markets Monitor*, December 8, 2003.

"Modern Portfolio Theory dictates this is not a stock-pickers market. Stock pickers chronically underperform the broad equity gauges."

Fact: They still do.

105. *Money and Capital Markets Monitor*, December 22, 2004.

"Once war finance fears take hold [investors] will run as a herd and dump their bonds and mortgages. Interest rates will soar and bankruptcies abound."

Fact: The great meltdown of "toxic" debt now shows up in a financial meltdown and risks of a severe recession.

106. *Money and Capital Markets Monitor*, May 16, 2005.

"A unilateral, preemptive [military] attack on false grounds is dangerous and immoral."

Fact. The US attack and occupation of Iraq was illegal and immoral. The Iraq war will bring with it untold damage to the United States.

107. *Journal News*, March 18, 2007.

"'This is the biggest financial bubble in US history,' Parks told the *Journal News* in January 2000. 'You [should] worry about Internet stocks. [They are] butterfly stocks, blindingly beautiful but without substance. I mean I can't see earnings in 98 percent of them.'"

Fact: "Parks was right about his forecasts of a stock market crash."

108. *Money and Capital Markets Monitor*, September 1, 2007, titled, "The Predicted Bursting of the Housing Market."

I concluded, "All big bubbles burst. Housing is an unprecedented big and dangerous bubble."

Fact. The bubble burst as predicted. As of today (January 2011), home sales and prices continue to tumble, inventories soar, and foreclosures mount.

109. *Money and Capital Markets Monitor*, January 8, 2008.

"The supply-side economists are back. They wail that corporate share holders are bleeding to death from high tax rates. No, the US corporations enjoy lower taxes than most of [their] competing foreign nations."

Fact: Listen to David Ricardo, not George W. Bush. Ricardo wrote, "A tax on hats will raise the price of hats, a tax on shoes the price of shoes. If this were not the case, the tax would be paid by the manufacturer." Also, US corporate tax avoidance and tax evasion in fact mean far lower effective tax rates in the United States than in foreign countries.

110. *Journal News*, March 18, 2008.

"While many economists are predicting that the problems in the banking system could lead to a recession, Robert H. Parks is more pessimistic. The Pace University finance professor said the economy could become mired in its first depression since the Great Depression. He said that 20 percent of US banks, hedge funds, brokerage houses, and other financial institutions could ultimately fail."

Fact: I forecast 20 percent or more would fail. Even that forecast proved to be too low.

111. *Christian Science Monitor*, March 24, 2008.

"When economist Robert Parks predicted early last week that there was more than a 60 percent probability the current financial meltdown would lead to the 'Bush depression, [Parks's] phone began ringing like crazy with calls from the media."

Fact: The recession worsened week by week to signal a high risk of depression.

112. *Money and Capital Markets Monitor*, September 27, 2008, titled "Triple Nightmare: Depression, Deflation, and Dollar Downgrade."

I repeated my conclusions of the March 18 and April 25 Monitors. I wrote, "Recession could easily degenerate into deflation, depression, and a downgrade of the once mighty dollar. The slump will spread globally. The White House, the Federal Reserve, and the Treasury have no policy to prevent a triple nightmare."

Fact: Policies of the bumbling White House, the Fed, and the Treasury are all too weak, too late, and too confused to ward off a major economic implosion.

Additional published forecasts in refereed articles and books

Refereed articles published in 2005-2006: (1) "Ex Ante Recognition of Bubble Stock Gauges and Forecasts of their Bursting in the United States and Japan": Lead Article, Best Author Award, and Keynote Speaker: *Journal of the American Academy of Business, Cambridge*, Vol. 8, No.1, March 2006; (2) "U.S. Monetary Policy, Bubble Stock Gauges, and the Over-Investment Boom-to-Bust Cycle 1997-2002," *International Journal of Business Disciplines*, Vol.16, No. 2, Fall 2005; (3) "Dominion of Flawed Fiscal and Monetary Policies over Economic Science," Lead article in the *Business Review, Cambridge*, Vol. 5, No. 1, September 2006.

Published Books: *Unlocking the Secrets of Wall Street* (Prometheus Books, 1998); *The Witch Doctor of Wall Street* (Prometheus Books, 1996); *Financial Institutions and Markets*, co-author (Prentice Hall, 1970); "Foreword," *The End of Laissez Faire/The Economic Consequences of the Peace*" by John Maynard Keynes (Great Mind Series/Prometheus Books, 2004).

Appendix C

EX ANTE RECOGNITION OF BUBBLE STOCK GAUGES AND FORECASTS OF THEIR BURSTING IN THE UNITED STATES AND JAPAN

(*Journal of the American Academy of Business*,
Cambridge, March 2006)

ection I of this article summarizes the *ex ante* identification of four major stock gauges as bubbles fated to burst. Section II presents the pure theory of a fully integrated stock valuation model coupling the Gordon (1962) dividend model with the Miller-Modigliani dividend irrelevancy model (1961), hereafter the G-MM model.

Section III, the applied analysis, presents four matching valuation recipes I used to identify bubble stock gauges. Given its still current relevance, I devoted the core of this article in Section III (A) to the bursting of the S&P 500 in 2000. Section III (B) reviews the predicted collapse of the "megabubble" NASDAQ Composite. Section III (C) tracks, but briefly, my forecast of the bursting of the S&P 500 in 1987. Section III (D) also reviews briefly the predicted crash of the megabubble Nikkei 225 in 1990.

I stress throughout the role of fiscal and monetary policy. A principal theme is that Federal Reserve policy 1997-2000 fueled and fired an over-investment boom that collapsed and bubble stock gauges that crashed, predictably. A related thesis is the failure of the regulatory officials and the central bank to suppress systemic financial fraud.

Section IV sets forth my conclusions and suggestions for further research. The appendix lists all *ex ante* bubble recognition and forecasts. All forecasts there are press documented, and each bubble burst as forecasted. The notes include additional press documentation and further *ex ante* evidence of bubble gauges in published articles.

I: Summary of *Ex Ante* Factors in Spotting Stock Bubbles

Defining and identifying bubbles *ex ante* are inseparable tasks. In addition to the valuation analysis I constantly tracked the emerging systemic depressants. The two analyzed together put in stark relief the theoretically maximum valuations under ideal conditions versus the depressants that lay waste to valuations.[1] For immediate perspective just glance at the treacherous roller coaster ride of the major stock indexes for the S&P 500, the NASDAQ Composite, and Japan's Nikkei 225.

Figure 1: Charts
The S&P 500, NASDAQ Composite, and Japan's Nikkei 225

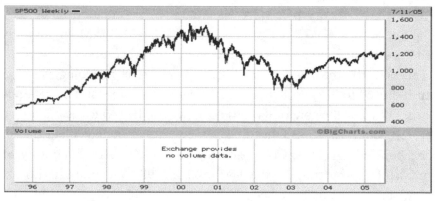

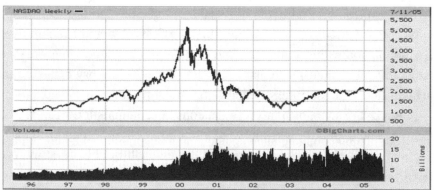

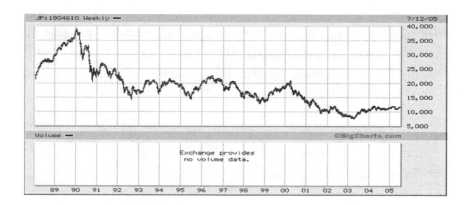

The legacy of bursting stock gauges included damaging and dangerous recessions, except for the 1987 crash. (Bubbles can sometimes exist in otherwise healthy economies.) But Japan after 1990 and the United States after 2000 suffered recessions, widespread bankruptcies, evaporating profits, major unemployment, outright deflation in Japan, and the specter of deflation in the United States. Massive boom-to-bust cyclical swings and crashing stock gauges contradicted the prematurely celebrated "wealth effect" and "new era" views. Crowd mania crowded out efficient market theory.[2]

II: The Pure Theory of a Fully Integrated Gordon-MM Valuation Model

A simple hypothetical example (Parks, 1998) may help in following easily the applied theoretical, mathematical, and empirical evidence in Section III. Assume two companies, A and B, with identical growth rates (g) = 8% for earnings, dividends, and capital gains; a 10% required return (k); and starting identical earnings ($E_0 = 200$). To show maximum potential valuations and price-earnings ratios under extremely optimistic but highly unrealistic assumptions one must posit (a) that earnings are always honestly reported and forecasted and (b) that the required return always matches the realized return. Assume further that the only difference in this ultrahappy hypothetical example is that A distributes 50% of its total earnings and plows back the 50% retained earnings into growth, and B plows back 100% of total earnings but pays zero dividends.

Consider first equation (1) for A under the Gordon dividend discount model *standing alone* with dividend distribution of 100. If the analyst mistakenly overlooks the additional 100 of retained earnings beyond the 100 of dividend distribution, the price, P_0 would be 5,400 on trailing earnings, and the price/earnings ratio, P_0/E_0, 27.

$$P_0 = (1+g)(D_0)/(k-g)$$
$$5,400 = (1.08)(100)/(0.10-0.08) \tag{1}$$
$$P_0/E_0 = 5,400/200 = 27$$

Consider next in equation (2) a fully integrated G-MM model with complete accounting of total earnings of 200, just as MM would insist. Assume now that A pays 100 in dividends but also plows back profitably 100% of the 100 of retained earnings. The alert analyst would calculate P_0 at 10,800 and the P_0/E_0 at 54.

$$P_0 = (1+g)(D_0)/(k-g) + (1+g)(E_0-D_0)/(k-g)$$
$$10,800 = 5,400 + 5,400 \tag{2}$$
$$P_0/E_0 = 10,800/200 = 54$$

Equation (2) for A generates identical maximum values with equation (3) for B, which assumes 100% earnings plowback. Of course. They are one and the same.

$$P_0 = (1+g)(E_0)/(k-g)$$
$$10,800 = (1.08)(200)/0.10-0.08 \tag{3}$$
$$P_0/E_0 = 10,800/200 = 54$$

Many investment texts fail to address the question of total earnings. That's unpardonable, the equivalent of ignoring the MM dividend irrelevancy theorem (1961).[3] My applied analysis, therefore, stresses how earnings were dishonestly hyped and how supposedly plowed-back earnings largely evaporated.

III (A): The Applied Analysis: The Predicted Bursting of the S&P 500 in 2000

I'll address here the bursting of the S&P 500 in 2000. But first consider four recipes for identifying bubble stock gauges. They provided useful cross checks for theoretical, empirical, and mathematical consistency. Recipe Four proved to be the most persuasive in analyzing the bursting of the S&P 500 in 2000 in Section III (A) and the Nikkei 225 in 1990 in Section III (D). But Recipe Four was hardly necessary in identifying the S&P 500 bubble prior to its collapse in 1987. High interest rates were the archenemy of the S&P 500 in 1987, as I'll document. Here are the four recipes.

1) Recipe One is the traditional approach for calculating fundamental value. Thus, when the calculated fundamental value lies far below market price and the macro-outlook is bleak, then one could conclude with high confidence that the gauge is a bubble. The recipe mixes in a high growth rate (g) despite forecasted cyclical weakness ahead and a low but insupportable required return (k) so that the k−g spread is positive but alarmingly thin. The floor to the required return (k) is taken as the yield on Treasury or AAA corporate bonds.

2) Recipe Two requires that one calculate how many years it would take for the derived fundamental value to catch up to the bubble market price, even assuming absurdly optimistic earnings growth and a very high earnings plowback. If the calculated time span is inordinately long, that itself would signal a bubble.

3) Recipe Three used extremely positive inputs to the Gordon dividend model designed to generate theoretical values exactly matching bubble prices. One input was a very high growth rate that I derived from the Gordon model. Since the inputs were insupportable, that itself was evidence of a bubble.

4) Recipe Four is the most compelling. It employed the same derived and high growth rate of Recipe (3) plus 100% earnings plowback.

For the S&P bursting in 1990, the inputs produced theoretical values far *above* the highest recorded bubble price. But these were "heavenly" inputs, that is, not of this earth. For the Nikkei 225 Recipe Four generated a theoretical value far *below* the market.[4]

Consider now the S&P 500 crash in detail. In doing so, one should recall that major cyclical depressants *preceded* the September 11, 2001 World Trade Center attack. While the attack reinforced my fears of collapse, I nonetheless had earlier and often projected that both the S&P 500 and the NASDAQ Composite would crash. Indeed, on March 24, 1998, the S&P 500 index looked like a budding bubble at 1105.[5] I should have classed it as an exploding bubble, for it rocketed to a record close of 1527 on March 24, 2000. It next plunged by 46% to 817 on February 13, 2003. By July 8, 2005, it had recovered to 1212, but still was 21% below its 2000 peak. The detailed analysis in this article, however, centers mainly on its closing price of 1409 on October 6, 2000.[6] The S&P 500 was then still very much a bubble. I could have chosen earlier dates for this article. Still the October 6, 2000 price of 1409 matched my repeated declarations of the S&P 500 as a bubble in late 1998, all through 1999, and early 2000 (see note 5).

Consider now the detailed evidence. Figure 2 includes the data for the S&P 500, my calculated annual growth rates for earnings and dividends, and the inputs for the market price of the S&P 500 priced at 1409 on October 6, 2000. You can see that my extremely high inputs ran far above any sensible reading of history. Indeed, *reported trailing* earnings plunged 45% from 51.92 on October 6, 2000, to 28.52 on December 24, 2001. Moreover, the 13.76% rapid earnings growth reported for 1992-2000 stood out as an aberration, one that I argued was laced with hype, deception, fraud, and bubble mania. It was a red flag waving far above the 6.01% annual growth rate for 1950 through 2000.

Figure 2:
S&P 500 Index: Reported Per Share Earnings and Dividends, Trailing Twelve Months

The table reports the S&P 500 index for the twelve-months trailing totals on dividends per share, and the four-quarters trailing totals on earnings per share, in US dollars, adjusted to the index.

Year	1926	1950	1992	10/06/2000	08/24/2001	12/24/2001
Earnings	1.24	2.84	19.09	51.92	45.44	28.52
Dividends	0.69	1.47	12.38	15.2	15.76	15.68

Source: The historical data for 1926, 1950, and 1992 on earnings and dividends per share are from requested printouts that "The S&P Rating Library" sent Parks on October 29, 1997, which are taken from S&P's *Security Price Index Record*. The data explicitly cited here are from the accompanying tables (pages 299 and 302) titled "Earnings, Dividends, and Price Earnings Ratios." They are also "per share" and "adjusted to the index." S&P 500 trailing total earnings and dividends per share for October 6, 2000, and later data are from the weekly publications of *Barron's* in its "Market Week" section.

Calculated Compound Annual Growth Rates for the S&P 500 Index

Period	Time Span	Earnings	Dividends
1926-2000	73.75 Years	5.19%	4.28%
1950-2000	49.75 Years	6.01%	4.81%
1992-2000	7.75 Years	13.76%	2.68%

Parameters in the Valuation of the S&P 500

The derived growth rate (g = 8.2765964%) and the dividend yields are based on the market price of 1408.99 on October 6, 2000, and the assumed required rate of return (k = 9.5%).

S&P 500 Price at close on 10/06/00	P_0	1408.99
Dividend Last 12 Months	D_0	15.92
Earnings	E_0	51.92
Required Total Return	K	9.50%
Calculated Growth Rate	G	8.2765964%
Price-Earnings Ratio	P_0/E_0	27.14 Times
Dividend One Year Ahead	$D_1 = D_0(1+g)$	17.23763415
Current Dividend Yield	D_0/P_0	1.1298874%
One-Year Ahead Dividend Yield	D_1/P_0	1.2234036%

Consider next what inputs one would have to employ in Recipe Three to derive a theoretical value matching to the penny the bubble S&P 500 price (P_0) of 1408.99 on October 6, 2000. (To show exact matching I had to carry many digits to the right of the decimal place.) Assuming a 9.5% required rate of return (k) that most money managers would then have deemed reasonable and a dividend (D_0) of 15.92 in the trailing twelve months, I derived the annual growth rate (g) from the Gordon model (equation 4) that, with the other inputs, would equate exactly the calculated value to 1408.99 (equation 5).

$$g = (k - D_0/P_0)/(1 + D_0/P_0) = (0.095 - 0.011298874)/(1.011298874) = 8.2765964\% \text{ (4)}$$

$$P_0 = D_0 (1+g)/(k-g) = (15.92) (1.082765964)/(0.095 - 0.082765964) = 1408.99. \text{ (5)}$$

I ignored in my inputs several factors that signaled additional troubles ahead. They included the nonsensical assumption of no slowdown cyclically in earnings or dividends, forever; a current 69.34% plowback of earnings forever maintained, with 30.66% of earnings paid out as dividends (recognizing that the higher the plowback the higher would be P/E levels and future capital gains); large stock buy-backs at bubble prices; zero taxes and commissions on capital gains, the equivalent of an eternal tax shelter; zero concern over the risks of bubble-high stock prices; and zero overstatement of reported *trailing* earnings or *projected proforma operating earnings.* I forecasted a growth recession degenerating into recession, but assumed in my valuation model *no growth recession or recession in sight.*[7]

Figure 2 (third panel) includes the inputs for my calculations applicable to the S&P 500 closing price on October 6, 2000. Figure 3 is designed to make explicit that the growth rate assumed for dividends applies also to earnings and capital appreciation. The example assumes that one buys at 1408.99, holds for five years, and then sells at the end of the fifth year for 2096.92 (figure 3). The capital gain is also 8.2765964%.

Figure 3
The Theoretical and Mathematical Bonding of the Gordon and MM Valuation Models

Analysis based on the S&P 500 closing price of 1408.99 on October 6, 2000 (and inputs in figure 2). Source: October 12, 2000 *Money and Capital Markets Monitor*

The ultrapositive (but insupportable) inputs I used in the Gordon model were deliberately designed to generate a theoretical value matching exactly the 1408.99 bubble price. The integrated G-MM model accounts explicitly for total earnings, including dividends and retained earnings plowed back into growth. Maximum potential values, with the derived growth of 8.2765964% for both models, are as follows:

The Gordon Model (with retained earnings ignored): $(D_0)(1+g)/(k-g) = 1408.99$
The Integrated G-MM Model: $(D_0)(1+g)/(k-g) + (E_0-D_0)(1+g)/(k-g) = 4595.15$
Inputs for 9.5% Required Return
$$k = IRR = (D_1/P) + g \ (1.2234036\%) + (8.2765964\%) = 9.5\%$$

The table for the Gordon model standing alone assumes a five-year holding period in which one purchases at 1408.99 and sells five years later at 2096.92, for a capital gain of 687.93. You can see that the assumed growth rate applies to dividends, earnings, and capital appreciation. But the table does not explicitly address any additional capital gains from retained earnings also plowed back for additional growth. The integrated G-MM model is indispensable in estimating maximum valuation even as real world forces decimated earnings and obliterated valuations. *But the bonded G-MM model is by no means the equivalent of the*

Gordon model standing alone whenever retained earnings are ignored. Hence the title of the table.

The Gordon Dividend Discount Model Standing Alone				
Year End (n)	Initial Dividend (D_0)	Dividend ($D_n = D_0(1+g)^n$)	Discount Factoor ($(1+k)^{-n}$)	Present Value $D_n(1+k)^{-n}$
1	15.92	17.2376	0.91324	15.7421
2	15.92	18.6643	0.83401	15.5662
3	15.92	20.2091	0.761654	15.3923
4	15.92	21.8817	0.695574	15.2204
5	15.92	23.69278	0.6352277	15.0503
6	15.92	25.65373693		

Present Value of Five-year Dividend Stream	76.9713
Price at End of Year Five ($P_5 = D_6/(k-g) = 2096.915272$) ($25.65373693/(0.0950-082765964) = 25.65373693/0.012234036 = 2096.915272$)	
Present Value of Price at end of Year Five = $P_5/(1+k)^5$ ($2096.915272/1.57423874 = 1332.0186$)	1332.0186
Sum of Theoretical Value Matching Bubble Price = 76.97 + 1332.02 =	1408.99

I also calculated what the fundamental value would be under Recipe One. In this case I entered somewhat less wildly optimistic inputs to the model. For example, I assumed a long-term growth rate g of 7.7%, which is still fairly optimistic and far higher than the 6.01% annual growth rate of earnings and the 4.81% annual growth rate for dividends in the long period of 49.75 years between 1950 and 2000 (figure 2). Even so, the calculated fundamental value of 953 lay far below the 1409 market price.

$$P_0 = D_0(1+g)/(k-g) = 15.92 \ (1.077)/(0.095/0.077) = 952.55 \ (6)$$

Consider next valuation under Recipe Four with the same derived and extremely high growth rate *plus* 100 percent earnings plowback. In this scenario, I assumed zero withdrawals from earnings where $E_0 = 51.92$, $D_0 = 0$, $\lambda = 100$ percent (the retention or plowback ratio), k = 9.5%, and g = 8.2765964 percent. Since $(1-\lambda)$ is zero with 100% plowback, I replaced in the Gordon model D_0 with E_0, and substituted 1 for $(1-\lambda)$.

$E_0(1+g) (1)/(k-g) = 51.92(1.082765964)(1)/(0.095-0.082765964) = 4595.15$ (7)

giving a price-to-earnings ratio of 4595.15/51.92 = 88.50443.

Earnings were 51.92. So, retained earnings were 51.92 less 15.92 of dividends, or 36. If 100% of the 36 of retained earnings were also profitably plowed back into growth (which never happened) the additional value of 3186.16 plus the 1408.99 would equate to the price of 4595.15 (equation 8). It matches, of course, the 4595.15 with 100% plowback (equation 7). They are one and the same (Section II).

$P_0 = (D_0)(1+ g)/(k-g) + (E_0-D_0)(1+g) /(k-g) = 4595.15$ (8)
$P_0 = 1408.99 + 3186.16 = 4595.15$

This static arithmetic makes sense in estimating *maximum* potential value (Section II). The same conclusions hold in a dynamic model with the focus on total earnings. The dynamics tell us that retained earnings plowed back into growth may instantly go to work in increasing the absolute levels of both earnings and dividends. *To appreciate fully the genius of MM, however, just imagine that years are shortened to seconds. Then a shift to a high plowback could quickly lift the valuation and P/E ratio, other things being equal.*[8]

A colossal catch, however, lies hidden in the phrase "other things being equal." The empirical world clashed violently with the purely theoretical world of a fully integrated G-MM model. Retained earnings were not profitably invested at the assumed growth rate. Realized returns plunged below required and expected returns. Earnings from 1995 to 2002 were frittered away in corporate acquisitions that often courted bankruptcy; in share buybacks at bubble prices that often burst; and in deception, looting, and fraud designed to enrich senior executives with stock options, exorbitant salaries, and enormous nonrepayable loans at the expense of shareholders and jobs.[9] Crashing market gauges remind us that Wall Street's mantra of *always* investing for the long run (or even the short run) gets precious little support from economic science.

I also wanted to test via Recipe Two. Remember that I derived a high growth rate that, with other optimistic inputs, generated a theoretical value matching the bubble price of 1408.99. The bubble price P_0 of 1408.99 divided by earnings of 51.92 meant a P_0/E_0 ratio of 27.14. My test was to assume instead a price-to-earnings ratio of 15, more in line historically with fairly priced stocks. With a 15 price-to-earnings ratio, the earnings per share would be 1408.99 divided by 15, or 93.93 per share. So, how long would it take under Recipe Two with a fast growth rate of 12% for 51.92 per share to grow to 93.93 per share? Answer: six years, even with a ludicrously rapid growth rate.

What can one make, though, of the celestial valuation of 4595.15 that lay far *above* the bubble price? To repeat, this value was based on "heavenly," hence insupportable inputs that include a derived and very high growth rate plus 100% earnings plowback. It's useful, I maintained, to note extreme valuations to point up the wild inputs that the crowd employs in denying the fact of bubbles.[10]

III (B): The Bursting of the NASDAQ
Composite in 2000

The NASDAQ companies had relatively little debt, but they raised trillions of dollars in the equity markets. They often substituted EBITDAM (earnings before interest, taxes, depreciation, amortization, and marketing costs) for EBIT in their *projected operating* earnings. NASDAQ analysts projected that *proforma-operating* earnings would be up sharply in 2000, 2001, and 2002 even as *trailing reported* earnings plunged over the same years. Marketing costs often represented a big multiple of *revenues*. The new mania-driven paradigm was to lock up market share now and get profits later.

Stock prices far outstripped earnings. The NASDAQ Composite P/E soared to 289 on March 31, 2001. By the summer of 2001 it sported an infinite P/E. The price peaked on March 10, 2000, at 5049, and then crashed.[11] It closed over four years later on July 8, 2005, at 2113, still 58% below its peak price. I could have used the rigorous Gordon-MM integrated model with the cross-check recipes to demonstrate a megabubble NASDAQ Composite, but that was hardly necessary. Why? Evidence of a megabubble was overwhelming in the celestial price-earnings ratio alone.

Stocks priced at bubble levels functioned often as the currency of choice in chasing after other companies and stocks at bubble prices. It also helps to explain the unprecedented climb in the M2 velocity of money from 1995 to 1999. Indeed, I classed it as the critical missing link in documenting Federal Reserve policy as ultra-easy.[12] According to the St. Louis District Reserve Bank, the extremely high M2 velocity lay in "the information technology revolution [that] permits more 'bang for the buck' in money management."[13] That said little analytically. Other district reserve banks found a fairly close correlation of M2 velocity and the opportunity costs of holding marketable three-month Treasury bills or five-year Treasury bonds over the years 1980 through 1992.[14] But from 1992 to 1999 the correlation collapsed: M2 velocity rocketed higher even as the opportunity costs with Treasury bonds fell. What was missing?

The lost link was the perceived huge opportunity cost of not holding stocks. Consider this example linking the crowd mania for stocks and its contribution to the unprecedented surge in M2 velocity.

Just how [did] the mutual fund stock boom and money velocity interact? When you draft a check against the Bank of New York to buy a [stock] mutual fund sold by Fidelity, (1) the Bank of New York experiences adverse clearings, (2) Fidelity's bank enjoys favorable clearings, and (3) Fidelity's balance sheet shows up with a liability (fund share) and an asset (dollar demand deposits in some Boston bank). Fidelity's [equity fund] manager (4) then buys newly issued or already outstanding stocks (5) shuffling deposits to the sellers of securities. The sellers . . . then have the cash (deposits) to buy labor, capital, and materials, and they (6) shuffle money to workers and consumers who (7) in turn spend to shuffle the funds to retailers and others[15] [with some checks redeposited in the Bank of New York to complete the sizzling circuit velocity of money].

Viewed alone, an unprecedented high-speed M2 velocity for a sustained period is incomplete. It must be coupled with its companion money aggregate to have any meaning. In the five years between 1995 and 1999 the M2 aggregate climbed beyond the Federal Reserve's maximum targets, and averaged annually 5.9%. Over the same time M2 velocity shot higher, averaging a 2.026 turnover. That scorching turnover rate stood far above the 1.7 average M2 velocity for the period from 1960 to 1995. So, what do you get when you multiply 5.9% by 2.026? Answer: a strong M2 monetary kick of 12% for the boom years,[16] which is just one dimension of an ultra-easy policy stance between 1995 and 1999.

Excessively easy money also showed up in *megaleveraging*, as I dubbed it. Thus net nonfinancial corporate borrowing exploded during the period between 1994 and 2000 by $1,867 billion even as net new equity financing imploded (contracted absolutely) by $627 billion.[17] Much of the borrowing by nonfinancial corporations funded buybacks of their own stocks at bubble prices that eventually crashed and the acquisition of other companies at bubble prices, which eventually saw the purchased companies go bankrupt. Exploding borrowing and imploding net equity funding contradicted the "grand illusion"[18] of a cautious and careful Federal Reserve policy over the boom years.

Private consumer and business spending speeded ahead while state and local governments went on a tax cutting and spending spree. Federal, state, and local budgetary surpluses soared, but the surpluses masked a booming economy fired by excessively easy monetary and fiscal policies that propelled income and capital gains tax revenues swiftly higher. Consumer price inflation advanced but it, too, was muffled by the ballooning US current account deficit (CAD) reflecting US imports of the highest quality at bargain prices. I dubbed CAD an unacknowledged ally of the Federal Reserve in fighting consumer inflation.[19]

The Federal Reserve during the period from 1995 to 1999 ignored *automatic* reserve cuts reflecting the fast creation of demand balances reservable at 10% that were then converted to nonreservable M2 items. It failed to slow heavy open-market buying of Treasury bonds (holdings jumped from $374 billion in 1994 to $478 billion in 1995)[20]; refused to increase margin requirements (to make sure that those buying stocks could cover the purchase price if the stock fell in value) despite rocketing stock prices to bubble heights; never *credibly* identified the overinvestment boom and bubble gauges as dangerous bubbles; and failed to restrain crowd mania or even warn resolutely of the damaging prospects for investors and workers of a boom slated to burst. Complementing central bank inaction, federal regulatory authorities and the self-regulating financial institutions failed appallingly to suppress systemic fraud.

The accumulated momentum of sustained Federal Reserve ease between 1995 and 1999 meant that the die had already been cast for a collapse of the overinvestment boom and the bursting of bubble stock gauges. An alternative explanation popularized by the press was that Federal Reserve boosts in the Fed funds rate in 2000 brought the boom to an end. No. The data on excessive monetary *and* fiscal stimulus for the period 1995 to 1999 had long signaled with high probability a collapse of investment spending and bubble stock gauges.

Most Wall Street analysts paid little attention to corporate stock buybacks or corporate acquisitions, both at bubble prices, and how this diluted earnings per share. They ignored how earnings were overstated by not expensing stock options; by repeated but illegal asset write-offs; by reckless corporate funding of suppliers in the race for market share; and by pension raiding of employee retirement funds. Wildly overstated *proforma operating earnings* meant that the P-E ratios for stocks were abhorrently understated.

How did chief investment officers fare? Many stayed invested in bubble stocks far too long; they and their clients lost heavily. How about chief financial officers? The contraction in "net new equity issues" for nonfinancial corporations (note 17) makes clear that this sector failed to raise a dime of net new equity capital despite the ultralow cost of equity funding (the other side of celestial P/E levels). Even after subtracting exercised stock options from gross corporate stock buybacks, this sector still failed to raise any *net* capital through equity funding. "Extraordinary popular delusions and the madness of crowds" held dominion over common sense, once again.[21]

III (C): The Bursting of the S&P 500 on Black Monday

I frequently dubbed the S&P 500 a bubble starting in early 1987 through the 10/7/87 and 10/14/87 *Monitors*. Recall that the bubble collapsed on 10/19/87. My timing was sheer luck. I calculated, using Recipe One, a fundamental value of 212.13 (equation 9). That fundamental value lay far below the 10/6/87 price of 319 (10/12/87 *Monitor*). The trailing twelve-month total of dividends was reported at 8.88, which meant a current dividend yield at $8.88/319 = 2.7837\%$. Assuming a high but insupportable growth rate of 7.5%, the dividend one year ahead (D_1) was $D_0 (1+g) = 8.88 \times 1.075 = 9.546$, and $D_1/P = 9.546/319 = 2.99\%$. Thus the implied or internal rate of return with these inputs was $((D_1/P) + g) = (2.99\% + 7.5\%) = 10.49\%$. I assumed a conservative (low) required return of 12%. It was low because AAA corporate bonds then yielded a high 10.8%. Since bond yields were the archenemy of the stock market, I assigned a triple-red warning. The equity premium (12% less 10.8%) was a thin 1.2%.[22]

$$FV = D_0 (1+ g)/(k-g) = (8.88)(1.075)/(0.12-0.075) = 212.13 \qquad (9)$$

Under Recipe Three I again calculated a derived growth rate (g). It was almost 9% (equation 10). As expected, it exceeded the 7.5% growth rate I first entered.

$$g = k-D_0/P_0/(1+ D_0/P_0) = (0.12-0.027837)/1.027837 = 0.0896667 \qquad (10)$$

Both growth rates (7.5% and almost 9%) ran far beyond historical experience.[23] To be sure, the 319 price and the 212 fundamental valuation now look very low as compared to present stock prices after their long and vigorous recovery to the present day. That's true, but the huge recovery contradicts not at all the fact of a bubble stock market in October 1987. Many Wall Street firms produced denials that were hilarious but wrong.[24] Black Monday teaches us that bubbles can exist in otherwise healthy economies. The crash barely fazed GDP. The market recovered fully in less than two years. Black Monday was a minor event in contrast with the huge damage of bursting megabubbles.

III (D): The Bursting of the Nikkei 225 Megabubble in 1990

I frequently calculated the fundamental value of the Japanese Nikkei 225, starting in 1987, 1988, 1989, and on several occasions after its early collapse in 1990. All calculations yielded the same answer: the Nikkei 225 was a *megabubble* fated to burst. The Nikkei 225 fell hard from its peak price of about 39,000 on December 29, 1989. But it still remained a bubble at a later price of 32,000 and a companion P/E of about 70. This induced me to make additional calculations. Consider that at a price of 32,000, the per-share earnings were 32,000/70 = 457 yen.

Focusing on Recipe Four, I included the following heavenly but insupportable inputs. They included (a) the reinvestment of all earnings at a 12% rate, forever; (b) 100% earnings plowback, which would all be happily reflected in eternal capital gains; (c) a high and constant 12% growth; and (d) a 15% required return. Even with these extremely positive inputs the calculated maximum potential value still lay at 17,061, far *below* the 32,000 bubble price:

$$P_0 = E_0(1+g)/ (k-g) = (457)(1.12)/(0.15-0.12) = 17,061 \qquad (11)$$

The denials of any bubble set forth in 1988 and 1989 by Wall Street analysts and others are best classed as crowd mania or deliberate deception, or both.[25]

Since the calculated theoretical value lay far *below* the bubble price, I was curious to find out under Recipe Two how long it would take for very fast earnings growth to catch up to the bloated Nikkei 225 at its peak of about 39,000, then later at 32,000. My shortcut was to see how many years it would take for earnings per share to grow at a very high 12% annual rate to support logically a more reasonable P/E ratio of 20 instead of the actual bubble P/E of 70, with the Nikkei 225 still priced at a bubble 32,000.

I calculated the yen earnings per share with an assumed P/E of 20. Thus 32,000/20 = 1,600. Next, I calculated how many years at a 12% annual rate it would take for 457 yen to grow to 1,600 yen, *other things being equal.* Answer: eleven years, a very long time to wait for any recovery. Indeed it was. The Nikkei 225 closed on July 8, 2005, at 11,566, still 64% below 32,000 and 70% below its peak of 39,000 in late 1989. The immediate catalyst for a stock market collapse was soaring global interest rates that helped to push the yields on Japanese sovereign bonds sharply higher, which in turn pushed the required return on the Nikkei 225 up sharply.

How destructive was the aftermath of a bursting Nikkei 225 bubble? For one thing, Japan's real GDP growth averaged an anemic 1.292% for the twelve years, from 1991 through 2002.[26] Economic anemia brought with it deflation, soaring sovereign debt, huge joblessness, widespread bankruptcies, and collapsing interest rates. Japan's plight paralleled the 1929 stock market crash in the United States that ushered in the Great Depression. The Nikkei 225 tracked eerily the NASDAQ Composite (figure 1). Both were megabubbles.

IV: Conclusions and Suggestions for Further Research

My debt to Gordon and MM is huge. Still, additional research is required to expand upon the contributions of these economic giants. New research could include (1) further analysis on the role of huge corporate indebtedness in predicting bankruptcy and (2) additional analysis on how the notion of zero risk-free borrowing, lending, and arbitrage can possibly be reconciled with the impossibility of divorcing the risks of asset management from the risks of liability management.

Imagine, for example, a borrower with AAA credit ratings. Assume he borrows short and invests in long Treasury bonds just before yield curves climb across their entire spectrums, and stay there for a sustained period. He could easily be forced into bankruptcy. While my example may seem extreme, financial history does make clear its reality. You may recall, for example, that thrifts borrowed short and invested long in the late 1970s just before yield curves rose abruptly across their entire spectrums in 1981 to produce the *death curve*.[27] A tidal wave of bankruptcies and the worst recession since the Great Depression followed.[28] That's strong evidence that even with the best credit-risk rating on the assets you acquire and the liabilities you assume, you still cannot rule out bankruptcy risk. Given also the limited human prescience noted in this article, zero-risk notions strike me as untenable.[29]

Another question is whether volatility can be taken as a reliable measure of risk. Modern portfolio theory and MM cost of capital theory both equate volatility to risk. Treasury securities so gauged are taken as risk free. Treasury securities, though, are extremely volatile, often more volatile than lower-rated corporate bonds.[30]

So, what is first and foremost in identifying risk? It surely is not volatility standing alone. At least equally important is the work of forecasting the cyclical and secular *direction* of earnings, interest rates, and stock prices. To do so requires the best of valuation tools and the best of macro forecasting tools. Indeed, this dual requirement is a key theme of this paper. It follows that economists could profit by paying far more attention to the integrated G-MM valuation model in trying to identify overpriced stock gauges. They could also focus far more on tracking, analyzing, and forecasting threatening systemic forces that underlie boom-to-bust developments, here and globally.

The parallels of the United States and Japan still trouble me. I forecasted a "megabubble" crash for Japan.[31] The reason was that Japan had fueled a runaway overinvestment boom that was unsustainable and bubble stock and real estate prices fated to crash. The United States did much the same, notwithstanding the much greater damage Japan suffered from the bursting of its property and stock markets.

Press Documentation of Major Bubble Stock Gauges Fated to Burst

The Bursting of the S&P 500 and the NASDAQ Composite in 2000

- *Barron's*, November 29, 1999 article by Alan Abelson: "'The Grand Illusion.' That's what . . . Parks calls the popular conception that Fed policy has been restrained. In fact, Fed policy, he insists, has been wildly expansionary."

- *Christian Science Monitor*, January 3, 2000 article by David Francis: "[Parks] is betting the NASDAQ bubble will burst in the next few months."

- *Journal News* (Westchester, New York), July 1, 2000 article by Phil Reisman: "Parks said [that] excessive Federal Reserve stimulation [created] a runaway boom, runaway stock market bubble, runaway real estate prices, and a mountain of debt."

- *On Wall Street,* July 10, 2000, article by Parks reads: "There has been enormous rise in stock prices [and] that's the bubble I hear about."

- *New York Times*, December 31, 2000 article by Alex Berenson on the "over investment boom": "[Parks] said 'all of a sudden you wake up with overcapacity and a pile-up of inventories.'"

- *Associated Press*, January 18, 2001 article by Dunstan Prial: "[Parks says that] speculation within . . . technology represents 'the biggest stock market bubble in US history. . . . Perform or die mania turned investment managers into gamblers.'"

- *Christian Science Monitor*, January 25, 2001 article by David Francis: "[Parks] said companies bought back their own stock at bubble prices."

- *Baltimore Sun*, September 29, 2002, p. 1 (Business). "On January 3, 2000, in the *Christian Science Monitor*, Parks described the boom in technology stocks as 'the biggest bubble in US history' and said the NASDAQ would deflate within months. In August last year [2002] after the NASDAQ had fallen to the then-unthinkable floor of 2000, Parks wrote that 'the bursting equity bubble has not run its course, especially among NASDAQ stocks.' He was right."

The Bursting of the S&P on Black Monday, October 19, 1987

- *Barron's*, September 21, 1987, p. 79. "[Parks] concludes that bonds' huge advantage over stocks' earnings and dividend yields makes prime fixed-income instruments attractive in the extreme."

- *New York Post*, February 9, 1988, p. 79. "[Parks] was for long a lonely voice in stating that the 1987 stock market boom in America was an insane development."

- *Market Chronicle*, February 26, 1987, p. 15. "[Parks advised that] stock market bulls could [now] profit by reading Charles Mackay's *Extraordinary Popular Delusions and the Madness of Crowds.*"

- *Barron's*, February 15, 1988, p. 102, in which reporter John Liscio wrote: "[Parks] recently told clients [that] Tokyo is flashing 'red-red.' Parks rated the US market red-and-yellow on August 18, 1987, and red-red on October 7 [1987]."

The Bursting of the Nikkei 225 in 1990 and Thereafter

- S&P's *CreditWeek*, January 29, 1990 lead article by Robert H. Parks insisting that "[The] Japanese stock market 'megabubble' [could] collapse."

- *Bond Week*, March 19, 1990, p. 13, quoted Parks as follows: "The Japanese are in a catch-22 situation of tightening monetary policy and watching the stock market . . . perhaps even crash" (see also *Barron's*, February 15, 1998.)

Appendix D

THE THREE-WAY FINANCIAL AND INVESTMENT REVOLUTION: THE WEB, GLOBAL ELECTRONIC TRADING, MODERN PORTFOLIO THEORY

Job Risks: Traders, Dealers, Stock Pickers, Money Managers
The Winner: King Customer as Investor (Not as Gambler)
(*The Money and Capital Markets Monitor*, June 12, 2009)

Ms. Lois Lurow of wallstreetlawyer.com asked me to expand on my views on market fragmentation and related blockbuster trading and investment changes straight ahead. Consider first these comments by Robert Kowalski of Street.com on June 12, 2009.

Robert Parks, a Wall Street economist and finance professor at Pace University in New York, thinks all the talk about fragmentation and stopping it is a ruse, that word fragmentation sounds like another word for intense competition. Within 10 years, Parks predicts all stock trading in the U.S. will be done electronically, leaving the NYSE trading floor and professional floor traders as relics of a bygone era. I think you'll have a centralized clearinghouse. Instead of fragmentation, over time electronic commerce will dominate. The trader's job will be at risk. Jobs will disappear.

Relics of a Bygone Era?

The NYSE and traders are not the only ones at risk. In the next ten years you will witness the explosive culmination of three revolutions. The first, the Worldwide Web, will expand at an accelerating pace to destroy old institutions and to create brand new ones. The second, electronic trading, still in [its] infancy, will soon sweep away with hurricane force inefficient, discriminatory, and often dishonest trading systems. The third, modern portfolio theory (MPT) will prove to be the most startling of all in making traditional money managers and many others obsolete. Operating simultaneously, the triple revolution signals enormous benefits to King Customer at the price, however, of a gambling-style casino society, which is already a plague. Consider these risk/reward specifics for the next ten years.

1) Global Best-Bid-and-Offer Electronic Trading

Why are traders, the NYSE, the Securities Industry Association, among others, afraid of CLOB (a central limit order book)? CLOB, which the SEC looks upon favorably, would route stocks through nationwide ECNs (electronic communication networks). It would also seek to assure that limit orders of public customers get "price and time priority" over the orders of dishonest security dealers operating for their own accounts. Both goals make sense. A national best-bid-and-offer (NBBO) system would be a big step ahead, too, but not big enough. Within ten years I would expect to see a global best-bid-and-offer system (GBBO) intertwined with the worldwide web and electronic communication networks (ECNs). That would add up to a global composite book.

It won't end there. Global electronic trading will become the rule not only for stocks but also for fixed-income contracts, currencies, derivatives, real estate, and countless other real and financial assets. Fierce international competition will see to that. Count on it. That very competition will slash trading commissions, costs, profits, and jobs. At risk will be the NYSE trading floor. Many professional traders will simply disappear.

2) The NYSE's Global Equity Market: A Badly Flawed GEM

The NYSE's proposed global equity market (GEM) linking key stock exchanges but excluding the NASDAQ is a step backward. The GEM cements fragmentation. The GEM would further isolate many public customers from an internationally linked and intensely competitive system. The GEM is but one of many self-serving schemes of monopolistic turfs from the ECNs and the ferocious competition they spawn. Count the GEM out.

3) The Intermarket Trading System (ITS)

The National Association of Securities Dealers and several national securities exchanges love ITS. Their pitch is that the ITS would allow all dealers to interact efficiently, thereby strengthening competition. They would indeed all get together. But is it possible that the ITS would try to sidetrack the ECNs and GBBO? Yes, the GEM, the ITS, and parallel proposals are but self-serving first cousins.

4) King Customer versus Gambling Customer

The GBBO will someday slice commission costs razor thin for the ultimate consumers, whether they be individual investors or giant institutional investment firms. It is hoped that the GBBO would make extinct the many online trading firms that now victimize their customers. The SEC estimates that more than half of the online trading firms reviewed (a) did not provide the best execution for their customers' trades, (b) improperly emphasized payment for order flow by routing orders to poorly qualified traders, and (c) suffered an inordinate number of delays and breakdowns in executing orders (General Accounting Report, *New York Times*, 6/11/00).

Other things being equal, lower trading costs should raise investment returns. But other things may not be equal. First, mania-driven, day-trading gamblers chasing bubble stocks can hardly expect to see higher investment returns. They go bankrupt instead. Second, the new exchange-traded funds (ETFs), traded like individual stocks, could easily foster more day-trading gambling consistent with the emerging casino society.

How about the highly trained and superbly educated institutional investors, money managers, and Wall Street senior strategists? Sad to say, many of the best and the brightest have also turned into gamblers. They chase rising bubble stocks via "momentum investing," a euphemism for gambling. They stay in expanding bubbles because they know that if they don't participate, they then risk losing their clients and possibly their jobs. The fund manager knows that if he does not chase momentum stocks, his clients will jump to these gambling funds. Yes, the best and the brightest have joined the casino society. It's true that the university professor must publish or perish. It's also true that money managers must perform or perish. Is it any wonder that many of them have turned into outright gamblers?

Could trading commissions charged directly to giant investment institutions approach zero, whether for indexed funds or individual securities? The huge holdings of TIAA-CREF come to mind. For example, when members shift from bond to stock funds, others may simultaneously shift from stock to bond funds. Other things being equal, the shifts would mainly offset each other. Managers would still have to make net trades, normally a fraction of member shifts, to realign TIAA-CREF's total holdings. Accountants would incur minor internal expenses to realign member accounts. The result overall for TIAA-CREF: extremely low trading costs.

Suppose that we extend this example of TIAA-CREF to a trading colossus. I have in mind a central electronic clearing (trading) unit encompassing all stock markets, all stock exchanges, all institutions, all Wall Street firms, and all consumers. What then? Stock trading costs could then plunge. King Consumer would reign but millions of traders would lose their jobs. Many would probably end up working for the giant trading firms.

That's not all. There is no technological reason why a central clearinghouse must be restricted to stocks alone. Most major real and financial assets could qualify within ten years. That's the ideal outlook, admittedly a frightening one for traders. Don't fret too much, though, for traders would find other jobs as technology expands existing markets, and spurs brand new markets, new products, and new efficiencies we can only vaguely picture now. Recall the wonders wrought by the printing press? What a happy irony.

5) Modern Portfolio Theory (MPT): Risks for Money Managers

The trader is not the only one at risk. Add to my risk list dealers, specialists, analysts, and money managers. I'll focus here solely on money managers. Consider this excerpt I chose from my book, *Unlocking the Secrets of Wall Street* (1998).

> MPT argues that you should not try to pick your own stocks because you can't beat the market. You should not pay money managers a dime to pick individual stocks because they can't beat the market either. To maximize total return and minimize nonsystemic risk (individual company risk) your best option for equities is to invest in a broadly based equity fund.

Let me explain. Modern portfolio theory (MPT) and a related cousin that, along with the Capital Asset Pricing Model (CAPM), argues that investors can maximize return for any given risk by investing in the ideal diversified market portfolio of equities. By ideal is meant the very highest return for any given risk, or the very lowest risk for any stipulated return. By market portfolio CAPM theorists mean a proxy for the broad equity market such as the S&P 500 index, the Russell 3000, or the Wilshire 5000, among others.

Nonsystemic Risk versus Systemic Risk

Nobel Prize winner William Sharpe argues that the only reason you should pay anybody to manage money is to pay for tracking and forecasting changes in systemic risk and reward. By systemic he means overall fluctuations in the stock market in response to abrupt cyclical or longer-run changes in interest rates, total profits, exchange rates, inflation rates, and unexpected shifts in fiscal, monetary, and international policies. But don't pay anybody a dime to pick individual stocks. That's already best done for you in the broadly based equity indexed funds that mirror the overall stock market.

What about that? My conviction is that Sharpe is about 90 percent correct because about 90 percent of investment performance reflects systemic changes in risk and reward. The hardest job is to figure out what indexed fund to buy. (It's not the NASDAQ, not now. The NASDAQ still trades at megabubble heights despite the recent plunge; its extreme volatility mirrors the antics of individual and institutional mania driven gamblers.)

MPT versus Allegedly Prescient Money Managers

In a July 24, 1997, report I wrote for institutional investment clients, I asked an irreverent question about stock pickers that generated howls of protest. Here's the question:

> Are the Warren Buffetts, Peter Lynches, John Templetons, among other icons, best viewed (a) as extreme statistical oddities on the right side and tail end of a normal distribution curve or (b) as extremely prescient and sophisticated money managers who year-after-year and decade-after-decade beat the market indexes?

You should have picked (a). Modern portfolio therory argues that stock pickers and actively managed stock portfolios chronically underperform in competition with an unmanaged and indexed stock fund that (a) best diversifies away nonsystemic or specific company risk and (b) closely mirrors systemic risk and reward prospects that translate into overall stock market cyclical fluctuations and trends. Burton Malkiel puts it this way in *A Random Walk Down Wall Street* (W.W. Norton, 1996): "No scientific evidence [exists] that the investment performance of professionally managed portfolios has been any better than that of randomly selected portfolios." Actually, the performance of managed accounts is far worse than Malkiel states. To see why, first try to answer this question:

> Since almost nine out of ten equity money managers on average over time underperform the S&P 500, just who does outperform?

That's the question. Please try to answer it before you read ahead. Again, who are those who outperform? A quick answer is that they change places. The average manager underperforms nine years straight, then outperforms in the tenth year. They shift chairs.

But what about the money managers who allegedly outperform year-after-year, decade-after-decade? Well, I would first check their data because many of them hype their performance results. Second, and more important, MPT and probability theory tell us that someone will always pick five horses straight, that someone has to win the lottery ticket. Translated into MPT and the normal distribution curve, you will predictably find among many thousands of professional money managers a few who outperform the herd by wide margins. You find them, consistent with probability theory, on the right side and skewed tail end of the normal distribution curve. In plain English they are plain lucky.

MPT argues further, in line with Nobel Prize-winner Harry Markowitz, that a portfolio indexed to the market itself is your best course in reducing nonsystemic or company risk. To repeat, the job of stock picking is already done for you. William Sharpe's revolutionary contribution that earned him the Nobel Prize focuses on systemic (overall market) risk.

The Blockbuster Investment Impact of William Sharpe

Money managers should devote their time and efforts to analyze and anticipate major systemic forces impacting the stock market, not on picking individual stocks. That's smart money. Simply put, investment plan sponsors should bypass self-proclaimed hotshot stock pickers to farm out company pension money to managers of indexed stock funds. That's smart money. Money managers who advertise themselves as great stock pickers should not then engage in secret "closet" indexing (investing in indexed funds). That's deceptive advertising. That's dishonest money.

Thanks to MPT, and especially the brilliant insight of William Sharpe and Harry Markowitz, it is no longer a mystery why so many money managers hate MPT. They do, you know. They know their jobs are at high risk. They know that trying to hold back MPT is on a par with King Canute's efforts to hold back the ocean waves from the shore.

Theoretical Nonsense on the Measure of Investment Risk

After complimenting so highly William Sharpe's view on systemic risk and reward, I cannot overlook the many problems of modern portfolio theory. The notion, for example, that volatility is a good measure of risk is absurd. It makes zero sense unless you define the length of your investment holding period. Is it ninety days or twenty years? Even more important, consider that if you did in fact have a valid measure of risk, you could then conclude with high probability that your realized return would match your expected return. In that never-never land you could get rich overnight. The truth is that economists have no reliable measure of investment risk, and never will.

Conclusions

Three revolutions will sweep across the investment and trading world with hurricane force in the first decades of the third millennium. They are the worldwide web, the global electronic communication networks, and modern portfolio theory. The three will operate simultaneously, magnifying each other, to benefit King Customer even as they blow away and destroy institutions and jobs many now take for granted.

Economists and money managers who truly understand systemic risks and rewards impacting investment markets will do well. One hundred percent stock pickers not trained in analyzing systemic forces will lose ground, and fast. Lawyers will run fast and profitably to deal with the complicated legal problems of the three-pronged revolution.

Appendix E

US RECESSION RAISES RISK OF DEPRESSION IN JAPAN: A SIMULTANEOUS US AND JAPANESE DOWNTURN RISKS GLOBAL BUST

Double Illusion: Easy Money in Japan and Tight Money in the United States
(*The Money and Capital Markets Monitor*, December 28, 2000)

I reached this conclusion in the August 23, 2000 *Monitor*.

> Almost always misunderstood, Japan's policy is procyclical and constrictive. That's the equivalent of a confused lifeguard pushing a drowning swimmer under water. The collapse of Japanese sovereign interest rates is not explained by easy money but rather by a bumbling central bank whose constrictive policies come straight on top of a weak and failing economy.

Many analysts argue that near-zero interest rates in Japan are firm evidence of Japan's extremely easy central banking policy. Incredible but true, the *Economist* (April 11, 1998) wrote of "Japan's super-loose monetary policy." What utter rot. Japan's central bank has in fact suppressed money growth for many years.

Even as we write this monitor, Japan's money M2 aggregate (which roughly matches ours) is higher by a minuscule 2% for the past twelve months. Meanwhile, deflation devastates consumption and investment demand, and now signals outright depression. The much-heralded economic recovery will, again, falter and die. Just as analysts mistake Japan's monetary stance to mean easy money, they also misinterpret US monetary policy to be constrictive. They are wrong. Let's review each in turn.

The First Illusion: Easy Money in Japan

The repeated but mistaken chorus of Japan's economic recovery is the story of the last ten years, ever since the collapse of its stock market. That was an easy call for me (Standard & Pool's *Credit Week*, 1/29/90), though a lucky one on timing. My present fears are worse. Consider Japan's current descent into an economic maelstrom.

> Output, prices, jobs, profits, and incomes fall; tax revenues evaporate and, as night follows day, budget deficits soar. Yet Japan still fails to monetize [create money] to fund huge deficits, but borrows instead from the public (nonmonetized deficits), which mops up private incomes and buying power, which "crowds out" private demand, which causes a further slide in output, jobs, profits, and incomes [in a self-reinforcing spiral downhill].

In plain English, the failure to create brand new money to fund huge deficits can kill any economy. It was precisely the failure to monetize huge deficits that also induced us to forecast the1981-82 recession (*Wall Street Journal*, 10/20/80). Why? The rationale was the same. Thus we maintained that huge deficits from the Reagan tax cuts that were not monetized would kill the economy. So, we got the "minidepression" we forecast.

The big difference with our experience in 1981 and Japan's experience today is critical. In 1981 huge nonmonetized deficits killed private financing and demand in a roaring, inflationary economy. We constricted to fight a wild, inflationary boom. Today in Japan, its huge, nonmonetized deficits resulting from disappearing jobs and tax revenues and poorly conceived public works kill demand by crowding out private financing and spending. Japan constricts to fight an imaginary ghost of inflation, even as its economy falls and deflationary forces grow stronger. What a suicidal mix that is!

The Second Illusion:
Tight Money in the United States

The widespread conviction that the Fed has tightened is simply not supported by the data. The error here compounds the opposite error of mistaking Japanese low interest rates with monetary stimulus. Consider this from the December 12, 2000 *Monitor*: *Fed-manufactured boom? Yes. Fed ultra-easy policy shows up (1) in fast M2 money growth consistently beyond the Fed's 5% [maximum] target; (2) in an unprecedented surge in M2 velocity, which the Fed appears to have ignored; (3) in skyrocketing business and consumer borrowing at roughly a 28% annual pace 1992-99; (4) in the explosion in CAD [the current account deficit]; and [5] in automatic cuts in reserve requirements as demand deposits, reservable at 10%, are converted to CDs, time deposits, and money market funds, reservable at zero percent. The [reserve] cuts alone swamped the tiddlywinks boosts in the Fed funds rate [fueling] the biggest mutual stock fund boom in US history, exploding stock prices, and a junk-bond market now threatening major bankruptcies. Fed-manufactured excessive liquidity soared in recent years. Tight money is a fiction.*

Excesses degenerate into opposite excesses. In the case of the United States, the Fed's ultra-easy stance creating boom now degenerates into a bust. A pile up in inventories and overcapacity here and abroad won't go away easily, to say the least. If this downturn worsens, which I expect, the focus should be overwhelmingly on a broadly based tax cut to lift consumption. A second goal should be a far more progressive tax structure.

Would that please the supply-siders counseling President Bush? Of course not. They will insist on cutting (a) the capital gains tax, (b) the highest tax rates on corporate income, (c) the highest marginal tax rates on personal income, and (d) estate and inheritance taxes. They might even try down the road (e) to legislate a flat tax or a comprehensive sales tax on the grounds of simplicity. Yes, simple but regressive. Indeed, (a) through (e) would add up to a brutally regressive policy.

Conclusions

As noted in the title to this monitor, both the United States and Japan face serious recessions for different reasons. The evidence has been building for years that both countries are headed for extremely rough times ahead. [As repeatedly argued throughout *The End of Capitalism*, the specter of depression now (2011) haunts not only the United States and Japan but also the entire world. The outlook grows even darker because of Japan's weak efforts to cool down some of the nuclear reactors damaged by the recent tsunami following the powrful earthquake off of its eastern coast in March 2011. The danger of radiation poisoning of its own people and the risk of radiation spreading to the western shore of the United States has placed significant added pressure on Japans's already overburdened economy.] RH

Appendix F

TWO ROADS TO MAJOR RECESSION: THE TUG OF WAR

(*The Money and Capital Markets Monitor*, April 20, 2005)

In the February 25, 2005 *Monitor* I warned of a perilous Tug of War. I wrote:

> "Collapsing stock gauges and the bursting overinvestment boom still tend to keep long interest rates down while runaway budget deficits, acutely for war, tend to push rates up. To be sure, excess capacity and accelerating bankruptcies still rule in suppressing recovery and signaling deep slumps." Looking ahead much further, the very worst way to finance a huge and expanding war is via monetized deficit spending [by both printing more money and the government selling more US Treasury notes]. A borrow and spend policy spells big trouble ahead, especially in the event of an unexpected surge of the economy coupled with headline news on soaring and deliberately understated Treasury and current account deficits. That poisonous mix can kill the economy.

The First Road to Recession

While nobody can quantify precisely the road to recession, the present economic slowdown could easily degenerate into a deep and prolonged slump. First, tax cuts for the wealthy are largely a spent force in sustaining economic recovery. [The claimed] trickle-down policy stimulus [that is used to support such tax cuts] cannot generate a sustained and satisfactory recovery in investment. Second, the huge overlooked crowding out of jobs by war spending is being ignored. [Except for the production of war materiel, the money that is pulled from the economy for war-related spending is not being pumped into the economy as investment and consumer spending.]

Famed economist Alfred Marshall (*Principles of Economics*, 1890) made clear that to raise investment one must lift final consumer demand. The demand for labor, materials, and investment is a "derived demand," meaning it is derived from final consumption. Keynes in his *General Theory* (1936) went further. Government might well let out on a competitive bid basis contracts to private business to repair bridges now subject to collapse, to build housing for the homeless, to fund university science, to construct both inter-and intracity rapid transit, to fund good schools, to provide medical care for all the children still left behind, to upgrade parks for all of us, and to institute programs to take the poison out of our water and air.

This liberal agenda is anathema to supply-siders. Beyond the failed Bush policies to promote sustained and satisfactory economic recovery, Bob Herbert (*New York Times*, April 4, 2005) cites Bush's moral failure. Herbert reminds us of three devils. "We're now in the age of Bush, Cheney, and DeLay, small men committed to the concentration of big bucks in the hands of the fortunate few."

The crucial problem now is the slide in real wages, the pitifully poor growth in jobs, the huge burden of consumer debt, and the legacy of excess capacity [too many consumer items seeking fewer and fewer consumer dollars] from bursting bubbles and a collapsing overinvestment boom. Most important of all, there appears to be no end to the massive crowding out by war spending of a wide array of social services and jobs. This is the huge but understated opportunity cost of a misguided and dreadful war.

The Second Road to Recession

Consider a perilous mix of trillion-dollar budget deficits and exploding current account [trade] deficits, and a strong economic surge. What then? Well, then [we should expect] investment managers (bond vigilantes) to dump their bonds. That group includes foreign holders of dollar denominated bonds, domestic banks imitating hedge funds [lending larger and larger sums for long-term use with less capital in reserve in the event of a downturn in the economy], and huge mortgage companies with ultra-thin capital such as Fannie Mae.

The Road to Bankruptcy:
Borrowing Short and Lending Long

All have been borrowing short and lending long, and profiting handsomely to date on the positive interest-rate spread [higher expected return on investment] and lower interest rates (rising bond prices) [the lower cost of borrowing money]. But when fears of soaring interest rates and inflation take hold they will run as a herd and sell their long bonds and mortgages. Rates will soar and bankruptcies abound [as people sell their financial assets to cover their borrowing, the price of those assets falls making it impossible to pay off debt]. [The Fed] will then speak of unexpected turmoil, powerless to counter the vigilantes.

In earlier *Monitors* I wrote of the impossibility of separating out the risks of borrowing and lending. Suppose you were rated AAA as a borrower. Now assume that you borrowed short term to buy thirty-year Treasury bonds just before long interest rates unexpectedly soared. In that case, you could easily tumble into bankruptcy. This example may sound extreme to you. But that's exactly what happened to the savings banks in 1981-82. They borrowed short and invested long just before interest rates across the board soared [forcing them to sell their bonds fast, which flooded the market and dramatically dropped the price of the bonds they were selling, which resulted in] throwing them into bankruptcy.

The same things are happening now. Moral: You cannot separate how you invest with how you fund what you invest. A second moral, as we all can now witness, is not to put your trust in the rating agencies. The AAA ratings were fictions, predictable fictions.

Two Perilous Peas in a Pod: Bush and his Allied Sycophant

Allied sycophant? Who? [At the time it was]Alan Greenspan [and the Fed]. Could prospects get even worse? Yes. The reason is that [the Fed] helped George W. Bush to finance a huge war largely via the money printing press. Greenspan is an old favorite in these *Monitors*. One of many examples of failed monetary policies is the 1997–2002 boom-to-bust cycle. That cycle was a central bank-fueled-and-fired cycle.

Ultramonetary ease in 1997 through 2000 showed up overwhelmingly in the data. It included corporate megaleveraging, the explosive rise in M2 [the actual money supply in circulation] times M2 velocity [the multiple turnover of this money as it is spent over and over again in the market-place], soaring asset inflation [e.g., the exploding home values, stock prices, and the like], the failure to raise margin requirements [for corporate and private investors thus more people were borrowing more to own stocks and property that they were sure would balloon in value very quickly and they would make a killing], the Fed's refusal to slow its heavy open-market purchases of Treasury bonds, and the failure to warn resolutely of the dire consequences of bursting stock gauges. What were the consequences? They included (1) a giant overinvestment boom that predictably collapsed and (2) flyaway bubble stock gauges that predictably burst.

Summary and Conclusions

Which of the two roads to recession is more likely? You choose, but choose one or the other, or both. [It appears now (2010) that deflation is sinking its deadly teeth into the economy. Also, the credit freeze; the collapsing economy; the crashing equity, debt, and property markets all signal deep and lasting troubles that come squarely on top of a hollowed out economy, soaring foreclosures and bankruptcies, and an overindebted and cash-poor business and consumer public.]

What does recession mean for the stock market? It's worth repeating my conclusion in the February 25, 2005 *Monitor*: Beware recession as severe as that of 1981–82 that could clobber the stock market.

What about the overinvestment boom? [Well, it is now dead.] What about corporate bonds and mortgages now ["under water" and] priced far below their purchase prices? [They are now called the walking dead, the zombies.] Economists call them toxic or acid securities, now piled up in unsalable inventories of banks, mortgage companies, insurance companies, and a wide array of hedge funds and private investment funds. This is only a partial list of toxic (poisonous) real and financial assets that now sends corporations and countries across the globe into bankruptcy and collapse.

What does this all mean for the stock market? *Chicago Tribune* reporter John Lux (April 4, 2005) reported, "Parks thinks that now's the time to show the markets your heels. He shifted every penny to money-market funds." Not quite. By 2007 and 2008 I had shifted all my funds to thirteen-year duration Treasury Inflation Protected Bonds (TIPS). Unlike zombies they have little or no credit risk, at least for now. RH

Appendix G

TEN FORECASTING SINS OF CAPITALISM: PROBABILITY OF DEEP DEPRESSION JUMPS FROM 60% TO 75%

(The Money and Capital Markets Monitor,
Updated and Expanded April 2, 2009)

Why is it that the giant consensus forecasts of economists, including the Blue Chip Consensus, seldom identifies bubble stock gauges until after they have burst, or runaway overinvestment booms until after they have collapsed? Why does this same critique apply to senior US officials?

I'll address in this *Monitor* the multiple reasons why private and government forecasters paint rosy scenarios no matter how bleak the outlook. Dreadful is the word that best describes the forecasting records of the Federal Reserve, the Treasury, the Council of Economic Advisers, and the Budget Bureau.[1] Consider first the record of the Federal Reserve, which I have recounted throughout this volume. Over many years I graded the Fed with an F for failure, and I still do.

Many Strikeouts in a Row

As I have shown time and again, the Fed policy of excessive constriction preceded recession every time. In each case the Fed pursued an excessively expansionary policy to produce a runaway boom and then an excessively constrictive policy to produce recession.

The Fed's policy of ultra-ease from 1997 to 2002 fired the overinvestment boom that predictably collapsed and the megabubble stock gauges that predictably burst. Did the Fed question the inanity of targeting interest rates?[2] No.

Were the fiscal and monetary "experts" at the Fed, the Treasury, and the private sector (1) blind, (2) confused, or (3) trapped by the same "extraordinary popular delusions and the madness of crowds"[3] of private investors? You should have chosen all three.[4]

The Reasons for Appallingly Bad Forecasts

Let's check the reasons for the seeming blindness of consensus forecasters. They range from forecasters' personal fears, to extreme right-wing ideology, to deficient knowledge of basic forecasting tools, to delusional crowd mania, and to deliberate distortion of the truth. Here are ten reasons I find most relevant to the current financial meltdown and major recession.

1) The Missing Policy Stimulus: I constantly read of the need for a massive public works program to create jobs and incomes for many millions of Americans. Where are these programs? For the last three years I argued in these *Monitor*s and in refereed journal articles that job creation should be the first priority of federal government stimulus. But I find only weak jobs programs in place, even at this late hour. One example is in the funds President Obama provided to the states for repair and rebuilding of America. But its size is peanuts in relation to what is needed. Have we already run out of time? Here is my forecast:

> **No satisfactory and sustained economic recovery is possible without a swift program to put people to work that at least matches or exceeds that of the massive federal jobs stimulus of the Great Depression. Deflation has now sunk its teeth into the economy and fosters expectations of continuing price declines and huge job losses. A full-blown jobs program is critically needed here and now.**

2) Extreme Right Ideology. The US history of economic science constantly preaches that the best of all worlds is that of extreme laissez faire capitalism with minimal regulation and controls. We constantly hear that the free market always knows what is best for the people. Adam Smith (1776), Milton Friedman, and current supply-side theorists preach this doctrine. But the theory is not supported by economic science. *An economy without controls can quickly become out of control.* The absence of regulation can help to produce a catastrophic financial meltdown and a severe and sustained global recession.

Famed economist John Maynard Keynes, a stern critic of capitalism without controls, taught us that ultrafree markets can backfire with frightful consequences. Keynes also destroyed the notion that major economic slumps would automatically generate economic recovery. Karl Marx forecasted that capitalism would implode (collapse) because of its internal contradictions. The neoclassicist Alfred Marshall (1842-1924) warned in his *Principles of Economics*, published in 1890, that a collapse in consumer demand would bring with it a collapse in investment spending. All three—Keynes, Marx, and Marshall—wrote how ultrafree and uncontrolled markets held the seeds of their own destruction. Extreme free-market thinkers, supply-side theorists, and ultralaissez faire Republicans repeatedly dismissed their views as flawed. Who was right and who was wrong? You now know.

3) Unreliable Macroeconomic Forecasts. One would hardly expect laissez faire market adherents to forecast any economic slump. Classical economic theory insisted that recession is impossible under capitalism. Keynes destroyed that economic nonsense in his *General Theory* (1936). He wrote also that there is no automatic recovery from depression. Yet other problems stalk free-market disciples. They passed off their right-wing ideology as economic science. They still bellow free-market gobbledygook, as do the right-wing Washington, DC, think tanks. They still oppose any role for big government in solving huge problems. The huge problem now is how to block major recession from spinning into a depression. The first step is to show the door to the ultraright.

4) Unreliable Stock Market Forecasts. What about Wall Street forecasts of the stock markets? To forecast reliably one must first master the theory and mathematics of a fully integrated stock model that combines the work of Myron Gordon, Franco Modigliani, and Merton Miller (see appendix C). That is the only trustworthy way to calculate fundamental value, which then permits one to compare fundamental value to actual market prices. With these Nobel Prize winners as my guide, I managed to forecast *ex ante* every stock market collapse from 1969-1970 to the 2008-2009 crash.[5] I have yet to meet many economists who are thoroughly at home with these three Nobel Prize winners. The RR's (Registered Wall Street Brokers) and senior investment managers I counseled over thirty years were seldom even familiar with the names of Gordon, Modigliani, or Miller.

5) Failed Microeconomic Analysis. But poor reasoning is just one explanation for bad macroforecasts. Others include the propensity to hype profit forecasts, to be blind to mania-driven markets, and to ignore pure greed. Yet another is the wasted time analysts spend on micro-analysis of individual companies but with zero understanding and attention paid to the macroforces. Remember the Titanic? The microengineers and others insisted that the ship was unsinkable. But it sank to the bottom of the sea on its first voyage. Why? It ran into an iceberg, a huge and destructive macroforce. The analogy was relevant then. The current collapse of the United States and foreign nations can also be analogous to a massive macro-force. Macrodestruction now warns of a full depression straight ahead.

6) Poor Theory on Coincident Indicators. Yet another forecasting error is the heavy reliance on the coincident indicators of economic activity. They include GDP, industrial production, employment, retail and wholesale sales, consumer confidence data, and incomes, among others. I have always labeled the coincident indicators as "rear-view mirror indicators." They tell you where you have been but not where you are going. Though coincident indicators are the most popular, they are largely useless for forecasting purposes.

To improve your forecasting abilities, focus mainly on the forward indicators such as new orders, unfilled orders, contracts, inventories (whether huge or in short supply), among other leading indicators. The most important leading indicators by far are the initial and likely lagged effects of monetary policy, fiscal policy, and international financial policy. While most important, forecasters rarely track or even understand the lagged impact of government actions that often prove to be devastating.

Moreover, never pay a whit of attention to what government policy makers say they do. Instead, track like a hawk the theory and data that tell you what they actually do. Never forget that government officials invariably paint to the positive side no matter how bleak the outlook. Remember that government policy makers often deceive and lie. On that count, the disgraced George W. Bush and his Republican supporters receive first prize for dishonesty. Who knows, maybe Barack Obama can teach the whole world to start telling the truth.

7) Treacherous Risk Models. Risk models are also out of date, including deviations from the standard deviation. Indeed, all of the risk models I have studied are based on historical data, including the once revered econometric models. The big problem today is that traditional forecasting models based on past data are largely irrelevant. Why? "Bayesian Analysis" tells us why. The Bayesian models deal with catastrophic forces almost universally left out of traditional models. These forces include massive floods, wars, global warming, and the proliferation of nuclear bombs. The recent global meltdown and recession should also be included as potentially catastrophic. These multiple Bayesian signals now warn us of a second great global depression.

8) "Quants" and Their Broken Mathematical Models. One of the most devastating forces that led to the present financial meltdown and recession was the inane work of financial quants, the quantitative mathematical economists. The quants substituted mathematics and patterns of past data for sound economics. But their models suffered major flaws. One key missing ingredient was their total inability to identify in advance the initial and often the lagged destructive impact of bumbling monetary, fiscal, and international financial policies. I have already reviewed that breakdown in depth. Today nobody would pay a nickel to rely on econometrics, including Wharton econometrics.[6]

9) Excessive and Deliberate High-Risk Leveraging. Want to be extremely profitable? Just borrow short term and invest long term in much higher yielding mortgages. The savings banks did that for many years. But during the period 1981-1982 long-term interest rates soared to record heights. Mortgage market prices plunged to bankrupt the thrifts and the federal government had to bail them out. They overleveraged. But it's far worse this time. Banks, private individuals, house buyers, and the broad mix of hedge funds, private funds, and Wall Street investment banks again overleveraged just before long-term interest rates soared. Again, they experienced huge losses, capital impairment, and many now risk bankruptcy. This time the holdings of the "shadow market" of investment bankers and others include countless millions of toxic instruments still market priced February 2011 far below initial costs. Toxics are the walking dead. The issuers apologize but their deeds smack of deliberate grand theft. Think AIG.

10) Value at Risk Drivel. Another broken down mathematical model goes by the name VaR, meaning value at risk. Grounded on statistical and probability theories that are centuries old, the VaR came into being in the early 1990s according to Joe Nocera, a business columnist for the *New York Times*. Well, I was around in the early 1990s and found myself virtually alone as a harsh critic of the quants and their collateralized mortgage bonds, credit default swaps, VaR, and other lethal creations.

One of the most specious enchantments of VaR was that it was supposed to measure the amount of risk in a trader's portfolio and firm-wide risk, all in one number. What rot! Still, the Securities and Exchange Commission and the Basel Committee on Banking Supervision both validated VaR. Preposterous but true, both regulators said that firms could rely on their own internal VaR calculations to set their capital reserves. That's a perfect example of zero controls.

Indeed, the VaR and related quant gibberish was all part of the attempt by financial economists to carve out a separate and higher-valued niche for themselves, separate and superior to economic science. That attempt failed predictably. It ruined the reputations of financial quants and cost millions of investors their jobs, incomes, homes, and life savings. Again, the quants' downfall is explained by their failure to see that finance has always been and always will be subservient to sound economic science. Quants damaged the image of many finance professors, but not those who always pay first allegiance to economic science.

Conclusions

Over three years ago I began writing *The End of Capitalism*. Meanwhile the devastation of capitalism has accelerated at high speed. As of early 2011, I fear we may have run out of time to ward off a major and sustained depression of many years. I see no reason now to alter the title of my work.

Appendix H

DINOSAUR BANKS: TOO BIG NOT TO FAIL

(The Money and Capital Markets Monitor, May 9, 2010)

Is there any parallel between huge monopoly banks and huge dinosaurs? Yes indeed. Both run out of control and can quickly destroy just about everything they touch. Specifically, huge banks, time and time again, borrow far too much money and become overloaded with debt. Sharp-eyed rating agencies may then jump together to cut their ratings on bonds and mortgages. Investors take note and abruptly discover that they can't borrow except at much higher interest rates. Economists dub this dangerous state of affairs "overleveraging," which first shows up in a wave of bank defaults followed by systemic bankruptcies in the United States. Why do banks over-leverage? Simply put, they want to grow bigger and bigger with cheap money in order to boost reported earnings and fill their pockets with giant-sized salaries and bonuses. The financial meltdown in the United States from overleveraging was a critical reason that explained the giant recessions here and abroad in the 1980s, the very worst recessions since the Great Depression. The State of New York's attorney general started an investigation of eight banks to determine whether they provided misleading information to rating agencies in order to inflate the grades they are given for the stock they sell.

These financial meltdowns are made far worse by the heavy use of derivatives. Right-wing Republicans are strong supporters of derivatives. Their argument is that derivatives help to protect corporations, investors, and the public from bankruptcy. Yes, they can help, but the grand old GOP wants little or no control by government on these derivatives.

What's the result? As I write this (winter of 2011) a major argument among liberal Democrats and angry Republicans unfolds as to why the markets, especially the stock markets, abruptly crashed, including the very biggest Wall Street firms such as Goldman Sachs. Why? The answer lies in the large banks that once again are making high-risk loans so they can to grow to dinosaur size or at least elephant size. That's not the only danger to the public when reliance on derivatives expands out of control. Huge banks also create toxic stocks that are deliberately designed to fail (i.e., the stocks are based upon financial instruments of highly questionable value). The banks then sell their own stocks "short" (at a discount) to make even more money to boost their obscene salaries and bonuses. Stocks now priced far below the purchase price, as I have often noted, are also toxic. A number of new stocks created by mathematical experts (called quants) are not only toxic but also exotic. The average investor cannot figure out what they mean. To make matters even worse, electronic trading has also run out of control and is poorly regulated. Several years ago, I wrote that eventually all stocks would be bought and sold electronically, a powerful force that would largely cripple the New York Stock Exchange. I neglected, however, to warn against unregulated electronic trading.

So, what is the biggest danger of all? It lies in giant dinosaur banks and other oversized financial institutions. They must be cut down in size. They should never be too big not to fail.

NOTES

Introduction: Destructive Contradictions of Capitalism

1. For my forecasted collapse of financial markets and housing see my epilogue to *Unlocking the Secrets of Wall Street* (Amherst, NY: Prometheus Books, 1998) and my article titled "Ex ante Recognition of Bubble Stock Gauges and Forecasts of Their Bursting in the United States and Japan," *The Journal of the American Academy of Business, Cambridge* 8: 1 (March 2006). The article won the best author award and appeared as the lead article. I was invited to make the keynote address at a conference the Cambridge journal hosted in New York City.

2. Lobbyists declare that guns in the home can protect us from intruders. Quite the contrary is in fact the case. The data show that firearms in the home lead to a dramatic increase in deaths as a result of gun accidents and angry reactions to domestic violence. See chapter 1 for details.

3. The US Supreme Court ruled in June 2008 that imprisoned suspects have the right to petition US courts and challenge the legality of their open-ended detention. The ruling stands as "a major setback to the Bush administration and its illegal and cruel treatment of 'enemy combatants.'" See *Christian Science Monitor*, June 13, 2008, p. 1.

4. Bertrand Russell, philosopher and mathematician, first noted the arithmetic-geometric link. See the *Autobiography of Bertrand Russell 1872-1914* and his *Autobiography 1914-1944*, both published by Little Brown and Company in 1967 and 1968, respectively. I view Russell as one of the most prescient and brilliant philosophers of all time. His warnings long ago of a nuclear holocaust are still relevant today.

5. *Economist,* August 6-12, 1994, and *Unlocking*, pp. 391-92.

6. I wrote the September 27, 2008 *Money and Capital Markets Monitor* specifically for investors and the press.

7. As a liberal economist virtually all of my clients were ultraconservative right-wing Republicans. They were far more interested in getting sound advice than in exploring my liberal philosophy. Strange.

8. See "Taxes and the Budget, Triumph of Self-Deception," *Unlocking*, pp. 214-24.

9. J. C. Flugel. *Man, Morals, and Society* (London: Duckworth, 1945).

10. See chapter 17, "The Tokyo Stock Mega bubble: The Role of Delusion and Deception" in *Unlocking*.

11. One of the very best books on myths, bad theory, and fake data is by the famed scientist Carl Sagan's *The Demon-Haunted World*: (New York: Random House, 1995).

12. See Plato's most famous dialogue, *The Republic*. He wrote it about 370 BCE.

13. Quoted from Rudolph Flesch, *The Art of Clear Thinking* (New York: Harper and Row, 1951).

1. The Plague of Gun Violence across America

1. "No Endgame," *New Yorker*, May 12, 2008 (emphasis added).

2. "Next Mortgage Bust," *New York Times*, May 18, 2008. I recommend this short but serious analysis.

3. See chapter 14 "Tax and Budget: The Triumph of Self-Deception over Scientific Method" in my *Unlocking the Secrets of Wall Street* (Amherst, NY: Prometheus Books, 1998) for my forecast of the 1981-82 recession under Reagan.

4. For a detailed analysis of my forecast of the present recession, see the epilogue of *Unlocking* titled "Entering the Third Millennium: Global Economic Shocks in an Electronically Bonded World."

5. I based this description of the NRA on Wikipedia, the free encyclopedia, and other confirming sources.

6. My comments on the Brady Center to Prevent Gun Violence and the American Medical Association are based mainly on Wikipedia and the free encyclopedia available on the Internet.

7. The Brady Center to Prevent Gun Violence see http://www.brady-center.org accessed on November 15, 2008.

8. Ibid.

9. Ibid. The cases are set forth in articles titled "Law Enforcement and Communities Less Safe Since Expiration of the Assault Weapons Ban," "US Supreme Court Should Reject Attempt to Weaken Law on Gun Possession by Domestic Violence Abusers," "Brady Center Takes Alaska Dealer to Court for Supplying Rifle to Murderer."

10. "The Medical Costs of Gunshot Injuries in the United States," *Journal of the American Medical Association*, http://jama-assn.orglcgc/content/full, August 4, 1999.

11. These data were taken from a fourteen-page Wikipedia listing of school-related attacks.

12. "Man in Santa Suit Kills 9, Self on Christmas Eve," *Yahoo News*, December 26, 2008.

13. I listed only the American schools. If you are interested in a full global listing with explanation of what happened in each individual attacked, just go to Wikipedia and click "List of School-Related Attacks." The full listing of both the US and foreign schools makes clear that the horror of death by gun is global.

14. The Brady Center for the Prevention of Gun Violence.

15. Ibid.

16. Ibid.

17. The numbered reports are documented as follows: (1) *New York Times*, June 16, 2005; (2) *New York Times*, June 17, 2005; (3) *New York Times*, June 17, 2005; (4) *New York Post*, June 26, 2005; (6) *New York Post*, June 29, 2005; (7) *New York Times*, July 8, 2005; (8) *New York Times*, July 11, 2005; (9) *New York Times*, July 12, 2005.

18. My encounter with furious NRA members is a true experience that took place at a health club, the Vertical Club, in New York City many years ago.

19. What can you do the next time you hear a slogan that makes no sense? Just create a similar but even more illogical slogan to show that both are false. Then explain the error theoretically and empirically. Two great books on how to spot fallacy and dishonest arguments are *How to Write, Speak, and Think Effectively* by Rudolf Flesch (New York: Signet Book, New American Library, 1960) and *Straight and Crooked Thinking* by Robert H. Thouless (London: Pan Books, 1964).

20. *New York Times*, March 22, 2005.

21. *New York Times*, February 2, 2006.

22. *Christian Science Monitor*, May 10, 2005.

23. *Wall Street Journal*, February 16, 2006.

24. Former Vice President Dick Cheney opposes gun controls but managed to shoot a fellow hunter in the face. Was Cheney brought to justice despite his failure to report immediately his deadly folly? No. Is there any linkage of macho hunters' fun with deadly guns and macho support for a war waged on false pretenses? Yes. That at least is the conclusion I reach in chapter 2 on "The Macho War Dogs," and earlier in *Unlocking*.

25. *New Republic*, June 27, 2006.

26. Meanwhile, the NRA celebrates the news that citizens can shoot intruders in their homes, see *Christian Science Monitor*, February 24, 2006. It insists, falsely, that guns at home save lives.

27. The mayor of New York City, Michael R. Bloomberg, *New York Times,* August 26, 2006.

28. CDC National Center for Health Statistics.

29. Brady Center to Prevent Gun Violence.

30. Brady Campaign to Prevent Gun Violence, "Firearm Facts," www.brady campaign.org/issues/gvstats/forearmoverview/

31. CDC National Center for Health Statistics and the online data collection system.

32. Harvard School of Public Health (February 2007).

33. I based some of this material on research posted on Yahoo Internet articles.

34. Brady Center to Prevent Gun Violence.

35. Ibid.

36. Ibid.

37. Note this headline from the *New York Times*, November 20, 2005: "As Deer Season Opens in Wisconsin, Tensions Remain a Year after the Killing of 6 Hunters."

38. Once an investment officer asked me if he could bring his friend to a luncheon I hosted that also included cocktails. I spotted a gun under his friend's jacket. I said no, politely. It made no sense to expose my guests, all senior investment executives, to anyone toting a gun and drinking alcohol.

39. The following material is based largely on Yahoo's study of "Guns and Gangs" and "A Bid to Talk to Angry Young Men with Guns" in the *Christian Science Monitor*, June 17, 2008, p. 1.

40. The Internet provides a full listing: Try http://www.u-s-history.com/pages/h3697.html.

2. The Macho War Dogs

1. Robert H. Thouless, *Straight and Crooked Thinking* (London: Pan Books, Ltd., 1964).

2. Lord Action (1834-1902) wrote "Power tends to corrupt and absolute power corrupts absolutely."

3. The manual restrictions are also listed in the *New York Times,* March 2, 2008, editorial page.

4. See the *Christian Science Monitor,* May 22, 2008 report on US torture and false imprisonment, p. 1.

5. Newspaper reports on Obama's criticism of torture techniques in the military and intelligence gathering agencies were ubiquitous.

6. For more enraged reactions to torture see the *Christian Science Monitor,* May 22, 2008, p. 1.

7. *Boumediene v. Bush* 476F. 3d 981 (2008).

8. Ibid.

9. The evidence of harsh treatment for immigrants is reported in "Dying in Detention," *New York Times,* June 11, 2008, editorial page.

10. Ibid.

11. Ibid.

12. Raymond T. Bye and William H. Hewett, *Applied Economics: The Application of Economic Principles* (New York: Alfred A. Knopf, 1928).

13. My comments lean a bit on scientist Carl Sagan's story of the fire-breathing dragon in *The Demon Haunted World* (New York: Random House, 1996) and Amir Aczel's *Complete Business Statistics* (New York: Richard D. Irwin, 1993).

14. Government officials lied about the reasons for war, WMD, and the bloated war budget. A grand jury indicted I. Lewis Libby, one-time senior aide to former Vice President Dick Cheney, for obstruction of justice, lying to the FBI, and perjury. See *New York Times,* March 7, 2007. There was some possibility that Cheney could face a civil suit, a congressional investigation, or both, but thus far no action has been taken.

15. Michael Dobbs, *One Minute to Midnight* (New York: Alfred A. Knopf, 2008).

16. Richard Holbrooke, "Real W. M. D.'s," *New York Times Sunday Book Review,* June 22, 2008.

17. Bertrand Russell warned repeatedly of the horrible dangers of nuclear war. Eminent scientists, including Einstein, joined Russell in trying to ban WMD for all nations. The world's best scientists were ignored.

18. These estimates are from the Natural Resources Defense Council and reported in the *New York Times,* May 8, 2005. But the risk is far greater than suggested by *present* warheads. William Langewiesche warns in his article "The Atomic Bazaar: The Rise of the Nuclear Poor" that many poor nation-states will acquire

nuclear weapons in the years straight ahead, *New York Times,* May 20, 2007. Bertrand Russell, far ahead of his time, was brilliantly yet horrifyingly prescient.

19. See "Russia and China Condemn U.S. Missile Shield Plan." *New York Times,* May 24, 2008.

20. Benjamin Franklin, *Autobiography of Ben Franklin* (New York: Collier & Son, Harvard Classics, 1937), pp. 79-80.

21. Estimates by John Hopkins Bloomberg School of Public Health, *New York Times,* November 11, 2006.

22. I graded former President Bush with an F- in my *Money and Capital Markets Monitor,* November 10, 2000. I wrote it for institutional investors and the press (available on request). That was before Mr. Bush took office as president. Over a quarter of the economics professors polled by the *Economist* (September 30, 2000) also "reckoned Mr. Bush's plans merited either a D (unsatisfactory) or F (outright fail)."

23. "A Focus on Violence by GI's Back from War," *New York Times*, January 2, 2008, p. 1.

24. The "compassionate conservative" Bush failed to get prompt aid to New Orleans despite this national catastrophe. Sick and hungry people waited and waited for food, water, and medicine that arrived five days too late. Many died.

25. Presidents Lyndon Johnson, Ronald Reagan, and George W. Bush ran huge deficits that persuaded me to forecast recession in each case. And that's what we got. See *Unlocking.*

26. War spending "outside the regular budget" was $400 billion. See *New York Times,* December 14, 2006.

27. *New York Times,* May 16, 2007.

28. Ramsey Clark drafted articles of impeachment. For details see www.impeachBush.org.

29. Torture is well documented. See "American Recalls Torment as a U.S. Detainee in Iraq," *New York Times,* December 18, 2006. Scandals, cruelty, and torture at other US prisons are also well documented.

30. The atrocities are detailed in many newspapers, including the *New York Times,* December 12, 2006.

31. The failed surge was reported in several newspapers, television, and radio reports. Reporter Richard A. Oppel Jr., wrote one of the clearest and best-documented articles I have yet seen. See his "Another Female Suicide Bomber Strikes Iraqi Province, Killing 15 Near Courthouse," *New York Times*, June 23, 2008, p. A6.

3. Religious Assaults on Science

1. Andrew Ross Sorkin on Tom Wolfe, *New York Times*, June 24, 2008, C1 and C3.

2. *Unlocking the Secrets of Wall Street* (Amherst, NY: Prometheus Books, 1998).

3. Ibid.

4. Richard Dawkins Oxford University professor, wrote *The God Delusion* (Boston: Houghton Mifflin, 2006).

5. Martin Rees, *Our Final Hour* (New York, Basic Books, 2003).

6. See Carl Sagan, *The Varieties of Scientific Experience: A Personal View of the Search for God* (New York: Penguin Press, 2007) and *The Demon-Haunted World* (New York: Random House, 1995).

7. Sagan, *The Demon-Haunted World*, pp. 171-73.

8. Inta, who died in 2008, was my wife and the mother of my three children. She told me on our first date that a fortune-teller in Atlantic City said she would marry someone born on the same date as she was. Then she asked me when I was born. I said September 20. She was startled, for her birth date was also September 20. I reminded her that many millions of people were born on September 20. Thus the probability was understandable that we might share the same birth date, thus a coincidence. I also said that we should rely on scientists for good forecasts, not fortune-tellers. Then I had no idea I would end up working for over twenty-five years as a Wall Street chief economist and forecaster.

9. These definitions are consistent with *Webster's New Universal Unabridged Dictionary* (Avenel, NJ: Barnes and Noble Inc., by arrangement with The Outlook Book Company, 1992).

10. This dialogue is based upon my own reading of the historical facts and double-checking the events in the *Encyclopedia Britannica* and on relevant Internet sites.

11. George Seldes, *The Great Quotations* (Secaucus, NJ: Jersey Castle Books Sales Inc., 1966).

12. Prisoners under cross-examination by the US Army at Guantanamo Bay and elsewhere were, like Galileo, forced to confess to crimes they did not commit in order to avoid extreme torture or death. How in the world could any such confessions be taken as truth? They can't. Torture can never be justified! Torture often sparks extreme anger and revenge, two powerful emotions that can ignite a global nuclear war.

13. The data cited here are from a 2007 survey by the Pew Research Center (available on the Internet). The results were also published by the *Christian Science Monitor* and other newspapers.

14. Jesus said (John 14:7): "No one comes to the Father [God] except through me."

15. Allah is the one and only creator. "If you ask them who it is that created the heavens and the earth…they will say 'Allah.' How then can unbelievers turn away from Him?" (Koran: X XIX: 61).

16. Jesus is reported to have said, "He that believes in me, though he were dead, yet he shall live; and whosoever lives and believes in me shall never die" (John 11: 25, 26).

17. See "New Findings about U.S. Religious Life," *Christian Science Monitor*, June 24, 2008, p. 2.

18. See Seldes, *The Great Quotations*, and *New York Times Review of Books,* April 10, 2007. In *Einstein: His Life and Universe* (New York: Simon & Schuster, 2008) Walter Isaacson writes, "Einstein, immersed in science, concluded that biblical stories could not be true and [he] eschewed orthodox religious practices the rest of his life."

19. One ludicrous example is that humans in their present form showed up on Earth only 10,000 years ago.

20. See additional information on Dr. Porco's scientific views in the *New York Times*, October 21, 2006.

21. Seldes, *The Great Quotations.*

22. The selected quotes are taken from James Joyce's *A Portrait of the Artist as a Young Man*, a Signet Classic with an introduction by Hugh Kenner (New York: Penguin Putnam paperback, 1991).

23. See Barbara Tuchman's *Distant Mirror, The Calamitous 14th Century* (New York: Random House, 1978).

24. Amelia England Parks, deceased, wrote the poem. She is the mother of four sons, John, Paul, David, and Robert (RH). The greatest thing she ever taught us was just to love and be loved in return.

25. For more details on scientists Stephen Hawking and Martin Rees see the *New York Times*, March 1, 2007.

26. See The American Atheist on Yahoo.com.

27. For more details on religious discrimination see *New York Times*, May 31, 2008, p.1.

28. For more details see the *Economist*, June 14, 2008, p. 75.

29. Discrimination against atheists is widespread despite the constitutional ban on any religious test for public office. See *Christian Science Monitor,* January 4, 2007, p. 1. A computer search of "atheist" turns up many atheist groups, including the creed of *The American Atheist* that we quoted in the text at some length.

30. This part is based somewhat on "The New Evangelicals," *New Yorker,* June 20, 2008, p. 28.

4. Business and Government Collusion

1. See *Unlocking the Secrets of Wall Street,* chapter 23 titled "The All-American Protectionists: Delusion Wrapped Up in Deception," (Amherst, NY: Prometheus Books, 1998), especially pages 354 and 355 for the unlawful acts of General Electric.

2. Floyd Norris, "Inside G.E., A Bit of Enron," *New York Times*, August 7, 2009, p. B1.

3. This quote is from "Lock and Load" on the editorial page of the *New York Times,* June 27, 2008, p. A18.

4. The Brady Center to Prevent Gun Violence and the American Medical Association, see chapter 1.

5. *New York Times,* June 27, 2008, p. A18.

6. This definition is from *Webster's New Universal Unabridged Dictionary* (Avenel, NJ: Barnes and Noble Inc., by arrangement with The Outlook Book Company, 1992).

7. These examples of discrimination are reported in *New York Times*, June 28, 2008, p. A 20.

8. This material is based on chapter 1 of my *Unlocking the Secrets of Wall Street* (Amherst, NY: Prometheus Books, 1998), pp. 33 and 34.

9. This list is a tip of the scandal iceberg. See "The Scandal Scoreboard," *Wall Street Journal*, October 3, 2003, and Robert H. Parks: "Ex Ante Recognition of Bubble Stock Gauges and Forecasts of Their Bursting in the United States and Japan," *Journal of the American Academy of Business*, 8: 1 (March 2006), recipient of the Best Author Award. See also *Unlocking*, chapter 4.

10. A few reporters deserve high praise for spotting crime and corruption. They include Pulitzer Prize winner Gretchen Morgenson of the *New York Times*, Nobel Prize winning economist Paul Krugman of the *New York Times*, Alan Abelson of *Barron's*, and David Francis of the *Christian Science Monitor*, among many others.

11. Robert H. Parks, "Ex Ante Recognition of Bubble Stock Gauges and Forecasts of Their Bursting in the United States and Japan," p. 4.

12. These are the words of Charles Mackay's 1852 book titled *Extraordinary Popular Delusions and the Madness of Crowds* (L. C. Page and Company, 1852; reprinted 1932; Amherst, NY: Prometheus Books, 2001, reprint). It seems little has changed since then.

13. For the details see my *Unlocking*, chapter 17 titled "The Tokyo Stock Megabubble: The Role of Delusion and Deception."

14. For details, analysis, and forecasts see *Unlocking*, the preface and pages 40 and 53.

15. Sustained and excessive Federal Reserve easing fueled the housing bubble. See my "Predicted Bursting of the Housing Market" in *Money and Capital Markets Monitor*, August 11, 2005, and "Ex Ante Recognition of Bubble Stock Gauges and Forecasts of Their Bursting in the United States and Japan."

16. The information contained in many of the appendices to this volume will be appreciated by trained economists and financial experts.

17. This is taken mainly from *Unlocking,* pp. 84 and 85.

18. Louis Uchitelle, "Forecasters See Fast Recovery; Others Doubt Their Eyesight," *New York Times*. January 3, 2009, p. 1.

19. See *Unlocking*, chapter 5, p. 85, for the details on incredibly poor Blue Chip forecasts.

20. See Joe Nocera's article on VaR and quants, *New York Times Magazine*, January 4, 2009, p. 26.

21. I came to Wall Street in 1968 in time to forecast recessions 5 through 10. Flawed fiscal, monetary, and US international policies made forecasting recessions "a piece of cake." All is documented in appendix A of *Unlocking*.

22. This tenth case is discussed in my refereed article "Ex Ante Recognition of Bubble Stock Gauges."

23. The *Journal News*, August 18, 2007, reported the following: "Robert H. Parks, a finance professor at Pace University, said, 'The collapse of the housing bubble could drive the economy into a recession and push financial stocks down another 30 percent. Those who say the worst is past must be dreaming.'"

24. Targeting interest rates is reviewed in *Unlocking*, pp. 18 and 87-93.

25. The step-by-step explanation of targeting interest rates is taken from *Unlocking*, pp. 87, 88, and 89.

26. I was the real chief economist and Twist a senior executive officer at

Blyth Eastman Dillon. See chapter 5 of *Unlocking* titled "Mephistopheles on Wall Street," especially pp. 66-67.

27. The moral here is not to remain silent when you see abuse. Speak up even if you risk trouble. You will still have integrity. You will also discover that life can be wonderful and exciting.

28. Frederic Bastiat, "Petition from the Manufacturers of Candles," in *Selections from Bastiat's* Economic Sophisms: *Readings in the History of Economic Thought* (New York: McGraw-Hill, 1932), pp. 433-34. Also see *Unlocking*, p. 23.

29. See *Unlocking* chapter 23, "The All-American Protectionists: Delusion Wrapped in Deception," especially pages 354-55.

30. I gave then President-Elect George W. Bush a grade of F- in my *Money and Capital Markets Monitor,* October 25, 2000 (available on request).

31. See *Unlocking* chapter 6, "President Reagan and Haywire Fiscal Economics."

32. Dr. Carmona's testimony made headlines in the *New York Times*, July 11, 2007, and in other newspapers.

33. The Bush administration fought the need for basic sex education to avoid AIDS, sickness, and death. Who suffers most from religious based censorship? Answer: Adults and children of all ages. See chapter 3, "The Religious Assault on Science," on how censorship blocked truth and science for many centuries.

5. Industrial Corporate Predators

1. See Chris Roberts, *Heavy Words Lightly Thrown* (New York: Gotham Books, 2005).

2. *New York Times*, May 13, 2007.

3. A major scientific study titled "Low Fat Diet Does Not Cut Health Risks," was described in the *New York Times*, January 8, 2006. Its findings contradicted long-held views of earlier science, and caused great anguish. As we'll see, however, true scientists never claim they have found *final truths for all time*.

4. "Better to Be Fat and Fit Than Skinny and Unfit," *New York Times*, August 19, 2008, p. F 15, quoting the *Archives of Internal Medicine*.

5. As a star cross-country runner in high school and a crazed runner thereafter, I have all the pains I cited.

6. The chemical term is methamphetamine, a deadly drug. "Local officials

[said] methamphetamine [is] the nation's leading law enforcement scourge–a more insidious drug than cocaine–and blamed it for crowding jails, theft, violence, and social welfare problems." *New York Times*, July 16, 1995.

7. Professor of Science David Siegel so argued, *New York Times*, January 28, 2007. Secondhand smoke can cause infections, asthma, lung cancer, heart disease, and death.

8. Data are from the National Highway Traffic Safety Administration (NHTSA). See also Mothers Against Drunk Driving (MAAD).

9. Details in the *New York Times*, June 27, 2008, p. 83.

10. *New York Times*, March 2, 2007.

11. "Stronger Label Sought for Diabetes Drug Byettta," *New York Times*, August 19, 2008, p. C 5.

12. "After a Recall, Risks Remain for Consumers," *Wall Street Journal*, August 19, 2008, p. D1.

13. "Merck Vioxx Study Aimed at Marketing," *Wall Street Journal*, August 19, 2008, p. B 3.

14. I was on Vioxx and stopped using it. My son and other surgeons warned me of its dangers just in time.

15. "Youth Access to Drugs Increases," *Christian Science Monitor*, August 14, 2008, p. 3.

16. "The Health Care Racket," *New York Times,* February 16, 2007. Paul Krugman does not mince words. Health expert Dr. Michaels declares, "Concern of OSHA [for] workers has gone out the window," *New York Times,* April 25, 2007.

17. The World Health Association ranks the United States as thirty-seventh in healthcare, one notch above Slovenia (article by Philip Boffey). Timothy Egan writes, "If our healthcare system doesn't kill you–infant mortality and life expectancy bring up the rear–it can put you in the poor house," *New York Times*, July 7, 2007.

18. The LIAA changed its name to The American Council of Life Insurance.

19. This entire discussion is in chapter 14: "Taxes and the Budget: The Triumph of Self-Deception over Scientific Method" of my *Unlocking the Secrets of Wall Street* (Amherst, NY: Prometheus Books, 1998).

20. Daniel Holland, *1969 Proceedings of the National Tax Association,* "Effects of Taxation on Compensation and Effort: The Case of Business Executives."

21. This truth is also falsified by "supply-side," right-wing ideologists. See Robert H. Parks, "Theory of Tax Incidence, International Aspects," *National Tax Journal* (June 1961), and Robert Frank's article "In the Real World...Trickle Down Theories Don't Add Up," *New York Times*, April 12, 2007.

22. See Parks, *Unlocking*, pp. 222-23 for a full explanation of tax impact and tax incidence, or Parks, "Theory of Tax Incidence, International Aspects," *National Tax Journal* (June 1961).

23. "The Meat and Produce Industry Put Children at High Risk," *New York Times*, January 1, 2007.

24. Dr. David Ludwig's warnings are reported in the *New York Times*, January 9, 2006. The abuse of anti-anemia drugs is cited in the *New York Times, September 9, 2007. The *Christian Science Monitor*, May 8, 2007 reports, "The FDA inspects only 0.7% of all imports." The FDA lists the most frequent violations (filth, salmonella, and pesticide) in food from India, Mexico, and China, *New York Times*, July 12, 2007.

25. The American Enterprise Institute creates flawed research for those who block effective controls.

26. Study by A. Gary Shilling Company, *Christian Science Monitor*, June 6, 2008, p. 11.

27. The Department of Labor report was included in the *Christian Science Monitor*, June 6, 2008.

28. *New York Times*, January 26, 2007.

29. "Researchers Fail to Reveal Full Drug Pay," *New York Times*, June 8, 2008.

30. The airline industry is in a "desperate" situation, *New York Times*, June 6, 2008. It cancels flights and grounds planes to cut costs and avoid more bankruptcy. Fuel prices still rise.

31. All bubbles burst, as noted in the introduction. Oil prices jumped to $145, then collapsed to $50. What's new?

32. Tailpipe pollutants can cause serious problems for children. The journal *Lanclet* warns that children who live within one-third of a mile of freeways suffer lung damage, *New York Times*, January 30, 2007.

33. The Department of the Interior says oil companies with federal leases will escape paying $10 billion in royalties over the next five years, *New York Times*, February 16, 2007. The Government Accountability Office warns that deep drilling companies could escape paying "$60 billion over 25 years," *New York Times,* March 3, 2007.

34. Big Oil is "the largest recipient of federal largesse," *Christian Science Monitor*, January 18, 2007. Big Oil is also the subject of recent suits over the vast oil spill in the Gulf of Mexico that has brought catastrophic loss and destruction to New Orleans and much of the gulf coast.

6. Racial, Sexual, and Economic Predators

1. This is the fourth meaning of "culture" as defined by *Webster's New Universal Unabridged Dictionary* (New York: Barnes and Noble Books, 1992).

2. Paul Krugmen, "Averting the Worst," *New York Times*, August 10, 2009.

3. Robert H. Parks, "Ten Forecasting Sins of Capitalism," *Money and Capital Monitor*, April 2, 2009.

4. Ibid.

5. Edmund Andrews, "An Upbeat Fed Views Recession as Near an End," *New York Times*, August 13, 2009, pp. 1 and A17.

6. Robert H. Parks, "Ex Ante Recognition of Bubble Stock Gauge and Forecasts of Their Bursting in the United States and Japan," *Journal of the American Academy of Business*, Cambridge, Best Author Award, 8:1 (March 2006).

7. Ibid.

8. My recession forecasts are listed in appendix B of this work, and in the index of my *Unlocking the Secrets of Wall Street* (Amherst, NY: Prometheus Books, 1998), p. 487.

9. Gretchen Morgenson, "The Fannie Mae and Freddie Mac Fallout," *New York Times*, July 13, 2008, p. 1.

10. Kelefa Sanneh, "Discriminating Tastes," *New Yorker*, August 17, 2009, p. 21.

11. Jim Rutenberg and Jackie Calmes, "Getting to the Source of the 'Death Panel' Rumor." *New York Times*, August 14, 2009, pp. 1 and A13.

12. John Maynard Keynes, *The General Theory of Employment, Interest, and Money* (New York: Harcourt Brace and Company, 1936).

13. I thank the Withy Law Firm for all of these listings as reported on the Internet via Google.

14. "Silent No More," the *Economist*, July 12, 2008, p. 18.

15. As noted, I witnessed a wide range of sexual and racial discrimination when employed as a chief economist with three major firms. I witnessed even worse discrimination as a young boy in New Orleans and later in Virginia. Virginians are extremely proud of their heritage, so proud that their pride could easily be labeled one of the seven deadly sins. Here is a cruel but hilarious example. One day I saw a cartoon in the *New Yorker*. It pictured a well-dressed white man and lady having cocktails at a party. The man said, "I am the only one from Virginia not related to Pocahontas." I thought the cartoon was funny, and sent it to my relatives. They were annoyed, and sent me a long history of my supposed blood link to Pocahontas.

16. *New York Times*, December 12, 2006.

17. *New York Times*, November 7, 2006.

18. *New York Times*, December 12, 2006.

19. *New York Times*, March 14, 2007.

20. *New York Times*, March 27, 2007.

21. *New York Times*, May 18, 2008, p. A18.

22. Ibid.

23. *New York Times*, July 16, 2008, p. 1.

24. *New York Times*, July 17, 2008, p. A21.

25. Quoted from chapter 3, "Mephistopheles on Wall Street," in *Unlocking*.

26. See also the racist research in wikipedia.org/wikipedia/wiki/Racism.

27. Robert Herbert, "Women at Risk," *New York Times*, August 8, 2009, p. A19. Herbert writes in this article of many crimes inflicted on women. He declares that mainstream culture is filled with gruesome forms of misogyny. Killers riddled with shame and sexual humiliation, which they invariably blame on women and girls. The answer to their feelings of inadequacy is to get guns and begin killing women and girls, among others.

28. *New York Times*, April 25, 2007.

29. *New York Times*, March 17, 2007.

30. *New York Times*, March 8, 2007.

31. *New York Times*, October 6, 2006.

32. *Christian Science Monitor*, October 6, 2006.

33. *New York Times*, November 2, 2006.

34. *New York Times*, March 23, 2007.

35. For an Internet search type "The Great Apes." Scientists warn that the great apes may vanish within fifty years because of loss of their forest habitats to humans, hunting, disease, poaching, and other vile acts.

36. See "Why Human Rights Extend to Nonhumans," *New York Times*, July 13, 2008, p. 3.

37. Published by Prometheus Books (1996).

38. For the full exchange see chapter 7 of *Frankenstein* (New York: Bantam Classic Edition, US/Canada, 1981).

39. Foreword to John Maynard Keynes, *The End of Laissez Faire* and *The Economic Consequences of the Peace* (Amherst, NY: Prometheus Books, 2004). See appendix A.

40. This section also borrows from RH's *Foreword* to Keynes's work *The End of Laissez Faire*.

41. See Parks's refereed articles (a) in the March 2006 issue of the *American Academy of Business* and (b) "U.S. Monetary Policy, Bubble Stock Gauges, and the Overinvestment Boom-to-Bust Cycle" in the *International Journal of Business Disciplines*, Volume 16-Number 2, Fall/Winter 2005.

42. See David Leonhardt's review of Doherty's "Radicals for Capitalism," *New York Times*, January 1, 2007.

43. See chapter 1 as an example of Covington in *Covert Action*, winter 1998.

44. I also found a right-wing bias in the National Bureau of Economic Research. See the details in chapter 4.

45. Paul Krugman wrote a scathing critique of the *Club for Growth* on its twisted supply-side ideology in support of business tax cuts, privatization, secrecy, and prejudice. See *New York Times,* April 21, 2007.

46. Want to meet the ultraright-wing and extreme laissez faire government supply-siders? See chapter 6 of *Unlocking* titled "President Reagan, Chairman Volcker, and Haywire Fiscal Economics."

47. RH hosted many meetings with government officials, the Congress, the International Monetary Fund (IMF), the World Bank, the Pentagon, and supply-side, think-tank ideologists. His guests were always senior investment officers, most of whom were extremely conservative. At the bar after dinner in the Madison Hotel, the supply-side government officials sometimes blurted out the truth, but not often (see chapters 3-6 of *Unlocking*).

48. The Mojave rattlesnake is the most venomous of any North American rattlesnake.

49. "Three Charged in Attacks on Election Night," *New York Times*, January 8, 2009, p. A 25.

50. "Latinos Recall Pattern of Attacks before Killing," *New York Times*, January 9, 2009, pp. A1, A2.

51. Snakes with warning rattles are often killed. Would natural selection then favor snakes without rattles? Darwin noted that species evolve to better survive long term (h*ttp://en.wikipedia.org/wiki/Rattlesnake*).

52. The Mojave rattler is widespread in southern California.

53. Chris Roberts, *Heavy Words Lightly Thrown* (New York: Gotham Books, 1980), p. 28.

7. Environmental Degraders and Destroyers

1. This definition of arson from *Webster's New International Unabridged Dictionary* (New York: Barnes and Noble Books, 1992).

2. Al Gore, *An Inconvenient Truth*, a documentary film about the threat of global warming.

3. See chapter 2 on "The Macho War Dogs."

4. This listing is from the following press reports: *New York Times*, January 7, 2007; *New York Times*, March 11, 2007; *Christian Science Monitor*, April 6, 2005; *New York Times*; August 8, 2005; *New York Times*, September 2007; *Christian Science Monitor*, July 12, 2005; *New Yorker*, December 12, 2005.

5. For more details on the suppression and censorship on global warming see "Climate Report Cites Role of Cheney's Office," *Wall Street Journal*, July 21, 2008, p. 1.

6. *Report of the Select Committee on Energy Independence and Global Warming* (July 18, 2008).

7. For additional details see, *Christian Science Monitor*, April 5, 2007.

8. See *New York Times*, April 4, 2007, for extended details.

9. It is true that China and India are the worst polluters with their use of coal plants. See *Christian Science Monitor*, March 22, 2007.

10. *The Great Global Warming Swindle* is the title of a documentary film dismissing global warming as a hoax. See Andrew Revkin, "Climate Film Draws Rebuke," *New York Times*, June 22, 2008, p. F 3.

11. International tariffs were a key factor in worsening the Great Depression of the Thirties. As we have seen, the fallacy also applies to military weapons build-ups and their deadly international repercussions (see chapter 2 on the "The Macho War Dogs").

12. To understand the simple math of comparative advantage see chapter 23 of Robert H. Parks, *Unlocking the Secrets of Wall Street* (Amherst, New York: Prometheus Books, 1998), pp. 346-47.

13. See chapter 5 of the present volume on the plague of obesity and chapter 2 on war and international lawbreaking.

14. The sources of these reports are as follows: (1) *Christian Science Monitor*, April 5, 2007; (2) New *York Times*, February 4, 2007; (3) *New York Times*, March 3, 2007; (4) *New Yorker*, March 20, 2006; (5) *WNYC* April 12, 2007 science interview of a Los Angeles science reporter; (6) *New York Times*, December

15, 2005; (7) *New York Times*, January 16, 2006; (8) *New York Times*, March 12, 2007; (9) *New York Times*, April 15, 2007; (10) *New York Times* March 3, 2007.

15. I listened to this interview on April 4, 2007, at the very time I was writing a daft of this chapter.

16. The scientific report by the Intergovernmental Panel on Climate Change.

17. *New York Times*, June 22, 2008, p. 1.

18. *Christian Science Monitor*, June 16, 2008, p. 10.

19. *Wall Street Journal*, May 22, 2008, p. 1.

20. *Wall Street Journal*, June 28, 2008, p. A3.

21. *New York Times*, July 12, 2008, p.1

22. *New York Times*, June 22, 2006, p. 1,

23. Ibid.

24. Ms. Meghan Russo conducted the interview that was published in the student paper of Pace University.

25. *National Geographic*, January 2008, p. 66.

26. Much of the material on "Planet Ocean" is based on the research of "The Nature Conservancy, Nature New York Issue" and their letter to me on "Climate Change' dated June 10, 2008.

27. The list is largely based on "The Greening of Geopolitics" by Thomas L. Friedman, *New York Times*, April 15, 2007. Friedman has long been a prescient and persuasive critic of George Bush's folly and farce.

28. High-tech trash problems are outlined in Chris Carroll and Peter Essick, *National Geographic*, January 2008, p. 66, and the *Nature Conservatory*. I based some of my comments on both sources, among others.

29. Carroll and Essick, *National Geographic*, p. 66.

30. See "Racing to Hug Those Trees" in the *Economist*, March 29, 2008.

31. See chapter 3 on the "Religious Assault on Science" and the listing I made of the world's famous scholars who say humankind risks extinction before this century is over.

8. The Perils of the Military, Industrial, and Big-Oil Complex

1. Andrew Kramer, "U.S. Advised Iraqi Ministry on Oil Deals," *New York Times*, June 30, 2008, p. 1.

2. The editorial was titled "The Iraq Oil Rush," *New York Times*, June 22, 2008, p. 9.

3. Kramer, "U.S. Advised Iraqi Ministry on Oil Deals," p. 1.

4. Ibid.

5. *New York Times*, "The Iraqi Oil Rush," p. 9.

6. Ibid.

7. Ibid., (emphasis added).

8. My review of oligopoly leans heavily on *Unlocking the Secrets of Wall Street* (Amherst, NY: Prometheus Books, 1998) and a bit on *Wikipedia*, the Internet encyclopedia.

9. Beyond the maintenance fee for my apartment I pay a separate fuel surcharge each month and another charge for electricity. Electric companies depend on fuel oil. They also boost fuel surcharges and turn off the electricity on the increasing number of customers who cannot afford to pay their utility bills.

10. "Unhappy America," *Economist*, July 26, 2008, p. 15.

11. Congressional investigators say they may subpoena former Vice President Cheney in an effort to force him to reveal his secret discussions with big oil executives.

12. Real oil prices are nominal oil prices (i.e., the market price paid irrespective of the value of the commodity) adjusted for inflation.

13. I forecasted a "maxirecession" in chapter 3 of *Unlocking* titled "Night Walkers in Washington, DC."

14. I also forecasted a financial meltdown and disastrous recession for 1981 and 1982. See the analysis and documentation in chapter 6 of *Unlocking* titled "Reagan, Volcker, and Haywire Fiscal Economics."

15. The exchange depicted here is a reconstructed composite of discussions I had with the Federal Reserve officials, International Monetary Fund (IMF) financial officers, and World Bank executives who spoke informally in the many forums I hosted for them and institutional investors. See "Dialogue of the Insane" in chapter 3 of *Unlocking*.

16. President Dwight D. Eisenhower's Farewell Speech to the Nation, January 17, 1961, available from many online sources.

17. This section borrows from "The 1973-75 Maxi-Recession," chapter 4 of *Unlocking*.

18. "Mr. Ford and the New Intellectuals," Advest Institutional Services, September 16, 1974.

19. For the broader post-World War II analysis of monetary overkill that led me to forecast every recession starting with the 1969-1970 recession, see *Unlocking* and an updated analysis in chapter 4 of the present work.

20. I was then chief economist for the investment firm of Blyth Eastman Dillon. I refused to wear the WIN label, which irritated the senior officers. The ludicrous label urged policies that in fact helped to undermine the economy.

21. He was kidding. In any case, stagflation and the predicted recession struck hard. It was well documented in advance by the press. The *Wall Street Journal*, August 20, 1973, wrote, "Even a fairly optimistic assumption on the Mideast and oil would require, according to Parks, a forecast of recession." The *Christian Science Monitor*, November 11, 1974 wrote; "Parks expects that real gross national product will fall 1.5 to 2.0 percent and that unemployment will rise to 8 percent or higher." The *New York Post,* November 24, 1975, reported, "Calling it a minidepression, Parks said it will be short lived in contrast with the protracted economic earthquake of the 1930s. He said his turn to guarded optimism is based on 'new government stimulus not yet announced and a slowing of inflation.'"

22. Thomas W. Evans, "Sue OPEC," *New York Times*, June 19, 2008, p. A26.

23. Ibid.

24. "The Arctic Is Said to Be Rich in Undiscovered Oil and Gas," *New York Times*, July 24, 2008, p. C4.

25. "Flaring Up Again," *Economist*, July 26, 2008, p. 65.

26. "The Puzzle of Oil Production, *Economist*, June 21, 2008, p. 59.

27. "Fuel Prices Overseas Take a Toll on U.S.," *New York Times*, July 28, 2008, p. 1.

28. "In Volatile Times, Investors Tune in to All Predictions," *New York Times*, July 28, 2008, p. C1.

29. For details on the huge importance of monetary and fiscal policies see chapters 1 and 2 of *Unlocking*.

30. "Beijing Considers New Curbs as Pollution Threatens Games," *New York Times*, July 29, 2008, p. 1.

31. Lung cancer killed Inta, the mother of my three children. She did not smoke but she did work as a senior fiduciary accountant in a major law firm in a polluted New York City. She persuaded me to leave the city because pollution worsened my bronchitis. I often wonder if the poisonous air of 9-11 killed my love.

32. I listed the dire forecasts in this work in chapter 7, "US Environmental Degraders and Destroyers."

33. See his "Terror in the Weather Forecast," *New York Times*, April 24, 2007.

9. The Dangers of Global Ascetics at War with WMD

1. *Selected Poems of T. S. Eliot*, (New York: Harcourt Brace Inc, 1958), p. 80.

2. Based upon comments Stephen Hawking made at a conference in Hong Kong as reported in the *New York Times*, March 1, 2007.

3. Martin Rees, *Our Final Hour: A Scientist's Warning* (New York: Basic Books, 2004).

4. Robert Frost, "Fire and Ice," *Harpers* magazine, December 1920. The deadly mix of hate, the fallacy of composition, and the proliferation of nuclear, chemical, and biological bombs dropped from the sky would also suffice. I so argue in chapter 3 of this work.

5. Milan Kundera, *Art of the Novel* (New York: Grove Press Inc., 1988), pp. 11 and 12.

6. Edgar Allen Poe, *Masque of the Red Death* (New York: W. Black Inc., 1927).

7. William Gilbert, "H.M.S. *Pinafore*" in *Bartlett's Familiar Quotations* (Boston: Little Brown Company, 1980), p. 627.

8. Poe, *The Masque of the Red Death*, also quoted in chapter 3.

9. Albert Camus, *The Plague* (New York, Random House, the Modern Library, 1947).

10. This section is based to some extent on chapter 24 of Robert II. Parks, *Unlocking the Secrets of Wall Street* (Amherst, NY: Prometheus Books, 1998). See also David Hume, *Inquiry Concerning the Principles of Morals* (New York, Charles Scribner's Sons, 1927). The full quote can be found in *Unlocking*, p. 59.

11. William Gilbert, H.M.S. *Pinafore* in *Bartlett's Familiar Quotations*, p. 627.

12. Based largely on Yahoo, "Selected Nuclear Quotations," http://www.edi.org/nuclear/nukequo.html.

13. My review of bioterrorism draws in part from "Bioterrorism's Threat Persists as Top Security Risk," *Wall Street Journal*, August 4, 2008, p. A 10, and "Anthrax Case Renews Questions on Bioterror Effort and Safety," *New York Times*, August 3, 2008, p. 1. I also checked numerous other sources.

14. After quoting Robert Frost's "Fire and Ice," I wrote, "The fallacy of composition warns that the present deadly mix of hate, nuclear bombs, anthrax, and warring ascetics would also suffice," see *Unlocking*, p. 392.

15. Eric Lipton and Scott Shane, "Anthrax Case Renews Questions on Bioterror," *New York Times*, August 3, 2008.

16. Ibid.

17. According to reports in the *New York Times*, the *Wall Street Journal*, the *Economist*, and others.

18. "Anthrax and the FBI," *New York Times*, editorial, August 4, 2008, p. A12.

19. Eric Lichtblau and Nicholas Wade, "FBI Details Anthrax Case, But Doubts Remain," *New York Times*, August 19, 2008.

20. "FBI Paints Chilling Portrait of Anthrax Attack Suspect" and "Hints of [Dr. Ivins's] Delusions," *Wall Street Journal*, August 7, 2008 p. 1; and *New York Times*, August 7, 2008, p. 1.

21. Howard Zinn, *A People's History of the United States* (New York: Harper Collins, 1999), pp. 298 and 408.

22. Ibid.

23. "Dangerous Driving in the Heavens," *Economist*, January 19, 2008, p. 13; and "Look Out Below: The Arms Race in Space May Be On," *New York Times*, March 19, 2008, p. wk 3.

24. Mark Mazzetti and David E. Sanger, "Israeli Air Strike Reignites Debate on Syrian Nuclear Ambitions," *New York Times*, September 22, 2007.

25. "Dangerous Driving in the Heavens," *Economist*, January 19, 2008.

26. Ibid.

27. "Rods from God," *New York Times*, March 9, 2008, p. wk 3.

28. Mike Moore, *Twilight War: The Folly of U.S. Space Dominance* (Washington, DC: Independent Institute, 2008).

29. This section is taken mainly from chapter 25 of *Unlocking* titled "Scientists on Economic Man."

30. Milan Kundera, *The Art of the Novel*, pp. 11 and 12.

31. I based most of this section on chapter 26 of *Unlocking*.

32. See a partial list on page 392 of *Unlocking*.

33. "500: Deadly U.S. Milestone in Afghan War," New York Times, August 7, 2008, pp. 1 and 18.

34. Sheryl Gay Stolberg, "Obama Defends Afghanistan as a 'War of Necessity,'" *New York Times* August 16, 2009, p. A6.

35. See the first two pages of chapter 8 on the real reason America decided to invade Iraq.

10. Can Science and New Liberal Leaders Save Capitalism?

1. *Scientific American* and many other scientific publications have fully documented the fact of evolution in the human species, just as Charles Darwin elaborated a century and a half ago. See also the fascinating, "Evolution: Beetle Drive," in the Science and Technology section of the *Economist,* August 30, 2008, p. 77; the introduction to the present volume; and "Scientists on Economic Man," especially Charles Darwin in my *Unlocking the Secrets of Wall Street* (Amherst, NY: Prometheus Books, 1998), p 379.

2. H. F. Parzer and A. P. Moczek, "Rapid Antagonistic Coevolution between Primary and Secondary Sexual Characters in Horned Beetles," *Evolution* 62, no. 9, pp. 2423-28.

3. Ken Muneoka, Manjong Han, and David M. Gardiner, "Re-growing Human Limbs," *Scientific American*, April 2008, pp. 57-64.

4. Ibid. If this isn't completely clear, then I urge you to turn to the *Scientific American* of April 2008 for the step-by-step pictures on pages 58 and 59.

5. Andrew K. Geim and Philip Kim, "Carbon Wonderland," *Scientific American*, April 2008, pp. 90-95.

6. Ibid.

7. Jeffery D. Sachs, "Keys to Climate Protection," *Scientific American*, April 2008, p. 1; and "Environmental Degraders and Destroyers," chapter 7 of the present work.

8. "The Doping Dilemma: How Game Theory Helps to Explain the Persuasive Abuse of Drugs in Cycling, Baseball, and Other Sports," *Scientific America*, April 2008, pp. 81-85; and "What Is the Prisoner's Dilemma?" *Geekwise.com*, December 13, 2009.

9. "What Is the Prisoner's Dilemma?" *Geekwise.com*, December 13, 2009.

10. Steven Cundiff, John Hall, and Jun Ye, "Rulers of Light," *Scientific American*, April 2008, pp.75-80.

11. Robert Nadeau, "The Economist Has No Clothes," *Scientific American*, April 2008, p. 42.

12. See chapter 4 of this volume for the failures of both government and business on macrofinancial and macroeconomic forecasting to identify *ex ante* emerging booms and busts and collapsing equity and debt markets.

13. I based this listing largely on "The Technology Quarterly," *Economist*,

September 6, 2008, pp. 3-27; several issues of *Scientific America*, and chapter 26 of *Unlocking* titled, "The Nature of Economic Man."

14. The detailed history of preemptive and unjustified US military attacks are in chapter 9 titled "The Dangers of US and Global Ascetics at War with WMD."

15. Bob Herbert, "[Liberals] Hold Your Heads Up," *New York Times*, September 8, 2009, p. A27.

16. See chapter 3 in this work titled, "Religious Assaults on Science."

17. For detailed documentation of these and other forecasts, see appendix A of *Unlocking*.

11. Summary and Dire Conclusions

1. "Home Frenzy Was a Bank Ad Come True," *New York Times*, August 15, 2008, page 1.

2. See the preface of this work and chapters 1 and 2 of *Unlocking the Secret of Wall Street* (Amherst, NY: Prometheus Books 1998) for useful and useless forecasting tools.

3. I documented the strong linkage between scientists as atheists in chapter 3.

4. "Scientific experts believe we are in the midst of the fastest mass extinction in Earth's history," American Museum of Natural History Survey, September 20, 2006.

5. The scientists quoted here are listed in "Extinction," *Wikipedia*, August 9, 2008.

6. Gautam Naik, "Mosquitoes Bred to Die," *Wall Street Journal*, June 22, 2008, p. 1.

7. "Guiding Light," *Economist*, July 12, 2008, p. 89.

8. "Stub Out that Weed Forever," *Economist*, July 26, 2008, p, 70.

9. "Win Some, Lose Some," *Economist*, August 9, 2008, p. 75.

10. Ibid.

11. "Superbugs: Resistant Infections Almost Impossible to Treat," *New Yorker*, August 11 and 18, pp. 46-55.

12. Chris Roberts, *Heavy Words Lightly Thrown* (New York: Gotham, 2005).

13. The "cherry pick" concept was reported in "The Immigration Deal," *New York Times*, editorial, May 20, 2007.

14. Alan S. Blinder, "Six Blunders En Route to a Crisis." *New York Times*, January 25, 2009, p 7.

15. Lizette Alvarez, "Suicides Reach New High," *New York Times*, January 30, 2009, p. A19.

16. Peter Lohr, "Something to Fear, After All," *New York Times*, January 27, 2009, pp. 1, 5.

17. Michael Cooper, "U.S. Infrastructure," *New York Times*, January 28, 2009, p. A16.

18. Susan Dominus, "Madoff Apologizes for the Ultimate Co-op Crime," *New York Times*, January 12, 2009), p. A19.

Epilogue: The Last Days of Capitalism?

1. Chapter 25 titled "Scientists on Economic Man: Their Disdain for Economist Preachers" in *Unlocking the Secrets of Wall Street* (Amherst, NY: Prometheus Books, 1998), hereafter *Unlocking*.

2. I documented the dangers of the risk of nuclear warfare sparked by collapsing states in chapter 8 of the present work on the "Perils of the Military, Industrial, and Big-Oil Complex," and in chapter 26 of *Unlocking*, where I stated that "The Americans' biggest fear about North Korea is its collapse, in which a starving and broke state simply implodes and sends everyone on a mad scramble for the country's arsenal—including the Chinese, the South Koreans, the Russians, and the Americans." These are the words of Jonathan Pollock, a North Korean expert at the Naval War College. For details see, "We May Miss Kim Jong-Il, and Maybe Musharraf," *New York Times*, September 14, 2008, p. 14. For a related press report that indirectly bears on the proliferation of WMD see "With Push from White House, U.S. Arms Sales Rise Sharply," *New York Times*, September 14, 2008), pp. 1 and 14. My fear is that many other nations are currently at risk of their economies imploding, which would multiply the odds of a worsening global economic meltdown but also the threat of cataclysmic global warfare with these highly lethal weapons.

3. Recent bankruptcies include Bear Stearns, Lehman Brothers, Merrill Lynch, AIG, Fanny Mae, Freddy Mac, among others. See "Crisis on Wall Street," *Wall Street Journal*, September 15, 2008, p. 1.

4. Erich Fromm, *The Anatomy of Human Destructiveness* (New York: Holt, Reinhart and Winston, 1973), p. 219.

5. I borrowed some of this material from chap. 25 of Parks, *Unlocking*.

6. John Dewey, *Morals and Conduct*, reproduced in *The World's Great Thinkers, Man and Man: The Social Philosophers* (New York: Random House, 1947), p. 465.

7. Charles Darwin, *The Descent of Man* (New York: W. W. Norton & Company, 1979), pp. 200 and 208.

8. Ernest Becker, *The Structure of Evil* (New York: George Braziller, 1968), p. 37.

9. Ernest Becker, *The Denial of Death* (New York: The Free Press, 1973), p. ix.

10. Hans Zinsser, *Rats, Lice, and History* (Boston: Little, Brown, and Company, 1936) p. 12, and *Unlocking*, p. 382. The word "util" means a unit of pleasure, a "disutil" a unit of pain. If you try to add (or aggregate) your pleasure plus mine, you end up with nonsense. Economists pretend to calculate total utils in their demand and supply curves. Still, nobody can measure demand and supply. Why? Because economists have only rough measures of ability and no measures of desire. Neither the Conference Board in New York nor Michigan's Consumer Survey Center has yet to learn these basic truths.

11. Ron Suskind, *The Way of the World: A Story of Truth and Hope in an Age of Extremism* (New York: Harper, 2008). See also *New York Times*, September 14, 2008), p. 12.

12. "Reign of Counter-Terror," *New York Times Book Review*, September 14, 2008, p. 12

13. The data I cite on price inflation, gross domestic product, industrial production, US corporate defaults, and unemployment are included in tables produced by the *Economist*. See "Economic and Financial Indicators," *Economist*, April 2, 2011 p. 93. Over several decades I found these tables to be a rich and accurate source. But sometimes the *Economist* was carried away with error. See, for example, its mistaken view that the Bank of Japan was pursuing a "super loose monetary policy" in "Misreading of the Collapse of Interest Rates [in Japan]" in the epilogue of Parks, *Unlocking*, p. 402.

14. See "Seven Blasts around Baghdad Kill at Least 24," *New York Times*, June 23, 2009, p. A10.

15. "Spate of Attacks Tests Iraqi City and U.S. Withdrawal," *New York Times*, June 24, 2009, p. 1.

16. See chapter 6, "President Reagan, Chairman Volcker, and Haywire Fiscal Economics," in Parks, *Unlocking*, pp. 95-109. The chapter documents

step-by-step my forecast of what I had dubbed the "1981-1982 minidepression." A good parallel is the 2009 recession.

17. Frederic S. Mishkin, *Monetary Policy Strategy* (Cambridge, MA: MIT Press, 2007). My comments relate to his article titled "How to Get the Fed Out of the Box," *Wall Street Journal*, June 22, 2009, p. A15.

18. Paul Krugman, "Not Enough Audacity," *New York Times*, June 26, 2009, p. A25. My guess is that his article will enrage the extreme right wing and please Obama's supporters.

19. Sara Murray, "Numbers on Welfare See Sharp Increase," *Wall Street Journal*, June 22, 2009, p. 1.

20. "Financial Reform in America," *Economist*, June 20, 2009, p. 77. I used some of this material but was in disagreement with much of it. Most important, I don't believe the *Economist* stressed as much as it should have that a truly frightening future faces America because of a failure to implement a strong public works program swiftly, with funding provided fully by the Federal Reserve. See also footnote 15.

21. *New York Times*, November 12, 2009, p. B1.

22. For Japan's collapse see Robert H. Parks, "The Tokyo Stock Megabubble: The Role of Delusion and Deception," in chap. 17 of Parks, *Unlocking*, pp. 257-73.

23. Bob Herbert, "What the Future May Hold," *New York Times*, November 7, 2009, p. A33.

24. Reed Abelson, "Taking on an Industry," *New York Times*, November 17, 2009, p A20.

25. Alex Berenson, *New York Times*, September 12, 2009, p. 1.

26. Leon Wieseltier, "Washington Diarist: Common Grounded," *New Republic*, November 4, 2009. He wrote, "so long as our relationship is defined as our differences, we will empower those who sow hatred rather than peace."

27. David Streitfeld, *New York Times*, November 13, 2009, p. 1. He notes: "The FHA [Federal Housing Authority] said just a few weeks ago, 'even under the bleakest economic forecast, its cash cushion would quickly recover.' On Thursday, it abandoned that position." Yes, not only do Wall Street, the banks, and the hedge funds forecast blue skies ahead, but government bunglers do the same. Their confidence, or pretended confidence, speeds far ahead of their knowledge.

28. Christopher Drew, *New York Times*, November 15, 2009, pp. 1 and 14. Drew writes, "The latest government estimate places the cost of adding 40,000

American troops at $40 billion to $54 billion a year." Yes, just imagine what $54 billion could do to increase jobs in America. My own conclusion is that the actual costs of war and its opportunity costs are always understated by the military and by the corporations who produce arms.

29. The data I cite are all taken from "The Economic and Financial Indicators," *Economist,* November 14, 2009, pp. 117 and 118. These are the most recent data, though the *Economist* always includes them in each of its issues. I believe any serious study of finance and economics by reporters, students, and economists can be improved by regularly tracking these indicators, which are updated every week in the publication. As a forecaster and economist I find their weekly empirical update indispensable.

Appendix C: *Ex Ante* Recognition of Bubble Stock Gauges and Forecasts of Their Bursting in the United States and Japan

1. My dual roles over a quarter century as a finance professor and Wall Street economist represented an indispensable mix, and a fortuitous one. Without this mix I could not have possibly written this article.

2. One might also consider this question: What constitutes *credible* forecasting? My answer would stress four requirements. First, all forecasts must be documented by the press and published articles. Second, consistent with modern portfolio theory, the forecaster should focus on a fully integrated G-MM model in his valuation analysis of the major *indexed* gauges. Third, he must warn over and over again that all big bubbles will burst, though nobody can say just when. Fourth, he must dismiss any criticisms or ridicule for his negative and often lonely views. After all, many normally alert investors and officials lose their common sense in times of bubbles. They accept without evidence the poppycock of the mania-driven crowd. Crowd denial constitutes a fairly strong forward signal of bursting bubbles. It has always been thus.

3. The identical valuation of A and B in equation (2) holds only with *identical starting earnings*. Only if A plows back an additional 100 to offset dividend payout, which is unlikely, could it match the values of B year-after-year. With 100% earnings plowback for B the 10,800 value would rise 8% annually for the

very *maximum valuations*. My compliments to Francis and Ibbotson for their focus on total earnings in their *Investments: A Global Perspective* (Upper Saddle River, NJ: Prentice Hall, 2002), p. 699. Many texts still fail on this count.

4. The extremely high P/E ratios of the NASDAQ Composite, Section III B, and the Nikkei 225, Section III D, led me to classify them both as megabubbles fated to burst.

5. See analysis in Robert H. Parks, *Unlocking the Secrets of Wall Street* (Amherst, NY: Prometheus Books, 1998), pp. 411-12, hereafter *Unlocking*. Subsequent press documentation of its forecasted bursting is in the appendix and in the *Money and Capital Markets Monitors* 1998-2001 sent to institutional investors and the press (available on request). Dates and titles of monitors follow: 4/9/98, "Wealth Effect: [M2], M2 Velocity, and the Mutual Fund Stock Boom"; 12/2/98, "Extraordinary Popular Delusions and the Madness of Crowds"; 12/9/98, "Butterfly Internet Stocks and Day-Trading Retail Mania"; 8/2/99, "Cardinal Sign of the Present Stock Market Bubble: Denial"; 12/8/99, "Current Accounts Deficit (CAD): An Angel Against Inflation"; 1/8/00, "Perform or Die Mania Turns Investment Managers into Gamblers"; 3/10/00, "The S&P 500 Is a Bubble, the Nasdaq [Composite] a Megabubble"; 4/17/00, "Growth Recession or Recession in Old Economy Will Clobber Profits in New Economy"; 5/24/00, "Debt Explosion, M2 Money [times] Unprecedentedly High M2 Velocity [documents] Excessively Easy Monetary Policy"; 7/20/00, "Red Flag for Stocks: Corporate Megaleveraging"; 8/8/01, "Megaleveraging 1994-2000 Signals New Wave of Bankruptcies"; 8/17/01, "Global Slump Will Push 30-Year Treasuries Below 5%."

6. The October 6, 2000 price of 1409 was the basis for my forecast in the October 12, 2000 *Money and Capital Markets Monitor* sent to the press and institutional investors (see figures 2 and 3).

7. The collapse of the overinvestment boom and crashing stock markets would, I maintained, degenerate into a growth recession or outright recession. I concluded, "There's a good chance of a fairly severe and prolonged recession" (*On Wall Street*, 7/1/2000, p. 144). One of my major concerns early on was the huge investment boom that generated productive capacity running far ahead of the rise in final demand. The Internet dot.com and telecommunications companies in particular invested heavily and frenetically. Many declared that their huge marketing expenditures would generate market domination, which never happened for the great majority. Instead, they tripped as a crowd over the fallacy of composition (not all can command top market shares). The resulting excess

capacity produced predictably tumbling prices and huge losses. Other major industries, such as the airlines and autos, also overexpanded and faced overcapacity and skidding prices. Although investment is normally a lagging indicator, this time I dubbed it a leading indicator of collapse. See also chap. 1 in Parks, *Unlocking* on (a) why the coincident indicators are unreliable forecasting tools and (b) why the forecaster should always track closely the initial and lagged effects of fiscal, monetary, and international financial policies. The focus on (b) dominates this article.

8. For a detailed analysis of MM identities and MM dividend irrelevancy see Parks, *Unlocking*, pp 247-49.

9. The *Wall Street Journal* (October 3, 2003, pp. B1, B4) article titled "Scandal Scoreboard" listed many corporate criminal acts for Adelphia Communications, Arthur Anderson, Citigroup, Enron, Global Crossing, Health South, Imclone Systems, Merrill Lynch, etc. The almost daily headlines still report fraudulent actions by Wall Street officers, insurance brokers, mutual funds, mortgage companies, and many others. Did ineffective regulation permit robber barons to run free to fleece the people? It looks that way.

10. Recipe Four with an extremely high growth rate plus 100% plowback generated a value for the Nikkei 225 still *below* the bubble price. But the hard evidence led me to class it as a megabubble (Section III D).

11. By July 2000 total losses exceeded total earnings on the NASDAQ Composite to produce an infinite P/E. See Browning for data on the NASDAQ and other gauges, *Wall Street Journal*, June 11, 2001, p. C1. As of October 14, 2003, the NASDAQ Composite's P/E was 236 times, largely on depressed earnings.

12. From 1997 through 2000 the *Money and Capital Markets Monitors* warned of an ultra-easy monetary policy. For example, the June 2, 1997 *Monitor* was subtitled "Overlooked Enormous Fed Stimulus: M2 x Rocketing M2 Velocity." The November 11, 1998 *Monitor* was titled "Red Flag: M2 Times M2 Velocity and the Mutual Fund Stock Boom."

13. *Monetary Trends*, October 1998, Federal Reserve Bank of St. Louis.

14. The details of opportunity cost are set forth in the November 11, 1998 *Money and Capital Markets Monitor*, which also included my critical comments on the St. Louis Fed *Monetary Trends*, October 1998.

15. This example reproduces that of the 8/31/98 and 12/12/98 issues of *Money and Capital Markets Monitor.*

16. The annual rise in M2 was 4.1% in 1995, 4.8% in 1996, 5.7% in 1997, 8.8% in 1998, and 6.1% in 1999, which averaged 5.9% for the five years. M2

velocity was 2.03 in 1995, 2.05 in 1996, 2.06 in 1997, 2.00 in 1998, and 1.99 in 1999, for an average turnover of 2.026 times. That was far above the 1.7 average M2 velocity for the period from 1960 to 1995. All data for M2 and nominal GDP underlying these updated calculations are from CEA *Economic Indicators*, August 2003 and December 2001, pp. 1, 26.

17. The climb in net borrowing for the nonfarm nonfinancial corporate business in billions of dollars was 227.1 in 1995, 182.8 in 1996, 291.8 in 1997, 408.4 in 1998, 377.2 in 1999, and 380.1 in 2000. The total net for these years was $1,867 billion. Net new equity issues, also in billions of dollars, were -58.3 in 1995, -47.3 in 1996, -77.4 in 1997, -215.5 in 1998, -110.4 in 1999, and -118.2 in 2000. I calculated the total contraction in equity financing over these years at -$627 billion. To calculate the net cash drain to the corporate sector, this amount of $627 billion would be reduced somewhat by any cash returned to corporations for exercised stock options plus any corporate tax benefit resulting from the exercised options. Still, the major corporate loss reflected stock buybacks at bubble prices that burst. I used updated and revised data for this article (CEA *Economic Indicators*, September 2003, p. 29).

18. I frequently labeled Federal Reserve caution a "grand illusion." See article by Alan Abelson in *Barron's*, November 29, 1999; *Christian Science Monitor*, January 3, 2000, p. 17; *On Wall Street*, July 1, 2000, p. 144; and the article "*Gloom with a View*" in *Financial Planning*, August 2001, p. 144.

19. See the December 8, 1999 *Monitor* titled "Current Account Deficit (CAD): An Angel Against Inflation." The US current account deficit (CAD) soared from $82 billion in 1993 to $481 billion in 2000. The consumer price index (CPI) for all items stood at 148.2 for 1994 and 166.6 for 1999, which translated into a five-year annualized advance of only 2.37% despite sustained ultra-easy and excessive monetary and fiscal stimulation that contributed to the great asset inflation for the period 1995 to 1999. The Federal Reserve did not acknowledge the CAD (or its statistical twin, capital inflow) as a huge counter-inflationary ally reflected in the CPI. It never admitted to any complicity in helping to fuel the great asset (property and stock) inflation. The updated data on the CPI are in CEA *Economic Indicators*, September 2003, pp. 36, 22, 24.

20. *Federal Reserve Release Z1*, September 9, 2003, p. 68, and *Federal Reserve Bulletin*, June 1997, p. A27.

21. Charles Mackay (1852) titled his work *Extraordinary Popular Delusions and the Madness of Crowds*.

22. On 10/19/87 Black Monday struck, but my timing was sheer luck. See also

chap. 14 of Parks, *Unlocking*, titled "Stock Valuation Tools: Forecasting Black Monday" and the *Money and Capital Markets Monitor*s dated 8/18/87, "Stock Valuation Models Flash Yellow and Red"; 10/7/87, "Stock Valuation Models Now Flash Red"; and 10/14/87, "Stock Valuation Models Still Signal Red."

23. Extremely high interest rates were then a huge problem. For that reason alone it seemed to me pointless to employ Recipe Four in 1987. The archenemy of stocks, interest rates, was sufficient in itself to kill the bubble. See Parks, *Unlocking*, especially chap. 15 titled "Forecasting Black Monday."

24. See chap. 16 titled "Monday Morning Quarterbacks on Black Monday" in Parks, *Unlocking*.

25. Parks, *Unlocking* documents deception in chap. 17 titled "The Tokyo Stock Megabubble: The Role of Delusion and Deception," in the January 29, 1990 S&P *CreditWeek*, and the appendix. The warnings were also included in the *Money and Capital Markets Monitor.* The 6/3/88 *Monitor* concluded: "The Japanese stock market superbubble will indeed burst, sooner rather than later." The 6/23/88 *Monitor* warned: "[Look for] bursting bubbles in the Japanese real estate and securities markets."

26. Real growth in Japan was 3.3% in 1991, 0.9% in 1992, 0.4% in 1993, 1.1% in 1994, 1.8% in 1995, 3.5% in 1996, 1.9% in 1997, a negative 1.1% in 1998, 0.2% in 1999, 2.8% in 2000, 0.4% in 2001, and 0.3% in 2002. I calculated the twelve-year average real growth at 1.29%, based on the annual data (Federal Reserve Bank of St. Louis, *International Economic Trends*, July 2003). Sustained anemia presages much more pain.

27. I called it the *death curve* (*Bond Week*, 7/20/ 81). It led me to forecast the dreadful 1981-82 recession (*Wall Street Journal*, October 20, 1980). Are there parallels in today's massive tax cuts and exploding war deficits with 1981-82, or 1965-69? Well, the Vietnam War was financed not with taxes but with largely monetized deficits, the worst way to finance a war. It persuaded me to forecast accelerating inflation and the 1969-70 recession (*Commercial and Financial Chronicle*, January 22, 1970). Are we making the same mistakes today? Yes, but a satisfactory answer is beyond the scope of this article.

28. Milton Friedman (1953) wrote that "the 'assumptions' of a theory [are] not whether they are . . . 'realistic,' for they never are, but whether they are sufficiently good approximations for the purpose in hand." Of course.

29. The MM arbitrage proof *before* a point of actual or even perceived excess leverage is surely one of the most original and powerful ideas in all financial literature. But the assumption of zero bankruptcy costs collapses *beyond* a

point of extreme leverage. Consider that the major premise (All men are immortal.) and the minor premise (Socrates is a man.) logically support the conclusion (Socrates is immortal.), which is empirically false though logically valid, given the relationship of the premises. But logic alone won't do; one also needs empirical support. It follows, as day follows night, that the assumption of zero bankruptcy costs is also false in *a volatile world* economy *beyond extreme leverage*. See Parks *Unlocking* for additional evidence and a step-by-step analysis of the MM arbitrage "proof," pp. 305-315.

30. Treasury bonds are *inherently unstable*. The often greater instability for Treasury bonds than lower-grade corporate bonds is largely explained via the "pure" rate. (See Parks (1959a, 1959b) and Parks (1998), pp. 163-66.)

31. Lead article in Standard and Poor's *CreditWeek*, January 29, 1990, and the Epilogue of Parks *Unlocking*.

Appendix G: Ten Forecasting Sins of Capitalism

1. I came to Wall Street in 1968 in time to forecast recessions 5 through 11. Flawed fiscal, monetary, and US international policies made forecasting recessions "a piece of cake."

2. The theory and failures of "targeting" are addressed at length in *Unlocking*.

3. Charles Mackay (1852) wrote his classic *Extraordinary Popular Delusions and the Madness of Crowds*.

4. The *Journal News*, August 18, 2007, reported: "Robert H. Parks, a finance professor at Pace University said, 'The collapse of the housing bubble could drive the economy into a recession and push financial stocks down another 30 percent. Those who say the worst is past must be dreaming.'"

5. Parks, "*Ex Ante* Recognition of Bubble Stock Gauges," March 2006.

6. I received both the Master's degree and the PhD at the Wharton School of Business when their econometric model was the talk of the land. I have never seen it or any other econometric model identify in advance major cyclical or secular changes in the economy. Econometric reliance on the past to forecast was sheer folly, and still is. The mix of irrelevant data and poor macroeconomic and financial models will continue to plague forecasters.

GLOSSARY

Abnormal returns. Returns beyond that required in a perfectly competitive market. Investors chased after abnormally high returns in the mania-driven boom from 1993 to 2009. The huge profits came with systemic lying, cheating, and stealing in the markets. The securities and property bust predictably followed.

Absorption thesis (tax incidence). The argument is that the final burden (incidence) of the corporate income tax reduces corporate cash flow and net profits, hence it rests on corporate shareholders. This is the opposite of the shifting thesis, which argues that higher income taxes are shifted backward to suppliers or labor in lower prices or wages, or forward into higher consumer prices, or both.

Acid financial contracts. Acid or "toxic" securities include stocks, bonds, mortgages, collateralized debt bonds, credit default swaps, and many other financial instruments that collapsed in price far below original costs. Toxic securities also include commercial and consumer investments in houses, hotels, and apartment buildings. Often, there is no trading market for toxic securities or properties. Nobody knows what these securities are worth.

Tumbling prices weaken the economy, which in turn pushes prices lower, which further weakens the economy. In 2009 a cyclical downward spiral meant that millions of Americans lost their homes, jobs, incomes, health insurance, and pensions. According to the January 31, 2010 *Christian Science Monitor*, "the typical length of unemployment [as of December 31] jumped to 20.5 weeks, double the time in the 1982-83 recession (then the worst recession since the Great Depression of the thirties).

Millions of Americans lost any hope of finding a job. They stopped looking for work. So what did the census do? It simply removed them from its count of the labor force. What nonsense! To include them in the

451

labor force together with those who work for poverty wages and zero benefits would mean a real unemployment rate of about 40 percent. What did our fiscal and monetary officials do to spur "Bottoms-Up" stimulus to provide jobs and incomes to the unemployed? The answer: they did far too little to ward off a second Great Depression. All President Obama had to do was to emulate President Franklin Delano Roosevelt's works programs. He did not. What a colossal and needless failure of federal government policy to create jobs and ward off depression.

Alpha. The difference between the expected return on a security and its equilibrium return in perfectly competitive markets (i.e., the return at the point at which supply meets demand).

American option. The right to purchase a bond or security at a specified price any time up to and including the stated expiration date for the financial instrument.

Arbitrage. The simultaneous purchase and sale of two securities that are essentially identical in order to profit from a disparity in their prices. The law of one price is that identical assets in the same market command identical prices. But that assumes honest trading, not the lawbreaking and dishonest trading I have identified throughout this work.

Arbitrage pricing theory. A model stating that the expected return on a security is dependent on many factors (e.g., exchange rate fluctuations, cyclical fluctuations and trends in profits, interest rate, and inflation swings, etc.) in addition to those specifically stipulated in the capital asset pricing model (CAPM). *See* **Capital asset pricing model**.

Bears. Investors who expect securities prices to fall.

Beta. A relative measure of the variability of an asset's return as compared with the overall market portfolio.

Black Monday. The October 19, 1987 stock market decline, the biggest one-day fall ever for the Dow Jones Industrial index.

Blue chip economists. Consensus forecasts of some fifty economists published by a private organization. Their forecasts are all too often dead wrong. One reason is that they pay far too little attention to macroeconomic forces, especially the initial and lagged effects of government fiscal, monetary, and debt policies. The lagged effects all too often prove to be highly destructive.

Bottoms-up forecasting. A forecasting method that estimates the values of individual companies and industries with the goal, among others, of gauging prospects for the overall economy.

Broker. An agent who buys and sells securities for investors, generally compensated with a commission on such sales and purchases.

Building permits. Authorization by local governments to begin construction on houses, apartments, etc.

Bulls. Investors who expect securities prices to rise.

Call option. A contract that gives the buyer the right to buy a stipulated number of shares of a security at a specified price and over a specified time period. *See* **Put option**.

Capacity utilization. Labor and capital (plant, equipment, and other facilities) employed as a percentage of the labor force and potential output. Operating below capacity is characterized by unemployed labor and idle factories.

Capital Asset Pricing Model (CAPM). An equilibrium investment model stating that the expected and required return on a portfolio of securities is the risk-free rate plus a premium for portfolio (unsystemic) risk and market (systemic) risk. Among other problems, the CAPM assumes risk-free lending, risk-free borrowing, and risk-free arbitrage, all of which are pure fictions. The parallel Modigliani and Miller model (MM) in corporate finance suffers for the same reason.

Capital inflow. In international finance, capital inflow is identical to the current account deficit. When, for example, the United States runs a deficit, foreigners increase their net claims against the United States, which is called net capital inflow to the United States. The ex post identities, the current account deficit and capital inflow, are widely misunderstood and account for serious errors of analysis.

Capital market line. A linear charting of return versus risk of a set of portfolios of stocks (the ideal or market portfolio) combined with risk-free borrowing or lending under the assumptions of perfect markets and homogeneous expectations of investors.

Capital markets. Financial markets with securities having maturities of one year or longer.

Capitalized value. The present value of an asset calculated by discounting all projected future net receipts at the required return (cost of capital). The rational and well-informed investor may, of course, come up with higher or lower values than that of the market. Markets can go haywire.

Capital investment. In real terms, this is investment in plant and equipment and other productive facilities.

Carrying costs. Out-of-pocket costs incurred in holding an inventory of goods or property, e.g., insurance and financing (interest) charges. It's also the difference between the future and spot prices of an asset or security, and can entail interest income foregone in order to invest in spot (cash) assets.

CATS. Certificates of accrual on Treasury-backed zero-coupon securities sold at a deep discount from face value. CATS pay no interest at any time but return the full face value at maturity.

Chaos. Confusion and disorder. Mathematicians, though, define a chaotic series as one that can be predicted with precision provided (a) you can define the beginning of the series and (b) you assume no intervening events will alter your prediction. Economists, needless to say, have no such power. Still, chaos theory now challenges conventional theory.

Checkable deposits. Accounts at banks and other financial institutions against which you can draw checks for payment without prior notice. You can also withdraw cash from your checkable (demand) deposits using automatic teller machines.

Chief economist. The top economist and normally the economic spokesperson for a company or other organization. His/her job may include analysis and forecasting, and managing others on staff, including junior economists.

Circuit velocity of money. As an extension of Irving Fisher's concept of velocity, I mean the turnover of money as it circulates within the complex of commercial banks and nonbank financial intermediaries. Circuit velocity is little understood among economists and Fed policymakers.

Classical preachers. Contemporary economists who misunderstand the views of classical economists set forth two centuries ago. They apply the classical solutions of the eighteenth century, which focused on long-run trends, to short-run cyclical swings of the twentieth and twenty-first centuries—a mighty error. Key Federal Reserve officers often do just that.

Closing price. The last trade price of the day for any given security or commodity.

Coincident indicators. Economic components like income, production, employment, sales, and Gross Domestic Product (GDP) that rise and fall at roughly the same time as the overall economy. These "rearview mirror" data are among the most popular but the very worst forecasting tools.

Collateralized mortgage obligation (CMO). A collateralized mortgage obligation, that is, a bond backed by a portfolio of mortgages, with the mortgages separated into short-term, medium term, and long-term portfolios (also called tranches) to meet different investor tastes. Each CMO bond is paid a fixed interest stream derived from the interest earned on the underlying mortgages. CMOs can be extremely risky investments.

Compounding. The interest earned on interest.

Conglomerates. A corporation involved in a number of unrelated businesses.

Consensus forecast. Just add up and rank the forecasts of Gross Domestic Product (GDP) or other economic series, and calculate the arithmetic mean or median to represent consensus thinking. Consensus forecasts can be dangerous to your financial health.

Consumer price index (CPI). A cost-of-living price index for a representative mix of goods and services. It compares these costs in the present time period with the cost of the same items in an equivalent previous time period to determine the rate at which prices have risen or fallen.

Convexity. Asymmetrical changes of bond prices to changes in yields. For example, for a given percentage change in yield to maturity, a bond will rise more in price with a fall in yields than it will fall in price with a rise in yields.

Cost of capital (composite or weighted average). The average cost involved in raising, say, debt and equity with the weights defined as the market values of the debt and equity.

Cost of debt capital. The required return (e.g., interest or dividend) for investing in any given debt security reflecting the multiple risks that could be involved. *See* **Risk components of interest rate**.

Cost of equity capital. The required return (e.g., interest or dividend) for investing in stock calculated as the return on the highest grade corporate bonds (sometimes US Treasury bonds) plus an additional return, the equity premium, for any additional risk. The premium would reflect company risk, the risk of the individual stock, plus the risk of overall stock market fluctuations. Despite the claims of modern portfolio theory, no satisfactory measure of risk exists now; it never has and never will.

Countercyclical policy. A policy designed to offset cyclical swings in the economy to provide sustained and satisfactory economic growth.

Coupon (zero) strips. Zero-coupon bonds using Treasuries.

Crowding in. *Monetized* government tax cuts or expenditures that increase private income, financing, spending, and output in an economy operating below capacity. Monetized borrowing refers to central bank credit creation to provide funds to private individuals, investment funds, or other federal expenditures to help create jobs and spur consumer and investment spending. *See* **Monetize**.

Crowding out. Government deficits via *nonmonetized* tax cuts and higher spending that displace or depress private financing, income, spending, and output to often cause recession. The government's borrowing in the private sector "crowds out" the individuals and companies who are seeking to borrow from the same limited pool of money.

Current production. Consumption, investment, and government goods and services measured in current prices or adjusted for inflation to measure "real" output, that is, nominal output in current prices minus inflation.

Cyclicals. Stocks or other assets that fall or rise sharply with the swings of the economy.

Default. Failure to pay contractual payments of principal and interest.

Defensive stocks. Stocks that have less variability (a beta less than one) than the overall market variability (beta is one). These stocks are less likely to fluctuate in price compared to the majority of stocks in the market.

Deflation. When prices fall to attract consumers but those consumers are waiting on the sideline (not spending) to see if prices fall even more before making a purchase.

Demand deposits. *See* **Checkable deposits**.

Demand elasticity. The percentage change in quantity of (e.g., goods and services) for any percentage change in price.

Demand for money to hold. The reciprocal of the velocity of money. A slower velocity means people spend less, hence they hold more of the money that is not spent.

Demand-pull inflation. When the prices that rise as a result of the growth of demand for goods and services rise faster than the supply of goods and services offered to the market.

Derivative. A financial instrument whose value is "derived" from the value of expected fluctuations in an underlying financial instrument, with percentage fluctuations in the underlying asset reflected in magnified percentage fluctuations in the value of the derivative. For example, a security is created and sold on the basis of the fluctuating price of some commodity—say, gold. The value of this new security is derived not from the purchaser's actual buying or selling of gold but from the price at which others buy or sell the commodity. Weak government regulation of derivatives can generate major losses for investors and others.

Direct (private) placements. Sale of debt or equity securities to professional investors such as life insurance companies or pension funds.

Discounted value. The present value of future receipts for a given good or service discounted at the required cost of capital to create that good or service.

Disinflation. A slower rate of inflation.

Dividend irrelevancy theorem. Other things being equal, the idea that the market price of stock should rise to reflect the plowback of earnings, the same earnings that otherwise might have been paid directly as dividends.

Dogs: overpriced gung-ho stocks. I argued that investors should avoid DOGS in favor of lovable CATS or high-grade bonds prior to an expected cyclical fall of the economy. *See* **CATS**.

Duration of a bond. That point in time between the purchase and the maturity of a bond when swings in interest income received from reinvestment of the coupon interest just offset the opposite swings in price so that the realized yield approximates the initially computed yield to maturity. Thus if interest rates were to fall, the lower interest stream from reinvestment of coupon income at lower rates would roughly offset at the point of duration any price gains on the bonds. Also a measure of potential price volatility of a bond.

Price-to-earnings ratio. Earnings, either those for the past twelve months or those projected for the next twelve months, divided by the present market price of a stock. Turned upside down, the earnings ratio becomes the price/earnings multiple.

EBIT. Earnings before interest and taxes.

Econometrician. An economist whose statistical model is based mainly on past correlations of economic series. These models rarely if ever take note of a cyclical turn in the economy. They have failed to help forecasters. Once in great favor, econometricians are now a lonely group.

Economic man. Those attributes of human beings that explain economic decision making and overall conduct in society. The focus of this book chapter-by-chapter highlights the opposing views of economists and competing scientists.

Efficient portfolio. A mix of securities that provides maximum returns for stipulated risks or minimum risks for a given return.

Equity premium. The extra return investors require and expect over and above the stated return on, say, low-risk, high-grade corporate bonds or Treasury securities. This premium is a function of the risk the investor is taking.

Ex ante. Expected. Also effective demand and supply, meaning, for example, the desire and ability to buy or sell a commodity at a given price. Often confused with *ex post* statistical identities.

Ex post. Historical accounting identities like purchases and sales, borrowing and lending, the current account deficit and capital inflow in international finance, terms often confused with effective demand and supply.

Exercise price. For a call option, the price at which the option buyer may contract to purchase an underlying asset, and for a put option, the price at which the option buyer may contract to sell the underlying asset.

Expected yield-to-maturity. The initially discounted return of all future receipts that just equals the purchase price.

Financial leverage. The extent to which debt is used as a percentage of the total funds raised by a company.

Fisher effect. In economic models in which the inflation rate is assumed to be steady, the unadjusted rate of interest changes with the inflation rate. (Named after US mathematician and economist Irving Fisher [1867-1947]).

Fixed cost. Costs that may remain unchanged as a function of sales and output. But many fixed costs can be highly variable. For example, fixed machinery and other capital costs can become quickly obsolete.

Fixed income group. Money managers of fixed-income securities like bonds, Treasury bills, and mortgages. These securities generate a stable or fixed amount of interest for investors.

Forward investment commitments. Contracts to provide financing in the future with terms stipulated at the time the contracts are drawn. *See* **Direct (private) placements**.

Fundamental (equilibrium) value. The present value of all future receipts discounted at a required discount rate (cost of capital) by well-informed analysts who pay strict attention to good theory and data. The actual market price may be far above or far below fundamental value.

Gold bugs. The quintessence of naive but highly motivated and often highly emotional analysts who see heaven in gold and the old gold standard, while paying no attention to sound theory, history, and data. Deeply conservative, they have strong convictions on how government is supposedly stripping our freedoms away and debasing the currency.

Growth recession. Anemic growth of the economy below its potential, signaling rising unemployment.

Gross domestic product (GDP). Total value of goods and services produced within the United States.

Gross national product (GNP). Total value of goods and services produced in the United States *minus* (roughly) our imports from abroad *plus* our exports to foreign nations.

High-grade bonds. High-quality bonds with a high-probability that all contract terms for repayment will be kept.

Idiocy Circle. The attempt by the Federal Reserve, for example, to keep interest rates from rising by greatly expanding the supply of reserves and money and credit, but with the result that excessive and continued monetary easing unintentionally backfires to produce accelerating inflation and higher interest rates.

Implied (internal) rate of return. That rate of return that equates the present price of an investment with the discounted value of all projected future receipts.

Incidence (tax). The final resting place or burden of the tax, or who ultimately pays the tax.

Income velocity. Spending for current production divided by the money stock (money supply).

Index fund. A passively managed fund designed to produce the same investment performance as that of a stock index such as the S&P 500 or the Russell 3000. It reduces the investor's risk compared to the potential volatility of investing in individual stocks in the index.

Inflation. A rise in the general price level, which is the same as a fall in the real purchasing power of the currency used to buy goods and services.

Institutional investor. Investors such as banks, insurance companies, pension funds, etc.

Interest-sensitive stocks. Stocks, like high-grade utility stocks, that tend to move up when interest rates fall, and vice versa. Any major cyclical fall in the stock market, though, could send interest-sensitive stocks down, too.

Inverse correlation. Things that move in opposite directions. For example, throughout most of the post-World War II period, interest rates generally declined or softened when the size of the federal budget deficit increased, and interest rates generally rose when the budgetary deficit contracted. With few exceptions, the magnitude of the deficit and interest rates went their opposite ways, a fact almost universally misunderstood.

Inverted yield curve. A plot of yields on the vertical axis and time to maturity on the horizontal axis such that short-term rates are higher than intermediate-term rates, which are higher than long-term rates. The slope of the yield curve provides a poor signal for where interest rates are headed.

J curve. The initial versus the lagged impact of, say, a fall in the value of the dollar in foreign exchange markets.

Lagging indicators. Economic data that generally follow movements in the overall economy. For example, economic series like plant and equipment expenditures and commercial and industrial loans tend to continue to rise after the overall economy has moved into recession. They are unreliable indicators of the future.

Leading indicators. Economic data that generally precede movements in the overall economy. Examples of such indicators are: orders for durable goods, new housing starts, the price of raw materials, etc.

Liquidity. The ability to sell at a price close to the current market prices, the near-term receipt of cash for any asset close to the current market price of that asset, or the ready ability to borrow on an asset by pledging the asset as collateral for a loan. The ability to secure ready cash for conducting a transaction.

Long run. That period of time when all costs are variable, when business wants to generate revenues that cover all costs plus a normal (satisfactory) profit at the minimum.

Long Treasury bonds. Any Treasury bond with a maturity beyond ten years.

Loose quantity theorist of money. The smart analyst who always pays attention to money, money velocity, and output.

Margin purchase. A purchase financed by borrowing a portion of the purchase price.

Market period. Economic time frame in which goods are already produced. Past costs of production may be irrelevant to your decision to hold or sell.

Market weights. The proportions using market values in, say, calculating the average composite cost of raising both debt and equity capital.

Microeconomic focus. A thorough analysis of the individual parts or components of the economy, which can be highly misleading.

MM arbitrage "proof." The risk-free borrowing and lending proof offered by economists Modigliani and Miller. They contend that the average weighted cost of capital of a corporation is independent of leverage (i.e., the capacity of the corporation to borrow money at an acceptable interest rate).

Momentum investing. Investing in a stock or security because its price is falling or rising. One is investing because of the momentum of the price (whether up or down).

Monetarist. A monetary theorist following the views of Nobel Prize winner Milton Friedman. Monetarists have lost ground as poor forecasters.

Monetary aggregates. Various measures of the money supply defined as M1, M2, and M3.

Monetize. To print or mint more money.

Monetized borrowing (deficits). Borrowing and simultaneously printing money to finance the borrowing. The Federal Reserve and the Treasury define monetization as direct Federal Reserve purchases of Treasuries, but that concept is far too narrow.

Money markets. Financial assets with terms-to-maturity generally of one year or less.

Money supply. M0 = total amount of paper currency and coin in circulation at any given time.

M1 = all currency plus the value of current checking accounts and what is waiting to be deposited into those checking accounts.

M2 = all currency in circulation plus savings accounts and non-interest bearing bank deposits.

New stock issues. Stock offerings just brought to the market such as IPOs (initial public offerings) to raise capital.

Nominal interest rate. The actual or current interest rate, unadjusted for inflation.

Nominal returns. Dollar returns not adjusted for inflation, the actual reported return.

Nonmonetized borrowing (deficits). Borrowing existing money that is available in the marketplace (not increasing the existing money supply).

Nonsystemic risk. Individual company risk. Systemic risk refers to swings in the overall economy. *See* **systemic risk.**

Normative economics. Economic analysis that focuses on what should be, not what is.

Oligopoly. When economic power is held in the hands of a few.

Operating earnings. *See* **EBIT.**

Opportunity cost. The income or rewards foregone. If you invest in a Japanese bond at 5 percent but could earn 9 percent on a British government bond, your gross opportunity cost is 9 percent, and your net opportunity cost is 4 percent. Investors frequently overlook the area of opportunity cost, to their sorrow.

Options. A contract between two investors that permits one to buy or sell from another a specific asset at a specific price at a specific time.

PacMan Interest. Fixed charges on debt that can gobble up cash flow and all earnings, and perhaps cause default or bankruptcy.

Par. The stated value of a stock or bond at issue.

Parrot. A naive investor who repeats what others have to say without understanding. Parrots populate both the buy side and sell side of Wall Street in great numbers.

Parrot circle. Chasing your tail by confusing definitions with analysis.

Perpetual bonds. Bonds with no fixed date of maturity but with a fixed stream of interest payments.

Portfolio. The mix of investment securities held.

Present value. Future receipts discounted to the present.

Price-to-earnings ratio. The price of a firm's stock as a proportion of the firm's actual earnings.

Program trading. Automatic purchase and sale of a group of securities treated as one security in response to changes in economic and financial data.

Projected earnings. Hyped up profit forecasts.

Pros. The despicable intellectual prostitutes (including top Wall Street executives as well as senior government and corporate officials) who rampage throughout the pages of this work. They represent the very worst features of "economic man."

Procyclical fiscal and monetary policy. Policies that make a bad situation worse. Examples would include increasing interest rates or sharply cutting federal expenditures in time of recession, thus deepening the recession.

Productivity (economic). Output per hour of all workers.

Progressive tax. A graduated tax system in which those who earn higher incomes pay higher tax rates than those who earn lower incomes.

Protectionists. These are the Parrots and Pros who would keep us from importing foreign goods by, for example, raising tariffs that tax incoming goods. Their naivete and self-serving arguments lead them to falsely think that these tariffs won't be countered by other countries when the United States attempts to export its goods.

Purchases (MV). Money (M) times the income velocity of money (V), or total spending for current production.

Pure interest rate. The rate you demand for waiting for your interest and principal to be returned to you even with no perceived risk of nonpayment. It is a volatile rate widely misunderstood, and influenced mightily by fluctuations in the demand for and supply of credit.

Put option. A contract that gives the buyer the right to sell a specified number of shares of stock at a specific price and at a specific time or within a specified time span.

Quant. A securities analyst who specializes in quantitative analysis.

Random. Each item of a given set has an equal probability of being chosen.

Reaganomics. Supply-side economic theory associated with President Ronald Reagan. It argued for tax cuts as a panacea to spur incentives, productivity, and economic growth. The theory was seriously flawed along with current supply-side notions.

Real gross national product (GNP). The inflation-adjusted GNP.

Real interest rate. The inflation-adjusted nominal interest rate.

Recession. A cyclical fall in the economy, often thought to be a contraction of GDP for six consecutive months or two quarters.

Reference (cyclical) dates. Peaks and troughs of the business cycle as estimated by the National Bureau of Economic Research.

Registered representatives (RRs). Brokers with security firms.

Reinvestment-rate risk. The risk involved in reinvesting either interest or principal reflecting unanticipated changes in interest rates.

Required investment return. The return you demand to compensate you for investment in any given alternative (e.g., bond, security, savings account, loan, etc.).

Reserves. Mainly the vault cash or deposits held at the Federal Reserve by other financial institutions that are members of the Federal Reserve.

Retained earnings. Profits generated by a company but are not distributed as dividends to stockholders. Instead they may be reinvested in the company or saved for future use.

Risk. The chance that investors will face actual loss or below-expected returns on any given investment instrument. Economists use volatility of return as a measure of risk. In fact, economists and investment strategists have no reliable measures of risk despite pretensions to the contrary.

Risk (components) of an interest rate. These include: credit risk, inflation risk, capital risk, marketability risk, reinvestment risk, liquidity risk, pure-rate risk, call risk, event risk, prepayment risk, and exchange-rate risk.

Sales (PT). The index of prices P times an index of output T in the Fisherian equation of exchange MV = PT. Simply put, P is the average price paid for current production (T), where PT = GDP. Money (M) times the turnover of money or velocity (V) is the total expenditure (MV) for current production. So, MV = PT = GDP.

Security analyst. A researcher who focuses on a company's future prospects by analyzing its debt and equity contracts.

Shading (painting to the bright side). A euphemism for deception and deceit, conscious or unconscious. One example is that of a government official who publicly talks about bright economic prospects while privately forecasting recession. Another example is that of economists who dare not forecast recession for fear of antagonizing their employers.

Shadow open-market committee. A private group of economists made up of monetarists who track and appraise Federal Reserve policies.

Shifting thesis (tax incidence). The view that the burden of a corporate tax (the ultimate payer) is shifted either forward to consumers in the form of higher prices or backward to suppliers and labor in the form of lower prices paid for wages or raw materials. *See* **Absorption thesis.**

Short run. Period of time analytically when fixed (sunk) costs have already been incurred.

Spot price or rate. The current or market price or rate.

Stagflation. Recession combined with higher inflation.

Stimulate an economy. To lift private spending, output, and employment via expansionary fiscal and monetary policies.

Stock market bubble. A highly overpriced stock market that bursts and leads to a financial meltdown, severe recession, and today (winter of 2010) high risk of another Great Depression. There can also be housing bubbles, corporate real estate bubbles, commodity bubbles, etc.

Stocks. Equity ownership in a corporation.

Subpar growth. Growth below potential.

Supply-side theory. *See* **Reagonomics.**

Systemic risk. Overall market risk reflecting fluctuations and trends (of output, profits, prices, interest rates, exchange rates, etc.) in stock and bond markets.

Tax incidence. *See* **Absorption thesis** and **Shifting thesis.**

Time preference theory. A theory of interest in which the equilibrium rate just matches (a) the demand for credit for those who want to borrow in order to consume now rather than later with (b) the supply of credit provided by those who forego current consumption by lending from current income.

Trailing earnings. Revenues minus all legitimate costs.

Tranche. *See* **Collateralized mortgage obligation.**

Transactions velocity. Spending for all purposes (current production plus purchases and sales of financial instruments, foreign exchange, secondhand goods, etc.), which means a much higher velocity. For example, the turnover of demand deposits runs about 4,000 times a year for large New York City banks.

Trickle-down theory. *See* **Reagonomics.**

Underwriting. The sale of newly issued securities by a brokerage firm to raise debt or equity capital for corporations, either through a best-efforts basis (for a commission fee as agent) or through buying the issue outright from the corporate issuer and selling it to investors (acting as a principal) with the hope of making a profit on the resale.

Variable labor costs. Labor and materials and other costs that fluctuate with the volume of output.

Velocity of money. The turnover or rate of speed at which money is spent.

Yield-to-maturity. The interest rate that equates the discounted or present value of all future receipts to the current market price of the asset.

Zero-coupon bonds. Bonds with no interest payments, but a single sum (principal) payable at maturity. These bonds are sold at deep discounts from maturity value. An example would be a government savings bond.

BIBLIOGRAPHY

Abken, Peter A. "Innovations in Modeling the Term Structure of Interest Rates." Federal Reserve Bank of Atlanta, *Economic Review*, 75, no. 4 (July/August 1990): 2–27.

Acel, Amir. *Complete Business Statistics*. New York: Irwin, 1993.

Bastiat, Frederic. "Economic Sophisms," in S. H. Patterson (ed.), *Readings in the History of Economic Thought*. New York: McGraw Hill Book Company, 1932.

Batra, Ravi. *Regular Economic Cycles*. New York: St. Martin's Press, 1985.

Becker, Ernest. *Denial of Death*. New York: The Free Press, 1973.

———. *Structure of Evil.* New York: George Braziller, 1968.

Blake, William. *The Marriage of Heaven and Hell*. London: J. M. Dent and Sons, Ltd., 1927.

Bloom, Allan. *The Closing of the American Mind*. New York: Simon and Schuster, 1987.

Bok, Sissela. *Lying: Moral Choice in Public and Private Lives*. New York: Random House, 1978.

Brigham, Eugene F. *Financial Management: Theory and Practice*, Fourth Edition. New York: Dryden Press, 1985.

Brigham, Eugene F. and Louis Gapenski. *Financial Management: Theory and Practice*, Seventh Edition. New York: The Dryden Press, 1994.

Buckley, William F., Jr. *Right Reason*. New York: Doubleday, 1985.

Bye, Raymond T., and William H. Hewett. *Applied Economics: The Application of Economic Principles*. New York: Alfred A. Knopf, 1928.

Camus, Albert. *The Plague*. New York: Random House, 1947.

Creswell, Julie. "Speedy New Titans of Wall Street Make Waves Far from Wall Street." *New York Times*. May 17, 2010 (Business), p. 1.

Darwin, Charles. *The Descent of Man*. New York: W. W. Norton, 1979.

Dawkins, Richard. *The God Delusion*: New York: Houghton Mifflin, 2006.

DeMandeville, Bernard. "Fable of the Bees," in S. H. Patterson (ed.), *Readings in the History of Economic Thought*. New York: McGraw Hill Book Company, 1932.

Dewey, John. *Morals and Conduct*, in Sax Commins and Robert N. Linscott (eds.), *The World's Great Thinkers, Man and Man: The Social Philosophers*. New York: Random House, 1947.

Dickens, Charles. Quote from Tyron Edwards, *Useful Quotations*. New York: Grosset & Dunlap Publishers, 1934.

Dobbs, Michael. *One Minute to Midnight*. New York: Alfred A. Knopf, 2008.

Eiteman, Wilford, Charles Dice, and David Eiteman. *The Stock Market*. New York: McGraw Hill, 1969.

Eliot, T. S. *Selected Poems*, New York: Grove Press, 1988.

Elton, Edwin J., and Martin J. Gruber. *Modern Portfolio Theory and Investment Analysis*. New York: John Wiley, 1991.

Epictetus. "The Manual," in Sax Commins and Robert N. Linscott (eds.), *The World's Great Thinkers, Man and Man: The Social Philosophers*. New York: Random House, 1947.

Etzioni, Amatai. *Moral Dimension: Towards a New Economics*. New York: The Free Press, 1988.

Ewing, Jack, and Judy Dempsey. "Credit Pinch Is Spreading in Europe." *New York Times*, May 17, 2010 (Business), p. 1.

Fama, Eugene F. *Foundations of Finance*. New York: Basic Book, 1976.

Federal Reserve Bank of New York. *Quarterly Review* (Fall and Spring 1988).

Federal Reserve Bank of Richmond. *Economic Review* (March/April, May/June, and July/August 1990).

Federal Reserve, Board of Governors. *Flow of Funds: Flows and Outstandings*. Washington, DC: published quarterly.

Feldstein, Martin. *Capital Taxation*. Cambridge, MA: Harvard University Press, 1983.

Fisher, Irving. *Why the Dollar Is Shrinking*. New York: The Macmillan Company, 1914.

Flesch, Rudolf. *The Art of Clear Thinking*. New York: Harper & Row, 1951.

Flugel, J. C. *Man, Morals, and Society: A Psychoanalytical Study*. New York: International Universities Press, 1945.

Friedman, Milton, and Anna J. Schwartz. *Monetary History of the United States*. Princeton, NJ: Princeton University Press, 1963.

Fromm, Erich. *Anatomy of Human Destructiveness*. New York: Holt, Rinehart and Winston, 1973.

Givens, C. J. *Wealth without Risk: How to Develop a Personal Fortune Without Going Out on a Limb*. New York: Simon and Schuster, 1988.

Gleick, James. *Chaos*. New York: Penguin Books, 1988.

Gordon, Alexander J., and Jack Clark Francis. *Portfolio Analysis*. Englewood Cliffs, NJ: Prentice Hall, 1986.

Gregory, Deborah H., and Miles Livingston. "Development of the Market for U.S. Treasury STRIPS." *Financial Analysts Journal* (March/April 1992): 68–74.

Hauser, Christine, and David Jolly. "Concerns in Europe Flare Again, Pushing U.S. Shares Lower." *New York Times*, May 17, 2010.

Holland, Daniel. "Effect of Taxation on Compensation and Effort: The Case of Business Executives." *Proceedings of the National Tax Association*, 1969.

———. *Dividends under the Income Tax*. Princeton, NJ: Princeton University Press, 1962.

Homer, Sidney, and Martin L. Leibowitz. *Inside the Yield Books: New Tools for Bond Market Strategy*. Englewood Cliffs, NJ: Prentice Hall, 1972.

Hu, Winne. "Teachers Facing Weakest Market Battered by Recession." *New York Times*, May 20, 2010, p. 1.

Hume, David. Selections from *Inquiry Concerning the Principles of Morals*, in *Hume Selections*, edited by Charles W. Hendell. New York: Charles Scribner's Sons, 1927.

Ibbotson, Roger, and Rex Sinquefield. *Stocks, Bonds, Bills, and Inflation*. Financial Analysts Research Foundation, 1983.

James, William. *Pragmatism*. Cambridge, MA: Harvard University Press, 1975.

Kennedy, Paul. *The Rise and Fall of the Great Powers*. New York: Random House, 1987.

Keynes, John Maynard. *General Theory of Employment, Interest, and Money*. New York: Harcourt Brace and Company, 1936.

———. *How to Pay for the War*. New York: Harcourt Brace and Company. 1940.

———. *A Tract on Monetary Reform*. London: Macmillan and Co., Ltd., 1923, p. 80.

———. *Treatise on Money*, Volume II. Cambridge, England: The Royal Economic Society, 1930.

Kidwell, Davis S., Richard L. Peterson, and David W. Blackwell. *Financial Institutions, Markets, and Money*. Orlando, FL: The Dryden Press, 1997.

Kindleberger, Charles P. *Manias, Panics, and Crashes*. New York: Basic Books, 1978.

Klima, Ivan. *Waiting for Dark, Waiting for Light*. New York: Picador, 1993.

Kundera, Milan. *Art of the Novel*. New York: Grove Press, Inc. 1988.

———. *Book of Laughter and Forgetting*. New York: Penguin Books, 1981.

Larrain, Maurice, and J. Pagano. "Nonlinear Dynamics and the Chaotic

Behavior of Interest Rates," *Financial Analysts Journal* (September/October 1991).

Lerner, Abba. *The Economics of Control*. New York: The Macmillan Company, 1959.

Lintner, John. "The Market Valuation of Risk Assets and the Selection of Risky Investments in Stock Portfolios and Capital Budgets." *Review of Economics and Statistics*, 47, no. 1 (February 1965): 13–37.

Mackay, Charles. *Extraordinary Popular Delusions and the Madness of Crowds*. New York: L. C. Page and Company, reprint, 1932

Malkiel, Burton G. *A Random Walk Down Wall Street*. New York: W. W. Norton & Company, 1996.

Mao, James, and Andrew W. Lehren. "Accelerting Pace of War, American Deaths Surpass 1,000." *New York Times*, May 17, 2010, p. 1.

Markowitz, Harry M. *Porfolio Selection: Efficient Diversification of Investments*. New York: John Wiley, 1959.

Marx, Karl. *Capital*, Volumes I, II, and III. New York: Charles Keer & Company, 1906, reprinted in 1932.

———. *The Communist Manifesto*, in Sax Commins and Robert N. Linscott (eds.), *The World's Great Thinkers, Man and Man: The Political Philosophers*. New York: Random House, 1947.

McColton, Caleb C. Quote from Tyron Edwards, *Useful Quotations*. New York: Grosset & Dunlap, 1938.

McLuhan, Marshall. *The Medium Is the Massage*. New York: Random House, 1967.

Mikkelson, Wayne H., and Partch Megan. "Stock Price Effects and Costs of Secondary Distributions." *Journal of Financial Economics* (June 1958).

Miller, Merton H. "The Modigliani-Miller Propositions After Thirty Years," *Journal of Economic Perspectives* (Fall 1988).

Mishkin, Frederic S. *The Economics of Money, Banking, and Financial Markets*. Glenview, IL: Scott, Forseman & Co., 1989.

Mitchell, David. *Introduction to Logic*. Garden City, NY: Doubleday & Company, Inc., 1970.

Modigliani, Franco, and Merton H. Miller. "The Cost of Capital, Corporation Finance, and the Theory of Investment," *American Economic Review*, June 1958.

Morgenson, Gretchen, and Louise Story. "Clients Worried over Goldman's Dueling Goals." *New York Times*, May 17, 2010, p. 1.

Parks, Robert H. *Unlocking the Secrets of Wall Street,* Amherst, NY: Prometheus Books, 1998.

————. *The Witch Doctor of Wall Street.* Amherst, NY: Prometheus Books, 1996.

————. "Foreword" to *The End of Laissez Faire/Economic Consequences of the Peace* by John Maynard Keynes. Amherst, NY: Prometheus Books, Great Mind Series, 2004.

————. "The Cost of Capital Crossover [and the Nikkei 225 Mega Bubble]," Standard & Poor's *Credit Week* (January 29, 1990).

————. "Dominion of Flawed Fiscal & Monetary Policy over Science," *Business Review,* Cambridge, lead article, (September 2006).

————. "*Ex Ante* Recognition of Bubble Stock Gauges and Forecasts of Their Bursting in the United States and Japan," *Journal of the American Academy of Business,* Cambridge, Best Author Award (March 2006).

————. "Fed 'Targeting' Risks Economic Anemia or Full Recession," *Standard & Poor's Credit Week* (November 13, 1995).

————. "Monetarist Mania," *Standard & Poor's Credit Week* (April, 1995).

————. "Monetary Policy and the Creation of Near Money," *Financial Analysts Journal* (September/October 1965).

————. "Portfolio Operations of Commercial Banks and the Level of Treasury Security Prices," *Journal of Finance* (March 1959).

————. "Theory of Tax Incidence: International Aspects," *National Tax Journal* (June 1961).

————. "The Trouble with M1," *Banking, Journal of the American Bankers Association* (November 1970).

————. "U.S. Monetary Policy, Bubble Stock Gauges, and the Over Investment Boom-to-Bust Cycle 1997-2002," *International Journal of Business Disciplines,* no. 2 (Fall 2005).

————. "Use and Abuse of Financial and Monetary Data," *Journal of Portfolio Management* (Spring 1975).

Patterson, S. H. (ed.) *Readings in the History of Economic Thought.* New York: McGraw Hill Book Company, 1932.

Poe, Edgar Allen. *Masque of the Red Death.* New York: W. Black Inc., 1927.

————. *The Power of Words,* in *The Works of Edgar Allan Poe.* New York: P. F. Collins & Sons, 1927.

Polakoff, Murray E., Thomas A Durkin, et al. *Financial Institutions and Markets.* New York: Houghton Mifflin, 1970.

Porter, Michael. *The Competitive Advantage of Nations*. New York: The Free Press, 1990.

Powell, Michael. "Howard Zinn, 87, Author Who Revisted U.S. History and Inspired Students, Dies," *New York Times* (January 29, 2010), p. B10.

Prestowitz, Clyde. *Swarthmore College Bulletin* (February 1990).

Riley, William B., and Austin H. Montgomery. *Guide to Computer-Assisted Investment Analysis*. New York: McGraw Hill Book Company, 1982.

Roberts, Chris. *Heavy Words Lightly Thrown*. New York: Gotham Books, 1980.

Roll, Richard. "A Critique of the Asset Pricing Theory's Tests." *Journal of Financial Economics*, 4, no. 2 (March 1997): 129–76.

Root, Franklin R. *International Trade and Investment*. Cincinnati, OH: South Western Publishing Company, 1990.

Sagan, Carl. *The Demon-Haunted World*. New York: Random House, 1995.

_____. *The Varieties of Scientific Experience: A Personal View of the Search for God*. New York: Penguin Press, 2007.

Schienemann, Gary S. "Japanese P/E Ratios," in *Prudential Bache Securities Investment Report* (June 20, 1988).

Schwartz, Robert A. *Equity Markets*. New York: Harper Collins, 1998.

Shakespeare, William. Quotation from *Measure for Measure*, in John Bartlett's *Familiar Quotations*. Boston: Little, Brown & Company, 1980.

Shakespeare, William. *Tragedy of Macbeth*, Act IV, Scene I, New York: Lancer Books, 1968.

Sharpe, William F., Gordon J. Alexander, and Jeffrey V. Bailey. *Investments*. Englewood Cliffs, NJ: Prentice Hall, Inc., 1995.

Siegel, Jeremy. "The Equity Premium, Stock and Bond Returns Since 1802." *Financial Analysts Journal* (January/February 1992): 28–38.

Singer, Junk K. *The Unholy Bible, a Psychological Interpretation of William Blake*. New York: G. P. Putnam's Sons, 1970.

Smith, Adam. From *The Wealth of Nations* and *Lectures on Justice, Police, Revenue and Arms*, in S. H. Patterson (ed.), *Readings in the History of Economic Thought*. New York: McGraw Hill Book Company, 1932.

Sprinkel, Beryl W. *Money and Markets: A Monetarist View*. Homewood, IL: Richard D. Irwin, Inc., 1971.

Stigam, Marcia. *The Money Market*. Homewood, IL: Business One, Irwin, 1990.

Stiglitz, Joseph. *Economics*. New York and London: W. W. Norton and Company, First Edition of Two Volumes, 1993.

Strunk, William, and E. B. White. *Elements of Style*. New York: Macmillan Company, 1959.

Strachey, John. *The Nature of Capitalist Crisis*. New York: J. J. Little and Ives Company, 1935, p. 7.

Thouless, Robert H. *How to Think Straight: The Technique of Applying Logic Instead of Emotion*. New York: Simon & Schuster, 1947.

_____. *Straight and Crooked Thinking*. London: Pan Books, Ltd., 1964.

Toffler, Alvin. *Future Shock*. New York: Random House, 1970.

Weston, J. Fred, et al. Articles by prominent economists on Modigliani Miller Cost of Capital Theory. The Financial Management Association (Summer 1980).

Wood, John H., and Norma L. Wood. *Financial Markets*. San Diego: Harcourt Brace Jovanovich, 1985.

Zinn, Howard, *A People's History of the United States: 1942–Present*. New York: New Edition, Harper Collins Publishers, 2003. The famed historian died of heart failure on January 27, 2010, at the age of eighty-seven. (See reporter Michael Powell's review of Howard Zinn who inspired students to "rethink American history" in *New York Times* (January 29, 2010), p. B10.

Zinsser, Hans. *Rats, Lice, and History*. New York: Little, Brown and Company, 1936.

INDEX